THE CITY BOSS IN AMERICA

THE
CITY BOSS
IN AMERICA
An Interpretive Reader

edited with commentary by

Alexander B. Callow, Jr.
University of California, Santa Barbara

New York
OXFORD UNIVERSITY PRESS
London   1976   Toronto

❧ for Marie ❧

❦ PREFACE ❧

Without the city boss and his machine, the story of the city is only half-told. The boss is a reflection of the growing pains of the American city. As such, he is, for the past and the present, eminently relevant and our book takes cognizance of this perennial phenomenon, covering not just one time segment but the entire history of the boss—from, roughly, the middle of the nineteenth century to the present. The six chapter divisions illuminate the critical features of machine politics: the rise of the boss, running the machine, the boss and the immigrant, corruption, the boss and the reformer, and the modern machine. Each such chapter is preceded by an essay designed not merely to interpret the selections, but to supplement them as well.

The selections come from a motley but knowledgeable group of specialists in urban affairs, including historians, political scientists, journalists, sociologists, politicians, and even a novelist, the late Edwin O'Connor. The essays are more interpretive than descriptive. They were chosen for their insight, literary flair, information on the subject, and, not the least, to make this book entertaining to read.

I wish to thank Ms. Darcy De Lazzer, who typed the manuscript, and the editorial staff of Oxford University Press, especially my editor, Nancy Lane, and Herbert Mann (whose advice suggests that he would have made a grand ward leader).

Santa Barbara   *A. B. C.*
October 15, 1975

~CONTENTS~

❧ ONE ❧
The Rise of the Boss

↬ COMMENTARY ↫

The city boss is an American original. He affected the shape and contour of American urban history; his political clout often reached from the state legislature to the Oval Office itself. And in his own bailiwick he invested politics with a pith, a vitality, an excitement compounded of an astonishing mixture of ruthlessness and compassion, corruption and good deeds, hate and love. Today there are some who look back with nostalgia at the booming days of the city boss. With city government run by huge, impersonal agencies with tongue-twisting names, with politics scrubbed cleaner with nonpartisanship, something seems missing today—a sense of community, a feel of neighborhood, a chance for commitment.

One may wince at the waste, the inefficiency, the graft; yet the boss and his machine, his ward system, his political clubs, his favors, his hi-jinks, his torchlight parades and picnics, bound the citizen to his neighborhood, the neighborhood to the machine, and the machine to a people's politics, humanizing and personalizing the political system, offering to that always endangered species—the underdog—the chance to survive. Unlike some present-day public officials, he brought to urban affairs not the mentality of an efficiency expert or the skills of a cost-accountant but the flair of a seasoned professional politician, a manager of men, a broker among competing interests, an arbiter of conflict, a man who viewed politics as a great game—fun, profitable, volatile. City bosses like William Marcy Tweed, Richard Croker, George Cox, James Michael Curley, Tom Pendergast, or Frank Hague could well repeat after Huey Long, "I was born into politics, a wedded man with a storm for my bride."

Before the rise of the city boss, urban affairs were managed by the gentry, the "respectabilities" whose political credentials were based on family fame, grandeur of fortune, or eminence as professional, merchant, or businessman. Such men accepted public office as part-time volunteers, feeling it their duty as gentlemen of social distinction to perform a stint of disinterested public service. They were, after all, by their own modest admission, the "best men" and the "natural" leaders. They governed cities that had the appearance of overgrown towns, "walking cities" where a man could comfortably stroll to work from his home, where municipal services were performed not by the city but largely by private companies or by voluntary organizations such as the volunteer fire department. While plagued with problems strikingly similar to those of our own time—poverty, violence, housing, racial and ethnic discrimination—cities were smaller, less complex, and ethnically more homogeneous—islands in an agrarian sea.

Roughly from the 1840s on, however, the city became an integral part of a massive transformation in American life, one that changed an agrarian society into a modern, urban, industrial society, and created the city boss in America. While there were many different types of bosses, at different times, in different kinds of cities, several critical factors converged to bring about the birth of the boss: rapid urbanization, immigration (foreign and domestic), obsolescence of formal governmental structure, demand for more municipal services, and the rise of the full-time professional politician.

Rapid growth, increased immigration, and the Industrial Revolution shattered old boundaries, scrambled and expanded the urban map. A population explosion made the American city equal to its European counterparts in size. The decade of the 1850s was unprecedented in urbanization: from 1860 to 1900, city dwellers increased from slightly more than six million to more than thirty million. In the 1880s alone, Chicago doubled in size from a half-million to more than a million people. By 1910 Philadelphia's population trebled and New York's increased four-fold. The interior cities—St. Louis, Cleveland, Detroit, Milwaukee, Columbus—showed massive gains as well. Demographically, the city split into more specialized financial, commercial, and residential areas, and this had profound political implications. Each made special and often conflicting demands on the political process, demands complicated by the hostility of diverse ethnic, religious, class backgrounds—Catholic *vs.* Protestant, middle class *vs.* lower class, Yankee *vs.* immigrant—that could be exploited politically.

The transformation from walking city to metropolis carried with it institutions and ideas that were highly resistant to change, so that it was painful if not impossible for the existing structure to adapt successfully to increasing urbanization. City charters, rooted in the eighteenth or early nineteenth century, became obsolete. City government became a thicket of little governments, fragmented, overlapping, and dispersed, often at odds with county and state agencies. Chicago, for example, had eleven major government units in 1890, each a powerful fiefdom with its own hierarchy, regulations, and taxing authority, each vying for power; yet, because of the diffusion of responsibility, none was held fully accountable for the successful or disastrous execution of that power. Edward Banfield has counted fourteen hundred separate governmental agencies in later twentieth-century New York. The extreme decentralization occasioned by urban growth called for the centralization of political authority. But the long memory of British rule created among Americans a fear of centralization as the source of potential tyranny.

The problem was compounded when cities incorporated into local politics another eighteenth-century notion, the system of checks and balances: mayor checked by the municipal legislature, both checked by the state legislature. The initiation of public policy under a system smothering in a strait jacket of checks and balances can lead to political paralysis, especially when checked (*read*: interfered with) by the state legislature. Indeed, from the Colonial period to this instant, cities have struggled with varying degrees of success for more independence from state legislatures dominated by agrarian solons indifferent or hostile to the interests of the city. Cities have been treated by state legislatures as incompetent, ill-behaved, wicked, or even illegitimate children, to be controlled by the state's assuming key powers in home rule—powers such as those involving the purse and taxation, appointments, and licensing legislation. Moreover, many state legislatures became the haven of railroad and utility magnates and factory and real-estate owners who fought against city dwellers "who howled for low trolley and subway fares, 80 cent gas, cheap electricity, workmen's compensation, minimum wage and maximum hour laws, factory and tenement house inspection."[1]

Growth triggered as well a demand for an array of new services providing both necessities and amenities of city living. As the cities expanded

1. Warren Moscow, *What Have You Done for Me Lately?* (1967), pp. 51-52.

5

horizontally and vertically, streets had to be paved, sewers dug, fires fought, crime combatted, disease controlled, garbage removed, and schools built. Cities urgently needed taxes and bonds to fund gas, light, water, telephones, playgrounds and parks, rapid transit, and professional fire and police departments. But many Americans clung tenaciously to the ideal of an older and simpler rural America that was served by a small, economy-minded government based on the proposition that the best government was the government that governed and taxed least.

Attitudes such as these, together with this kind of governmental structure and urban environment, set the stage for the rise of the city boss. The boss exploited the inability of government to supply the demands of the emerging city. He created a mechanism—the machine—for coping with the complex political, economic, and social adaptations entailed in the transformation of American society that began in the nineteenth century. It was not the only mechanism, as reformers would insist; it was not the most honest, or the most efficient; yet as a response to urban needs, it was, to put it in its simplest terms—a way of getting things done. The machine was an extra-legal political organization that won elections, controlled key public offices and agencies, negotiated among competing special interests, and brought a semblance of order to the chaos of dissipated and decentralized political structures. The machine flourished because it provided material and psychological incentives and obligations, and a system of rewards called patronage, oriented not toward realizing such aspirations as "good government" or programs for the "public interest" but toward satisfying the craving for the things men crave: for money, power, prestige, respect, security, and order. It survived for at least three generations because it reflected the realities of the specialized neighborhoods—financial, industrial, commercial—and above all, the inner-city residential areas.

If there was a "secret" to the rule of the boss, it was his flair for reaching, in spite of the asphalt, the roots of urban life—the street, the block, the neighborhood of working- and lower-class urbanites. He recognized their problems of poverty, unemployment, alienation, and their hunger for a share of the American bonanza. He exploited ethnic, religious, and working-class loyalties, reconciled hostilities, cemented family and personal affiliations, and created a kind of people's politics that gave the neighborhood an access to the political process. Here universal suffrage provided a vast potential army of the political faithful where a favor would get a vote; here were ethnic and religious blocs, like the "little

Italy's" or "little Athens's" in New York, to be wooed and mobilized by a material reward of a job and the psychological reward of "recognition" on the ticket. Here, too, were both a political division and an electoral process that allowed more people involvement in urban politics.

The neighborhood of the machine was divided into wards, districts, and precincts. Under the so-called ward system an alderman represented a relatively small number of people who were usually socially homogeneous. Having a small number of constituents, the alderman became intimately acquainted with the problems of his ward. The long ballot of the ward system, with its large number of elected officials ranging from mayor, alderman, constable, a host of county officials, board officers (for education, sanitation, and other services) to every kind of county, superior, and circuit district court judge, gave more people of the neighborhood a chance to hold public office and produced in turn a rich harvest of patronage for the boss to increase his power.

If the neighborhood was the domain of the boss, his power did not end here. It was a power base to extend his authority over and attract support from the other neighborhoods, which could benefit from the building, running, and cleaning of the city. Control of municipal services was the key to that expansion. Municipal services provided power, profit, and patronage for the emerging city boss, and the stakes of the political game soared as the cities grew. The boss became the arbiter of who got what, when, and at what price. Thus, he was able to mobilize coalitions among the businessmen, financiers, and contractors to combine with the huge pool of unskilled labor from the neighborhoods into a formidable organization where mutual cooperation spelled political might. And there were fringe benefits. New demands created new municipal bureauracies—petty sovereignties with their own built-in systems of reward and punishment: taxes to levy—or to vary, licenses to grant—or refuse, inspections to make—or ignore, rules to enforce—or break. As a kind of political Santa Claus, the boss could reward with low tax assessments the contractors who had been "good," he could leak plans to widen Ann Street to friendly real-estate operators who could speculate without gambling, and he could give Mrs. Higgins's boy Mike a job in the police court. He who giveth could taketh. A bad-mouthing saloonkeeper might be visited by a health inspector who would enforce a long-forgotten ordinance; a disloyal banker might find city deposits removed to a competitor's vault.

The final element in making machine politics possible was the dramatic change in leadership in the cities: the emergence of a new breed, the full-time professional politician, men of slender social distinction, whose training came not from the countinghouse or the university, but from the street gang, the saloon, the fire department, the political club. Unlike the gentry, the old ruling class, whose manners, education, and culture gave it a distaste for direct contact with the masses, the professional never hesitated to invoke the rhetoric and symbols of mass support and to perform personal services. Steeped in the tactics of practical neighborhood politics, he organized the bleak, sprawling areas inhabited by the poor into political strongholds, devoted himself to the business of building and entrenching a political organization, and outmaneuvered the old elite by exploiting the growing complexities of urban life. During the last half of the nineteenth century, the gentry, in Arthur Mann's words, "were outnumbered, overrun, and displaced" by the professional politicians of more humble origins, principally the city boss and his lieutenants, the district and ward leaders.

Thus the city boss entered the mainstream of American urban political life. What kind of a man was he? For generations the public imagination has pictured him as a bull-necked, beefy thug, with a derby hat cocked over a beetle brow, chomping on an enormous stogy, Irish eyes smirking, decked out in a gaudy vest and black pantaloons, diamonds in his stickpin, diamonds on his fingers; a brutish plug-ugly—arrogant, boisterous, jolly, utterly immoral—his gravel voice barking orders, grunts, snarls. Vintage Tweed, a shade of Croker, a touch of Butler, and a few others. James Bryce, the scholar-aristocrat, summed it up with incisive English brevity: "vulgar figures with good coats."

Once this grotesque stereotype is cleared away, we can begin to get a better idea of the type of man he was. The fact is that the city boss was as diverse as American political life itself. Like men from most other professions, among them there were similarities but also some striking differences. One of the first scholarly studies to attack the stereotype of the boss was Harold Zink's *City Bosses* published in 1930. Of the twenty bosses studied, fifteen were either immigrants or the children of immigrants; thirteen never received an education beyond grammar school, most entered politics at an early age and held at one time or another a public office (Frank Hague, not included in the Zink study, was elected to public office before he could legally vote). Fifteen were raised in abject poverty or modest circumstances, and most went on to become prosperous. There was for several a rags-to-riches theme that Horatio Alger might have written of this way: "Could a lowly stonecutter become a mighty leader of Tammany Hall? John Kelly did. Could a hoodlum conquer New York? Richard Croker did. Can you imagine a seedy, squat, Irish horsecar driver rising to be one of the most powerful city bosses in our history? Charles Murphy did."

But there others who did not fit this mold. Abraham Ruef was graduated from the University of California at eighteen with highest honors, loved music and philosophy, and spoke seven languages. Ed Flynn, boss of the Bronx, was a bookish college graduate and a brilliant lawyer. William Flinn, an elegant and charming man, was listed in the *Pittsburgh Social Register* for twenty years.

There were differences in background that shattered the notion that the tough lad who chewed and bit his way out of Hester Street to scramble up the greasy pole of urban politics was always Irish. Tweed was of Scotch descent; Martin Behrman, boss of New Orleans, and Abe Ruef of San Francisco were Jews; George Cox of Cincinnati was English, and Fred Ludin,"the mystery man" of Chicago, was of Swedish extraction.

Nor were all the bosses jolly, boisterous, crude, or swinging loose-livers. For all the genial ones, like Bill Tweed, Chris Magee, and James Michael Curley, there were the grim, silent, cold ones, like John Kelley, Charles Murphy, and George Cox. If Boss Tweed and Frank Hague had magnificent estates, and Richard Croker lived like a robber baron in New York, others like John Kelley and Ed Flynn lived modestly (as Richard Daley still does), shunning conspicuous consumption. True, Tom Pendergast of Kansas City was psychologically crippled by compulsive gambling, and "Doc" Ames of Minneapolis was a notorious drinker (although he was "exceptionally kind to children"), and Martin Behrman, at 230 pounds, was a pathological eater who ran up $200 luncheon bills at Antoine's in New Orleans. There were many others, however—even the infamous Tweed—who never smoke or drank and were good family men. So celebrated was Ed Crump's love for his mother—he visited her every Sunday— that one of his supporters said that it made him "the finest bygod peckerwood in these parts." As Peter McGuinness of Brooklyn explained:

> I don't smoke, drink, chew, nor gamble. And I never go to any of them
> Jesse James night clubs. As the fellow said, "If you don't do none of
> them things, Peter, what the hell do you do?" I say, all I do is take
> God's beautiful air and sunshine. And I play politics.

9

Some bosses, Crump, Curley, and Hague among others, even legislated the morals of their cities by cracking down on hard liquor and loose women. Tim Sullivan, the saloonkeeper-politician, and king of gambling and prostitution in the Bowery, was capable of delivering the same indignant tut-tuts as any strait-laced reformer. When Elinor Glyn published her *Three Weeks*, a shocking book for the early twentieth century, Sullivan declared, "Anybody that reads *Three Weeks* should get three months." As Andy Logan put it: "Though motherhood touched him—the tears came to his eyes when the Occidental piano player broke into 'Mother Machree'—he didn't care to hear how Mother had got in that fix."[2]

The city boss, then, was a crazy mix of many shades and sizes of physical, mental, ethnic, and moral qualities. The qualities shared by most of them were executive ability, tenacity, a flexible, pragmatic approach to problems, and, above all, a gift for playing the great game of politics. Just as the boss and his machine changed over time in response to new developments, so the popular image of machine politics changed. The essays of this first chapter were selected to reveal shifting interpretations of the city boss over an eighty-year period from a variety of men: an evangelistic reformer, a journalist, an urban historian, and a modern sociologist. The first selection is from *Our Country* by the Reverend Josiah Strong (1886), a book that sold more than 175,000 copies in thirty years. *Our Country* has been compared in its moral intensity to another all-time best seller, *Uncle Tom's Cabin*. It has also been seen as a kind of historic document, inasmuch it reflected the attitudes, hopes, and fears of the dominant segment of American society in the 1880s—the white, Protestant middle and upper classes.

This piece is only in part a tirade against the boss, showing the moral fervor of nineteenth-century reformers; it also places local politics within a national context and reflects the acute anxiety of Americans as they were emerging from an agrarian to an urban, industrialized nation. What made Strong so compelling to the dominant group of Americans was his flair for moral suspense on a heroic level.

Our country, according to Strong, was on the threshold of either national fulfillment or national disaster. Americans ("native" Americans, that is) were God's favorite, yea, chosen people, the cream of the world's racial stock. It was America's divinely inspired mission to become the

2. *Against the Evidence* (1970), p. 57.

instrument for the world's redemption. Before redemption, however, must come purification, and this process was threatened by a host of perils alien to the traditional rural values of Protestant America. The city was to be the testing ground for the values symbolized by American democracy. Into the city were funneled forces destructive of the American mission: socialism, anarchism, intemperance, monopolies, and the spoils system. The core of democracy—self-government—was imperiled by the boss, the machine, and the "rabble"—the immigrants. Countless variations on the nineteenth-century definition of machine rule (politics dominated by "evil" men) could be heard from the pulpit, in the classroom, at political rallies, and read in newspapers, magazines, and books. No wonder that the American WASP felt engulfed in crisis. The city threatened the farm; the boss and his machine could reduce democracy to a mockery and a shambles; and the purity of the Protestant could be diseased by infusions of Catholic and Jewish immigrant blood. It was at once a question of morality and survival.

While a crusade may increase the pitch of moral indignation, it does not illustrate the nature of urban politics, the way the machine developed, or the way the boss ran the machine. One may hate the enemy, but it is not enough to call him a wicked fellow. One must understand his strategy as well. What was needed was a more realistic interpretation of the boss and his machine, and this appeared in Lincoln Steffens's *Shame of the Cities* (1904), a section of which constitutes the second essay of this book. Steffens attacked the moralizing reformers, the public apathy, and the business community. His aspiration was to shatter public indifference and alert both the reformers and the people at large to the way power was exercised and what he considered the real sources of political corruption. Disenchanted with the reformers' political sermons, he found those reformers to be simplistic innocents building a howitzer to kill a mouse. The reformers' panacea of routing the rascals and making city government more efficient missed the point. While, in the Steffens theory, the public in general must share responsibility for allowing graft, it was the "respectabilities," the businessmen with easy consciences, who helped to make "the system" work. Where, indeed, did the money come from? Who slipped the boss the bribe? Who received the government contracts? How was that ninety-nine-year lease for a streetcar line negotiated?

Steffens's exposé of the alliance between the boss and the businessman provided a new dimension to urban politics and helped puncture the public's trust in the moral superiority of the American business community. Steffens advanced the shocking argument that city bosses were human, often generous, thoughtful, witty; they were buccaneers—yes, but, as measured against grasping businessmen, certainly not the worst ones. Steffens interpreted the boss in economic rather than moral terms. The boss performed a service—if an illegitimate one—for the banker, the contractor, the merchant, the utilities and transportation corporations, for those who could not or would not satisfy their economic self-interest through regular channels. It was a view that set the stage for another major shift in interpreting the city boss in America. For here was the suggestion that the machine played a positive role: it performed a function dictated by the nature of political life in the city.

Sociologist Robert Merton, in the next essay, expands this idea into a general functional theory to account for both the rise and the operation of the boss and his machine. Light-years away from the evangelism of a Strong and the crusading of a Steffens, Merton argued that the machine, centralized and disciplined, developed as an alternative to the confused, decentralized nature of formal government. It flourished, says Merton, because it provided services unavailable from formal government to a variety of operators whose survival depended upon it: not merely the "legitimate" member of the business community but the illegitimate businessman and the racketeer and gangster as well.[3] More important, the machine functioned to humanize politics for the "deprived" classes. Through patronage, gifts, and friendship the machine gave the poor Yankee from the farm or the immigrant Irishman or German a chance at some degree of social mobility.

The final essay in this section reflects the view of a modern urban historian, a view that became still another turning point in the interpretation of the city boss. Whereas the preceding essays deal with the boss in more general terms, Zane Miller examines the rise and fall of a specific boss, George Cox of Cincinnati, but is less concerned with Cox the grafter than with Cox the politician and reformer. Miller fleshs out the so-called Periphery theory initiated by Richard C. Wade, in which it is argued that by the outset of the Progressive period the classic conflict of the city *vs.* the country was replaced by a struggle within the city itself.[4] Accord-

---

3. This relation is epitomized by the dying words of Johnny Lazia, overlord of organized crime in Kansas City during the era of the Pendergast machine: "Tell Tom Pendergast I love him."
4. "Urbanization," from *The Comparative Approach to American History,* ed. C. Vann Woodward

ingly, Miller traces the demographic spread of Cincinnati into three out-lying ("Hilltop") sections occupied by the upper and middle classes, with the poor and newly-arrived confined to the central city (the "Basin"). The contest was between the inner city and the peripheries, and no longer a matter of conquering the inner city. If the boss was to sustain his power, as Cox realized, he must woo the periphery neighborhoods; and in so doing Cox achieved several reforms.

Cox, then, was no free-booting graftmonger like Tweed or Croker, exploiting the chaos of rapid urbanization. Rather, he helped to soothe the cultural and racial antagonisms inherent in the widely disparate neigh-borhoods, ease the growing pains of a metropolis, and institute a program of moderate reforms which set the tone for the city of Cincinnati. In a word, he brought stability out of chaos. In contrast to older images of the city boss, Cox was "not necessarily a public enemy" (in Miller's words). And so, through time, the city boss has been scrubbed cleaner, although his paws may still remain sticky from the muck of corruption (even Cox was not above suspicion). Perhaps that is not the point.

We have come a long way from the "perils" of Josiah Strong, in both rhetoric and analysis. The city boss is seen no longer as a snarling Satan or as an amusing swashbuckler, but as an integral figure in the history of American urban politics, often a dynamic one performing a role vital to the growth of both the city and its citizens. Demographic analysis has increased our understanding of boss rule, but future studies examining other vital catalysts of political behavior, such as religion, race, class, and ethnicity will effect an even greater balance.[5] Yet for all his rhetorical excesses, does Strong still speak to a point necessary for the measure of the boss? For all his analytical perception, does not Merton execute a moral whitewash of the boss? The urban historian Bruce Stave poses the problem neatly: "If the observer divorces himself from the moral issues, does he thereby distort his understanding as much as if he saw everything in terms of good and evil?"[6] It is a nagging question that persists through-out the history of the city boss—and one that needs to be pondered.

(1968). For a similar argument, that of the boss reaching for new sources of power, see Lyle W. Dorsett, *The Pendergast Machine* (1968).

5. See Joel Arthur Tarr, *A Study in Boss Politics: William Lorimer of Chicago* (1971), chap. 1.

6. Bruce Stave, ed. *Urban Bosses, Machines, and Progressive Reformers* (1972), p. x.

PERILS—
THE BOSS, THE MACHINE, THE IMMIGRANT
A Nineteenth-Century View

Josiah Strong

Political optimism is one of the vices of the American people. There is a popular faith that "God takes care of children, fools, and the United States." We deem ourselves a chosen people, and incline to the belief that the Almighty stands pledged to our prosperity. Until within a few years probably not one in a hundred of our population has ever questioned the security of our future. Such optimism is as senseless as pessimism is faithless. The one is as foolish as the other is wicked.

Thoughtful men see perils on our national horizon. Our argument is concerned not with all of them, but *only with those which peculiarly threaten the West*.

America, as the land of promise to all the world, is the destination of the most remarkable migration of which we have any record. During the last ten years we have suffered a peaceful invasion by an army more than four times as vast as the

From *Our Country* (New York: Baker and Taylor Co., 1891), pp. 41-42, 54-55, 171-73, 179-81, 184-85.

estimated number of Goths and Vandals that swept over Southern Europe and overwhelmed Rome. During the past hundred years fifteen million foreigners have made their homes in the United States, and three-quarters of them have come since 1850, while 5,248,000 have arrived since 1880. A study of the causes of this great world movement indicates that perhaps as yet we have seen only beginnings. These controlling causes are threefold. 1. The attracting influences of the United States. 2. The expellent influences of the Old World. 3. Facilities for travel. . . .

Moreover, immigration not only furnishes the greater portion of our criminals, it is also seriously affecting the morals of the native population. It is disease and not health which is contagious. Most foreigners bring with them continental ideas of the Sabbath, and the result is sadly manifest in all our cities, where it is being transformed from a holy day into a holiday. But by far the most effective instrumentality for debauching popular morals is the liquor traffic, and this is chiefly carried on by foreigners. In 1880, of the "Traders and dealers in liquors and wines," (I suppose this means wholesale dealers) sixty-three per cent were foreign-born, and of the brewers and maltsters seventy-five per cent while a large proportion of the remainder were of foreign parentage. Of saloon-keepers about sixty per cent were foreign-born, while many of the remaining forty per cent of these corrupters of youth, these western Arabs, whose hand is against every man, were of foreign extraction.

We can only glance at the political aspects of immigration. As we have already seen, it is immigration which has fed fat the liquor power; and there is a liquor vote. Immigration furnishes most of the victims of Mormonism; and there is a Mormon vote. Immigration is the strength of the Catholic church; and there is a Catholic vote. Immigration is the mother and nurse of American socialism; and there is to be a socialist vote. Immigration tends strongly to the cities, and gives to them their political complexion. And there is no more serious menace to our civilization than our rabble-ruled cities. These several perils, all of which are enhanced by immigration, will be considered in succeeding chapters.

Many American citizens are not Americanized. It is as unfortunate as it is natural, that foreigners in this country should cherish their own language and peculiar customs, and carry their nationality, as a distinct factor, into our politics. Immigration has created the "German vote" and the "Irish vote," for which politicians bid, and which have already been decisive of state elections, and might easily determine national. A mass of men but little acquainted with our institutions, who will act in concert and who are controlled largely by their appetites and prejudices, constitute a very paradise for demagogues. . . .

The city is the nerve center of our civilization. It is also the storm center. The fact, therefore, that it is growing much more rapidly than the whole population is full of significance. . . . The city has become a serious menace to our civilization, because in it, excepting Mormonism, each of the dangers we have discussed is enhanced, and all are focalized. It has a peculiar attraction for the immigrant. Our fifty principal cities in 1880 contained 39.3 per cent of our entire German population, and 45.8 per cent of the Irish. Our ten larger cities at that time contained only nine per cent of the entire population, but 23 per cent of the foreign. While a little less than one-third of the population of the United States was foreign by birth or parentage, sixty-two per cent of the population of Cincinnati was foreign, eighty-three per cent of Cleveland, sixty-three per cent of Boston, eighty per cent of New York, and ninety-one per cent of Chicago. A census of Massachusetts, taken in 1885, showed that in 65 towns and cities of the state 65.1 per cent of the population was foreign by birth or parentage.

Because our cities are so largely foreign, Romanism finds in them its chief strength. . . .

If moral and religious influences are peculiarly weak at the point where our social explosives are gathered, what of city government? Are its strength and purity so exceptional as to insure the effective control of these dangerous elements? In the light of notorious facts, the question sounds satirical. It is commonly acknowledged that the government of large cities in the United States is a failure. "In all the great American cities there is to-day as clearly defined a ruling class as in the most aristocratic countries in the world. Its members carry wards in their pockets, make up the slates for nominating conventions, distribute offices as they bargain together, and—though they toil not, neither do they spin—wear the best of raiment and spend money lavishly. They are men of power, whose favor the ambitious must court, and whose vengeance he must avoid. Who are these men? The wise, the good, the learned—men who have earned the confidence of their fellow-citizens by the purity of their lives, the splendor of their talents, their probity in public trusts, their deep study of the problems of government? No; they are gamblers, saloon-keepers, pugilists, or worse, who have made a trade of controlling votes and of buying and selling offices and official acts." It has come to this, that holding a municipal office in a large city almost impeaches a man's character. Known integrity and competency hopelessly incapacitate a man for any office in the gift of a city rabble. In a certain western city, the administration of the mayor had convinced good citizens that he gave constant aid and comfort to gamblers, thieves, saloon-keepers and all the worst elements of society. He became a candidate for a second term. The prominent men and press of both parties and the ministry of all denominations united in a Citizens' League to defeat him; but he was triumphantly returned to office by the "lewd fellows of the baser sort." And again, after a desperate struggle on the part of the better elements to defeat him, he was re-elected to a third term of office.

Popular government in the city is degenerating into government by a "boss." During his visit to this country, Herbert Spencer said: "You retain the forms of freedom; but so far as I can gather, there has been a considerable loss of the substance. It is true that those who rule you do not do it by means of retainers armed with swords; but they do it through regiments of men armed with voting papers, who obey the word of command as loyally as did the dependents of the old feudal nobles, and who thus enable their leaders to override the general will, and make the community submit to their exactions as effectually as their prototypes of old. Manifestly those who framed your Constitution never dreamed that twenty thousand citizens would go to the polls led by a 'boss.' "

As a rule, our largest cities are the worst governed. It is natural, therefore, to infer that, as our cities grow larger and more dangerous, the government will become more corrupt, and control will pass more completely into the hands of those who themselves most need to be controlled. . . .

The fundamental idea of popular government is the distribution of power. It has been the struggle of liberty for ages to wrest power from the hands of one or the few, and lodge it in the hands of the many. We have seen, in the foregoing discussion, that centralized power is rapidly growing. The "boss" makes his bargain, and sells his ten thousand or fifty thousand voters as if they were so many cattle. Centralized wealth is centralized power; and the capitalist and corporation find many ways to control votes. The liquor power controls thousands of votes in every considerable city. The president of the Mormon Church casts, say, sixty thousand votes. The Jesuits, it is said, are all under the command of one man in Washington. The Roman Catholic vote is more or less perfectly controlled by the priests. That means that the Pope can dictate some hundreds of thousands of votes in the United States. Is there anything unrepublican in all this? And we must remember that, if present tendencies continue, these figures will be greatly multiplied in the future. And not only is this immense power lodged in the hand of one man, which in itself is perilous, but it is wielded without the slightest reference to any policy or principle of government, solely in the interests of a church or a business, or for personal ends.

The result of a national election may depend on a single state; the vote of that state may depend on a single city; the vote of that city may depend on a "boss," or a capitalist, or a corporation; or the election may be decided, and the policy of the government may be reversed, by the socialist, or liquor, or Roman Catholic or immigrant vote.

THE SHAME OF THE CITIES
A Progressive's View

Lincoln Steffens

... Even in government we have given proofs of potential greatness, and our political failures are not complete; they are simply ridiculous. But they are ours. Not alone the triumphs and the statesmen, the defeats and the grafters also represent us, and just as truly. Why not see it so and say it?

Because, I heard, the American people won't "stand for" it. You may blame the politicians, or, indeed, any one class, but not all classes, not the people. Or you may put it on the ignorant foreign immigrant, or any one nationality, but not on all nationalities, not on the American people. But no one class is at fault, nor any one breed, nor any particular interest or group of interests. The misgovernment of the American people is misgovernment by the American people.

When I set out on my travels, an honest New Yorker told me honestly that I

From Lincoln Steffens, *The Shame of the Cities* (New York: McClure, Phillips and Co., 1904), pp. 4-12, 14-16.

would find that the Irish, the Catholic Irish, were at the bottom of it all everywhere. The first city I went to was St. Louis, a German city. The next was Minneapolis, a Scandinavian city, with a leadership of New Englanders. Then came Pittsburg, Scotch Presbyterian, and that was what my New York friend was. "Ah, but they are all foreign populations," I heard. The next city was Philadelphia, the purest American community of all, and the most hopeless. And after that came Chicago and New York, both mongrel-bred, but the one a triumph of reform, the other the best example of good government that I had seen. The "foreign element" excuse is one of the hypocritical lies that save us from the clear sight of ourselves.

Another such conceit of our egotism is that which deplores our politics and lauds our business. This is the wail of the typical American citizen. Now, the typical American citizen is the business man. The typical business man is a bad citizen; he is busy. If he is a "big business man" and very busy, he does not neglect, he is busy with politics, oh, very busy and very businesslike. I found him buying boodlers in St. Louis, defending grafters in Minneapolis, originating corruption in Pittsburg, sharing with bosses in Philadelphia, deploring reform in Chicago, and beating good government with corruption funds in New York. He is a self-righteous fraud, this big business man. He is the chief source of corruption, and it were a boon if he would neglect politics. But he is not the business man that neglects politics; that worthy is the good citizen, the typical business man. He too is busy, he is the one that has no use and therefore no time for politics. When his neglect has permitted bad government to go so far that he can be stirred to action, he is unhappy, and he looks around for a cure that shall be quick, so that he may hurry back to the shop. Naturally, too, when he talks politics, he talks shop. His patent remedy is quack; it is business.

"Give us a business man," he says ("like me," he means). "Let him introduce business methods into politics and government; then I shall be left alone to attend to my business."

There is hardly an office from United States Senator down to Alderman in any part of the country to which the business man has not been elected; yet politics remains corrupt, government pretty bad, and the selfish citizen has to hold himself in readiness like the old volunteer firemen to rush forth at any hour, in any weather, to prevent the fire; and he goes out sometimes and he puts out the fire (after the damage is done) and he goes back to the shop sighing for the business man in poli-

tics. The business man has failed in politics as he has in citizenship. Why?

Because politics is business. That's what's the matter with it. That's what's the matter with everything,—art, literature, religion, journalism, law, medicine,—they're all business, and all—as you see them. Make politics a sport, as they do in England, or a profession, as they do in Germany, and we'll have—well, something else than we have now,—if we want it, which is another question. But don't try to reform politics with the banker, the lawyer, and the dry-goods merchant, for these are business men and there are two great hindrances to their achievement of reform: one is that they are different from, but no better than, the politicians; the other is that politics is not "their line." There are exceptions both ways. Many politicians have gone out into business and done well (Tammany ex-mayors, and nearly all the old bosses of Philadelphia are prominent financiers in their cities), and business men have gone into politics and done well (Mark Hanna, for example). They haven't reformed their adopted trades, however, though they have sometimes sharpened them most pointedly. The politician is a business man with a specialty. When a business man of some other line learns the business of politics, he is a politician, and there is not much reform left in him. Consider the United States Senate, and believe me.

The commercial spirit is the spirit of profit, not patriotism; of credit, not honor; of individual gain, not national prosperity; of trade and dickering, not principle. "My business is sacred," says the business man in his heart. "Whatever prospers my business, is good; it must be. Whatever hinders it, is wrong; it must be. A bribe is bad, that is, it is a bad thing to take; but it is not so bad to give one, not if it is necessary to my business." "Business is business" is not a political sentiment, but our politician has caught it. He takes essentially the same view of the bribe, only he saves his self-respect by piling all his contempt upon the bribe-giver, and he has the great advantage of candor. "It is wrong, maybe," he says, "but if a rich merchant can afford to do business with me for the sake of a convenience or to increase his already great wealth, I can afford, for the sake of a living, to meet him half way. I make no pretensions to virtue, not even on Sunday." And as for giving bad government or good, how about the merchant who gives bad goods or good goods, according to the demand?

But there is hope, not alone despair, in the commercialism of our politics. If our political leaders are to be always a lot of political merchants, they will supply any demand we may create. All we have to do is to establish a steady demand for good government. The bosses have us split up into parties. To him parties are nothing but means to his corrupt ends. He "bolts" his party, but we must not; the bribe-giver changes his party, from one election to another, from one county to another, from one city to another, but the honest voter must not. Why? Because if the honest voter cared no more for his party than the politician and the grafter, then the honest vote would govern, and that would be bad—for graft. It is idiotic, this

devotion to a machine that is used to take our sovereignty from us. If we would leave parties to the politicians, and would vote not for the party, not even for men, but for the city, and the State, and the nation, we should rule parties, and cities, and States, and nation. If we would vote in mass on the more promising ticket, or, if the two are equally bad, would throw out the party that is in, and wait till the next election and then throw out the other party that is in—then, I say, the commercial politician would feel a demand for good government and he would supply it. That process would take a generation or more to complete, for the politicians now really do not know what good government is. But it has taken as long to develop bad government, and the politicians know what that is. If it would not "go," they would offer something else, and, if the demand were steady, they, being so commercial, would "deliver the goods."

But do the people want good government? Tammany says they don't. Are the people honest? Are the people better than Tammany? Are they better than the merchant and the politician? Isn't our corrupt government, after all, representative?

President Roosevelt has been sneered at for going about the country preaching, as a cure for our American evils, good conduct in the individual, simple honesty, courage, and efficiency. "Platitudes!" the sophisticated say. Platitudes? If my observations have been true, the literal adoption of Mr. Roosevelt's reform scheme would result in a revolution, more radical and terrible to existing institutions, from the Congress to the Church, from the bank to the ward organization, than socialism or even than anarchy. Why, that would change all of us—not alone our neighbors, not alone the grafters, but you and me.

No, the contemned methods of our despised politics are the master methods of our braggart business, and the corruption that shocks us in public affairs we practice ourselves in our private concerns. There is no essential difference between the pull that gets your wife into society or for your book a favorable review, and that which gets a heeler into office, a thief out of jail, and a rich man's son on the board of directors of a corporation; none between the corruption of a labor union, a bank, and a political machine; none between a dummy director of a trust and the caucus-bound member of a legislature; none between a labor boss like Sam Parks, a boss of banks like John D. Rockefeller, a boss of railroads like J. P. Morgan, and a political boss like Matthew S. Quay. The boss is not a political, he is an American institution, the product of a freed people that have not the spirit to be free.

And it's all a moral weakness; a weakness right where we think we are strongest. Oh, we are good—on Sunday, and we are "fearfully patriotic" on the Fourth of July. But the bribe we pay to the janitor to prefer our interests to the landlord's, is the little brother of the bribe passed to the alderman to sell a city street, and the father of the air-brake stock assigned to the president of a railroad to have this life-saving invention adopted on his road. And as for graft, railroad passes, saloon

and bawdy-house blackmail, and watered stock, all these belong to the same family. We are pathetically proud of our democratic institutions and our republican form of government, of our grand Constitution and our just laws. We are a free and sovereign people, we govern ourselves and the government is ours. But that is the point. We are responsible, not our leaders, since we follow them. We *let* them divert our loyalty from the United States to some "party"; we *let* them boss the party and turn our municipal democracies into autocracies and our republican nation into a plutocracy. We cheat our government and we let our leaders loot it, and we let them wheedle and bribe our sovereignty from us. True, they pass for us strict laws, but we are content to let them pass also bad laws, giving away public property in exchange; and our good, and often impossible. laws we allow to be used for oppression and blackmail. And what can we say? We break our own laws and rob our own government, the lady at the customhouse, the lyncher with his rope, and the captain of industry with his bribe and his rebate. The spirit of graft and of lawlessness is the American spirit. . . .

The people are not innocent. That is the only "news" in all the journalism of these articles, and no doubt that was not new to many observers. It was to me. When I set out to describe the corrupt systems of certain typical cities, I meant to show simply how the people were deceived and betrayed. But in the very first study—St. Louis—the startling truth lay bare that corruption was not merely political; it

21

was financial, commercial, social; the ramifications of boodle were so complex, various, and far-reaching, that one mind could hardly grasp them, and not even Joseph W. Folk, the tireless prosecutor, could follow them all. This state of things was indicated in the first article which Claude H. Wetmore and I compiled together, but it was not shown plainly enough. Mr. Wetmore lived in St. Louis, and he had respect for names which meant little to me. But when I went next to Minneapolis alone, I could see more independently, without respect for persons, and there were traces of the same phenomenon. The first St. Louis article was called "Tweed Days in St. Louis," and though the "better citizen" received attention the Tweeds were the center of interest. In "The Shame of Minneapolis," the truth was put into the title; it was the Shame of Minneapolis; not of the Ames administration, not of the Tweeds, but of the city and its citizens. And yet Minneapolis was not nearly so bad as St. Louis; police graft is never so universal as boodle. It is more shocking, but it is so filthy that it cannot involve so large a part of society. So I returned to St. Louis, and I went over the whole ground again, with the people in mind, not alone the caught and convicted boodlers. And this time the true meaning of "Tweed Days in St. Louis" was made plain. The article was called "The Shamelessness of St. Louis," and that was the burden of the story. In Pittsburg[h] also the people was the subject, and though the civic spirit there was better, the extent of the corruption throughout the social organization of the community was indicated. But it was not till I got to Philadelphia that the possibilities of popular corruption were worked out to the limit of humiliating confession. That was the place for such a study. There is nothing like it in the country, except possibly, in Cincinnati. Philadelphia certainly is not merely corrupt, but corrupted, and this was made clear. Philadelphia was charged up to—the American citizen.

It was impossible in the space of a magazine article to cover in any one city all the phases of municipal government, so I chose cities that typified most strikingly some particular phase or phases. Thus as St. Louis exemplified boodle; Minneapolis, police graft; Pittsburg[h] a political and industrial machine; and Philadelphia, general civic corruption; so Chicago was an illustration of reform, and New York of good government. All these things occur in most of these places. There are, and long have been, reformers in St. Louis, and there is to-day police graft there. Minneapolis has had boodling and council reform, and boodling is breaking out there again. Pittsburg[h] has general corruption, and Philadelphia a very perfect political machine. Chicago has police graft and a low order of administrative and general corruption which permeates business, labor, and society generally. As for New York, the metropolis might exemplify almost anything that occurs anywhere in American cities, but no city has had for many years such a good administration as was that of Mayor Seth Low. . . .

THE LATENT FUNCTIONS OF THE MACHINE
A Sociologist's View

Robert K. Merton

... In large sectors of the American population, the political machine or the "political racket" [is] judged as unequivocally "bad" and "undesirable." The grounds for such moral judgment vary somewhat, but they consist substantially in pointing out that political machines violate moral codes: political patronage violates the code of selecting personnel on the basis of impersonal qualifications rather than on grounds of party loyalty or contributions to the party war-chest; bossism violates the code that votes should be based on individual appraisal of the qualifications of candidates and of political issues, and not on abiding loyalty to a feudal leader; bribery, and "honest graft" obviously offend the proprieties of property; "protection" for crime clearly violates the law and the mores; and so on.

In view of the manifold respects in which political machines, in varying

Reprinted with permission of Macmillan Publishing Co., Inc., from *Social Theory and Social Structure* by Robert K. Merton, pp. 71-82, © Copyright The Free Press, a Corporation, 1957.

degrees, run counter to the mores and at times to the law, it becomes pertinent to inquire how they manage to continue in operation. The familiar "explanations" for the continuance of the political machine are not here in point. To be sure, it may well be that if "respectable citizenry" would live up to their political obligations, if the electorate were to be alert and enlightened; if the number of elective officers were substantially reduced from the dozens, even hundreds, which the average voter is now expected to appraise in the course of town, county, state and national elections; if the electorate were activated by the "wealthy and educated classes without whose participation," as the not-always democratically oriented Bryce put it, "the best-framed government must speedily degenerate";—if these and a plethora of similar changes in political structure were introduced, perhaps the "evils" of the political machine would indeed be exorcized.[1] But it should be noted that these changes are often not introduced, that political

23

machines have had the phoenix-like quality of arising strong and unspoiled from their ashes, that, in short, this structure has exhibited a notable vitality in many areas of American political life.

Proceeding from the functional view, therefore, that we should *ordinarily* (not invariably) expect persistent social patterns and social structures to perform positive functions *which are at the time not adequately fulfilled by other existing patterns and structures,* the thought occurs that perhaps this publicly maligned organization is, *under present conditions*, satisfying basic latent functions.[2] A brief examination of current analysis of this type of structure may also serve to illustrate additional problems of functional analysis.

SOME FUNCTIONS OF
THE POLITICAL MACHINE

Without presuming to enter into the variations of detail marking different political machines—a Tweed, Vare, Crump, Flynn, Hague are by no means identical types of bosses—we can briefly examine the functions more or less common to the political machine, as a generic type of social organization. We neither attempt to itemize all the diverse functions of the political machine nor imply that all these functions are similarly fulfilled by each and every machine.

The key structural function of the Boss is to organize, centralize and maintain in good working condition "the scattered fragments of power" which are at present dispersed through our political organization. By this centralized organization of political power, the boss and his apparatus can satisfy the needs of diverse subgroups in the larger community which are not adequately satisfied by legally devised and culturally approved social structures.

To understand the role of bossism and the machine, therefore, we must look at two types of sociological variables: (1) the *structural context* which makes it difficult, if not impossible, for morally approved structures to fulfill essential social functions, thus leaving the door open for political machines (or their structural equivalents) to fulfill these functions and (2) the subgroups whose distinctive needs are left unsatisfied, except for the latent functions which the machine in fact fulfills.[3]

Structural context. The constitutional framework of American political organization specifically precludes the legal possibility of highly centralized power and, it has been noted, thus "discourages the growth of effective and responsible leadership. The framers of the Constitution, as Woodrow Wilson observed, set up the check and balance system 'to keep government at a sort of mechanical equipoise by means of a standing amicable contest among its several organic parts.' They distrusted power as dangerous to liberty: and therefore they spread it thin and erected barriers against its concentration." This dispersion of power is found not only at the national level but in local areas as well. "As a consequence," Sait goes on to observe, "when *the people or particular groups* among them demanded

24

positive action, no one had adequate authority to act. The machine provided an antidote."[4]

The constitutional dispersion of power not only makes for difficulty of effective decision and action but when action does occur it is defined and hemmed in by legalistic considerations. In consequence, there developed "a much *more human system* of partisan government, whose chief object soon became the circumvention of government by law. . . .The lawlessness of the extra-official democracy was merely the counterpoise of the legalism of the official democracy. The lawyer having been permitted to subordinate democracy to the Law, the Boss had to be called in to extricate the victim, which he did after a fashion and for a consideration."[5]

Officially, political power is dispersed. Various well-known expedients were devised for this manifest objective. Not only was there the familiar separation of powers among the several branches of the government but, in some measure, tenure in each office was limited, rotation in office approved. And the scope of power inherent in each office was severely circumscribed. Yet, observes Sait in rigorously functional terms, "Leadership is necessary; and *since* it does not develop readily within the constitutional framework, the Boss provides it in a crude and irresponsible form from the outside."[6]

Put in more generalized terms, *the functional deficiencies of the official structure generate an alternative (unofficial) structure to fulfill existing needs somewhat more effectively*. Whatever its specific historical origins, the political machine persists as an apparatus for satisfying otherwise unfulfilled needs of diverse groups in the population. By turning to a few of these subgroups and their characteristic needs, we shall be led at once to a range of latent functions of the political machine.

Functions of the political machine for diverse groups. It is well known that one source of strength of the political machine derives from its roots in the local community and the neighborhood. The political machine does not regard the electorate as an amorphous, undifferentiated mass of voters. With a keen sociological intuition, the machine recognizes that the voter is a person living in a specific neighborhood, with specific personal problems and personal wants. Public issues are abstract and remote; private problems are extremely concrete and immediate. It is not through the generalized appeal to large public concerns that the machine operates, but through the direct, quasifeudal relationships between local representatives of the machine and voters in their neighborhood. Elections are won in the precinct.

The machine welds its links with ordinary men and women by elaborate networks of personal relations. Politics is transformed into personal ties. The precinct captain "must be a friend to every man, assuming if he does not feel sympathy with the unfortunate, and utilizing in his good works the resources which the boss puts at his disposal."[7] The precinct captain is forever a friend in need. In our prevailingly impersonal society, the machine, through its local agents, fulfills the important social *function of humanizing and personalizing all manner of assistance* to those in need. Foodbaskets and jobs, legal and extra-legal advice, setting to rights minor scrapes with the law, helping the bright poor boy to a political scholarship in a local college, looking after the bereaved—the whole range of crises when a feller needs a friend, and, above all, a friend who knows the score and who can do something about it,—all these find the ever-helpful precinct captain available in the pinch.

To assess this function of the political machine adequately, it is important to note not only that aid *is* provided but *the manner in which it is provided*. After all, other agencies do exist for dispensing such assistance. Welfare agencies, settlement houses, legal aid clinics, medical aid in free hospitals, public relief departments, immigration authorities—these and a multitude of other organizations are available to provide the most varied types of assistance. But in contrast to the professional techniques of the welfare worker which may typically represent in the mind of the recipient the cold, bureaucratic dispensation of limited aid following upon detailed investigation of *legal* claims to aid of the "client" are the unprofessional techniques of the precinct captain who asks no questions, exacts no compliance with legal rules of eligibility and does not "snoop" into private affairs.[8]

For many, the loss of "self-respect" is too high a price for legalized assistance. In contrast to the gulf between the settlement house workers who so often come from a different social class, educational background and ethnic group, the precinct worker is "just one of us," who understands what it's all about. The condescending lady bountiful can hardly compete with the understanding friend in need. In *this struggle between alternative structures for fulfilling the nominally same function* of providing aid and support to those who need it, it is clearly the machine politician who is better integrated with the groups which he serves than the impersonal, professionalized, socially distant and legally constrained welfare worker. And since the politician can at times influence and manipulate the official organizations for the dispensation of assistance, whereas the welfare worker has practically no influence on the political machine, this only adds to his greater effectiveness. More colloquially and also, perhaps, more incisively, it was the Boston ward leader, Martin Lomansey, who described this essential function to the curious Lincoln Steffens: "I think," said Lomansey, "that there's got to be in every ward somebody that any bloke can come to—no matter what he's done—and get help. *Help, you understand; none of your law and justice, but help*."[9]

The "deprived classes," then, constitute one subgroup for whom the political machine satisfies wants not adequately satisfied in the same fashion by the legitimate social structure.

For a second subgroup, that of business (primarily "big" business but also "small"), the political boss serves the function of providing those political privileges which entail immediate economic gains. Business corporations, among which the public utilities (railroads, local transportation and electric light companies, communications corporations) are simply the most conspicuous in this regard, seek special political dispensations which will enable them to stabilize their situation and to near their objective of maximizing profits. Interestingly enough, corporations often want to avoid a chaos of uncontrolled competition. They want the greater security of an economic czar who controls, regulates and organizes competition, providing that this czar is not a public official with his decisions subject to public scrutiny and public control. (The latter would be "government control," and hence taboo.) The political boss fulfills these requirements admirably.

Examined for a moment apart from any moral considerations, the political apparatus operated by the Boss is effectively designed to perform these functions with a minimum of inefficiency. Holding the strings of diverse governmental divisions, bureaus and agencies in his competent hands, the Boss rationalizes the relations between public and private business. He serves as the business community's ambassador in the otherwise alien (and sometimes unfriendly) realm of government. And, in strict business-like terms, he is well-paid for his economic services to his respectable business clients. In an article entitled, "An Apology to Graft," Lincoln Steffens suggested that "Our economic system, which held up riches, power and acclaim as prizes to men bold enough and able enough to buy corruptly timber, mines, oil fields and franchises and 'get away with it,' was at fault."[10] And, in a conference with a

hundred or so of Los Angeles business leaders, he described a fact well known to all of them: the Boss and his machine were an *integral part* of the organization of the economy. "You cannot build or operate a railroad, or a street railway, gas, water, or power company, develop and operate a mine, or get forests and cut timber on a large scale, or run any privileged business, without corrupting or joining in the corruption of the government. You tell me privately that you must, and here I am telling you semi-publicly that you must. And that is so all over the country. And that means that we have an organization of society in which, *for some reason*, you and your kind, the ablest, most intelligent, most imaginative, daring, and resourceful leaders of society, are and must be against society and its laws and its all-around growth."[11]

Since the demand for the services of special privileges are built into the structure of the society, the Boss fulfills diverse functions for this second subgroup of business-seeking-privilege. These "needs" of business, as presently constituted, are not adequately provided for by conventional and culturally approved social structures; consequently, the extra-legal but more-or-less efficient organization of the political machine comes to provide these services. To adopt an *exclusively* moral attitude toward the "corrupt political machine" is to lose sight of the very structural conditions which generate the "evil" that is so bitterly attacked. To adopt a functional outlook is to provide not an apologia for the political machine but a more solid basis for modifying or eliminating the machine, *providing* spe-

27

cific structural arrangements are introduced either for eliminating these effective demands of the business community or, if that is the objective, of satisfying these demands through alternative means.

A third set of distinctive functions fulfilled by the political machine for a special subgroup is that of providing alternative channels of social mobility for those otherwise excluded from the more conventional avenues for personal "advancement." Both the sources of this special "need" (for social mobility) and the respect in which the political machine comes to help satisfy this need can be understood by examining the structure of the larger culture and society. As is well known, the American culture lays enormous emphasis on money and power as a "success" goal legitimate for all members of the society. By no means alone in our inventory of cultural goals, it still remains among the most heavily endowed with positive affect and value. However, certain subgroups and certain ecological areas are notable for the relative absence of opportunity for achieving these (monetary and power) types of success. They constitute, in short, sub-populations where "the cultural emphasis upon pecuniary success has been absorbed, but where there is *little access to conventional and legitimate* means for attaining such success. The conventional occupational opportunities of persons in (such areas) are almost completely limited to manual labor. Given our cultural stigmatization of manual labor,[12] and its correlate, the prestige of white-collar work, it is clear that the result is a tendency to achieve these culturally approved objec-

tives *through whatever means are possible*. These people are on the one hand, "asked to orient their conduct toward the prospect of accumulating wealth [and power] and, on the other, they are largely denied effective opportunities to do so institutionally."

It is within the context of social structure that the political machine fulfills the basic function of providing avenues of social mobility for the otherwise disadvantaged. Within this context, even the corrupt political machine and the racket "represent the triumph of amoral intelligence over morally prescribed 'failure' when the channels of vertical mobility are closed or narrowed *in a society which places a high premium on economic affluence, [power] and social ascent for all its members*."[13] As one sociologist has noted on the basis of several years of close observation in a slum area:

The sociologist who dismisses racket and political organizations as deviations from desirable standards thereby neglects some of the major elements of slum life. . . . *He does not discover the functions they perform for the members* [of the groupings in the slum]. The Irish and later immigrant peoples have had the greatest difficulty in finding places for themselves in our urban social and economic structure. Does anyone believe that the immigrants and their children could have achieved their present degree of social mobility without gaining control of the political organization of some of our largest cities? The same is true of the racket organization. *Politics and the rackets have furnished an important means of social mobility for individuals, who, because of ethnic background and low class position,* are blocked from advancement in the "respectable" channels.[14]

This, then, represents a third type of function performed for a distinctive subgroup. This function, it may be noted in passing, is fulfilled by the *sheer* existence and operation of the political machine, for it is in the machine itself that these individuals and subgroups find their culturally induced needs more or less satisfied. It refers to the services which the political apparatus provides for its own personnel. But seen in the wider social context we have set forth, it no longer appears as *merely* a means of self-aggrandizement for profit-hungry and power-hungry *individuals*, but as an organized provision for *subgroups* otherwise excluded from or handicapped in the race for "getting ahead."

Just as the political machine performs services for "legitimate" business, so it operates to perform not dissimilar services for "illegitimate" business: vice, crime and rackets. Once again, the basic sociological role of the machine in this respect can be more fully appreciated only if one temporarily abandons attitudes of moral indignation, to examine in all moral innocence the actual workings of the organization. In this light, it at once appears that the subgroup of the professional criminal, racketeer or gambler has basic similarities of organization, demands and operation to the subgroup of the industrialist, man of business or speculator. If there is a Lumber King or an Oil King, there is also a Vice King or a Racket King. If expansive legitimate business organizes administrative and financial syndicates to "rationalize" and to "integrate" diverse areas of production and business enterprise, so expansive rackets and crime organize syndicates to bring order to the otherwise chaotic areas of production of illicit goods and services. If legitimate business regards the proliferation of small business enterprises as wasteful and inefficient, substituting, for example, the giant chain stores for hundreds of corner groceries, so illegitimate business adopts the same businesslike attitude and syndicates crime and vice.

Finally, and in many respects, most important, is the basic similarity, if not near-identity, of the economic role of "legitimate" business and of "illegitimate" business. *Both are in some degree concerned with the provision of goods and services for which there is an economic demand*. Morals aside, they are both business, industrial and professional enterprises, dispensing goods and services which some people want, for which there is a market in which goods and services are transformed into commodities. And, in a prevalently market society, we should expect appropriate enterprises to arise whenever there is a market demand for certain goods or services.

As is well known, vice, crime and the rackets *are* "big business." Consider only that there have been estimated to be about 500,000 professional prostitutes in the United States of 1950, and compare this with the approximately 200,000 physicians and 350,000 professional registered nurses. It is difficult to estimate which have the larger clientele: the professional men and women of medicine or the professional men and women of vice.

29

It is, of course, difficult to estimate the economic assets, income, profits and dividends of illicit gambling in this country and to compare it with the economic assets, income, profits and dividends of, say, the shoe industry, but it is altogether possible that the two industries are about on a par. No precise figures exist on the annual expenditures on illicit narcotics, and it is probable that these are less than the expenditures on candy, but it is also probable that they are larger than the expenditure on books.

It takes but a moment's thought to recognize that, *in strictly economic terms*, there is no relevant difference between the provision of licit and of illicit goods and services. The liquor traffic illustrates this perfectly. It would be peculiar to argue that prior to 1920 (when the 18th amendment became effective), the provision of liquor constituted an economic service, that from 1920 to 1933, its production and sale no longer constituted an economic service dispensed in a market, and that from 1934 to the present, it once again took on a serviceable aspect. Or, it would be *economically* (not morally) absurd to suggest that the sale of bootlegged liquor in the dry state of Kansas is less a response to a market demand than the sale of publicly manufactured liquor in the neighboring wet state of Missouri. Examples of this sort can of course be multiplied many times over. Can it be held that in European countries, with registered and legalized prostitution, the prostitute contributes an economic service, whereas in this country, lacking legal sanction, the prostitute provides no such service? Or that the professional abortionist is in the economic market where he is legally taboo? Or that gambling satisfies a specific demand for entertainment in Nevada, where it constitutes the largest business enterprise of the larger cities in the state, but that it differs essentially in this respect from motion pictures in the neighboring state of California?[15]

The failure to recognize that these businesses are only *morally* and not *economically* distinguishable from "legitimate" businesses has led to badly scrambled analysis. Once the economic identity of the two is recognized, we may anticipate that if the political machine performs functions for "legitimate big business" it will be all the more likely to perform not dissimilar functions for "illegitimate big business." And, of course, such is often the case.

The distinctive function of the political machine for their criminal, vice and racket clientele is to enable them to operate in satisfying the economic demands of a large market without due interference from the government. Just as big business may contribute funds to the political party war-chest to ensure a minimum of governmental interference, so with big rackets and big crime. In both instances, the political machine can, in varying degrees, provide "protection." In both instances, many features of the structural context are identical: (1) market demands for goods and services; (2) the operators' concern with maximizing gains from their enterprises; (3) the need for partial control of government which might otherwise interfere with these activities of businessmen; (4) the need for an efficient, powerful and centralized agency to provide an effective liaison of "business" with government.

Without assuming that the foregoing pages exhaust either the range of functions or the range of subgroups served by the political machine, we can at least see that *it presently fulfills some functions for these diverse subgroups which are not adequately fulfilled by culturally approved or more conventional structures.*

Several additional implications of the functional analysis of the political machine can be mentioned here only in passing, although they obviously require to be developed at length. First, the foregoing analysis has direct implications for *social engineering*. It helps explain why the periodic efforts at "political reform," "turning the rascals out" and "cleaning political house" are typically (though not necessarily) short-lived and ineffectual. It exemplifies a basic theorem: *any attempt to eliminate an existing social structure without providing adequate alternative structures for fulfilling the functions previously fulfilled by the abolished organization is doomed to failure.* (Needless to say, this theorem has much wider bearing than the one instance of the political machine.) When "political reform" confines itself to the manifest task of "turning the rascals out," it is engaging in little more than sociological magic. The reform may for a time bring new figures into the political limelight; it may serve the casual social function of re-assuring the electorate that the moral virtues remain intact and will ultimately triumph; it may actually effect a turnover in the personnel of the political machine; it may even, for a time, so curb the activities of the machine as to leave unsatisfied the many needs it has previously fulfilled. But, inevitably, unless the reform also involves a "re-forming" of the social and political structure such that the existing needs are satisfied by alternative structures or unless it involves a change which eliminates these needs altogether, the political machine will return to its integral place in the social scheme of things. *To seek social change, without due recognition of the manifest and latent functions performed by the social organization undergoing change, is to indulge in social ritual rather than social engineering.* The concepts of manifest and latent functions (or their equivalents) are indispensible elements in the theoretic repertoire of the social engineer. In this crucial sense, these concepts are not "merely" theoretical (in the abusive sense of the term), but are eminently practical. In the deliberate enactment of social change, they can be ignored only at the price of considerably heightening the risk of failure.

A second implication of this analysis of the political machine also has a bearing upon areas wider than the one we have considered. The paradox has often been noted that the supporters of the political machine include both the "respectable" business class elements who are, of course, opposed to the criminal or racketeer and the distinctly "unrespectable" elements of the underworld. And, at first appearance, this is cited as an instance of very strange bedfellows. The learned judge is not infrequently called upon to sentence the very racketeer beside whom he sat the night before at an informal dinner of the political bigwigs. The district attorney jostles the exonerated convict on his way to the back room where the Boss has called a meeting. The big business man may complain almost as bitterly as the big racketeer about the "extortionate" contributions to the party fund demanded by the Boss. Social opposites meet—in the smoke-filled room of the successful politician.

In the light of a functional analysis all this of course no longer seems paradoxical. Since the machine serves both the businessman and the criminal man, the two seemingly antipodal groups intersect. This points to a more general theorem: *the social functions of an organization help determine the structure (including the recruitment of personnel involved in the structure), just as the structure helps determine the effectiveness with which the functions are fulfilled*. In terms of social status, the business group and the criminal group are indeed poles apart. But status does not fully determine behavior and the interrelations between groups. Functions modify these relations. Given their distinctive needs, the several subgroups in the large society are "integrated," whatever their personal desires or intentions, by the centralizing structure which serves these several needs. In a phrase with many implications which require further study, *structure affects function and function affects structure*. . . .

NOTES

1. These "explanations" are "causal" in design. They profess to indicate the social conditions under which political machines come into being. In so far as they are empirically confirmed, these explanations of course add to our knowledge concerning the problem: how is it that political machines operate in certain areas and not in others? How do they manage to continue? *But these causal accounts are not sufficient*. The functional consequences of the machine, as we shall see, go far toward supplementing the causal interpretation.

2. I trust it is superfluous to add that this hypothesis is not "in support of the political machine." The question whether the dysfunctions of the machine outweigh its functions, the question whether alternative structures are not available which may fulfill its functions without necessarily entailing its social dysfunctions, still remain to be considered at an appropriate point. We are here concerned with documenting the statement that moral judgments based *entirely* on an appraisal of manifest functions of a social structure are "unrealistic" in the strict sense, i.e., they do not take into account other actual consequences of that structure, consequences which may provide basic social support for the structure. As will be indicated later, "social reforms" or "social engineering" which ignore latent functions do so on pain of suffering acute disappointments and boomerang effects.

3. Again, as with preceding cases, we shall not consider the possible dysfunctions of the political machine.

4. Edward M. Sait, "Machine, Political," *Encyclopedia of the Social Sciences*, IX, 658 b [italics supplied]; *cf.* A. F. Bentley, *The Process of Government* (Chicago, 1908), chap. 2.

5. Herbert Croly, *Progressive Democracy* (New York, 1914), p. 254, cited by Sait, *op. cit.,* 658 b.

6. Sait, *op. cit.,* 659 a. [italics supplied].

7. *Ibid.,* 659 a.

8. Much the same contrast with official welfare policy is found in Harry Hopkins' open-handed and non-political distribution of unemployment relief in New York State under the governorship of Franklin Delano Roosevelt. As Sherwood reports: "Hopkins was harshly criticized for these irregular activities by the established welfare agencies, which claimed it was 'unpro-

fessional conduct' to hand out work tickets without thorough investigation of each applicant, his own or his family's financial resources and probably his religious affiliations. 'Harry told the agency to go to hell,' said [Hopkins' associate, Dr. Jacob A.] Goldberg." Robert E. Sherwood, *Roosevelt and Hopkins, An Intimate History* (New York: Harper, 1948), 30.

9. *The Autobiography of Lincoln Steffens* (Chautauqua, New York: Chautauqua Press, 1931), 618. Deriving largely from Steffens, as he says, F. Stuart Chapin sets forth these functions of the political machine with great clarity. See his *Contemporary American Institutions* (New York: Harper, 1934), 40-54.

10. *Autobiography of Lincoln Steffens*, 570.

11. *Ibid.*, 572-3 [italics supplied]. This helps explain, as Steffens noted after Police Commissioner Theodore Roosevelt, "the prominence and respectability of the men and women who intercede for crooks" when these have been apprehended in a periodic effort to "clean up the political machine." *Cf.* Steffens, 371, and *passim.*

12. See the National Opinion Research Center survey of evaluation of occupations which firmly documents the general impression that the manual occupations rate very low indeed in the social scale of values, *even among those who are themselves engaged in manual labor*. Consider this latter point in its full implications. In effect, the cultural and social structure exacts the values of pecuniary and power success even among those who find themselves confined to the stigmatized manual occupations. Against this background, consider the powerful motivation for achieving this type of "success" by any means whatsoever. A garbage-collector who joins with other Americans in the view that the garbage-collector is "the lowest of the low" occupations can scarcely have a self-image which is pleasing to him; he is in a "pariah" occupation in the very society where he is assured that "all who have genuine merit can get ahead." Add to this, his occasional recognition that "he didn't have the same chance as others, no matter what they say," and one perceives the enormous psychological pressure upon him for "evening up the score" by finding some

means, whether strictly legal or not, for moving ahead. All this provides the structural and derivatively psychological background for the "socially induced need" in *some* groups to find some accessible avenue for social mobility.

13. Merton, "Social structure and anomie,"

14. William F. Whyte, "Social organization in the slums," *American Sociological Review*, Feb. 1943, 8, 34-39 (italics supplied). Thus, the political machine and the racket represent a special case of the type of organizational adjustment to the conditions described in chapter IV [of Merton work]. It represents, note, an *organizational* adjustment: definite structures arise and operate to reduce somewhat the acute tensions and problems of individuals caught up in the described conflict between the "cultural accent on success-for-all" and the "socially structured fact of unequal opportunities for success." . . . Other types of *individual* "adjustment" are possible: lone-wolf crime, psychopathological states, rebellion, retreat by abandoning the culturally approved goals, etc. Likewise, other types of *organizational adjustment* sometimes occur; the racket or the political machine are not *alone* available as organized means for meeting this socially induced problem. Participation in revolutionary organizations, for example, can be seen within this context, as an alternative mode of organizational adjustment. All this bears theoretic notice here, since we might otherwise overlook the basic functional concepts of functional substitutes and functional equivalents. . . .

15. Perhaps the most perceptive statement of this view has been made by Hawkins and Waller. "The prostitute, the pimp, the peddler of dope, the operator of the gambling hall, the vendor of obscene pictures, the bootlegger, the abortionist, all are productive, all produce services or goods which people desire and for which they are willing to pay. It happens that society has put these goods and services under the ban, but people go on producing them and people go on consuming them, and an act of the legislature does not make them any less a part of the economic system." "Critical notes on the cost of crime," *Journal of Criminal Law and Criminology*, 1936, 26, 679-94, at 684.

BOSS COX'S CINCINNATI
A Historian's View

Zane L. Miller

Many observers of the turn-of-the-century urban scene have depicted bossism as one of the great unmitigated evils of the American city, as a tyrannical, authoritarian, relentlessly efficient and virtually invulnerable political system. Between 1904 and 1912, for example, George B. Cox was castigated by writers in four national magazines. Gustav Karger called him the "Proprietor of Cincinnati." Lincoln Steffens declared that "Cox's System" was "one great graft," "the most perfect thing of the kind in this country." Frank Parker Stockbridge claimed that "The Biggest Boss of Them All" had an organization "more compact and closely knit than any of the political machines which have dominated New York, Philadelphia, Chicago, St. Louis or San Francisco." And George Kibbe Turner concluded that in the 1890s "the man from Dead Man's Corner ... seated himself over the city of Cincinnati. For twenty years he remained there—a figure like no other in the United States, or in the world."[1] Yet these knowledgeable and sensitive journalists obscured as much as they revealed about the nature of Queen City politics in the Progressive era. A new kind of city had developed, and "the boss" comprised only a fraction of its novel political system.

Paradoxically, Cox and his machine[2] were produced by, fed on, and ultimately helped dispel the spectacular disorder which engulfed Cincinnati in the late-nineteenth century and threatened the very survival of the democratic political process. In these years, increasing industrialization, technological innovations in communication and transportation—especially the coming of rapid transit—and continued foreign and domestic migration had reversed the physical pattern of the mid-century walking city and transformed Cincinnati into a physically

From "Boss Cox's Cincinnati: A Study in Urbanization and Politics, 1880-1914," *The Journal of American History* 54 (March 1968): 823-38. Reprinted by permission of the publisher.

enlarged, divided, and potentially explosive metropolis.[3]

Old citizens were shocked as familiar landmarks and neighborhoods vanished. By 1900, railroads and warehouses had monopolized the Ohio River bottoms. The financial and retail districts had moved up into the Basin around Fountain Square, the focus of the street railway system; new club, theater, and tenderloin districts had developed; and industries had plunged up Mill Creek Valley, converting Mohawk-Brighton into "the undisputed industrial bee-hive of the Great Queen City of the West," surrounding once fashionable Dayton Street, creating a new community called Ivorydale, and reaching out to the villages of Norwood and Oakley in search of cheap land, ready access to railroads, and less congested and more cheerful surroundings.[4]

The Over-the-Rhine entertainment section along Vine Street became tawdry with commercialism. It now had, complained one habitué, "all the tarnished tinsel of a Bohemianism with the trimmings of a gutter and the morals of a sewer"—a repulsive contrast, he felt, to "the old-time concert and music halls . . . where one could take wife, sister, or sweetheart and feel secure . . . that not one obnoxious word would profane their ears."[5]

The fashionable residential districts which had flanked the center of the walking city began to disintegrate. One family after another fled the East End for the hills around the Basin, leaving only a small coterie led by the Charles P. Tafts to stave off the advance of factories and slums.[6] The elite West End seemed to

disappear overnight. It "did not go down imperceptibly," recalled one old resident. "It went to ruin almost as if a bombshell sent it to destruction."[7]

The Hilltops, at mid-century the private preserve of cemeteries, colleges, and a handful of wealthy families,[8] became the prime residential district in the new city. The crush to get in generated new tensions. In 1899 one observer acidly remarked: "When rapid transit came the Hebrews . . . flocked to" Walnut Hills

until it was known by the name of New Jerusalem. Avondale was then heralded as the suburb of deliverance, but again rapid transit brought the wealthy Hebrews . . . in numbers greater than the flock of crows that every morning and evening darkens her skies, until now it has been facetiously said that the congregation has assembled in force and . . . when Avondale is roofed over the synagogue will be complete.[9]

The diffusion of wealthy families, the reduction in casual social and business contacts, and the construction of new communities made ardent joiners of the Hilltops elite. Each neighborhood had an improvement association, and between 1880 and 1905 five new businessmen's organizations devoted to boosting the city's lethargic economy had appeared. In the same period six social clubs opened downtown facilities, and three country clubs were started. By 1913, moreover, there were twenty-two exclusive clubs and patriotic societies and innumerable women's groups.[10] These developments helped counteract the disruptive effects of the "country movement," as one visi-

Zane L. Miller

tor labeled it, which was "so general that church-going became an affair of some difficulty" and "society itself . . . more or less disintegrated."[11]

But not all those moving out were affluent. Liberated by rapid transit, skilled and semiskilled workers and moderately prosperous professional and white-collar men with life savings, the courage to take out a mortgage, an equity in a building and loan association, or a willingness to rent a flat in a double or triple decker, also fled the Basin.[12] They took refuge in a no-man's-land between the center of the city and the Hilltops frontier which was similar to an area dubbed the Zone of Emergence by Boston social workers.[13]

Zone residents formed what the Cincinnati *Post* referred to as "the so-called middle class . . . , the class that makes any city . . . what it is . . . [,] the class that takes in the great body of people between wealth and poverty" and builds up "many organizations, societies, associations, fraternities and clubs that bring together people who are striving upward, trying to uplift themselves, and hence human society."[14]

They, too, found life in the new city a novel experience. A retired leather factory porter who moved into the Zone lamented:

When I lived down on Richmond in a little house we cooked the corn beef and cabbage in the house and ate in there, and when we wanted to go to the toilet we went out into the yard, now I live in a fine house, I am made to eat . . . out in the yard, and when I want to go to the toilet I have to go into the house.[15]

Graham R. Taylor had noted that since most Zone residents commuted they suffered a severe "dislocation of the normal routine of factory and home": they had to adjust to "the need for travel and its curtailment of leisure and income. . . . ," to eating lunches away from home, to doing without "customary city facilities," and to knowing the feeling of "isolation from their fellows."[16] Price Hill—like the rest of the Zone a heavily Catholic area—felt itself conspicuously cut off. In the 1890s the editor of the *Catholic-Telegraph*, denouncing the traction company as the "octopus," joined the Price Hill Improvement Association in begging both city and traction company officials to bring the area "within range of the civilized world" and suggested secession as a means of dramatizing to the "people east of Millcreek" that a new public school, "granted by the unbounded munificence of the City of Cincinnati," did not amount to a redemption of the city's annexation pledges.[17]

The exodus, however, did not depopulate the Basin. Instead, a great residential Circle formed around the central business district. It filled with newcomers and those who lacked the means to get out—rural whites and Negroes from the South, Germans, Irish, Greeks, Italians, and Jews from eastern Europe. Working at the poorest paying jobs available, they were jammed into the most congested quarters. The Circle led all other areas of the city in arrests, mortality, and disease.[18]

Although the pressure to escape was enormous, the barriers were formidable. Ignorant of the ways of the city, as an Associated Charities report put it, Circle dwellers had to be "shown how to buy,

36

how to cook, how to make the home attractive, how to find employment." Many, "utterly friendless and discouraged," succumbed to "the damnable absence of want or desire" and grew "indifferent . . . to their own elevation."[19] Plagued by "physical bankruptcy,"[20] they found it difficult to find and hold jobs, let alone form and maintain the kind of organizations which enabled Zone residents to shield themselves from economic disaster, legal pitfalls, social isolation, and apathy.[21]

The immediate impact of the emergence of the new city pushed Cincinnati to the brink of anarcy. In March 1884, the *Enquirer* complained that the police had failed to choke off a crime wave although, in the last year alone, there had been twelve arrests for malicious shooting, twenty-nine for malicious cutting, forty-seven for cutting with intent to wound, 284 for shooting with intent to kill, ninety-two for murder and manslaughter, and 948 for carrying a concealed weapon. The total number of arrests came to 56,784. The city's population was 250,000.[22] Later that same month, a lynch mob descended on the county jail. While police and militia fought off the mob, gangs looted stores and shops on the fringe of the downtown district. In three days of riot the courthouse was burned to the ground, fifty-four people were killed, and an estimated 200 people wounded.[23]

During the fall elections, violence erupted in the lower wards; two policemen and one Negro were killed. Congressman Benjamin Butterworth remarked that he had "never witnessed anywhere such coarse brutality and such riotous

demonstrations. . . ." Cincinnati, he concluded, "seems . . . doomed to perdition."[24]

Less than two years later the city faced another major crisis. On May 1, 1886, Cincinnati workers joined in nationwide demonstrations for the eight-hour day. These were followed by a series of strikes. The militia was called out, and for two weeks the city resembled an armed camp. Only the show of force and, perhaps, the memory of the courthouse catastrophe prevented another riot.[25]

Yet labor remained restive, and a rash of strikes followed. By 1892, the paternalistic system which had dominated the breweries was smashed.[26] And in 1894, Judge William Howard Taft spent the hot days of June and July "trying to say nothing to reporters" and "issuing injunctions" in an effort to control and prevent the railroad strike from leading to mass violence.[27]

The Sunday-closing question was another explosive issue. The *Post*, the *Catholic-Telegraph*, a Committee of Five Hundred, and many Protestant clergymen all leveled scathing attacks on the continental Sabbath. "Sunday in Cincinnati," asserted one Methodist minister, "is a high carnival of drunkenness, base sensuality, reeking debauchery and bloody, often fatal crime." Other spokesmen tied the open Sunday to anarchism, atheism, corrupt politicians, a decadent daily press, indifferent public officials, and the ruthless exploitation of labor.[28] "The modern Puritan," insisted Charles P. Taft, "intends to rise up and oppose to the uttermost this kind of Sunday."[29]

When, in 1889, the mayor announced his intention to enforce the Sunday-closing law for saloons, the city almost faced another riot. Some 1,000 saloon-keepers vowed to ignore the new policy. When a cadre of police and firemen marched over the Rhine to close Kissell's saloon, an unruly crowd gathered, epithets were hurled, but no violence occurred. Kissell's was closed; the "era of the back door," with "front doors locked and curtains up, but back doors widened," had opened.[30]

These spectacular outbreaks plus other pressures overwhelmed city hall. Indeed, scarcely a residential area, economic interest, or social or occupational group was left unscathed by the multidimensional disorder. As the physical area of the city expanded, officials were besieged by demands for the extension, improvement, and inauguration of public services of all kinds and for lower taxes. Simultaneously, the relative decline of the city heightened the urgency of the agitation. Municipal institutions and agencies, established to meet the needs of the walking city, became overburdened, outmoded, and dilapidated.[31]

The new city, with old ways shattered, provided a fertile breeding ground for turmoil and discontent and, as it turned out, for innovation and creative reconstruction. Initially, however, this unprecedented change accompanied by unprecedented demands for government action produced only the hope of reform. In 1885, on the eve of the repudiation of a Democratic administration, William Howard Taft predicted that "the clouds are beginning to break over this Sodom of ours and the sun of decency is beginning to dispel the moral miasma that has

rested on us now for so many years. It's the beginning of an era of reform."[32]

Yet for almost a decade no party could put together a decisive ruling majority.[33] The city's political processes seemed frozen by a paralyzing factionalism. The division of the city into residential districts which roughly coincided with socio-economic lines made it difficult for the wealthy and well-educated[34] to keep in contact with and control ward politics. As a result, extreme factionalism developed which could, apparently, be surmounted only by appealing to a host of neighborhood leaders and by constructing alliances which crossed party lines.

According to close observers, the chief products of this system were the use of money in city conventions and the rise of what Charles P. Taft called the "bummer," a "queer creature" who "evolves somehow from the slums. . . ." In youth "a bootblack, a newsboy or a general loafer," he matured into "an Arab" who needed only "a good standing with a saloon that has a fine layout during the day." A "hustler at the polls and conventions," the bummer was in such demand that he could accept money from competing candidates, thus lengthening the convention and contributing to interfactional dealing. After studying the influence of the "bummer," Taft gloomily concluded that the "day of pure politics can never be . . . until a riot, a plague or flood kills off all the ward bummers."[35]

By 1897, however, and without divine intervention, all this had changed. In January of that year, three months before the city election, the *Post* gravely announced its intention to describe "impassionately and without bias the means employed" in Cincinnati's "superior and unrecorded government." It was controlled by "the boss, whose power is absolute"—George B. Cox.[36]

The *Post's* analysis closely paralleled those made after the turn of the century. It dissected the patronage system, outlined the sources of financial support, and noted the attempted appeasement of the city's various special groups—the soldiers, the Germans, the Republican clubs, the Reform Jews, the legal and medical professions, the socially prominent Hilltops businessmen, and certain cooperative Democrats. It excitedly reported the effectiveness of the organization's intelligence system, the way the "plugger" and the "knocker" wore "beaten paths to the office of the boss to urge the appointment of this man, the discharge of that [,] or to report some feature of misconduct or expression. . . ." The paper noted that Cox was always available for consultation with any citizen regardless of station or status and that he had been little more than one of several important factional leaders until, in 1886, Governor Joseph B. Foraker selected him to serve as chief advisor on patronage and political affairs in Hamilton County.[37]

Foraker made a shrewd choice; Cox had grown up with the new city and received a liberal education in its ways. The son of British immigrants, he was born in 1853 and reared in the Eighteenth Ward, a district which by the 1880s contained fashionable as well as slum housing, factories, and its share of saloons and brothels. His father died

when Cox was eight. Successively, Cox worked as a bootblack, newsboy, lookout for a gambling joint, grocery deliveryman, bartender, and tobacco salesman. His school principal, who later became superintendent of schools, claimed that Cox was frequently in boyish trouble in classes, exhibited an "undisguised love for his mother," and "never lied . . . bore malice, sulked, whined or moped." Cox had also been exposed to religion. Although not a churchgoer, as an adult he had, according to one journalist, "dormant powerful sentiments, which rest on foundations of the firmest faith."[38]

In the mid-1870s Cox acquired a saloon in his home neighborhood. He entered politics and served on the city council from 1878 until 1885 when, after joining forces with the Republican reform mayoralty candidate, he ran unsuccessfully for county clerk. He tried for the same post in 1888, failed, and never again stood for public office.[39]

At that time, moving away politically from the Circle, Cox worked with George Moerlein, perhaps the strongest of the GOP professionals in the Zone. In 1890, he and Moerlein quarreled over patronage; and in the city convention of 1891, Cox was able, with the support of the Blaine Club, a kind of political settlement house that he had helped to establish, to defeat Moerlein's candidate for police judge and nominate his own man.[40] Moerlein men now became Cox men. So, too, did Charles P. Taft and the *Times-Star*, which had been one of the last, the most influential, and the most outspoken of Cox's critics in the Hilltops Republican ranks. It accepted Cox, the paper announced, to secure a "New Order" for Cincinnati.[41] And the president of the gas company, sensing the political drift, confided to his diary that he had "concluded [an] arrangement with Geo. B. Cox for services at $3500 per year quarterly to last for three years."[42] In the spring election of 1894 the Republicans carried the city with a plurality of over 6,500 votes, the first decisive municipal election in a decade.[43] In 1897, Cox was the honest broker in a coalition composed of Circle and Zone Negroes, Zone politicians, the gas and traction companies, and Hilltops Republican reformers.[44]

Election returns after 1885 disclose a clear pattern. The GOP won five successive contests by uniting powerful Hilltops support with enough strength in the Zone to overcome the Democratic grip on the Circle.[45] Until 1894 the margins of victory were perilously thin. The substantial triumph of that year merely marked the completion of the alliance which pitted a united periphery against the center of the city.

The heart of the Republican "New Order" coalition, and the critical factor in the election of 1894, was its appeal to voters in the Hilltops fringe who demanded order and reform. To satisfy the Hilltops, Cox and his associates eliminated the bummer, provided brief and decorous conventions, enfranchised Negroes by suppressing violence at the polls, reduced the rapid turnover in office, and cut down the incidence of petty graft and corporation raiding.

Moreover, the "machine" heeded the advice of its reform allies from the Hilltops. Cox accepted the secret ballot, voter registration, and a series of state laws which, though retaining the mayor-council form of government with ward representation, were designed to give the city a stable and more centralized government. The administrations which he indorsed started to build a professional police force, expanded and re-equipped the fire department, pushed through a $6,000,000 water-works program, renovated municipal institutions, supported the growth of the University of Cincinnati, launched extensive street-paving and sewer-constructing projects, and tried to reduce the smoke problem and expand the city's park acreage. They also opened the door to housing regulation, suppressed the Sunday saloon, flagrant public gambling, and disorderly brothels (the city was never really closed), began to bring order into the chaotic public-utilities field by favoring privately owned, publicly regulated monopolies under the progressive management, and succeeded in keeping the tax rate low. The Republican regime, in short, brought positive government to Cincinnati.[46]

While this program also won votes in the Zone, it was not the sole basis for the party's popularity there. Many of the lieutenants and captains closest to Cox were Zone residents. They composed a colorful group known variously as "the gang," "the sports," or the "bonifaces"— a clique which met nightly Over-the-Rhine either at Schubert and Pels, where each had a special beer mug with his name gilded on it, or at the round table in Wielert's beer garden. Three of them owned or operated combination saloons, gambling joints, and dance halls; one was prominent in German charitable associations and the author of several textbooks used in the elementary schools; another served twenty consecutive terms as president of the Hamilton County League of Building Associations; and one was a former catcher for the Cincinnati Redlegs.[47]

Their tastes, behavior, and attitudes were conveniently summarized in the biographical sketches of ward leaders and city officials in the 1901 *Police and Municipal Guide*. All were characterized as friendly, well-known, "All Around Good-Fellows" who liked a story, belonged to several social and fraternal groups, gave generously to charity, and treated the poor and sick with special kindness. They were all among the most ardent supporters of any project to boost the city.

Cox is pictured in the *Guide* as an adherent to the code of the Zone who had risen to the top. He was a *bon vivant* who enjoyed good cigars and good jokes, a man of wealth whose recently completed Clifton mansion was luxuriously decorated and adorned with expensive works of art, a man of impressive but quiet and private charity. Above all, he was true to his word, loyal to his friends, yet quick to reprimand and replace those who betrayed his trust by misusing public office.[48]

Cox and his top civil servants—surrounded by a motley crowd of newspaper reporters, former boxers and ball players, vaudeville and burlesque performers, and other Vine Street characters—provided an attractive model for men awed by the glamor, wealth, and

power which was so visible yet so elusive in the new city. Cox's opponents in the Zone seldom attacked him or this inside group directly. Even in the heat of the 1897 campaign, the *Volksfreund*, the German Catholic Democratic daily, carefully described Cox as an "amiable man" who had to be "admired" for his "success" and, either ignoring or unaware of the process of negotiation and mediation by which he ruled, criticized him only for his illiberality in imposing "dictatorial methods" on the GOP.[49] Indeed, most Zone residents, like those of the Hilltops, found it difficult to object to a government which seemed humane, efficient, and progressive.

Yet it would be a mistake to overestimate the strength of the "New Order" Republican coalition. Its victories from 1885 to 1894 were won by perilously close pluralities. The organization, moreover, failed to carry a referendum for the sale of the city-owned Southern Railroad in 1896 and lost the municipal contest in 1897 to a reform fusion ticket, and the fall elections of 1897, 1898, and 1899 to the Democrats.[50] In all these reversals, crucial defections occurred in both the Hilltops and the Zone. Skittish voters grew indignant over alleged corruption, outraged by inaction on the traction and gas questions, piqued by the rising cost of new city projects, annoyed by the slow expansion of the educational program, or uneasy over the partial sacrifice of democracy to efficiency within the Republican organization.[51]

Thereafter, however, the Republicans rallied and won three of the next four city elections by unprecedented margins.

The strategy and tactics remained essentially the same. Although not wholly averse to raising national issues, Cox's group gave local affairs the most emphasis.[52] The organization was occasionally purged of its less savory elements. Cox and his Zone advisors continued to consult with the Hilltops allies on nominations. The party promised and, in fact, tried to deliver order and reform. Without abolishing ward representation in the city council, it strengthened the mayor and streamlined the administration. The party also broadened and deepened its program as civic associations, women's clubs, social workers, social gospellers, and spokesmen for the new unionism—all novel forces in urban politics—expanded and elaborated their demands.[53]

But voting patterns underwent a fundamental and, for the GOP, an ultimately disastrous change. By 1903 the Republicans dominated the entire city, carrying not only the Zone and Hilltops but also the center. The Circle was now the invincible bulwark of Cox's power.[54]

There were several factors involved in the conversion of Circle Democrats to Republicanism. First, Cox had extensive personal contacts with them which dated back to his unsuccessful races for county clerk in the 1880s. Second, the Democrats had been unable to put down factionalism. By the late 1890s there were two reform elements in the party, both of which belabored the regulars from the center of the city as tainted with corruption, too cozy with Cox, and perhaps worst of all, as a discredit and burden to the party because they wore the charred shirt of the courthouse riot.[55]

In the wake of the fusionist victory of 1897, Mike Mullen, the leader of a riverfront Democratic ward, explained why he would henceforth work with the Republican party.

I have worked hard [for the Democratic party] have suffered much and have won for it many victories. Yet all the while there was a certain element . . . that looked on me with distrust. . . . [L]eaders of the Fusionist Party did not think enough of me to let me look after the voting in my own ward, but sent down a lot of people to watch the count. That decided me.[56]

He was later joined by Colonel Bob O'Brien who, like Mullen, specialized in Christmas turkey, soupline, and family-service politics.[57] These Democrats led their constituents into the Republican fold.

It was this alliance with the Circle which ultimately destroyed Cox. Anti-machine spokesmen were convinced that they had to educate the city before they could redeem it. They felt, too, that politics was a potent educational tool. But campaigns had to be spectacular in order to engage the voters' attention and participation. As A. Julius Freiberg notes, the "psychology" of the electorate was such that years of "speaking, writing, explaining, even begging and imploring" had been "to no purpose." The "reformer and his fellow students may sit about the table and evolve high principles for action, but the people . . . will not be fed by those principles unless there is a dramatic setting, and the favorite dramatic setting is the killing of a dragon." And all the people "love the dramatic; not merely the poor, but the rich, and the middle class as well." All that was needed was a situation which would enable the right man to "bring to book the boss himself."[58]

Reformers hammered relentlessly at the theme that Cox was not a good boss; he was the head of a "syndicate" which included the worst products of slum life.[59] In "that part of the city where vice and infamy hold high revel," went one version of the charge, "the boss-made ticket finds its most numerous supporters. Every dive keeper, every creature who fattens upon the wages of sin . . . , all the elements at war with society have enlisted." Men "who claim to be respectable," the chief "beneficiaries of this unholy alliance . . . , go down into the gutter and accept office from hands that are reeking with the filth of the slums." Worse still, this "alliance of the hosts of iniquity with the greed of special privilege and ambition for power and place" plays so successfully "upon the prejudices and . . . superstition of the many that wrong is often espoused by those who in the end are the victims of the wrong."[60]

The reformers also inpugned Cox's personal integrity. Democratic County Prosecutor Henry T. Hunt secured evidence that Cox had perjured himself in 1906 when he said he had not received a cent of some $250,000 of interest on public funds which Republican county treasurers had been paid by bankers. In the spring of 1911, Hunt and the grand jury indicted Cox and 123 others during a broad investigation of politics, corruption, and vice.[61]

Finally, Hunt, stressing the issue of moral indignation, ran for mayor in the fall of 1911 on a Democratic reform ticket. Using the moral rhetoric of the muckraker, Hunt and his associates tied bossism, the chaos, poverty, and vice of the slums, and the malefactors of great wealth together and pictured them as a threat to the welfare of the whole city. Once again the Hilltops and Zone voted for order and reform. Hunt's progressive coalition swept the periphery, lost only in the Circle wards, and won the election.[62]

By that time, however, Cox was no longer boss. President Taft and Charles P. Taft had wanted Cox to step aside as early as 1905, but they found him indispensable. After the grand jury revelations, however, they were able to convince the "bonifaces" that Cox was a liability. With the organization against him, Cox retired. For a time, he insisted that his two chief assistants, August Herrmann and Rudolph Hynicka, should also quit, apparently convinced that they, like himself, could no longer command the confidence of the periphery. Charles P. Taft's *Times-Star* agreed. The two men, backed by the Blaine Club, merely resigned their official party positions but refused to get out of politics entirely.[63]

What, then, was Cox's role in politics and government in the new city? He helped create and manage a voluntary political-action organization which bridged the racial and cultural chasms between the Circle, Zone, and Hilltops. He and his allies were able to bring positive and moderate reform government to Cincinnati and to mitigate the conflict and disorder which accompanied the emergence of the new city. With the crisis atmosphere muted, ardent reformers could develop more sophisticated programs and agitate, educate, and organize without arousing the kind of devisive, emotional, and hysterical response which had immobilized municipal statesmen in the 1880s. In the process, while battering at the boss, the slums, and the special-privilege syndicate, they shattered the bonds of confidence which linked the Zone "bonifaces" and the moderate reformers of the Hilltops to Cox's organization. Cox, it seems, said more than he realized when, in 1892, he remarked that a boss was "not necessarily a public enemy."[64]

NOTES

1. Gustav J. Karger, "George Barnesdale Cox: Proprietor of Cincinnati," *Frank Leslie's Popular Monthly*, LVII (Jan. 1904), 273; Lincoln Steffens, "Ohio: A Tale of Two Cities," *McClure's Magazine*, XXV (June 1905), 309; Frank Parker Stockbridge, "The Biggest Boss of Them All," *Hampton's Magazine*, XXVI (Jan.-June 1911), 616; George Kibbe Turner, "The Thing Above the Law: The Rise and Rule of George B. Cox, and His Overthrow by Young Hunt and the Fighting Idealists of Cincinnati," *McClure's Magazine*, XXXVIII (March 1912), 580. See also Wallace S. Sayre and Nelson W. Polsby, "American Political Science and the Study of Urbanization," Philip M. Hauser and Leo F. Schnore, eds., *The Study of Urbanization* (New York, 1965), 115-23.
2. It operated, according to William Howard Taft, "as smoothly . . . as a nicely adjusted Corliss engine" Cincinnati *Enquirer*, Oct. 22, 1905.
3. Zane L. Miller, "Boss Cox and the Municipal Reformers: Cincinnati Progresivism, 1880-1914" (doctoral dissertation, University of Chicago, 1966), Part I. Introduction, 2-5.

4. For the quotation see Max Mosler, Jacob Hoffman, and James D. Smith, *Historic Brighton: Its Origin, Growth and Development* (Cincinnati, 1902), 91. See also James A. Green to Joseph C. Green, March 28, 1913, James A. Green Papers (Cincinnati Historical Society); Andrew Hickenlooper, "Reminiscences," 524, Andrew Hickenlooper Papers (Cincinnati Historical Society); Graham Romeyn Taylor, *Satellite Cities: A Study of Industrial Suburbs* (New York, 1915), 91-93; Willard Glazier, *Pecularities of American Cities* (Philadelphia, 1886), 135.
5. Frank Y. Grayson, *Pioneers of Night Life on Vine Street* (Cincinnati, Aug. 1924), 63-65, 123-25. Interviews: William C. Smith, Dec. 19, 1962; Alfred Segal, Nov. 2, 1962; Robert Heuck, Nov. 27, 1962; and Edward F. Alexander, Nov. 13, 1962.
6. Cincinnati *Post*, June 20, 1912; Ruth M. Heistand, "A Social History of Cincinnati's Eastern Basin Area: An Inquiry into the Character, Interests, Attitudes, and Social Services of this Primary Neighborhood" (master's thesis, University of Cincinnati, 1936), 55, 72-75.
7. James Albert Green, *History of the Associated Charities of Cincinnati, 1879-1937: A Record of Service* (Cincinnati, n.d.), 18-19.
8. Sidney D. Maxwell, *The Suburbs of Cincinnati: Sketches Historical and Descriptive* (Cincinnati, 1870), 2, 96-97, 99-100, 118-28, 148, 177-85.
9. Cincinnati *American Israelite*, Oct. 26, 1899.
10. Cincinnati *Civic News*, I (Oct. 1911), 3; Frank F. Dinsmore, Chas. W. Dupuis, Martin H. Fischer, and Walter A. Draper, *History of the Queen City Optimists Club* (Cincinnati, Jan. 1955), 1-2; *Mrs. Devereux's Blue Book of Cincinnati Society for the Year 1912-1913* (Cincinnati [1912?]), 183-241.
11. Charles Dudley Warner, "Studies of the Great West, Cincinnati and Louisville," *Harper's New Monthly Magazine*, LXXVII (Aug. 1888). 430.
12. For a full analysis of this region see Miller, "Boss Cox and the Municipal Reformers," Part I, 58-124.
13. Robert A. Woods and Albert J. Kennedy,

The Zone of Emergence (Cambridge, 1962), 31-183.

14. Cincinnati *Post*, June 11, 1913.

15. Quoted in Joseph Stacy Hill, "Further Chats With My Descendants," Typescript *ca.* 1933, p. 42 (Cincinnati Historical Society).

16. Taylor, *Satellite Cities*, 95-96.

17. Cincinnati *Catholic-Telegraph*, March 20, 1890, Nov. 2, 16, 1893.

18. For a detailed analysis see Miller, "Boss Cox and the Municipal Reformers," Part I, 15-57.

19. Cincinnati *Charities Review*, I (April 1908), 8; United Jewish Charities, *Fourteenth Annual Report, 1910* (Cincinnati, n.d.), 59.

20. One social worker speculated that the Circle dwellers' "lack of energy and initiative" was due "to physical bankruptcy . . . which, although largely imaginative, is the result of [a] neurotic and temperamental condition . . . and incapacitates . . . as effectively as real physical disability." See United Jewish Charities. *Eighteenth Annual Report, 1914* (Cincinnati, n.d.), 7-8.

21. Boris D. Bogen, "Politics in Jewish Settlements," *Jewish Charities*, II (Sept. 1911), 10-11.

22. Cincinnati *Enquirer,* March 9, 1884. See also Joseph D. Emery, *Thirty-Five Years Among the Poor and Public Institutions of Cincinnati* (Cincinnati, 1887), 16.

23. Perhaps the best among the many contemporary accounts of the riot is J. S. Tunison, *The Cincinnati Riot: Its Causes and Results* (Cincinnati, 1886). The casualty totals are from "Annual Report of the Department of Police," *Annual Reports of the City Departments of the City of Cincinnati for the Fiscal Year Ending December 31, 1884* (Cincinnati, 1885), 311.

24. Benjamin Butterworth to Alphonso Taft, June 5, 1885, Taft Papers, Family Correspondence, Box 25 (Manuscript Division, Library of Congress). For other accounts of the election disorders in the fall of 1884 see Cincinnati *Catholic-Telegraph*, Oct. 16, 1884; Butterworth to Joseph B. Foraker, Jan. 5, 9, 1885, Joseph B. Foraker Papers, Box 31 (Cincinnati Historical Society).

25. Oscar Ameringer, *If You Don't Weaken:*

The Autobiography of Oscar Ameringer (New York, 1940), 44-47; Sidney D. Maxwell to Mrs. Emma Maxwell, May 5, 6, 11, 12, 1886, Sidney D. Maxwell Papers (Cincinnati Historical Society); Cincinnati *Times-Star*, May 3, 13, 1886.

26. Cincinnati *Freie Presse*, Jan 23, 1921. For the strikes see Cincinnati *Times-Star*, Feb. 3, Oct. 6, 1892; Cincinnati Central Labor Council *Chronicle*, June 5, 1886, Sept. 29, 1901.

27. Henry F. Pringle, *The Life and Times of William Howard Taft: A Biography* (2 vols., New York, 1939), I, 134-36.

28. Rev. T. H. Pearne, *What Shall Be Done with the Cincinnati Sunday Saloon? An Address Before the Cincinnati Methodist Preachers' Meeting, May 13th and May 19th, 1887* (Cincinnati, 1887), 7. See also Cincinnati *Times-Star*, March 29, 1889; Cincinnati *Post*, March 29, 1889; Cincinnati *Catholic-Telegraph*, June 5, 1884; *Address of the Bund für Freiheit und Recht* (Cincinnati, May 1886), 4, 5, 6-7.

29. Cincinnati *Times-Star*, Dec. 2, 1889.

30. Jno. Pearson to Foraker, July 26, 1889; Foraker to John B. Mosby, July 26, 1889, Foraker Papers, Boxes 38, 29; "Report of the Non-Partisan Board of Police Commissioners," *Annual Reports of the City Departments of the City of Cincinnati for the Fiscal Year Ending December 31, 1889* (Cincinnati, 1889), 199-200; Joseph Benson Foraker, *Notes of a Busy Life* (2 vols., Cincinnati, 1916), I, 411-16. For the "era of the back door" see Grayson, *Pioneers of Night Life*, 18.

31. See the reports of the city boards, departments, and agencies, and the mayor's annual messages in the *Annual Reports* of the city, 1884-1891. See also Cincinnati Commercial Club, *Report of [the] Special Committee to [the] Commercial Club . . . on Deficient Water Supply to the City, Aug. 25, 1890* (Cincinnati, n.d.); Cincinnati Chamber of Commerce, *A Canal Town in a Railroad Era* (Cincinnati, Feb. 1887); Charles B. Wilby, "What is the Matter with Cincinnati?" *Extracts of a Paper Read before the Young Business Men's Club, Nov. 30, 1886* (Cincinnati, n.d.).

32. William Howard Taft to Mother [Louisa Taft], March 27, 1885, Taft Papers, Family Correspondence, Box 25.

33. In 1885 the Republican reform mayoralty candidate won by 4,000 votes out of a total of nearly 53,000. See Cincinnati *Times-Star*, April 6, 1885. But the elections of 1887 and 1889 were three-cornered affairs resulting in a total Republican plurality of 1,153. In 1891, with only two strong tickets in the field, the Republican mayoralty nominee won by a margin of 138 votes over his Democratic opponent. Cincinnati *Times-Star*, April 5, 1887; Hamilton County Board of Elections, "Record of City Elections, Commencing in 1888" (Offices of the Hamilton County Board of Elections, Cincinnati).
34. Richard C. Wade, *The Urban Frontier: The Rise of Western Cities, 1790-1830* (Cambridge, 1959), 112-17, 204-06.
35. Cincinnati *Times-Star*, Sept. 27, 29, 1890.
36. Cincinnati *Post*, Jan. 2, 1897.
37. Ibid., Jan. 2, 8, 15, 20, 16, 30, Feb. 1, 1897.
38. Karger, "George Barnesdale Cox," 274.
39. See notes 1 and 37.
40. George B. Cox to Foraker, Dec. 24, 1888; Foraker to T. W. Graydon, March 16, 1889; Foraker to Murat Halstead, March 18, 1889, Foraker Papers, Boxes 32, 29; Diaries, Feb. 2, 16, March 23, 25, 1891, Hickenlooper Papers; Cincinnati *Post*, Feb. 3, March 4, 9, 1891; Hickenlooper to Milton A. McRae, March 26, 1891, Hickenlooper Papers.
41. Cincinnati *Times-Star*, April 4, 1891.
42. Diaries, May 8, 1891, Hickenlooper Papers.
43. Hamilton County Board of Elections, "Record of City Elections."
44. Although Cox avoided publicity, his few public statements succinctly summarize his technique. Bossism, he believed, evolved with the modern city. He never consciously aspired to leadership but acquired it naturally—or had it thrust upon him. A good and successful boss, he felt, claimed and held power by adhering to a few principles. He kept graft at a minimum, kept his word, and demanded that those responsible for securing nominations and winning elections receive consideration when favors were passed out. See Cincinnati *Commercial-Gazette*, Jan. 29, 1892; Cincinnati *Post*, Feb. 22, 1911, May 20, 1916.
45. Election returns from Cincinnati *Times-Star*, April 6, 1885, April 5, 1887; Hamilton County Board of Elections, "Record of City Elections."
46. See *Annual Reports of the City Departments of the City of Cincinnati . . .*, 1885-1897; Cincinnati Municipal Reference Bureau, *The March of City Government, City of Cincinnati (1802-1936)* (Cincinnati, 1937), 15-16.
47. The Cincinnati *Times-Star*, March 27, 30, 1891, lists all the Republican councilmen, gives their occupations, and comments on their backgrounds. See also Cincinnati *Citizens' Bulletin*, Aug. 29, 1903.
48. Cincinnati Police Department, *Police and Municipal Guide, 1901* (Cincinnati, n.d.). Perhaps the best description of the "bonifaces" and the Vine Street characters is in Grayson, *Pioneers of Night Life*, 63-65. Grayson was a reporter for the Cincinnati *Times-Star* and a member of the coterie.
49. Cincinnati *Volksfreund*, March 8, 1897. The Cincinnati *Catholic-Telegraph* and the *Chronicle*, the Cincinnati Central Labor Council organ, both spoke essentially to a Zone constituency. Even when in a reform mood they did not attack the "bonifaces" personally in these years.
50. In the 1899 gubernatorial election the Zone, apparently attracted by the Democratic reform platform, went Democratic along with the Circle. The Hilltops, however, voted Republican. See Hamilton County Board of Elections, "Abstract of Votes Cast from 1896-1899, Incl., . . . 1899" (Offices of Hamilton County Board of Elections, n.d.). In 1897 both the Zone and the Hilltops went for the fusion reformers against the GOP. See Hamilton County Board of Elections, "Record of City Elections."
51. The accumulation of Zone grievances is quite clearly seen in the 1897 election which the fusionists won by 7,400 votes out of a total of 64,000. For the campaign and post-election analysis see Miller, "Boss Cox and the Reformers," 818-81. Nonetheless, it was the massive defection of the heretofore solidly Republican Hilltops which put the fusionists on top in 1897.
52. Although national issues were irrelevant,

Boss Cox's Cincinnati

the general pattern of politics in Cincinnati was similar to national developments. Carl N. Degler has suggested that the Republican party attained national dominance after 1884 in part because it was identified by urban voters as the party of positive action. See Carl N. Degler, "American Political Parties and the Rise of the City: An Interpretation," *Journal of American History*, LI (June 1964), 41-50.
53. For the new forces in politics see Miller, "Boss Cox and the Reformers," 305-37. The Cincinnati *Citizens' Bulletin*, Aug. 15, 29, 1908, Oct. 23, 1909, Sept. 30, 1911, among other contemporary sources, recorded Republican strategy. For the policy of the Republican administrations see the *Annual Reports of the City Departments of the City of Cincinnati*... for the years 1900-1905 and 1907-1911.
54. Before this time, only two Circle wards had been reliably Republican. One, the Eighteenth, was Cox's former district; and the other, the old Ninth, was entrusted to Rudolph K. Hynicka who, with August Herrmann, served as Cox's closest associates. See also Hamilton County Board of Elections, "Record of City Elections."
55. Cincinnati *Times-Star,* Nov. 7, 1888. For the Democratic factions see *ibid.*, March 25, 1885; C. W. Woolley to John Sherman, April 7, 1885, John Sherman Papers (Manuscript Division, Library of Congress); Cincinnati *Volksfreund*, April 8, 1887; Cincinnati *Times-Star*, April 2, 1889; Cincinnati *Post*, April 2, 1889, Feb. 26, 1894; and especially R. B. Bowler to Charles T. Greve, Sept. 13, 19, 20, Oct. 8, 29, Dec. 19, 26, 1893, Jan. 6, 12, March 23, 1894, Charles T. Greve Papers (Cincinnati Historical Society).
56. Cincinnati *Post*, April 12, 1897.
57. Cincinnati *Citizens' Bulletin*, April 11, May 9, Aug. 29, 1903; Cincinnati *Volksblatt*, April 7, 1903; Henry C. Wright, *Bossism in Cincinnati* (Cincinnati, 1905), 48-49.
58. A. Julius Freiberg, "Mayor Hunt's Administration in Cincinnati," *National Municipal*

Review, III (July 1914), 518.
59. See, for example, Cincinnati *Post*, Oct. 5, 11, 13, 1905; Cincinnati *Enquirer*, Nov. 1, 17, 1905; Cincinnati *Citizens' Bulletin*, May 6, July 8, Sept. 30, 1905, April 27, 1907.
60. Cincinnati *Citizens' Bulletin*, Oct. 19, 1907.
61. Ohio General Assembly, Joint Committee on the Investigation of Cincinnati and Hamilton County, *Who got the quarter million graft and who paid it back?... History and Work of the Special Committee Created Under and by Virtue of Senate Joint Resolution No. 54 and House Bill No. 1287* (Columbus, n.d.), 6-11; Cincinnati *Citizens' Bulletin*, Feb. 22, 1908, April 8, 1911; Charles P. Taft to William Howard Taft, Feb. 28, 1911, Taft Papers, Presidential Series, No. 3, Box 523.
62. Henry T. Hunt, *An Account of My Stewardship of the Office of Prosecuting Attorney* (Cincinnati, n.d.), 1-11; Cincinnati *Citizens' Bulletin*, Sept. 30, 1911; Cincinnati *Post*, Oct. 25, 1911; Hamilton County Board of Elections, "Abstract of Votes... 1908-1911" (Offices of the Hamilton County Board of Elections). The language of the Cincinnati reformers regarding democracy, morality, and politics was very much like that of the Muckrakers as described in Stanley K. Schultz, "The Morality of Politics: The Muckrakers' Vision of Democracy," *Journal of American History*, LII (Dec. 1965), 527-47. Yet they were primarily interested in devising institutions, including a positive government, which would mold moral citizens and make politics democratic. Their goal was not destructive, nor their rhetoric ceremonial.
63. Cincinnati *Times-Star,* Nov. 8, 1905; William Howard Taft to Rudolph K. Hynicka, July 15, 1910, Taft Papers, Presidential Series 8, Letterbooks; William Howard Taft to Horace D. Taft, Nov. [?], 1911, Taft Papers, Presidential Series 8, Letterbook; Cincinnati *Post*, May 22, 1911; Cincinnati *Commercial-Tribune*, Nov. 5, 1911.
64. Cincinnati *Commercial-Gazette*, Jan. 29, 1892; Cincinnati *Post*, Feb. 22, 1911.

❧ TWO ❧
Running the Machine

⤳ COMMENTARY ⤶

The city boss was a political entrepreneur in the business of politics, the business of running an organization that could get votes and win elections. In fact the boss ran a machine similar to a large corporation in makeup and goals.[1] While his executive suite might be the back room of a saloon, like the businessman-entrepreneur he was interested in profiting from the enormous opportunities presented by the city. Like a corporation, his organization was hierarchical in structure, offering a variety of inducements material, psychological, social—but demanding as well discipline obedience, and loyalty. Like the businessman, he had either to harmonize or to destroy competition. His products were power and affluence, his consumers were voters and party-workers. His methods were the dispensing of patronage, favors, city contracts, the stock-piling of obligations, the execution of the law—promising, cajoling, threatening. His road was charted not by signs of moral principles but by political expediency, for the boss tiptoed around Burning Issues with uncanny dexterity. ("What do I care who is President," Israel Durham once said, "so long as I can carry my ward.") His success ultimately depended upon getting the votes, winning the elections, perpetuating the machine—the business of playing politics.

In the matter of dealing with people, the demands on the city boss were greater indeed. The vagaries of the marketplace could confound the best of businessmen, but the vagaries of the human spirit—the insatiable appetite of a powerful ward leader, the ambitions of a rival, dissenting factions

1. See Joel Arthur Tarr, "The Urban Politician as Entrepreneur," *Mid-America,* **49** (January 1966): 55–67.

spoiling for a party civil war, the pretensions of the enemy party, the accusations of the reformers, the infinite variety of competing interests and class, ethnic, and religious groups within an American city—presented the most confounding problems to test the political executive. The ultimate goal of survival by winning elections depended upon the knack of leading men. As Lord Bryce put it, "The aim of a Boss is not so much fame as power, and not so much power over the conduct of affairs as over persons."

Politics, it has been said, is the art of the possible. The possible is achieved by leadership, the art of the city boss. George Washington Plunkitt, the sage of Tammany Hall, called it statesmanship, and people have laughed at that extravagant use of the word ever since. Perhaps Plunkitt should have the last laugh. Without statesmanship the finest of political machines declines. Today as the media play up a politician's personal qualities, one might be tempted to name personality as the first quality of leadership. Boston's James Michael Curley, for example, was a man of devastating charm; Israel Durham of Philadelphia inspired an almost mauldlin affection ("Everybody likes him, hundreds love him, and almost everybody calls him 'Iz' "). No one ever claimed that the dour Charles Murphy had charisma, and yet he exercised leadership and Tammany flourished. His successor, George Olvany, a pleasant man, did not have it—and Tammany slipped. Respect, not personality, was the first prerequisite of leadership—respect for the professionalism of an effective *practical* politician, i.e., a man who knew how to get things done and how to get men to do them. This, in turn, required other qualities of leadership: an intimate knowledge of one's constitutents—their likes and dislikes, fears, hostilities, and, especially, their needs; a command of the intricacies of not only municipal government but county and state government as well; the ability to make intelligent decisions—fair, incisive, and yet, if the occasion demanded, subject to negotiation, for compromise was at the heart of getting things done, and the inflexible politician rarely rose to any heights in machine politics. Respect without trust, however, was meaningless. The boast of Tom Pendergast could be echoed by most successful city bosses: "Put this down: I've never broken my word to any living human being I gave it to." The verbal promise, the contract by handshake, a trust fulfilled, was a badge of honor held in reverence by bosses as corrupt as Tweed or as honest as Flynn. Reformers called it honor among thieves.

Respect and trust, in turn, attracted loyalty and obedience, the cement to any kind of organization. For the city boss was first and foremost an Organization Man. Loyalty and obedience translated into hard work for the party was the supreme virtue right up the line, to the precinct captain, to the ward leader, to the boss, and, above all, to the organization. ("Join Tammany and work for it. Stay loyal. Stay put. Don't leave your party. Reward will come."). Machine politics had no room for the rugged individualist, that blithe spirit of independence. The term "ward heeler" is vividly apt. Despised by the general public, which celebrates self-reliance, the fellow who heels to the organization—subservient, obedient, loyal—is prized in a profession where disloyalty can be a cheap route to success and a threat to the machine. When, for example, Gov. Charles Edison recommended a man for a judgeship because of his integrity, Frank Hague yelled, "The hell with his integrity, Charlie. What I want to know is, can you depend on the S.O.B. in a pinch?" If there is one classic model of loyalty in American politics, it has to be O. K. Allen, elected Governor by Huey Long's machine in Louisiana. As Huey's brother Earl wrote of him: "A leaf blew in the window of Allen's office and fell on his desk. He signed it."

One of the greatest tests of leadership was delivering the vote. Unlike some of his counterparts in business, the boss did not operate from a penthouse suite, surrounded by vice-presidents and well-tailored aides. Working out of a saloon, political club, or city hall, beginning early and retiring late, the boss put in an exhausting seven-day week, "mending his fences" daily with his constituents. He might deal with as many as two hundred people in one day. Tom Pendergast was up by 4:30 A.M. and at work at his shabby office in the Jackson Democratic Club by six o'clock. During the day he was besieged by hordes of people asking for an infinite variety of favors. Wearing a gray flannel hat that he removed only for the ladies, Pendergast, a no-nonsense political executive, greeted each supplicant with a "Well, what's yours?"

To get the vote, the boss created a rude sort of public welfare system, jerry-built in comparison to the colossus created by the federal government in the 1930s, but in some ways more efficient and humane for the poor, illiterate, bewildered denizens of the great American cities. The boss performed services tuned to the daily pains and problems of urban living: jobs and cash for the needy, coal for a winter's chill, bail and pardons for the unlucky, flowers for the sick. He negotiated building permits, exten-

sions on commercial paper, railroad passes, contracts and franchises for
the businessman; he established foreign-language classes for immigrants,
patched up family quarrels, disciplined gouging landlords, and,
to console the bereaved, attended a host of funerals. Tim Sullivan, for
example, donated eight thousand pairs of shoes, and turkey besides, for
the poor of the Bowery at Christmas time. Social workers called him a
pest, because he gave aid "so unscientifically." Boss Tom Pendergast
would not agree: "When a poor man comes to old Tom's boys for help we
don't make one of those damn fool investigations like these city charities.
No, by God, we fill his belly and warm his back and vote him our way."
The boss, then, established his leadership as a broker in friendship, an ambassador of goodwill. He built and sustained his power by becoming what
Jane Addams called "a stalking survival of village kindness."

Political scientists have long noted that inasmuch as a national political
party is essentially a confederation of local and state organizations, the
success of the party depends ultimately upon the strength and leadership
in those local and state units. The same is true of machine politics. The
machine was a coterie of powerful ward leaders who gave allegiance to the
boss. Such leaders represented the grass-roots of urban politics, the neighborhood. They headed the most important social institution of the
neighborhood, the political club, and most city bosses learned their trade
by managing one. The club united the neighborhood, cemented political
loyalty, mustered votes for the organization, and became a powerful instrument for control of nominations to local offices. It was a simple political formula: the more neighborhood statesmen that advanced to office,
the more powerful the club and the ward leader became. It is doubtful,
for instance, that William Marcy Tweed could have reached the heights of
New York politics without the backing of his Seventh Ward and the club
that made him so powerful.

Deeply political as it was, the club functioned also as an important
social institution. Like the saloon, the clubhouse was a working man's
club, a haven for recreation and good fellowship, and a refuge from wives.
It was a pleasant place where a tired Manure Inspector or an Assistant
Health Warden could find relaxation at the billiard table or at the bar,
where he could chew over the latest political gossip. It provided a means,
too, by which the native poor, or an immigrant Irishman or German,
could advance to higher social status. Its social events paid off in political
dividends. By sponsoring clambakes, picnics, summer outings, at least two

balls or "rackets" a year, and exciting torchlight parades celebrating the sterling character of the leader, the club created a neighborhood *esprit de corps* and made politics fun. On July 30, 1902, Tammany Hall's William Devery and his club staged a bash that must set a record of its kind, by way of an outing for only the women and children of his district—ten thousand of them. He rented two steamboats, six barges, and one tugboat, for a joy ride up the Hudson. The fleet was equipped with six physicians and six nurses, forty-five musicians, and an opera troupe. Devery charmed the ladies and a few thousand screaming children with 6,000 pounds of candy, 1,500 quarts of ice cream, uncounted heaps of sandwiches and pies, rivers of soft drinks, and, practical politician that he was, 1,500 nursing bottles for the tiny ones. As Devery said, "You can't do nothin' with the people unless you do somethin' for 'em."

At the heart of the business of politics, the key inducement to mobilizing the vote, selecting candidates, keeping the cooperation of ward leaders, and, not least, winning elections, was patronage. Patronage was a system of reward and punishment, the giving or denying of jobs in public and party office. Patronage was power, the means to extend leadership by building a vast network of followers to control both the party organization and the many divisions of municipal government and (if the boss was powerful enough) county and state government as well. Here was the boss's army, the political sharpshooters, guerrillas, bushwackers, and light cavalry. Army is a metaphor of some precision. The Tweed Ring was in command of 12,000 jobs on the public payroll: powerful in its day of the 1860s and 1870s, but puny twenty years later when compared to Boss Croker's army of 40,000. In the 1930s, the Kelly-Nash machine in Chicago controlled 30,000 municipal jobs and, with its power in the Governor's office and the state administrative organization, 14,000 more. The dispensing of patronage was no routine or automatic affair. It was another test of leadership, a formidable challenge of political judgment. There were ticklish, delicate decisions to be made that could mean triumph or disaster: whom to reward? whom to trust? whom to punish?

The bosses varied in their approaches to control of patronage. Some held top jobs in city government. Hague of Jersey City, Daley of Chicago, and Curley of Boston served several terms as mayor. Others like Democrats Pendergast of Kansas City and Buckley of San Francisco, and the Republican bosses of Philadelphia, chose less visibility by way of minor (but lucrative) public offices such as Assessor or County Clerk. Tweed did both. He held a firm hand over the city administration as President of the Board of Supervisors, controlled a rich patronage mine as Deputy Street Commissioner and Commissioner of Public Works, enlarged the power of Tammany in the state legislature by becoming a State Senator, and held executive positions in banks, printing firms, railroads, and insurance companies.

All this suggests that the boss exercised leadership as an autocrat invested with absolute power. This is one of the enduring myths about the city boss in America—a myth not only created by reformers but enhanced by boasts from the bosses themselves. "I am the law," said Frank Hague. "I decide. I do. Me. Right here." Words were often matched with deeds. In a dazzling display of raw power, Charles Murphy masterminded the impeachment and conviction of William Sulzer, Governor of New York. Yet for all their rhetorical thunder and political muscle, none of the bosses were complete autocrats. All had to bargain for favors. Each was vulnerable to the attack of reform crusades. In the giant ebb and flow of population movement in the American city the neighborhood could change, and with it the boss's support. His power base was always shifting, for the city boss was not a dictator but a power broker, a manager of competing interests, always challenged by a mixed constituency in which satisfying one could enrage the other. It required a strategy of balance, persuasion, and give-and-take. Above all, it depended upon the crucial question of leadership: *Can he deliver*? As the man commented of the demise of the Hague machine, "When the Big Boy goes, it means he can no longer do anything for anybody."

The selections in this chapter constitute a kind of working manual on how to run a political machine, from the old-fashioned machine of the nineteenth and early-twentieth century to the new-fashioned machine of recent years. The first is from *Plunkitt of Tammany Hall*, a minor classic in the literature on the city boss. The thrust of the book is clear from its subtitle:

A Series of Very Plain Talks on Very Practical Politics, Delivered by Ex-Senator George Washington Plunkitt, The Tammany Philosopher, From His Rostrum—The New York County Court House Bootblack Stand

Plunkitt, the ex-butcher boy who became a millionaire, began his political career in the Tweed Ring era and became a seasoned professional politi-

cian under Croker and Charles Murphy. In this selection, Plunkitt makes it
clear why politics is too serious a business to be left to college professors,
philosophers, or (worse of all) reformers. The sidewalk ideologue, sassy
and cynical, gives "free" advice to young men "who are lookin' forward
to political glory and lots of cash."

The second selection is from another fine primer of practical politics,
The Great Game of Politics, by Frank R. Kent. A veteran reporter for the
Baltimore *Sun*, Kent was a knowledgeable observer of big city politics.
Since the business of the boss was winning elections, Kent discusses two
aspects crucial to running a successful organization: the importance of the
primary elections, and the way the boss picks his candidates. In the latter
connection one is reminded of a story told of Boss Croker. When he was
asked to appoint a certain young man as County Clerk of Manhattan,
Croker said, "He's a good boy, but that job requires brains and experience. He'll have to be satisfied with going to Congress."

The final two essays discuss the art of running the new-fashioned machine. Although George Washington Plunkitt would be outraged at the
presumption of college professors in writing about practical politics,
Martin Meyerson and Edward Banfield succeed admirably in discussing the
aldermen, running the City Council and the ward, the patronage system,
the functions of the precinct captain, financing the machine, and the
corruption of the Chicago machine in the mid-twentieth century. Finally,
from *Behind Closed Doors*, one of the best writings by a practicing politician on present-day urban politics, come the views of Edward Costikyan.
He is of a new breed of big-city politician, totally different in style and
tactics from a Richard Croker of the late-nineteenth century. An attorney,
he succeeded Carmine DeSapio as leader of Tammany Hall in the early
1960s. In this essay he discusses the way a modern political executive
manages the machine in three critical areas—the club, the constituency,
and the campaign.

HOW TO BECOME
A STATESMAN

George Washington Plunkitt

There's thousands of young men in this city who will go to the polls for the first time next November. Among them will be many who have watched the careers of successful men in politics, and who are longin' to make names and fortunes for themselves at the same game. It is to these youths that I want to give advice. First, let me say that I am in a position to give what the courts call expert testimony on the subject. I don't think you can easily find a better example than I am of success in politics. After forty years' experience at the game I am—well, I'm George Washington Plunkitt. Everybody knows what figure I cut in the greatest organization on earth, and if you hear people say that I've laid away a million or so since I was a butcher's boy in Washington Market, don't come to me for an indignant denial. I'm pretty comfortable, thank you.

From William L. Riordon, *Plunkitt of Tammany Hall* (New York: Alfred A. Knopf, 1948), pp. 9-14.

Now, havin' qualified as an expert, as the lawyers say, I am goin' to give advice free to the young men who are goin' to cast their first votes, and who are lookin' forward to political glory and lots of cash. Some young men think they can learn how to be successful in politics from books, and they cram their heads with all sorts of college rot. They couldn't make a bigger mistake. Now, understand me, I ain't sayin' nothin' against colleges. I guess they'll have to exist as long as there's bookworms, and I suppose they do some good in a certain way, but they don't count in politics. In fact, a young man who has gone through the college course is handicapped at the outset. He may succeed in politics, but the chances are 100 to 1 against him.

Another mistake: some young men think that the best way to prepare for the political game is to practise speakin' and becomin' orators. That's all wrong. We've got some orators in Tammany Hall, but they're chiefly ornamental. You never heard of Charlie Murphy delivering a speech, did you? Or Richard Croker, or John Kelly, or any other man who has been a real power in the organization? Look at the thirty-six district leaders of Tammany Hall to-day. How many of them travel on their tongues? Maybe one or two, and they don't count when business is doin' at Tammany Hall. The men who rule have practised keepin' their tongues still, not exercisin' them. So you want to drop the orator idea unless you mean to go into politics just to perform the sky-rocket act.

Now, I've told you what not to do; I guess I can explain best what to do to succeed in politics by tellin' you what I did. After goin' through the apprenticeship of the business while I was a boy by wrokin' around the district headquarters and hustlin' about the polls on election day, I set out when I cast my first vote to win fame and money in New York city politics. Did I offer my services to the district leader as a stump-speaker? Not much. The woods are always full of speakers. Did I get up a book on municipal government and show it to the leader? I wasn't such a fool. What I did was to get some marketable goods before goin' to the leaders. What do I mean by marketable goods? Let me tell you: I had a cousin, a young man who didn't take any particular interest in politics. I went to him and said: "Tommy, I'm goin' to be a politician, and I want to get a followin'; can I count on you?" He said: "Sure, George." That's how I started in business. I got a marketable commodity—one vote. Then I went to the district leader and told him I could command two votes on election day, Tommy's and my own.

He smiled on me and told me to go ahead. If I had offered him a speech or a bookful of learnin', he would have said, "Oh, forget it!"

That was beginnin' business in a small way, wasn't it? But that is the only way to become a real lastin' statesman. I soon branched out. Two young men in the flat next to mine were school friends. I went to them, just as I went to Tommy, and they agreed to stand by me. Then I had a followin' of three voters and I began to get a bit chesty. Whenever I dropped into district headquarters, everybody shook hands with me, and the leader one day honored me by lightin' a match for my cigar. And so it went on like a snowball rollin' down a hill. I worked the flathouse that I lived in from the basement to the top floor, and I got about a dozen young men to follow me. Then I tackled the next house and so on down the block and around the corner. Before long I had sixty men back of me, and formed the George Washington Plunkitt Association.

What did the district leader say then when I called at headquarters? I didn't have to call at headquarters. He came after me and said: "George, what do you want? If you don't see what you want, ask for it. Wouldn't you like to have a job or two in the departments for your friends?" I said: "I'll think it over; I haven't yet decided what the George Washington Plunkitt Association will do in the next campaign." You ought to have seen how I was courted and petted then by the leaders of the rival organizations. I had marketable goods and there was bids for them from all sides, and I was a risin' man in politics. As time went on, and my association grew, I thought I would like to go to the Assembly. I just had to hint at what I wanted, and three different organizations offered me the nomination. Afterwards, I went to the Board of Aldermen, then to the State Senate, then became leader of the district, and so on up and up till I became a statesman.

That is the way and the only way to make a lastin' success in politics. If you are goin' to cast your first vote next November and want to go into politics, do as I did. Get a followin', if it's only one man, and then go to the district leader and say: "I want to join the organization. I've got one man who'll follow me through thick and thin." The leader won't laugh at your one-man followin'. He'll shake your hand warmly, offer to propose you for membership in his club, take you down to the corner for a drink and ask you to call again. But go to him and say: "I took first prize at college in Aristotle; I can recite all Shakspere forwards and backwards; there ain't nothin' in science that ain't as familiar to me as blockades on the elevated roads and I'm the real thing in the way of silver-tongued orators." What will he answer? He'll probably say: "I guess you are not to blame for your misfortunes, but we have no use for you here."

RUNNING
THE OLD-FASHIONED MACHINE

Frank Kent

Right here is the place to explain exactly why the primaries are so much more vital than the general election to the precinct executive.

The same reasons that make this statement apply to the precinct executive, make it equally apply to the ward executive, the district leader, the boss, the machine as an entirety, and the country as a whole.

Unless these facts are clearly understood at the start, there can be no real grasp of machine power, methods, and control. No political knowledge is worth anything unless they are comprehended.

To think that the general election is more important than the primary election, as most voters do, is to magnify the wrong side of the political picture. It ought to be reversed, and instead of, as now, many more voters voting in the general election than in the primaries, the

From *The Great Game of Politics* (New York: Doubleday, 1923), pp. 6-13; 103-11. Reprinted with permission of the publisher.

public interest should be concentrated on the primaries first, and the general election second. As things stand to-day, the popular tendency is to regard primaries as the particular concern of the politicians, and not of real interest to the average voter. The result is that often an absurdly small porportion of the qualified voters participate in the primaries.

There could not be a greater mistake. This lack of appreciation of what the primaries really mean, and the general neglect to participate in them, plays directly into the hands of the machine. It makes it ridiculously easy for the machine, through the precinct executives, to control the situation. It actually permits the machine to run the country.

The reasons this is true are simple enough. Primaries are really the key to politics. There is no way for party candidates to get on the general election ballot except through the primaries. Primaries are the exclusive gate through which all party candidates must pass. Control of that gate in any community means control of the political situation in that community. It makes no difference whether the candidates who pass through that gate are knocked down in the general election or not, the next set of candidates must pass through the primary gate just the same. It ought to be plain, then, that so long as the machine controls the primaries, it is in a position to limit the choice of the voters in the general election to its choice in the primaries. That is the real secret of its power, and, so long as it holds the power, it cannot be put out of business. Defeating its candidates in the general election not only does not break its grip, if often does not make even a dent in it. It can and does continue to function after a general election defeat just as it did before. The only place a machine can be beaten is in the primaries. So long as it can nominate its candidates, so long is it an unbeaten machine. This is a government by parties, and under our system parties are essential to government. In all the states the two big parties—the Democratic and Republican—are recognized by law. These laws provide that these parties shall hold primaries, which are preliminary elections, participated in exclusively by party voters, for the purpose of nominating party candidates. The only way in which candidates may get on the ballot at the general election, other than through direct nomination in the primaries, or through nominations by conventions composed of delegates chosen in the primaries, is by petition signed by a designated number of voters. This gives a candidate a place on the ballot as an "outsider" and is rarely resorted to because of the extremely small chances of success of such candidate. Nothing short of a political tidal wave or revolution can carry an independent candidate to success. He may pull sufficient votes from one side or the other to bring about the defeat of one of the regular party nominees, but his own election is a thing so rare as to be almost negligible.

The fact that I wish to drive home now is that all over the country 99 per cent. of all candidates for all offices are nominated as a result of primaries. The obvious and inescapable deduction is that in 99 per cent. of all elections, the choice of the voters in the general election is limited to the choice of the voters in the primary elections. When the full significance of that statement sinks in, the tremendous importance of the primaries will be better appreciated. It ought to be clear that the man who votes in the general election and not in the primaries loses at least 50 per cent. of the value and effectiveness of his vote as compared to the man who votes in both. Before a candidate for any office can be elected, except the rare independents who escape the primaries and go on the general ballot by petition, he must first be nominated. In 99 per cent. of the cases, nominations are made in the primaries. In 1 per cent. of them they are made by petition. In the face of these facts, it would appear distinctly in the interest of every voter to be a primary election voter. The truth is, however, that the one class that regularly votes in the primaries is the machine voters—and, of course, they control, and always will control, under these conditions.

It is not too much to say that the great bulk of the men holding municipal, state, and federal offices throughout the country to-day were elected or appointed to these offices because of the support of the party organizations or machines. They are exactly the same thing. There are in the United States more than 2,000,000 political jobholders of one kind or another. They range all the way from the President of the United States to the city street sweeper.

Nearly all of these are strictly organization men. Practically of them vote strictly party tickets with unvarying regularity. Moreover, through family or other ties, every one of them is able to influence from two to ten votes besides his own. Some of them, of course, control a great many more. Five is the average. This means a powerful army. It is a lot of votes. They are divided between Republicans and Democrats, but the number is great enough to give each an exceedingly formidable force. They constitute the shock troops of the organization—the rank and file of the machines.

The potent thing politically about these machine men is that they vote. That is the real secret of machine power. They do not talk politics and then fail to register. Nor do they register and then fail to vote. Nor do they, when they vote, spoil their ballots. Every election day, regardless of wind or weather, "hell or high water," they march to the polls, cast their straight organization ballots, and they are counted. As voters they are 100 per cent. effective. Besides, they see that the voters they are supposed to influence or control likewise go to the polls. Voting is a business matter with them and they attend to it.

But the overwhelmingly big thing is that they are primary-election voters—not merely general-election voters. No clear comprehension of politics can possibly be had until these basic facts are grasped:

First, all candidates of the two great parties must first be nominated as a result of primaries. There is no other way for them to get on the ballot.

Second, it is more important to the machine to nominate its candidates than to elect them.

Third, that the primaries are the instrument that gives the organization its legal status, and that it is, therefore, the only instrument through which it can be destroyed.

Fourth, that in the general election, the two party machines compete in getting the vote to the polls, and thus largely nullify each other's effectiveness. In the primaries the machines have no organized competition. Hence they become enormously effective and, so long as the average voter fails to participate, are practically invincible.

Fifth, in nearly all the states, Republicans are barred from voting in Democratic primaries and Democrats must keep out of Republican primaries, which means that each party machine in the primaries is free from conflict with the other party machine.

Sixth, not only are the nominations made in the primaries, but members of the state central committee, control of which is the key to the whole machine, are elected in the primaries.

This is not the place to go into a detailed account of primary election variations in the different states. Some data concerning exceptions to the general rules here laid down are given in the Appendix to this book, but in the main the statements made in this chapter apply to the country as a whole.

When these things are considered, it ought to be plain why the primaries are so vital to the machine, and why it is a matter of political life and death to the precinct executive to carry his precinct in the primaries. The machine can lose its candidate time after time in the general election without greatly diminishing its strength or loosing the grip of its leaders. Of course, it is disheartening to the rank and file and it greatly lessens the number and quality of the political pies for distribution to the faithful. It could not be kept up too long without causing a revolt in the organization, but, I repeat, the machine cannot be smashed by defeating its candidate at the election.

But if it loses in the primaries, it is out of business. Any organization that cannot carry the primary election is a defunct organization. It either politically disappears or it makes peace and amalgamates with the faction that defeated it. In rare cases it waits for the wind of public sentiment that blew it over to die down, picks up the pieces, and crawls back into the saddle. But no political machine or precinct executive could possibe survive two primary defeats.

Apart from the lack of competition, it must be evident that the reason the machine is so much more potent in the primaries is that the total number of voters is so much smaller. The smaller the vote the more dominant the machine. Only the voters of one party are permitted to vote in that party's primaries. All the members of any political machine are members of one party, and they all vote.

Hence, in the primaries the machine polls its full strength, while the number of voters outside of the machine who can vote is very much cut down. It ought to be plain that every party voter outside of the machine who refrains from voting in the primaries adds to the strength of the precinct executive—which means the machine—by just that much.

It also ought to be plain that the man who poses as an independent in politics and declines to affiliate with either party, thus disqualifying himself as a primary voter, has greatly lessened his individual importance as a political factor as well as added to the strength of the machine.

He can be as independent as he pleases in the general election. He can refuse to vote for the party nominees if they do not suit him, but if he does not vote in the primaries, those who do are picking the men for whom he must vote, for or against, in the general election.

Boiled down, it comes to this: so long as the primaries are controlled by machines, the general-election voter, no matter how independent he may be, 99 per cent. of the time is limited in his choice to two machine selections. There is no getting away from that fact.

. . .

Placing just as much of his machine as he possibly can on the payroll is the primary purpose of the boss.

That is the fundamental idea back of a political organization. That is its *raison d'être*. All the labour and expense of building it up, all the time and trouble of controlling the primaries, all the fighting and working to elect the ticket after it has been nominated, from the machine standpoint, would be aimless and futile and foolish, if success were not to be rewarded with something more than the mere satisfaction of winning. If, after the machine has sweated, fought, and bled to nominate and elect a set of party candidates, somebody else is to get the jobs—why, what is the use?

Political organizations run politics because of the lack of active interest and clear understanding upon the part of the ordinary citizen. This general political inertia, these hazy and confused political ideas, this tendency to think of politics as something low and slimy, which ought to be left to the politicians—particularly the primaries—these are the things that make machines possible and powerful. In proportion as the average voter becomes interested and informed, the bulk and power of the machine decreases.

Under our party system, as has been shown, some sort of unofficial organization is essential to the orderly conduct of elections and the proper functioning of the Government. There has to be some human agency to do the actual party work of filling tickets, arranging details, providing election officials, bringing forward candidates, preparing for registration. These things do not do themselves. Nor can the state do them all. They call for voluntary activity upon the part of some one—and those who volunteer naturally form an organization and develop leaders. The whole thing is human and natural and inevitable. Nor can it be expected that the men who take over this work do so from patriotic or public-spirited motives. They take it over from purely practical and selfish motives and because there is an opportunity there for place, power, and money.

The point is that, although an organization of some sort is essential, under ideal conditions, with every citizen politically informed, and active enough to vote, the organization would be a simple, slender, inexpensive affair, easy to reward through proper patronage recognition without imposing a real burden on the taxpayers. Under existing conditions, with the voters lax, uninformed, inactive, and numerously not voting in every community—particularly in the primaries—the machine grows great and powerful, tremendously costly to the taxpayers, and develops bosses who are able to demand and get a far larger proportion of the positions under city, state, and federal governments than is good for them, for the state, the city, or the country. The basic truth is that the boss will go just as far in the patronage matter as he can—and the distance he can go is exactly measured by the indifference of the voters. Under conditions as they exist to-day in the big cities of the country, he goes very far, indeed. It becomes his chief occupation—this placing of his followers on the public payroll.

But that is not all he has to do. There are two things expected of him as boss—the nomination in the primaries of candidates friendly to the organization and the election of these candidates. It is here that the boss shows his quality. So long as more than half the qualified voters fail to vote, the kind of machine described in these pages has the power to put over in the primaries practically any one it wants.

It would be possible, for instance, in either New York, Philadelphia, Chicago, Boston, Baltimore, St. Louis, or Cleveland for the bosses to nominate almost any old "Muldoon" for mayor that they might choose—but electing him is another matter. There is no sense in putting up a candidate in the primaries merely to have him knocked down in the general election.

It is true that, so long as he holds control of the primaries, the boss still has his machine, but no machine will indefinitely follow a funeral director—and no boss not a fool would deliberately court defeat through a too-brazen exhibition of primary power. What he does is to try so to load the ticket in the primary with the precise proportion of "Muldoons" that can get by in the general election—but no more. Almost always, in the framing of the ticket which the machine supports in the primary, the boss looks for men of sufficient standing and independence not only to command a certain degree of public respect and support but also to enable him to nominate "Muldoons" for the bulk of the places without arousing a dangerous popular resentment.

It is a matter of judgment. The boss wants a ticket that will win, but, at the same time, he wants candidates, who when they win, will not turn around and kick him and his machine out of the City Hall. How far he has to go in taking chances with independent men on the machine ticket depends upon the strength of his party in the city, the temper of the people, and the weight, disposition, and force of the newspapers. It has been shown how the nominations for the legislatures, the city councils, and the smaller

or more numerous offices are made through the ward executives—and how it is easy in these instances to "get by" with tried and true deliverable machine men.

It is when it comes to picking the head of the ticket—the candidates for mayor or governor or judge—that the boss uses care and judgment. It is by the head of the ticket usually that the public judge the whole thing. If the head of the ticket is a good, strong man of standing and known integrity, or if some of the more conspicuous of the candidates are of this type, the rest of the ticket can be and is with impunity loaded down with "Muldoons."

In political circles this practice of putting a few of the conspicuously higher type on to leaven the organization loaf is known as "perfuming the ticket" or putting a "clean collar on the dirty shirt." In other words, the machine ticket is as clean as—and no cleaner than—the sentiment of the people of the community compels it to be. That is to say once more what has already been said in these pages a number of times—the quality of the ticket is exactly measured by the tolerance of the voters. Everything about the machine—everything in politics—is measured by this same yardstick, and it cannot be said too often. It is the heart of the whole thing from beginning to end.

There are various ways in which the boss, or bosses—because in some cities like Philadelphia and Norfolk the machine is run by a little oligarchic group of bosses, rather than by one man—get the "clean collar" or "perfumery." Sometimes he has nothing at all to do with bringing the candidate out, but places his machine behind a man who announces himself, without reference to the boss or the machine, but who looks like the strongest proposition in sight, and a dangerous one to beat in the primaries. It may be a matter of expediency, or to avoid a bruising fight, or to placate popular sentiment, or purely a question of finances.

Sometimes the boss manoeuvres the appointment of a group of prominent business men affiliated with the party, who canvass the field and induce some respectable citizen to enter with the assurance of a machine support, which leaves him unpledged and uncompromised. Sometimes the man thus chosen is friendly to the machine; sometimes not. There are no rules about this part of the game. It is purely a matter of what can be done, and depends upon the character of the candidate, the exigencies of the situation, the necessities of the machine, the political complexion of the community. There are times and places when the boss can himself inspire a mayoralty candidacy without the necessity of a camouflaged committee or any other set of false whiskers. The disadvantage of this, however, is that it is apt to make the boss and the machine more directly the campaign issue than is safe.

This fact may be set down as sure—whatever way the boss may get his candidate, he tries to pick one whom he can elect.

Right here it ought, in fairness to the boss, to be said that, even if he had a free hand and did not operate under the restraint of public sentiment, in only rare cases would he go to the limit in putting up wholly unfit or really bad men for conspicuous places. The boss may, and often does, live like a leech, on the public

purse, but, in spite of being a boss, he is also a citizen of his community, and there are mighty few of them who have not some sort of civic sense of right and wrong. His is not at all the civic view of the reformer, perhaps, but it is a distinct civic sense just the same. It is an unusual boss who does not take pride when his machine-made mayor turns out to be a good public official, and equally unusual that he is not disgusted when he commits some disgraceful or scandalous act.

There have been instances in most cities where the boss has sold out to the other side, "laid down" or "thrown the election," but they are rare. Often machines coöperate and help one another in the primaries. That is sensible and easy, but it is neither sensible nor easy in the general election. In the first place, the ward and precinct executives, very many of whom are decent fellows who play the game on the level, according to their lights, revolt against treachery. In the second place, if there is a chance to win they want to win, because to lose means hard times and no jobs. In the third place, the boss cannot "throw an election" without a good many people knowing about it and raising a howl that may split his machine.

Some of the cogs in the machine in a hard fight, with money on both sides, go crooked. District leaders and executives of the lower type may jump the track, but rarely the boss, and when there is treachery in the ranks it is sternly punished by the boss. All of this does not prevent an occasional general "sell out," but in these days it is rapidly getting almost as dangerous to "buy" as well as to "sell." Men are apt to hesitate before they give to the necessarily unscrupulous person with whom they must deal the power such knowledge affords him.

Now, when the boss gets his "clean collar" it is the simplest and easiest thing imaginable to swing the machine back of him. The balance of the ticket has been made up through recommendations of the ward executives and district leaders, by giving recognition to the various elements with voting strength sufficient to make it inexpedient to ignore them, or to individuals powerful enough to compel recognition, and to sections of the city which will resent being left unrepresented on the ticket. In some cases candidates are put on because of their ability, or the ability of their friends, to contribute to the campaign fund, and sometimes for purely personal reasons. Sometimes, too, it is a matter of luck with a candidate—lack of opposition, or a last-minute demand for a man. Take any machine ticket in any city and it is a queer conglomeration containing some of the best and some of the worst types in town—and put there through all sorts of influence and for all sorts of reasons.

When it is completed the boss closes the gate and "sends the word down the line." All this consists of is a curt phrase to the ward executives and the district leaders as they come in to see him at headquarters.

"It's Smith," says the boss, or "It's Jones," "go to it." In many cases, that is all he does say. Sometimes after the "It's Smith," the boss says, "What can you do down your way?" or "What will your ward give?" or "You ought to give him 1,000 majority," or some such thing. The ward executive is likely to reply, "All right, boss," and get out, or he may tell the boss about the sentiment of his people or express his judgment as to the selection's strength or weakness in his ward or district, but it is always an exceedingly brief conversation. There is no argument. What the boss says goes.

A bolter is an extremely rare bird in a well-run machine with a real boss. Once he gets the "word" the ward executive or district leader hurries off, calls a meeting of his ward club, and passes the "word" along that night to his precinct executives. Inside of twenty-four hours after the boss decides the whole machine, from top to bottom, has got the "word" and begins to function. The ward clubs meet and indorse the ticket, the business of lining up the office-holders begins, the candidates open up headquarters and the campaign is under way.

Sometimes the boss decides weeks in advance. Sometimes it is only a few days before the primaries when the decision is given out, but it makes no difference—the machine can be swung in line just the same. The executives prefer to know as far ahead as possible, because it gives a better chance to iron out the rough spots, and checks freelance candidates from tying up and committing precinct executives, and making inroads on the organization forces. But the manner in which, at short notice, the vast bulk of the machine workers can be swung in behind the boss's candidate is a marvellous illustration of discipline, when the looseness of organization construction is considered and the varieties of human beings taken into account.

RUNNING THE MACHINE
Chicago-Style

Martin Meyerson and Edward Banfield

The City Council, the body which would have to pass upon any sites proposed by the Authority, consisted of 50 aldermen, with the mayor as presiding officer. The aldermen were elected for four-year terms from wards of roughly 25,000 to 65,000 registered voters, only about a third of whom usually voted in aldermanic elections. (The number who voted in mayoralty elections was about twice as great.) Nominally the office of alderman was non-partisan. Actually, however, no one could win an election without the support of a powerful organization and (with some rare exceptions) the only powerful political organizations in the wards were the Democratic and Republican parties. An alderman who did not have the support of his party "machine"[1] ordinarily had no hope of reelection.

The Democratic "machine" had ruled Chicago since 1923. Catholics were in control of it; since 1930, with a few exceptions, they had held the major city offices: the mayor, city treasurer, county clerk, more than half of the county commissioners, and two-thirds of the aldermen were Catholics. And among the Catholics it was those of Irish extraction who were dominant in politics: one-third of the Council, including most of its leaders, were Irish-Catholics. The other aldermen were mostly of Polish, Italian, Bohemian, Lithuanian, Slovak, or Greek extraction (in descending order of importance, these were the principal nationality groups in the Democratic party) or of German extraction (these were Republicans). A few aldermen were Jews (unlike the Poles, Italians, and other ethnic minorities, the Jews did not usually endeavor to be recognized as a group on the party slate or in the award of patronage). Two were Negroes. The numerical importance of the Irish in the Council was to be accounted for not so much by their numbers in the electorate as by the fact that in wards where no one ethnic group had a clear majority they made the most acceptable compromise candidates. As one politician explained to an interviewer, "A Lithuanian won't vote for a Pole, and a Pole won't vote for a Lithuanian. A German won't vote for either of them—but all three will vote for a 'Turkey' (Irishman)."[2]

A few of the aldermen aspired to higher political office, especially (among those who were lawyers) to judgeships, but most of them were in the business of being aldermen as other men are in the business of selling shoes. Being an alderman was supposed to be a full-time occupation, but the salary was only $5,000, so most aldermen supplemented their salaries by selling something—most often insurance or legal service (more than half of them were lawyers). Being an alderman was, of course, very good for business.

Ordinarily, even if he were so inclined, an alderman could not concern himself deeply with the larger issues of city government or take a city-wide view of important problems. If he wanted to stay in office, he had to devote all of his available time and attention to the affairs of the groups that made up his ward. He was in the Council to look after the special interests of his ward and to do favors for his constituents: to get streets repaired, to have a playground installed, to change the zoning law, to represent irate parents before the school authorities, and so on. In addition to activities of this kind, he had to take an interest in the social life of his ward—to appear at weddings, funerals, and neighborhood occasions, and to say a few well chosen words and make a small donation when called upon. If he had any

time left, he might think about the problems of the city as a whole. But whatever he thought, he was expected to work for his ward first.

From a formal standpoint, the 50 aldermen governed Chicago.[3] The Council made appropriations for all municipal purposes, it awarded franchises to and regulated the rates of public utility companies, it passed on appointments presented by the mayor, and (within the authority given it by the state) it could create new city departments at will. The mayor could send or read messages to the Council, he could vote when there was a tie (or when more than one-half of the aldermen had already voted for a measure), and he had a veto (including an item veto over appropriations acts) which could be overridden by a two-thirds vote. In principle, each alderman was the independent agent of his ward. From a formal standpoint, then, the Council was a good deal like a league of independent nations presided over by a secretary-general.

In fact, however, there existed two sets of informal controls by which the aldermen's independence was very much limited and qualified. One set of controls was the leadership of the Council itself. Half a dozen of the most powerful Democratic aldermen—the "Big Boys," they were sometimes called—working usually with the mayor, effectively controlled the whole Council when matters of interest to them or to the mayor were at stake. They did this in part by controlling committee assignments. Unless an alderman could get on an important committee, his power in the Council was small. And unless he cooperated with the chairmen of the important committees and especially with the chairman of the Finance Committee (whose salary was $8,500, who was provided a limousine with a police chauffeur, and who had an office second only to the mayor's in splendor), he could not hope to get anything done for his ward. Any measure that required an appropriation had to go to the Finance Committee, and so, as one alderman explained, the chairman of that committee "sits at the gate of accomplishment for any alderman. . . ." Indeed, if an alderman fell foul of the Finance Committee chairman or of any of the "Big Boys" he might be punished by having some city service to his ward reduced or suspended. On the other hand, even if he were a Republican, he could expect generous treatment from the leadership if he "played ball."

The other set of informal controls operated through the party or machine. An alderman had to stay in favor with his ward committeeman—i.e., the party leader in his ward—or else be the committeeman himself. The ward committeeman made all of the important decisions for the party within the ward. The committee man was elected in the primary every four years (usually he could keep an opponent off the ballot by raising technical objections to his petitions) and so his power rested in part upon a legal foundation. From a legal standpoint, he was entitled to receive and disburse party funds, to manage campaigns, and to represent the leaders of the party within the ward. In fact he was commonly the "boss" of the ward; the party organization in the ward "belonged" to him. He

decided who would run on the party's ticket within the ward, he appointed and dismissed precinct captains at will, and he dispensed patronage. As a member of the City and County Central Committees of his party, he participated in selecting its candidates for all city, county, and state offices and for Congress. (Half of Illinois' 26 Congressional districts were in greater Chicago.) In each of the party governing bodies his vote was in proportion to the total primary vote for his party in the last election; this of course gave him an incentive to "turn in" the biggest vote possible.

No salary went with the office of committeeman, but most of the committeemen held one or more public jobs and some of them ran businesses which were profitable because of their political connections.

William J. Connors, Democratic boss of the 42nd ward (the district described by Zorbaugh in *The Gold Coast and the Slum*), may be taken as reasonably representative of at least some other ward committeemen. In 1950 Connors, who was in the insurance business, was on the public payroll in two capacities: as a state senator and as a bailiff of Municipal Court. His way of running his ward was described as follows:

That Connors provides well for his workers is undeniable. Not only does he have a great many jobs to distribute, but he is a source of funds if any of his men need to borrow. He supports them when they are in difficulty with the law, as sometimes happens, and takes an interest in their family affairs. His relationship with them is that of a benevolent despot. He holds the power to withdraw their source of livelihood and to banish them from active work in the party and from their power positions in the community. He is the sole dispenser of the campaign funds from the party superstructure and the candidates. He may establish the assessments of the jobholders at any rate he desires without consulting them. He makes the party commitments to the county and city organs without a canvass of the captains' opinions and then demands complete obedience to these decisions. He may move a captain from one precinct to another at his discretion and is, of course, the sole source of patronage distribution.

The committeeman generals his workers much like a military leader might. He plots the strategy of the campaign, estimates the difficulties that may be encountered, and decides the amount and allocation of money to be spent. He shifts captains from one point to another when called for. He attempts to "build" good precincts over a long period of time. Such building requires several years and may involve extensive trials and changes. Jobs arc distributed not only on the basis of the effectiveness of the captain but in regard to the total effects such distribution may have. It happens occasionally that a strong Democratic captain has a smaller number of jobs allotted to him than one who is attempting to build up a Democratic precinct in the face of strong Republican competition. Thus in one precinct which casts a heavy Democratic vote, there are only two jobs besides the captain's, while another precinct that turns in only a slight Democratic majority is staffed by nine jobholders in addition to the captain.

The committeeman respects the unity of the precinct organization and the authority of the captain and his workers. As long as the captain's activities are successful and his conduct does not threaten the party's vote-getting power, Connors does not interfere with the internal structure. The captain selects his own assistants and nominates his choices to receive public jobs. He assumes the responsibility for building an effective precinct organization. He decides how party funds allocated to him will be distributed and to a certain extent how they will be obtained. He and his men must share the responsibility of contributing whatever additional money is necessary beyond that sent from the party's headquarters. Connors respects the autonomy of the captain in this area of personal influence. Captains may or may not distribute campaign literature, pay cash for votes, engage in fraudulent activities, or arrange precinct meetings of the voters. The only important check on the captain's conduct is the final tabulation of votes at each election.

Any ward committeeman who cared to could have himself nominated alderman. If he chose not to run for the office himself (like Connors, he might prefer to be on the public payroll in another capacity), he made sure that the candidate was someone who would work closely with him in ward affairs and offer no challenge to his control of the organization. "Naturally," an alderman once explained, "he (the ward committeeman) doesn't want to get a man who will build himself into a power so he can take the organization away from the committeeman. If the alderman doesn't do what the ward committeeman wants him to do then the committeeman will dump him a the next election." Some committeemei treated their aldermen as errand boys other paid little attention to them, and still others treated them as friends, partners, and collaborators.

If an alderman became powerful enough, he might unseat his committeeman and become the ward boss himself. But even in this case he could not be independent of the machine. The leaders of the Central Committee could bring him into line by withholding patronage or discharging public employees from his ward, by denying him financial support from the party's general coffers at election time, or by allowing an investigation of graft and corruption to take place in his ward. If it saw fit, the Central Committee could destroy a ward organization—and thus a ward committeeman— by these means, but it could do so, of course, only at the cost of impairing, at least temporarily, the effectiveness of the machine. Since its purpose was to win elections, a major concern of the machine was "harmony." Only if a committeeman failed to support the party's slate was he likely to be disciplined severely. If they wanted a favor from him, party leaders would offer him a favor—usually patronage—in return.

To increase their power *vis-à-vis* the Central Committee leadership, ward committeemen formed factional alliances or "blocs." Usually these alignments were on a geographical basis—thus, for example, there were South Side and West Side blocs of ward committeemen.

In order to maintain itself and to accomplish its purposes, any organization must offer incentives of the kinds and amounts that are necessary to elicit the contributions of activity it requires. It must then use these contributions of activity so as to secure a renewed supply of resources from which further incentives may be provided—it must, in other words, maintain what Chester Barnard has called an "economy of incentives" or else cease to exist.

In Chicago a political machine distributed "gravy" to its officials, its financial backers, and to the voters. In this way it induced them to contribute the activity it required—to ring doorbells on election day, to give cash, and to go to the polls and vote for its candidates—and in this way it gained possession, through its control of the city or county government, of a renewed supply of "gravy."

As the word "gravy" suggests, the incentives upon which the machines relied were mainly material. Some prestige attached to being a ward politician; there was "fun" in playing the political "game"; there was satisfaction in being "on the inside"; and sometimes there was even an ideological commitment to an issue, the party, or a candidate. But these non-material incentives were not ordinarily strong enough to elicit the amound and kind of activity that a machine required from its workers. "What I look for in a prospective captain," a ward committeeman told an interviewer, "is a young person—man or woman—who is interested in getting some material return out of his political activity. I much prefer this type to the type that is enthused about the 'party cause' or all 'hot' on a particular issue. Enthusiasm for causes is short-lived, but the necessity of making a living is permanent."

The "material return" that the party

offered a worker was generally a job on the public payroll. Committeeman Connors, for example, had at his disposal in 1952 an estimated 350 to 500 jobs and the total public payroll to Democratic workers in his ward was conservatively estimated at $1,320,000.

Although jobs were the most visible of the material returns the party gave its workers, other opportunities to make money may have been more valuable. An alderman or committeeman who was a lawyer, an insurance man, or a tavern owner could expect to profit greatly from his association with the party. Whether he was profiting lawfully or unlawfully it was often impossible to tell. Alderman Sain and his ward committeeman, County Commissioner John J. Touhy, for example, were partners in an insurance business. "We handle a lot of business, no question about it," Touhy once blandly told a reporter. "I assume its just good business in the ward to carry insurance with us."[4]

Even with the voters the machine did not make its appeal on the basis of issues or ideology. It offered them certain non-material incentives—chiefly the friendship and protection of its precinct captains—but in the main with them, as with the party workers, it relied upon "gravy." Just as it gave its workers jobs and opportunities to make money in exchange for their services, so it gave its loyal voters "favors"—special services and preferential treatment at the hands of its members and dependents who held city or county jobs—in exchange for their votes.

The party's agent in exchanging friendship and favors for votes was the precinct captain.[5] In 1950 a representative captain described his work as follows:

I am a lawyer and prosecuting attorney for the City. I have spent 19 years in precinct work and have lived and worked in my present precinct for three and a half years.

I try to establish a relationship of personal obligation with my people, mostly small shopkeepers and eighty per cent Jewish. I spend two or three evenings a week all year round visiting people, playing cards, talking, and helping them with their problems. My wife doesn't like this, but it is in my blood now. I know ninety per cent of my people by their first names.

Actually I consider myself a social worker for my precinct. I help my people get relief and driveway permits. I help them on unfair parking fines and property assessments. The last is most effective in my neighborhood.

The only return I ask is that they register and vote. If they have their own opinions on certain top offices, I just ask them to vote my way on lower offices where they usually have no preferences anyway.

I never take leaflets or mention issues or conduct rallies in my precinct. After all, this is a question of personal friendship between me and my neighbors. I had 260 promises for Korshak in this primary.

On election day I had forty or fifty people to help me because this was a "hot" campaign. All they had to do was to get out their own family and friends. I used to lease an apartment near the poll where I gave out drinks and cigars, but I don't do this any more.

I stayed inside the poll most of election day, especially during the vote counting. If something went wrong, you could have heard me yell all over the precinct. Actually there isn't as much fraud now as there used to be.

Abner (the PAC candidate) was not really a threat in my precinct. He had seven workers but they contacted only their friends. No one feels obligated to them and they worked only during the campaign. Abner's campaigners were naive. They expected to influence people by issues, and they relied on leaflets and newspaper publicity which is not effective. Besides, Abner (Negro) is not hard to beat in a white precinct. I just carried a picture of both candidates around with me.

I can control my primary vote for sure because I can make the party regulars come out. I don't encourage a high vote here, just a sure vote. In the general election there is much more independent voting, and I can't be sure of control.

In the conservations areas, especially, the precinct captain was often active in the neighborhood improvement association and a leader in efforts to keep "undesirable people" out of the neighborhood. An interviewer who spoke to 30 precinct captains in 1951 found that 16 of them had been approached by voters who wanted help in preventing Negroes and Jews from moving into the neighborhood. Some of these captains invented slogans and ran campaigns on an issue such as: "The _____ neighborhood is a good clean neighborhood. Let's keep it that way!" A captain was likely to learn about it almost immediately if a landlord rented to an "undesirable"; very often the captain would go to the landlord to urge in the name of civic pride that he

discriminate and to point out that property values would decline if he did not.

In heavily Democratic precincts the owners of rooming houses sometimes consulted with their precinct captains about new roomers and assisted the party workers with their canvas at election time. In some cases these owners refused to permit Republican workers to enter their buildings. The loyalty of the rooming house owner to the Democratic party was not a matter of ideology: the owner who did not cooperate with the precinct captain could expect a visit from the city building inspector the next day.

In addition to the services of party workers and voters, the machine needed cash. (It usually cost about $40,000 to elect an alderman.) This it raised by assessing the salaries of people who owed their jobs to the party, from the proceeds of ward-sponsored affairs such as picnics, boxing matches, and golf days, and in contributions from individuals and organizations who wanted to be on good terms with the party or, perhaps, even to help its candidates win. These were all considered legitimate sources of revenue. In some wards, however, money was raised by promising favors or threatening injury to business interests, especially to those interests—e.g., taverns, hotels, and nightclubs—which were subject to inspection and licensing laws. Business people who wanted favors—a change in the zoning law, a permit to operate a tavern, a tax adjustment, and so on—were expected to pay for them in cash. In some wards there was even said to be a fixed schedule of prices for such favors. Whether the money so received went to support the party or to support personally the ward committeeman, the alderman, and their cronies was seldom clear; indeed, in many wards no real distinction could be made between the coffers of the party and pockets of the boss: the ward organization "belonged" to the boss.[6]

The most profitable favors were of course those done for illegal enterprise. In giving protection to gambling joints, unlawful taverns, and houses of prostitution some politicians joined with racketeers to form a criminal syndicate.[7] A by-product of their activity was the systematic corruption of the police force; in one way or another officers were either bribed or discouraged from doing their duty. "After you find out how many places are protected by the ward politicians," a patrolman of long service told an investigator, "you just stay out of the way so you won't be around when something happens."

The machines were most effective in delivering votes in the precincts where they were most corrupt. In general, these were in the "skid-row" districts and the slums, where votes were cheapest and illegal activities most numerous. The "river wards" in the decaying center and on the West Side of the city were the most solidly organized and the most corrupt. Here "social absenteeism"—the departure of socially articulate leaders of the community—had reached such a point that the machine politicians had the field to themselves.[8] It was almost unthinkable that an alderman in one of these wards might lose at the polls because he took an unpopular stand on an issue. If he lost, it was because his committeeman "dumped" him, because the committeeman sold out to

the opposition, or because the opposition managed to build a more powerful machine, but it was not because the voters disliked his stand on any issues. These "river wards" were in sharp contrast to the so-called "newspaper wards" particularly on the North Side where voters usually split the ticket in the way a newspaper advised. The aldermen in the "river wards" could afford to be contemptuous of the newspapers; in their wards editorials were words wasted.

Although corruption in varying degrees was widespread in both parties, it was by no means universal in either. Some Democratic and some Republican wards were probably almost entirely "clean" and even in wards which were not "clean" there were aldermen and other officials who were not parties to the "deals" that were made in the back rooms. The honest aldermen, however, got little credit or encouragement from the voters. Many people seemed to think that all politicians were corrupt and that if an alderman did not use his office for personal profit it was because he was a fool. When a North Side alderman bought his boy a football suit and helmet the other children in the neighborhood said, "Look at the alderman's son," suggesting ill-gotten funds. The alderman himself drove a two-year-old Dodge instead of the Cadillac that he could well afford, but even this did not convince his constituents that he was honest.[9] This widespread cynicism tended, perhaps, to give the aldermen a low conception of their calling and to encourage irresponsibility on their part.

Some of the honest men, the Mayor

among them, did less than they might have done to put a stop to corruption. The fact was that they needed for themselves or for their party the support of the powerful bosses in the corrupt wards. So, for that matter, did many other interests, both liberal and conservative, in city, state, and nation.

NOTES

1. Although written almost two generations ago, Lord Bryce's description of machines applies both in general and in detail to the Chicago machines of the present day. See *The American Commonwealth*, 1917 ed., Macmillan, New York and London, vol. II, chap. LXIII, for Bryce's account of the circumstances which give rise to machines.

"The elective offices are so numerous that ordinary citizens cannot watch them, and cease to care who gets them. The conventions come so often that busy men cannot serve in them. The minor offices are so unattractive that able men do not stand for them. The primary lists are so contrived that only a fraction of the party get on them; and of this fraction many are too lazy or too busy or too careless to attend. The mass of the voters are ignorant; knowing nothing about the personal merits of the candidates, they are ready to follow their leaders like sheep. Even the better class, however they may grumble, are swayed by the inveterate habit of party loyalty, and prefer a bad candidate of their own party to a (probably no better) candidate of the other party. It is less trouble to put up with impure officials, costly city government, a jobbing State legislature, an inferior sort of congressman, than to sacrifice one's own business in the effort to set things right. Thus the Machine works on, and grinds out places, power, and opportunities for illicit gain to those who manage it."

2. A candidate's ethnicity was often a decisive asset or liability; in mixed wards he was most fortunate if his name was such that he could be represented as belonging to more than one ethnic or nationality group. Thus, Alderman Benjamin M. Becker's ward committeeman introduced him to voters of German extraction as of German extraction, stressed to voters of Swedish origin that Becker's wife had lived in Sweden and must have Swedish blood herself, pointed out to Catholics that Becker was a graduate of the DePaul University College of Law and a teacher there (thus implying that he was a Catholic), and presented him to Jews as a Jew. If the Catholics were fooled, no great injustice was done, for Becker's predecessor as alderman for many years was Dr. Joseph Ross, a Catholic whom the Jews assumed was a Jew.

3. The city could exercise only those powers doled out to it by the state legislature, however, and so it might be more accurate to say that the city was governed by the state. See Barnet Hodes, "The Illinois Constitution and Home Rule for Chicago," 15 *Chicago Law Review* 78 (1947).

4. Some years earlier the *Chicago Daily News* compiled a list of the ordinances introduced by Sain over a five-month period and then inquired of the people who were specially benefited by these ordinances whether they had recently bought insurance of the firm of Touhy and Sain. It turned out that many of them had. (September 24, 1940)

5. In a vivid account by David Gutmann, the Chicago precinct captain is described as a "salesman." "Mr. Dolin [the precinct captain] is a go-between his party, which has services and favors to sell the public in exchange for the public's votes, and the public, or at least the segments of it which are willing to exchange their votes for services—often enough to swing a close election. In this relationship the vote stands for currency, the party is the manufacturer or the supplier, the public is the consumer, and Mr. Dolin the door-to-door salesman. . . . To the party the vote has 'commodity' or exchange value, in that it represents a fraction of the total sum of votes needed by the party to gain exclusive control over the 'tons' of patronage whereby it holds power, and to gain access to the financial resources of the community." David Gutmann, "Big-Town Poli-

tics: Grass-Roots Level," *Commentary*, 17:1 (February 1954) 155.

6. If he thought the transaction was likely to be profitable, the ward boss might sell the services of his organization to the opposition. He might be criticized for doing this, but he was not likely to be unseated; after all, the organization "belonged" to him.

7. "... the criminal syndicate," according to Aaron Kohn, chief investigator for the Emergency Crime Committee of the City Council, "can be described as consisting of political officials, having the power and responsibility to enforce the laws, who maliciously withhold that power in exchange for money and support from hoodlums, vice operators, professional gamblers, and other community enemies, to aid them in their political ambitions." Independent Voters of Illinois, *The Kohn Report; Crime and Politics in Chicago*, Chicago, 1953, p. iii. However, after two months inquiry a grand jury in

the Spring of 1954 gave up its efforts to uncover specific links between crime and politics in Chicago. "If an alliance exists," the jurors said, "it might be disclosed with funds to conduct undercover work." *Chicago Sun-Times,* May 1, 1954.

8. See the discussion of social absenteeism in Morris Janowitz, *The Community Press in an Urban Setting*, The Free Press, Glencoe, Illinois, 1952, p. 214. Janowitz notes that social absenteeism contributes to the decay of the ideological element in politics, thus creating "a new kind of hoodlumism in politics" and making possible sudden shifts from one party to another which have no significance in terms of the traditional political allegiances.

9. As this study went to press a committee of the Chicago Bar Association filed charges against this very alderman after the *Sun-Times* had accused him of fee-splitting in zoning cases.

RUNNING
THE NEW-FASHIONED MACHINE

Edward N. Costikyan

THE CLUB

Every local political leader in an urban area must have a permanent headquarters to which supporters and suppliants alike may go to see him. In New York County, there are in normal circumstances thirty-three such local headquarters.[1] They are the regular Democratic clubs of their respective areas.

Each club pays for its own rent, telephone bills, mailings, insurance, typewriters, addressograph and addressograph plates. It must pay for whatever social events it sponsors, and for it own charities.

The hardest organization in the world to manage and lead is such a volunteer organization. Neither executives nor envelope-stuffers are paid. Dereliction in duty cannot be controlled by discipline nor by the threat of discharge. Even if the miscreant is a public employee by reason

From *Behind Closed Doors*, copyright ©1966 by Edward N. Costikyan. Reprinted by permission of Harcourt Brace Jovanovich, Inc.

of the club's help, there is little that can be done; the city will not fire people because they fail to get out a political mailing or to ring doorbells even after they have promised, or even volunteered, to do so.

Once one of our club leaders insisted that at a particular election *every* captain be at his polling place at 6:00 A.M. sharp. We were then still an insurgent club. Our captains had no real function to perform at 6:00 A.M., since our Regular Democrat counterparts had their own staff of captains ready to handle early morning election-day details such as making sure the

1. In 1955 the party adopted rules which, defying all natural law, declared each district would be headed by two co-equals, one male and one female. In 1963 in three districts, the male from one club and the female from its opposition club won. So in those districts there are two co-equal headquarters, making the county total 36 for 33 leadership districts. But the number may vary every two years. In 1965, due to reapportionment the total was 39 districts.

polls opened on time. Our captains knew it, and few were inclined to rise at 5:00 A.M. in order to show the flag when no one else would be awake to see it. I knew this, and declined to issue the 6:00 A.M. directive.

"But they *have* to come," I was told.

"What if they ask why, and there's no good reason to be there?" I asked.

"Then fire them."

"Yeah," I said, "fire them and then what do we do?"

To this there was no answer. There was no waiting line of anxious applicants begging for appointment to a captaincy. In fact, over half the districts then had no captains. This is the unanswerable problem when one seeks efficiency in a modern volunteer political party—if you fire someone, then what do you do?

Even if every public jobholder who failed to carry out his political duties could be fired, one still could not maintain discipline. The maximum percentage of jobholders among the captains and workers in any club in New York County is about 35 percent—and that is very unusual. More often it's between 10 and 20 percent and frequently less. Even if job threats could insure discipline in this minority, little would be achieved. A 35 percent container—like a sieve—carries little water.

These being the facts, other techniques must be used. Appeals to idealism, personal friendship, supposed obligations—all of these are among the tools. But essentially the leader must create a spirit that can produce a desire to follow through among his supporters. To sustain such a spirit is the heart of the matter. Even

with it, running a club of this kind is a difficult and perpetually challenging task. The investment of time is incredible. Privacy, to a considerable extent, evaporates.

Budgets vary—from as low as $4,000 to as high as $30,000 a year. Memberships vary—from under 200 to over 4,000. The number of voters represented varies from under 10,000 to over 50,000. The degree of activity varies. In each case, the leader's responsibility is to keep the local headquarters open and functioning. Prospective new members must be sought and, once inveigled into the headquarters, welcomed. Someone else may have done the inveigling, but the leader had better personally show his happiness at their presence.

The headquarters usually looks dingy and needs repainting, which means money or labor or both. The leader must be prepared to see that the money or labor is there (or do it himself).

The Membership Committee is planning a new-member's party. The leader must be available.

The club's bank account is low and someone must be stimulated to set up a fund-raising affair. The leader's counsel is sought as to the best money-raising device to try this time.

Regular monthly membership meetings require a continuing supply of reasonably interesting speakers on important issues. Can the leader get the commissioner of correction or housing or something?

There is a growing feud between two key officers in the club. Will the leader talk to them and straighten them out?

Complaints are flowing in (to the leader) that club members are not receiving club mailings. The leader finds out that two volunteers, each looking to the other, have fallen five months behind in keeping the membership lists current.

So-and-so has moved out of the district, and no one is handling such-and-such committee. Does the leader have any ideas as to who might take over?

The treasurer has been away, the bills for annual dues (usually five or six dollars, with optional higher amounts for "sustaining members") have not been sent out, and the treasury is low. Where can we find some funds, borrowed or otherwise, for last month's rent?

The theater-benefit committee must put down a thousand-dollar deposit by next Tuesday. Can the leader suggest ten people to be asked to lend a hundred apiece?

And so it goes. The leader is always the first and last resort.

A good leader delegates—and then redelegates when the original delegatee flops. As a result, as time passes, more and more of the internal work is undertaken by the club president and other officers. But still the problems continue, and when they remain unsolved on the way up, they end in the leader's hands.

Every problem—paint, heat, rent, telephone, mailing costs, repairs, robberies, fires, insurance, location, cleaning—at one time or another are the leader's ultimate responsibility. Indeed, the hallmark of a real political leader is whether he has swept out his own clubhouse—*while he was the leader!* There's nothing like it to stimulate the club members and, if I may

say so, to clean up the headquarters the way they should be cleaned up.

The final club problem is *knowing* the members. They come and go. There are as many as a hundred new members a year. A leader who wants to survive must make sure that he spends enough time learning who they are, and meeting them, becoming *their* leader as well as the club's!

THE CONSTITUENTS

The second major area of the leader's activity is dealing with constituents. Depending upon the area serviced, a leader may have a heavy or light load of constituents *every* Monday and to a lesser extent, Thursday night, fifty-two weeks a year.

In some areas of New York, fifty to a hundred constituents arrive each week for help from the leader. In areas like mine, the number has varied—five to ten a week at the beginning, when the area was 60 percent tenements; one to two a week at the most now that the district is 80 percent middle, upper-middle, and luxury housing.

What do these people want?

Basically they want help with problems that are frequently impossible to solve and frequently quite simple.

Tenant disputes with landlords were once the bulk of our problem; the apartment hasn't been painted in six years; there's no heat; the plaster is broken; we need new windows; there are no lights in the halls. Sometimes it's worse: the landlord wants a rent increase; the building is going to be torn down and the landlord says I've got to get out; I was late on the rent and I have this eviction notice.

These problems, calling for various degrees of activity—from a phone call or a form to representing a tenant in court—are handled as the problem demands, either by the leader or his associates.

I always insisted that if anything more than routine form-filling or telephoning was necessary, one of the attorneys in the club assume the personal responsibility of becoming the attorney for the complainant—or else let someone else do the job.

On only two occasions did a constituent ask me to "talk to the judge," both times about a housing matter. One was a landlord. The other a tenant. In both cases I said no. In both cases, justice was done. Indeed, the tenant, who won her case without intervention, became a committed party worker and a firm believer in a nonpolitical judiciary.

There are constituents with problems in the criminal courts. A sixteen-year-old son was arrested; one of the club members, who was a good criminal lawyer, took that one on—and the boy was acquitted. The sister-in-law of a club officer was arrested for shoplifting and was on her way to night court when the leader was advised. The leader dropped everything, went to court, and ultimately worked out a disposition with the complaining witness.

A local neighborhood hotspot had repeated trouble with the State Liquor Authority, whose inspectors seemed to be harassing the place looking for a shakedown. Did the leader know anyone at the S.L.A.? He didn't, but he knew a leader

who did, the complaint of harassment was made, and the harassment ceased.

A constituent on welfare had violated the rules, taken a part-time job, and picked up an extra three hundred dollars over a four-month period. Welfare had found out and was demanding he repay the three hundred, but he didn't have it. There were criminal charges pending. Could the leader help? He could. A couple of phone calls to the appropriate authorities in the Welfare Department resulted in the obvious conclusion that the money simply wasn't there and that it wouldn't help anyone to send the man to jail. (That was over ten years ago—and the man has been in no trouble since.)

A constituent had lost his job in an advertising agency at the age of forty-five, his unemployment insurance had run out, so had his savings. Wasn't there some place his obvious talents could be used? There was. A city agency needed a skilled economic researcher at $6,500 a year.

A constituent had taken a civil-service exam and passed it, but an ancient matrimonial dispute had led the appointing authority to reject him. Could he get a chance to explain the whole matter in person? He could (though he didn't get the job).

A group of constituents were fighting the installation of a commercial parking garage in a residential building. Could the leader appear at the hearing before the zoning authority? He couldn't, but the club president could.

The residents of a building were going crazy because of excavation for a new apartment house across the street. The racket started at 7:00 A.M. every day, including Saturdays. Could the leader get the contractor to lay off on Saturdays? He could.

A constituent wanted to organize a program to plant trees down one street. Would the leader get permission—and some money—from the landowners? He would.

A taxi driver had three moving-traffic violations and was about to lose his license. Can we help? Not much.

A family found their welfare allowance wholly inadequate. Could the leader help? He could, if only to the extent of speeding a review of the allowances.

And so it goes, week in and week out, year after year.

A relatively small number seek jobs; many—often proprietors of single-man enterprises—seek relief from jury duty; once the general counsel of a major oil company (a Republican, by the way, although we never asked anyone their party affiliation—a constituent is a constituent) sought help because a new street light had been put up outside his third-story bedroom window on Beekman Place. It was shining in his eyes all night. Couldn't a shield be placed on the back of the light? It was—and it was carefully adjusted one evening, while the venerable gentlemen stuck his head out the window and shouted directions to the man on the ladder.

In other districts the problems will differ. Getting new street lighting; placing traffic lights where constituents—not traffic engineers—think them necessary; dealing with school location and other education problems; securing better parks, or getting existing parks cleaned up; law-enforcement problems and better police protection.

Indeed, every variety of problem that affects his district finds its way to the district leader. A composite of the problems brought to district leaders is a composite of the problems that affect the city.

In a tiny percentage—far less than one percent of the problems, in my experience—something illicit is sought: the fixing of a case or the calling-off of an inspector who insists that a sidewalk be repaired. In twelve years of handling these problems, I can remember only one case where I was offered a pay-off, three cases where communication with a judge or hearing officer was sought, and one other case of proposed misconduct. That's a low percentage, in light of the legends about politicians.

As a general rule, no one who asks for help from the club is expected to pay for it. Indeed, the ranks of former politicians are heavy-laden with unimaginative types who thought it appropriate to receive a slight token of appreciation for each favor undertaken, let alone satisfactorily performed.

The requests are of all degrees of difficulty. In many cases, the only answer that can be given ("I want a five-room apartment in a city housing project, and my income is ten thousand a year") is "Sorry, nothing can be done." In other cases—for example, when an aged couple, seeking a city housing-project apartment, is perplexed by a one-year delay after due application—the answer may be "We'll see what's wrong and what can be done."

Very rarely indeed can the district

leader say "Yes, it will be done." Perhaps in only one-third of the cases can anything be done—and for those cases months may be needed. And yet the district leader and his associates, who frequently take on responsibility for following through on problems, must make friends while doing no more than "their best," with no better than a one-third record of success except in purely routine matters. Dealing with constituents soon develops in the leader both a broad knowledge of government and considerable tact and diplomatic skill.

And when a local issue erupts that places the local community in conflict with city or state government—such as the proposal for the Lower Manhattan Expressway, which Robert Moses and various labor unions supported and which the local residents opposed; the destruction of a local hospital, which the hospital commissioner proposed and the local residents opposed; the closing of Washington Square Park to traffic, which was generally opposed by the city but violently supported by local residents; and so on—the party leader must be prepared to be the community spokesman, especially if he has an opponent or potential opponent for the leadership, who will be delighted to become the spokesman if the leader is silent.

Basically the leader cushions the impact of government upon his constituents and provides a pipeline for his constituents to the bureaucracy at the heart of every urban center.

Instead of the tenant calling a telephone number for the nth time to make a complaint about the absence of heat on a

freezing day in January, the leader calls or goes to see a deputy clerk he knows—and that impossible temperature and the freezing tenants become a far more human problem, and far more likely to receive attention than if they were merely one address on a long list of telephoned complaints.

The political rewards for effective handling of such problems are simple: votes for the leader and his club's candidates when, every two years, they run for re-election to party office, and, it is hoped, votes for the party's candidates for public office on every election day.

The first reward is far surer. When someone has been helped—or even treated decently—he doesn't forget the man or the club that helped him. Translating that memory into a vote for a President or governor or mayor or even an assemblyman is a far chancier business. But chancy or not, this is an essential part of the duty of a district leader. And his willingness to devote his time to this kind of activity is one of the credentials he must possess if he wishes to be accepted as a political leader who is entitled to be heard by other leaders when candidates are being nominated and policies being decided.

This description of tasks undertaken for constituents is not a careful distillation of the legitimate from the illegitimate ones. The percent of illegitimate requests to which the author was subjected was minuscule. True, other leaders might attract more illicit requests and might accept the assignments. I can issue no guarantees of probity for all politicians. But my experience tells me that the percentage of misconduct among political leaders in this area is relatively insignificant. For example, . . . the locus of corruption (to the extent that there is corruption) has shifted. The politician is no longer the middleman. Public officials amenable to corruption can be approached directly, and with less exposure. Why use an unnecessary middleman?

Moreover, most of the problems that concern constituents do not require illicit intervention. So why do it?

Indeed, the myth of the corruptibility of the political leaders is, I am convinced, to a large extent and in a substantial majority of cases a relic from ancient history and a carefully exploited legend designed to immobilize and minimize the significance of political leaders.

After all, many a civic leader and many a public official makes his reputation by periodically denouncing "the politician," "the bosses," and "the political hacks." Yet the evidence of graft and misconduct in recent years has in almost all cases involved civil servants and public officeholders—not political leaders—who have gone wrong.

THE CAMPAIGN

The final area of the leader's principal local activity is the management of the party's general election campaign in his area.

He has thirty election districts? He *must* have thirty captains—one for each district. If there are thirty captains but six are no good, he must find six new ones and ease the old ones out without too much of a fuss.

Every year one or two captains retire. They must be replaced—by trained people.

Does Captain A have enough help? How can we get him or her a couple of assistants? The Fourteenth E.D. has two good co-captains sharing the district. They've developed to the point that either one can handle it alone—if he or she will. Can we move one over to the Sixteenth E.D.?

Last year's campaign chairman, who deals directly with the captains and handles the execution of the campaign, has gotten too busy in his law practice, or has gotten married, or has moved. Whom shall we put in his place?

We will want to send out two mailings the week before election day—one to Democratic registrants and one to Republicans. Can we put X in charge of getting the 25,000 envelopes (or 50,000, or 75,000) addressed during the summer?

Who will write our local literature? What should it say?

How about a telephone campaign the last two weeks? Can we get so-and-so to organize that?

We need a mailing to new residents to tell them where to register, so we'll need someone to canvass all the new buildings before September 1 to get the names of new tenants.

And so on and on. By September 1, the campaign machinery must be set up. By September 30, it must be rolling. After that it's too late to start concocting new campaign plans, or even to do much more than feed the machinery that has been set up, to oil it, and to make minor adjustments and replacements.

All year round, therefore, as the leader meets new members, as he deals with constituents, he notes those who might be helpful in a campaign and passes on the names to the campaign chairman. The campaign chairman looks about too. The club president, the secretary, vice-president, ex-leaders, ex-presidents—they all look, and suggest. The campaign chairman assigns people to specific tasks or areas. One out of three delivers. Those who don't are forgiven, but then are forgotten as campaigners.

The campaign chairman keeps a chart; it shows captains and workers in each election district. Regularly the leader checks it. "We're light in the Eleventh. There's a fellow named so-and-so who was in to get some help who might work out. Why don't you try him?" And so the list grows. By election day there is, besides the captain, a list of five or six workers per election district. Two to four of them, moreover, are really prepared to work all day getting Democratic voters to the polls. The district is "manned"!

On election day, while voters sleep, the leaders and the campaign chairman and the lawyers and the captains and workers rise at 5:00 A.M. By 6:00 A.M. the leaders—male and female—are on the way around the polls to see they are open, manned by captains, functioning, peaceful, and happy.

All day long, the leaders check the polls—the voter turnout, the captains' attitudes, the morale. Where a district is light when it shouldn't be, the leaders or the campaign chairman find the captain and jack him up.

When there are legal problems at the polls, a lawyer is sent. When a machine breaks, the leader or the law chairman calls the Board of Elections again and again—until it's fixed. If a voter is denied the right to vote, one of the lawyers gets him a cab, and soon he's on his way to the Supreme Court to apply for a legal order authorizing him to cast his ballot.

When night falls, the leader gives his captains a last push to get out the Democrats, and then awaits the closing of the polls and the reports of the results.

The first four election districts often give the experienced leader a clue to the results—win, lose, or too close to tell. By 1:00 A.M. the results are finally in—good or bad.

The next morning—bright, early, and perhaps groggily—the leader and the campaign chairman and the captains are at work earning their livings, while their nonpolitical co-workers comment how nice it was to have had a day off. That night the leader may very well be at his headquarters—especially after a licking—surveying the wreckage, putting the election figures in the desk drawer so that they'll be available for later analysis, cleaning up the headquarters.

The week after election day, the leaders and the campaign managers go over the results and compare them with those of prior years. There was a new captain in the Fifteenth E.D. and that district went Democratic for the first time in ten years ("That guy looks good—I hope we can keep him interested"); the margin keeps going up in the Eighteenth; according to the captain in the Nineteenth, Y was a great help—maybe Y could take on a district.

And so the planning starts for the next year's campaign. More people, new people, different people. But the machinery is permanent, although the people who man it change and change and change.

There are "promotions"—a captain becomes assistant campaign manager, and then campaign manager, and then club president—and then perhaps district leader. Or a captain, after two or three or four (or ten) years grows tired of the drudgery, the stairs to climb, the doorbells to ring, and retires.

Out of the shifting but steady process grows a small, semipermanent, semiautonomous political institution—the leader's political home, and usually his successor's political home. The club is the symbol of his district. It is his headquarters, his meeting place, his responsibility, his ticket of admission to the meetings where candidates are selected and political policy made.

⚛ THREE ⚛
The Boss and the Immigrant

✦ COMMENTARY ✦

Had it not been for the immigrant this land would not have been settled. In the thirty-five years following the end of the American Revolution, only about 250,000 came. But within the hundred years after 1815, a series of massive folk wanderings from Europe brought thirty-five million immigrants to the United States to till the soil, dig the canals, lay the railroad tracks, work the factories, people and build the cities. While with the rise of the industrial city the Catholic Irish and German came to predominate, in the four decades from the 1880s the ethnic composition shifted dramatically to immigrants from Southern and Eastern Europe—Russian Jews, Poles, Italians, Greeks, and Bohemians; between 1882 and 1914 twenty million of them poured in, and in the peak year of 1907, almost 1,300,000 more. Unlike immigrants before 1840, most of the newcomers stayed in the cities, fewer were Protestant and middle-class, more were of rural peasant stock, desperately poor, often illiterate, and ignorant of American political and social institutions. In the New York of the 1880s, out of a population of two million, a half-million could not speak English. By 1920, when for the first time more Americans lived in urban centers than in the village or on the farm, more than three-quarters of the urban population were either of foreign birth or sons and daughters of immigrants.

Had it not been for the immigrant the city boss and his machine would not have become what they were. Each needed the other. The immigrant, a new kind of uprooted urban proletarian, was the disinherited of a new frontier, the frontier of the urban wilderness, untamed, exploitive, dingy. The quality of life left the urban immigrant vulnerable to the inducements of the boss. Theirs was a world of marginal subsistence, sweat shops, child labor, yellow-dog contracts; a world without public relief, workmen's compensation, old-age pensions, where private charity could be inadequate and humilating. When they could find work, many worked a sixteen-hour day, six-day week, for a wage of three cents an hour. A few days' illness could mean catastrophe. The death of a bread-winning father could shatter the family and send the children either to orphanages or to a life on the streets. As Denis Brogan has said, these people had "nothing to lose but their chains and little to sell but their votes."

To get those votes the boss set in motion a process, an Americanization process, that offered a commitment to American political and social institutions and at the same time provided a balm to urban life. The boss became an ethnic broker, bartering votes for patronage and a chance to achieve social and political mobility, however modest. If the sacredness of the ballot was abused, access to the political system, however limited, helped to ease the class tensions that so characterized the European urban proletariat. In his own way the city boss helped to maintain an open-ended society.

Often the process began at the instant the ship docked. Party workers met immigrants and helped them get settled. Martin Lomansey of Boston, for example, met every new immigrant ship and helped the newcomers find lodging or guided them to relatives. James Michael Curley set up naturalization classes to prepare newcomers for the citizenship examination. And Boss Tweed went to the heart of the Americanization process. In 1868 the New York Printing Company (William Tweed, president) printed 105,000 applications for citizenship and 69,000 certificates of naturalization. Friendly judges, anticipating election day, converted their courts into naturalization mills, grinding out a thousand new Americans a day, and thousands of new supporters for Tammany Hall.

Nor were the inducements of the Americanization process exclusively material favors. Several bosses cast themselves as super-patriots, and their organizations as the guardians of the blessings of American life so urgently sought by the immigrant. Flags were waved, prose turned purple, celebrations were wild on national holidays. Enemies of their organization and reformers in general were identified as opponents of true patriotism and American ideals. It was heady stuff for immigrants, because of their compulsion to be a part of America, on one hand, and because of the constant ridicule and contempt of Nativists, on the other. Patriotism became a means for the newcomer to prove himself worthy.

The immigrant's cultural baggage contained apparel out of style for urban living. The majority of the immigrants, landless peasants from a static agrarian environment, found themselves painfully ill-equipped to cope with a commercial, money-oriented urban world. With the skilled, specialized middle-class occupations closed to most of them, only the more menial, dirty, poorly paying jobs were available. Generations of political and religious persecution left them deeply suspicious of formal government. Conditioned by boss rule of one sort or the other—from the aristocracy, the nobility, or the Church—they were hardly shocked by the demands of machine politics and its seeming opposition to the self-help, self-reliance, and individualistic values of American political thought. The aspirations of boss and the immigrant were the same— survival. Survival through intimate, personal affiliation with friend, bene- factor, family, or church. The immigrants' goals were immediate, short- termed, bent to the business of eating, employment, protecting the young in a hostile, alien existence. The boss provided those personal services, opened the door to the political process, and exacted his reward: votes and loyalty.

It was the superb irony of machine politics that the boss had no better ally in solidifying immigrant support than his traditional enemy, the re- former. In the late-nineteenth and the early-twentieth century, the immi- grant and religion were the volcanic issues of the day, as communism and race have been to our generation. Whereas the reformer, especially the Protestant, middle- and upper-class variety, regarded the newcomer with contempt as well as fear that he and his culture would pollute the "na- tive" stock and pervert the ideals of American democracy, the boss sup- ported the immigrants' culture and traditions, exploited his old-world hostilities and new-world frustrations. The boss had the uncanny knack of being, as it were, able to ride the immigrant waves. For example, when Tim Sullivan's heavily populated Irish district in New York gave way to invasions of Jews and Italians, he adjusted with grace and sagacity, gleeful- ly donning a yarmulke for Bar Mitzvahs, learning enough Yiddish and the Neapolitan dialect for friendly chitchat, appearing prominently at all eth- nic festivities. The Italians loved him when he used his clout with the New York Legislature to have Columbus Day declared a state holiday. A pro- fessional Irishman with his own kind, James Michael Curley worked com- fortably with the Lithuanians of South Boston and the Italians of East Boston. He wept before 25,000 Italians at a memorial service for Enrico

Caruso, joined the N.A.A.C.P., and gave patronage to the blacks when
they moved in.

To the reformer, on the other hand, the urban crisis resulted largely
from an unholy marriage of boss and immigrant. To many of them, the
immigrant was a moral cripple. "These newcomers," said one high-minded
reformer, "were ignorant, clannish, and easily controlled. Their moral
sense had been blunted by ages of degradation." It was a head-on collision
of two different political styles. Politics to many reformers was the Protestant ethic preached and practiced. The public good must be put before
personal welfare. Politics must reflect correct business habits: efficiency
and low costs; above all, the politician must be a man of unblemished integrity and committed to high moral principles. Whereas to the immigrant,
politics meant not some misty goal of elegant principles but something
that would specifically advance his welfare. When a reformer ventured
into the immigrant slums to preach temperance, Sabbatarianism, civic
responsibility, the evils of patronage, the necessity of justice, and the logic
of practicing economics, the newcomer's reaction was one of suspicion
and fear. The call for efficiency and the end of patronage might mean the
end of his job. Economy might scotch the building of a school for his
child. To him civic responsibility was an understanding of his plight, justice was a playground for the children, or something to eat when times
were bad; and temperance reform, as Alfred Lewis put it, "got between
the people and its beer!"

This should not suggest the easy generalization that urban immigrant
politics pivoted exclusively around differences in class, with the Democrats representing the working and lower class and the Republicans claiming the middle and upper classes. "I s'pose you've noticed how that Pat/
Rhymes, beautiful, with Democrat," might explain Irish support of Democratic Tammany Hall in New York; but the Irish, Jews, Swedes, Bohemians, and Germans in other cities voted differently on the issues of the day.
Neither major party had an absolute monopoly on the immigrant or the
native vote. Recent studies have demonstrated that such ethnocultural
factors as religion were as important as class in party selection.[1]

Nor were all boss-ruled cities heavily populated with immigrants. The
large eastern cities and the great inland city of Chicago did attract an enormous number of immigrants, but Denver's Boss Speer and Kansas City's

1. See Joel Arthur Tarr's interesting discussion of ethnocultural factors in *A Study in Boss Politics:
William Lorimer of Chicago* (1971), pp. 17-23.

Boss Pendergast had relatively few immigrants (both had their poor, however). Whereas New York had a diversity of ethnic groups, a virtual ethnic Mulligan stew, which generally—but certainly not always—supported the Democrats, Milwaukee had only two dominant groups, the Germans and the Poles, and the Germans flocked to the Socialist Party. David Shannon in his *The Socialist Party of America* tells the story of a Socialist politician with a Polish name explaining why he failed to win an election. "If we had had someone with a good American name like Schemmelpfennig we could have won."

Despite these qualifications, however, the link between the boss and the immigrant helps substantially to account for the complexion of machine politics in America. It was an alliance, however, with a double-edge. If it explains in part how the boss flourished, it also explains in part how he either changed or declined. Over time a generation gap created a chasm between the machine and the sons and daughters and grandchildren of the original immigrants. As more and more second- and third-generation immigrant children were absorbed into the middle class, more adopted the attitudes of middle-class politics. Prosperity, education, "making it," made them less dependent upon personal welfare and more concerned with the public welfare. They became increasingly vote-conscious, issue-oriented, reform-minded, and ironically, anti-boss. Since the 1940s, the reform movement in New York has been dominated by second- and third-generation Jews, whose families of the Lower East Side had once supported the Tammany Hall of Richard Croker and Charles Murphy. In *The Irish and Irish Politicians* Edward M. Levine writes of the "new Irish" politicians of Chicago in the 1960s, many with college degrees and living in middle-class neighborhoods, many married to a woman of different ethnic background and raising children who are losing much of their ethnic identity. One, an official in city government appointed by virtue of his expertise rather than by patronage, could say; "I was never a precinct captain and don't even know who the captain in my precinct is." This is a far cry from the days of Hinky Dink Kenna and Bathhouse John Coughlin.

From the juxtaposition of the historian and the novelist, the first two selections in this chapter deal sympathetically, often poignantly, with the flair of the boss for dealing with the immigrant. The first, from Oscar

95

Handlin's Pulitzer Prize-winning *The Uprooted*, explores in a general fashion the urban setting and its ethnic heritage, the boss's arsenal of favors and his posture of compassion that wooed the immigrant to the machine. The second is from the novel *The Last Hurrah*, which narrowly missed a Pulitzer Prize in 1956 and is considered by many the best ever written on urban politics in America. Author Edwin O'Connor examines one specific event, Knocko Minihan's wake. Why, he asks, all the boisterous conviviality at such a solemn occasion as a funeral? Why wasn't the family of the deceased humiliated by all the political chatter? Why did so many people appear when no one really liked Knocko Minihan, a dull and sour fellow? The answer to these questions exhibits the master's touch of Frank Skeffington (modeled after James Michael Curley) and his bond with the Boston immigrant.

Less sympathetic is Daniel Patrick Moynihan, the ex-bartender who rose to the heights at Harvard University, and then in the U.S. government and diplomatic service. During the hundred years after 1820, roughly one-fourth of all the millions who immigrated to America were from Ireland. Moynihan writes of the genius of these Irish for politics, and the phenomenon of Tammany Hall politicians in the great days of Tammany's reign, from the Tweed era of the 1860s-70s to that of natty Jimmy Walker of the 1920s. He analyzes the structure and development of Tammany Hall as a political institution—certainly the most powerful (and notorious) political machine in American history. Moynihan makes a persuasive argument that Ireland's history, its political experience, its village life, prepared the Irish for their extraordinary success in American politics. What is striking is that Moynihan is an unsentimental Irishman. George Washington Plunkitt could say, "I saw my opportunities and took 'em." But Moynihan says that the Irish Tammany warriors had marvelous opportunities for social change and failed to take them. His characterization of the Irish as conservative custodians of the status quo should be measured against the notion of the boss as reformer, discussed in the commentary to chapter 5 of our book.

The final selection is an overview of boss and immigrant that brings us up to our own time. Political scientist Elmer E. Cornwell, Jr., discusses the patterns of integration and the political techniques under the classic machine, and then compares the situation with that of the most recent newcomers to the American city, the blacks and the Puerto Ricans. He examines the political integration of the blacks in Chicago and of the

Puerto Ricans and blacks in New York, and concludes on a note that might rate a last hurrah from immigrants of an earlier era: party government of the "bad" old days of the city boss served the immigrant well as a vehicle for integration into American life. Unfortunately, with the decline of urban party government from roughly the 1930s—a casualty of reform—the party plays a much lesser role in the newcomer's adaptation to the city than it did in the past.

WHY THE IMMIGRANT SUPPORTED THE MACHINE

Oscar Handlin

As a boy in Brooklyn, "Hughey" McLaughlin was already a leader among his cronies. Big and strong, handy with his fists in a fight, he commanded the respect of the lads who hung around the firehouse. One employment after another was not quite to his taste; but in the neighborhood he was well known, and favorably. In 1855 his opportunity came. Taken on at the Navy Yard, he was put in charge of a group of workers, a gang, with the title of Boss Laborer, soon shortened to Boss.

These were the essential elements. To hold his own position it was necessary that he retain the favor of the political authority that appointed him. He did so by the ability to deliver a certain number of votes. And he was able to deliver those votes because he controlled a fund of

From *The Uprooted*, Second Edition, by Oscar Handlin, reprinted by permission of Little, Brown and Co., in association with The Atlantic Monthly Press. Copyright 1951, © 1973 by Oscar Handlin.

desirable jobs. In time, McLaughlin extended the scope of his operations from the Navy Yard to the whole municipality. The relationship between votes and jobs remained the same.

Throughout the country in the great cities, other bosses became the heads of other gangs. Some had assembled followings as foremen or contractors, others by growing up in a district where they exercised continuing leadership as a gang of boys grew up to be a gang of voters. Everywhere the connection between these allegiances and the opportunity to work was plain. In an economy that condemned the immigrants to unskilled labor a large percentage of the available jobs were directly or indirectly dependent upon political favor. Aqueducts and streets the city built for itself; trolley, gas, telegraph, and electric lines were laid by companies franchised by the city; and every structure, as it went up, was inspected by the city. One pair of hands was much like another when it held the shovel; the employers of unskilled labor were wise enough to treat indulgently the wishes of the municipal officials in whose power it was to let contracts or grant permits.

The job was at the center of the boss's attractiveness. But he was also able to call forth a more general sense of attachment. Often the feelings of group loyalty focused upon him. He was a member of many associations, made friends on every block. In the columns of their own newspapers his name appeared frequently. His achievements cast their reflected glory on the whole community and he in turn shared its sense of solidarity. In that respect he stood at an advantage over every competitor for the immigrants' leadership. He had sprung from among them and substantially remained one with them.

Furthermore, he spoke for them. After the Civil War as the national parties in election after election chewed over the same stale issues, a great dullness settled down over their campaigns. Few people cared to take the trouble to distinguish how the position of the Democrats differed from that of the Republicans on civil service reform or the tariff. Few even bothered to learn what those problems were about. These were remote and abstract questions that did not directly touch on their own lives. The immigrant might sometimes read an article on such a matter in his newspaper but was less likely to be persuaded by any intrinsic ideas on the subject than by the character of the persuader. If a trusted source said that when a Democrat is President misery comes, that if the Republicans win the factories will open, the new citizen was likely to accept the statement without cavil.

The local issues were the important ones. Whether there should be a new public bathhouse in Ward Twelve, whether the city should hire extra laborers, seemed questions of no moment to the party statesmen. To the residents of the tenement districts they were critical; and in these matters the ward boss saw eye to eye with them. *Jim gets things done!* They could see the evidence themselves, knew the difference it made in their own existence.

The boss took command of the group in political matters. The old-line nationalist leaders still commanded the respect of their fellow countrymen but could not compete with the boss for votes. That fact Bourke Cockran discovered, in New York, when he met the opposition of Croker of Tammany Hall. Patrick Collins learned the same lesson in Boston, and an identical moral was pointed in other cities throughout the country. The machine gave form to the immigrant vote.

The ambitious politician, however, could not get very far if his power rested only on the loyalty of a bloc of immigrant followers. The instability of settlement prevented the consolidation of control on that basis. Tammany could not be sure how long its dominance of the East Side wards would last, or Lomasey in Boston of the West End, when the original Irish residents moved out and their place was taken by Jews and Italians. The successful chieftains were those who expanded their roles beyond the little group within which they had grown to power.

Hugh McLaughlin had perceived this. In his White House Saloon or in his office on Willoughby Street, he had made himself available to all comers. On the corner in Boston where his boyhood gang had whiled away the time, Martin Lomansey built the Hendricks Club. By the century's end, behind the whitened windows of an empty store, in the back room of a saloon, upstairs above the dance hall—under a variety of designations there was in every ward a place where a man could go and see the boss, or see someone who would in turn see the boss.

I think that there's got to be in every ward a guy that any bloke can go to when he's in trouble and get help—not justice and the law, but help, no matter what he's done. The old man reminisces as the incidents of a long career come back. What requests had not been made of him! And often enough he'd stepped in without waiting to be asked. Time and again one of the boys would let him know: the poor fellow had allowed his payments to lapse and now the widow had not the burial money; or, the furniture was being put out in the street and them with no place to go and the wife ailing at that. Baskets at Christmas, picnics, boat rides on the river or lake, and a ready purse at the mention of any charitable collection—these were all within his realm of obligations.

But mostly he had intervened at the points at which his people encountered the difficulties of the law. Between the rigid, impersonal rulings of the statute and the human failings of those ignorant of its complexities he stood as mediator. The poor lad who had an extra glass and by some half-remembered encounter ended the night in jail, the shopkeeper whose stand edged beyond the legal limit onto the sidewalk, turned to him whose contact set matters straight. They had all sat there explaining their troubles, the liquor dealer and the peddler worried about licenses, the contractor and the real-estate owner involved in deals with the city. They had to come to him because they knew he was *fair* with his *favors*.

Those vain fools up on the hill had laughed and then seethed with indignation when he had torn the legislature apart so that wretched Italian could vend his peanuts on the grounds. The fulminations against "peanut politics" had been all to the good. They had confirmed the popular impression that he championed the little men against the big, the humble against the proud. Hundreds who themselves never had the occasion to turn to him firmly believed in his accessibility. The image, his own and theirs, was that of the kindly overlord, the feudal noble translated from the manor to the ward—above the law and therefore capable, if properly approached, of doing better justice than the law.

There was a price, of course. An exception made for one lawbreaker could be made for another; if the frightened peddler could get off, so too could the swaggering tough. After all, the turkeys in the baskets, the bubbling kegs of beer at the ends of the long picnic tables, all cost money. Whose money?

There were persons who would pay

the bill. The thriving gambling industry of the 1870's stood on a tenuous relationship with the police. With expanded operations and greater capital investments, the operators of the keno, faro, and policy games could not tolerate a situation in which they were at the mercy of the extortions of every precinct lieutenant and his underlings. Nor would saloonkeepers willingly expose themselves to the assaults of temperance fanatics with their zealous insistence upon awkward closing hours or even upon total prohibition. An accommodating boss like Mike McDonald in Chicago provided protection in return for moderate occasional contributions from some two thousand gamblers in Chicago.

This source of support was not very secure, however. With time, the big promoters moved into the shadowland of legality and became less dependent upon protection. Some advanced to the ownership of bucket shops or indeed to the dignity of brokerage offices; others began to make book on horse racing and prize fighting, now legitimate enterprises. The older forms of speculation catered increasingly to the less profitable poor and were left to the attention of the petty promoter, from whom not much could be drawn in the way of assessments.

Some bosses and their wives were, at the same time, stricken with social aspirations. Having made their way in the world, they wanted the visible symbols of having done so. Mike McDonald had made Carter Harrison mayor. Why should not the one be as respectable as the other? Unfortunately there were limits to the enjoyment of success; when McDon-

ald moved to a fine suburb and began to play the gentleman, he lost his following and was unseated by Bathhouse John Coughlin and Hinky Dink Mike Kenna, two ungentle characters still close to the source of the votes.

If it was unsafe to desert one's proper district, at least some leaders hoped to surround themselves with other forms of respectability. They preferred not to deal with gamblers and saloonkeepers, but with nice people. And by this time there were some nice people quite eager to deal with the wielders of political influence. The perspicacious boss could become the familiar of the banker and the traction magnate, be taken to lunch in a good club (though not made a member), and puff his chest in the company of the financially mighty. Within the grant of government of these years were all sorts of profitable franchises, for laying trolley tracks, for building subways and electric and water lines, for the disposing of garbage. The interests concerned with these privileges were willing to aid the co-operative politician, aid to such an extent that he would not any longer be dependent on his emoluments from faro or overhours beer. The New York Dutch had a word for it, *boedel*.

Boodle was honest graft. When they floated the gas company they set aside a block of shares for the good fellows. No cash down—their credit was good. When the franchise came through and the stock prices rose in the market, the shares could be sold, the original purchase price paid, and a tidy balance would be left for the deserving. Or even if the capitalists were forced to lay out a flat sum without these complexities, that didn't hurt anyone. Such practices were not too far from the ordinary practices of legitimate business to offend any but the most tender consciences. Occasional revelations by shocked reformers did not alienate the boss's constituency; they merely endowed him with the additional romantic aspects of a Robin Hood.

Rivalry, not moral disapproval, provoked the serious troubles. In many matters the municipality shared jurisdiction with the state; and in the halls of the legislature, the city machines ran head-on into collision with the politicians who had long operated on a statewide basis. These men had not the assistance of the formal organization of the machine, but they had earlier consolidated their positions through alliances of key officeholders. Generally they were native American, as was the bulk of their following; and they drew their support from the farming areas and from the small towns. In most parts of the country they had the advantage of an anachronistic distribution of power which favored the rural at the expense of the urban districts. Years of bitter struggle followed the appearance of the immigrant organizations, as the state party chieftains attempted to mobilize minority national blocs to undermine the authority of their metropolitan competitors. In New York and Massachusetts, for instance, the Republicans attempted to woo the Italians and Jews to break the hold of the Irish Democrats on the city vote.

In time, however, there was an accommodation. Spheres of influence were defined and divided. Live and let live. Perhaps the appearance on the scene after 1900 of a crew of miscellaneous reformers and liberal independents drove the various manipulators of power into a union of convenience. In any case, shortly after 1910 the old acerbity was dulled and an era of more peaceful relationships ensued.

It was not surprising that the boss should see in the stirring of reform interests a threat to his own position. But it was significant that the mass of immigrants should regard the efforts of the various progressives with marked disfavor. In part this disapproval was based on the peasant's inherited distrust of radicalism; but it was strengthened by a lack of understanding among the radicals that deprived them of all influence among the newcomers.

In the case of the Italians and other central Europeans, the revolutions of the mid-nineteenth century had added fear of the pillaging reds to the traditional suspicion of revolutionaries. All these old misgivings crossed the ocean to the New World. Conservative enough at home, the peasants had become more conservative still in the course of migration. They dreaded political change because that might loosen the whole social order, disrupt the family, pull God from His throne; the radicals themselves talked that way and confirmed the worst such suspicions. Naturally the influence of the churches on both sides of the Atlantic was thrown in the balance on the side of stability and confirmed the unwillingness of the immigrants to be involved in any insurgent movements. . . .

KNOCKO MINIHAN'S WAKE

Edwin O'Connor

At 7:30, Adam [Skeffington's nephew] was waiting; Skeffington, on the other hand, was not. His unpunctuality inviolable, he was fifteen minutes late, and as the long official car pulled up he said genially, "Hop in. As a taxpayer, you're entitled to. Try the comforts of the vehicle you thoughtfully provided for me."

Adam got in. Determined to remove all mystery from the outset, he said, "By the way, when we were talking this afternoon I completely forgot to ask you where we were going."

"So you did," Skeffington said. "I took it as a rare mark of confidence; now I find it was only a lapse of memory. One more illusion lost." He chuckled and said, "Actually, we're going to a wake. Knocko Minihan's wake."

"A *wake?*"

"Surprised? I had an idea you might be: there was just the possibility that you

From *The Last Hurrah*, by Edwin O'Connor. Reprinted by permission of Little, Brown and Co., in association with The Atlantic Monthly Press. Copyright © 1956 by Edwin O'Connor.

weren't in the habit of spending your free evenings in visiting deceased strangers. But I felt that tonight it might be useful for you to come along. In its way, a wake can be quite an occasion."

"You may be underestimating me," Adam said. "I've been to a few wakes. Not many, but a few."

"I don't doubt it. Probably not exactly like this one, however. Not that poor Knocko's will be unique, but it might be a little different from those you've been to." ...

"And how did he make out after this terrible start?"

"Not too well. Save in one respect, that is. He [Knocko Minihan] married a grand woman who was a close friend of my wife's—your aunt's," he said. "In every other way he was a failure. He had a hardware store that he ran into the ground almost before the opening-day sale was over. Then he tried several other businesses, all of which petered out in no time at all. I don't know that people trusted him especially, and they certainly didn't like him. And neither," he said, rather surprisingly, "did I. However, *de mortuis* . . . ."

"If nobody liked him," Adam said, "I imagine we'll run into a fairly slim attendance tonight."

"Not at all," said Skeffington. "The place'll be crowded to the doors. A wake isn't quite the same as a popularity contest. There are other factors involved. Ah, here we are." . . .

While they stood in the hall, more people came in; clearly, the wake of Knocko Minihan was expanding. As it did, Adam was struck by the altered deportment of his uncle; it was almost as if, from being one of the visiting mourners, he had suddenly become the host. He nodded and spoke briefly to all the new arrivals; without exception, all responded in identical fashion: a muttered acknowledgment of the pitiful fact of Knocko's death, followed by a perceptibly more fervent statement of good wishes. . . . "That's a role I occasionally practice: the combination physician, caterer and master of ceremonies. It's something I might have to fall back on one day when I retire from politics."

"I am impressed," Adam said truthfully. "I hadn't realized that all this was a part of your job."

"Well, this is rather a special case. The widow's an old friend, and in her present condition she's in no shape to arrange for the usual civilities. So I just had a few things sent over." It was a detail he had taken care of that afternoon; the food had come from the ample commissariat of the Wadsworth Hospital. As this was a city institution, the food had been provided for by public funds; it was, in a word, a tax-supported wake. And all for Knocko Minihan; the beneficiary, thought Skeffington, was unworthy of the occasion. He said to Adam, "I'm not so sure that all the arrangements would meet with Knocko's approval, but then of course, when you come right down to it, he's not really in much of a position to complain, is he? Come along, I want to go in here."

They entered the next door down the hall; Adam found himself in a room which compared favorably with the parlor in its size and general hideousness, but which contained many more people and a great deal more noise. It was not until he had been in this room for a moment that he realized that there was still another difference: here, the mourners were exclusively male. To his surprise, he recognized some of them as the old familiars of his uncle's outer office. They had disdained the chairs which had been set out for them in a severe row which paralleled the wall; they preferred to stand, talking, smoking, moving, waiting. When Skeffington came in, the waiting was over. They surged around him, the noise grew, and Adam was soon separated from his uncle by a tight, struggling double ring of the self-appointed palace guard. He caught Skeffington's eye; in return he received a quick but unmistakable wink, the meaning of which was quite clear. For the moment at least, he was on his own; Skeffington had decided that it was time for his field of experience to be widened still further. . . .

Adam could not help marveling at the completeness of Knocko's failure to dominate, or even to intrude upon, his own wake. Here in the antechamber he was playing a bad second fiddle to the swapped vote and the living Skeffington; in the adjoining room, where the women were gathered before the bier, was he equally unfortunate? Presumably so: City Hall undoubtedly possessed its Ladies' Auxiliary. Yet there, perhaps the tactless presence of the casket and its contents might severely hamper political discussion; upon further consideration, however, he was inclined to doubt this. It was evident now that they had come tonight neither to bury Knocko nor to praise him; they had come to ignore him. The more one considered this neglect, Adam thought, the more callous one discovered it to be, and despite his resolutions to be prepared for all possible developments, he was somewhat shocked by this one.

Cuke and Ditto [two political small fry] had continued to talk; they were interrupted by the approach of old John Gorman. He had been standing to the left of the ring surrounding Skeffington, talking to petitioners with more modest or more localized requests. Now he came across the room, a remarkably neat, spare old man, straight as a string; when he reached them he said softly, "Ditto. Run down to the car now and tell Patsy to take you down to Ryan's for a half-dozen boxes of cigars. He'll know the kind. You'd best go along with him, Cuke. The fresh night air will do your lungs a world of good."

The two men obeyed instantly. It was,

for both, an errand of pleasure, and besides, an order from Gorman was an order from Skeffington. Gorman turned to Adam, smiling faintly.

"There's no greater turn you could do Ditto," he said. "Up in the back seat of the big black car, just himself and Cuke. Almost as good as if it was just himself. Well now, did the two of them tell you all about politics?"

"Not quite," Adam said. . . . "Although the subject did manage to come up, Mr. Gorman. As a matter of fact, it was just about the only subject that did come up."

"Ah well, that's natural enough," the old man said mildly. "If you met the Pope you'd talk about religion."

Adam smiled. "I suppose so. Still, wouldn't we also talk just a bit about Knocko Minihan? Particularly if we happened to meet at his wake?"

"It would be the pious thing to do, no doubt," Gorman agreed. "But then if you both knew Knocko, you might damn well want to talk about almost anything else in a hurry. Out of respect for the dead, you might say."

"Yes, I see. But what I don't see is this: if Knocko was such a generally disliked man, why are so many people here tonight? They didn't come to gloat, obviously; they're not ghouls. But then why did they come?"

"That I'm not sure about. Still," the old man said thoughtfully, "I wouldn't think you'd be far wrong if you said they came as you did yourself. For the very same reason, that is."

Adam stared at him. "But I came only because of my uncle."

"So you did," Gorman said. "So you did, indeed."

"Then you mean that all these other people came because of Uncle Frank, too?"

"Ah well, I wouldn't say all; that'd be a bit of an exaggeration. You had a little chat with Delia Boylan, I hear"—suddenly and irrelevantly, it occurred to Adam that there seemed to be very little that this old man did *not* hear—"and there's some that came like Delia: they just enjoy themselves going to a wake. It's like little boys and girls going to birthday parties. Then there's some that came on the widow's account: Gert's a fine woman, and she has her friends. And there may be a few no doubt came for Knocko himself; they say," he said wryly, "there's saints amongst us even today. I don't run into many myself. But most of them that are here tonight stopped by for the one reason: they knew your Uncle Frank was to come. And that's the long and the short of it." He saw no point in mentioning the delegations from the different city departments who were here in compulsory attendance; it would only complicate the issue. The boy, he reflected, was a good boy, but young; naturally, he could have no idea of the way things were done. To tell him would be to serve no purpose save perhaps an educational one, and John Gorman was really not wildly interested in telling the young the facts of life.

"And so," Adam said, "while it's Knocko's wake, it's really my uncle who's the main attraction?"

Gorman nodded. "It is."

Adam said, "And naturally business goes on as usual; Only here instead of at

the Hall?" His feeling of shock had increased; the whole business, he decided, was a really appalling mixture of hypocrisy and hardness.

"You have things a little twisty," the old man said softly, "if you don't mind me saying so." A little rap across the knuckles was in order, he decided; not a hard rap, to be sure, for he was a good lad and he was Skeffington's nephew, but a rap all the same. It was for the lad's own good; it would help to keep him from leaping about like a salmon to the wrong conclusions. He said, "You're a bit hard on your uncle, I think. The man has no need to go to wakes if he wants to collect a crowd about him; he can do that anywhere. All he has to do is stop on a street corner to light his cigar and fifty people come out of the cement to say, 'Hello Frank, and what can you do for me today?' And when he showed up here tonight it wasn't to talk politics. He can do that any minute of the day, any place he likes; he needs no dead man in the next room to help him tell Tommy Mulcahy that the polls are open from eight to eight on Election Day, and only one vote to a customer this year. What he came here for tonight is simple as simple can be: he came to bring a crowd to Knocko's wake so the widow would feel a little better. Knocko's been lying here all day yesterday, all last night, and all day today: how many people d'ye s'pose came in to see him in all that time? Maybe thirty-five, and ten of those came in to get out of the rain. Tonight there'll be hundreds here, and the widow'll think it's all Knocko's pals, waiting till the last moment to bid him good-by. But with all

106

those people in here, and your uncle here to bring them, what in the name of Heaven are they to talk about but what they like and what they know? God knows they can't talk about Knocko. Half of them never knew the man, and the other half that knew him didn't like him. That's not the kind of thing that makes for easy conversation. And you can't keep a roomful of men talking in soft voices about what a terrible thing death is, and will he go to Heaven, and maybe is he up there this very minute looking down on us all? Those are grand thoughts, but somehow nobody is able to keep thinking them for two hours whilst waiting for the priest to get here to say the Rosary. So they have a little food and they talk a little politics, and I don't know that they do a great amount of harm with either. And then when the priest does get in at last and they all kneel down to pray for Knocko, you might put your mind to this: there'll be ten times the people here praying for him as would be here without your uncle and all the chatter about politics. I don't s'pose they'll all be praying away as holy as St. Francis, but you never know about a thing like that; maybe some of them will mean it, and maybe it'll do Knocko a bit of good. I have the suspicion that he's in no mood at the moment to throw away any prayers from friend or foe; he's likely to be needing anything in that line that comes his way." He paused; it had been a speech of fantastic length for this ordinarily taciturn old man. Still, he reflected, sometimes a bit of gab was needed to drive a point home. He wondered: had it done the trick? He hoped

so; looking at the boy, he thought so. In any case, it was all he had to say on the subject. "So that being the way it is," he concluded, his mild blue eyes resting on Adam's face, and his thin old lips twisted once more into the just perceptible smile, "don't be too hard on us, boy. I don't doubt but that it's a bit different from what you're used to here tonight, but it's no terrible thing that's being done.". . .

. . . He considered the subject of Adam's instruction now closed. With his lips slightly pursed, he began to look slowly about the room, watching for developments that might have taken place while he had been talking. One of these was in the doorway even now. He said to Adam, "Now there's your man for you, over by the door. D'ye know him?"

Adam saw a short, stout man with oddly protuberant eyes who had paused to regard the room before entering; he was middle-aged, and dressed in a rumpled gray suit; under his right arm he carried what looked to be a small shoebox. Although he stood motionless in the doorway, there was something about him which suggested perpetual and hectic movement; one felt that to see him thus at a standstill was like seeing a hummingbird forcibly immobilized: it was somehow unfair. Or at least so Adam felt; it was the first time he had set eyes on Charlie Hennessey.

Evidently Charlie had chosen Gorman and Adam as his immediate goal. He came towards them with his curious little skating steps, and was on them even before Gorman had an opportunity to identify him for Adam. In any case, such

107

indentification would have been unnecessary, for Charlie identified himself.

"Hello, my dear man," he said to Gorman. "You're looking very well, John: a nice, even, healthy color. That speaks of a good circulation. Marvelous! The blood's the thing. And this must be Frank's nephew, Adam Caulfield by name. I'm Charles Hennessey, my dear man. I read you daily in the funny papers. Nice drawing, a good sense of humor. Marvelous! I read all the papers and everything that's in them. Well, my dear man," he said, turning again to Gorman, "I see the boss still has the touch. Oh, the grand touch! You have to hand it to the man. The most unpopular man in the ward dies and almost before he's cool there's a mob scene round the casket shouting, 'Three cheers for Skeffington for mayor!' Marvelous! Shrewd! Getting votes out of Knocko, like getting blood out of the turnip. They call it alchemy, a kind of old-time magic. And Frank's the master magician. Imagination! Foresight! The only man among us to realize that you could get a good turn out of Knocko after all: you only had to wait until the man was dead. Oh, clever! My hat's off to the man!"

Adam looked up sharply as this extraordinary man voiced what was substantially the charge he himself had made only minutes before; would he, too, suffer the Gorman rebuke? But the old man merely seemed amused; he said simply, "Ah, that's all moonshine, Charlie. All gas." To Adam he said significantly, "Charlie here is running against your uncle for mayor."

"Yes, yes, fighting tooth and nail," Charlie said briskly. "All in the interests of decent government. And of course what I'm saying is the very reverse of gas, my dear man. All truth! It's a matter of public record that Frank Skeffington has been campaigning at wakes for fifty years. Big wakes or small ones, it made no difference. If nobody died for the six months before an election he wouldn't know where to go. He's spent half a century with one eye on the coffin! A Skeffington maxim: Never neglect the relatives, friends or enemies of the deceased. I've studied the man all my life and I'm very familiar with his methods of operation, my dear man."

Gorman said, "Charlie—"

Charlie held up a warning finger, he bounced up and down for emphasis. "Which is not to say the man does no good," he said. "Far from it. Oh no no no, my dear man! In his way he does a world of good: I freely give him credit. He comes to a wake, he draws a crowd, and he keeps everybody in the house that should be crying so busy carting sandwiches they forget to cry. Occupational therapy, my dear man! The touch of a master psychologist! Another Skeffington maxim: Stampede them! Give them no time to think! And on top of that the man is charitable. A heart of gold, you can't take that away from him. If the widow here tonight should need a little cash, she'll get it without asking. If she needs a job, there'll be one waiting for her at City Hall tomorrow morning; she can sit around all day stuffing empty papers into envelopes and mailing them to herself. Nice light work and one of the best-paying jobs in the city. Marvelous! A likable trait in the man. Not good government, but likable. Generous! But by the same token, my dear man, it's not a one-way street. Oh, by no means! *Quid pro quo*, as Julius Caesar used to say. Which means, 'I'll do fine by the wake, but it'll do twice as fine by me!' Oh yes yes! Marvelous! Shrewd!"

Altogether, thought Adam, an amazing performance; however, its primary effect had been to leave him increasingly doubtful about the necessity for his own apology. Once more he looked at Gorman, anticipating some sign of rebuttal, but apparently the old man was done with argument. He said, "Charlie. Where's your cap? The one that's made out of tar or lumps of coal or whatever it is. Did you leave it home out of respect? Could you not get a nice little one made out of black sateen you could bring to funerals and wakes?" . . .

"Oh yes! I stand on the sound truck and say, 'Dear folks, don't underestimate the mayor. Don't think he has no capacity merely because the city is going to rack and ruin around us, our fine civic buildings are all held together with Scotch tape and library paste, our nice residential streets look like back alleys in South Timbuctoo, and every man among us who owns property is taxed like the Aga Khan. But dear folks, don't condemn the mayor totally for this! Be just, dear folks! Remember that while he may be a bum administrator, we have to admit two things about him. One, he has a grand heart, and two, he's the greatest orator and crowd psychologist that this part of the world has ever produced! These are

facts I'm telling you, dear folks! There's no one to touch him in that department! Oh yes,' " [Hennessey] cried, . . . weaving back and forth, his hand clutching an invisible microphone, the floor beneath his feet miraculously transformed into the platform atop his sound truck, "there's no one to touch him at all! The last surviving member of his species! Only last week I wrote letters to the sociologists down at Yale, Harvard, and Princeton, telling them to get their best men over here to watch Frank Skeffington in action before it's too late! Oh yes! Important! I told them to get them over here and watch him set the buffoons on fire, all laughing and jumping and cheering and stamping their feet, while he stands up there nodding his head and in the big air-conditioned voice telling them fifteen lies and a bedtime story to send them home happy! Marvelous! The talent is inborn, dear folks! A terrible mayor but a great entertainer! And what's the lesson in that, dear folks? Simply this: I say to you tonight that you have to make up your minds whether or not you want an entertainer in the mayor's seat. And if you do, dear folks, if you want a good laugh while the buildings of your city are falling to the ground one by one all around you, then by all means return Frank Skeffington to office!' "

This sustained performance won more laughter and applause; Skeffington had listened, greatly amused. He liked Charlie Hennessey, and while the liking was comfortably buttressed by the knowledge that, as a rival, Charlie could do him no serious damage, still, the feeling had more genuine roots. Skeffington knew that he had much common ground with this exuberant little pepperpot. They shared the same background, the same traditions, and even, to a considerable extent, the same gifts; it was just that in one of them, Skeffington reflected, somewhere along the line someone had forgotten to tighten a necessary wire, and the result was Charlie. Charlie, with all his volcanic but essentially purposeless eloquence, his thousand and one unrelated interests, his wild undisciplined quixotic pursuit of impossible ends! Looking at Charlie in full flight was for Skeffington a little like looking into a mirror in a fun house: through the lunatic distortions, he could always manage to discern just a little bit of himself. . . .

The Rosary over, it was time to go. Skeffington swiftly and efficiently made the rounds, saying the necessary good-bys; then he signaled to Adam, and uncle and nephew walked towards the front door together. They had almost reached the door when Skeffington, suddenly halting, said, "Hold on a minute. I want a word with that undertaker before we go."

They both turned and saw the head of Johnnie Degnan poking out of the kitchen at the far end of the hall; obviously he had been watching their departure. Skeffington beckoned, and he came running quietly to them.

"Ah, good evening, Governor," he said, in his swift hushed tones. "A very sad occasion. I wanted to see you before this evening, to make your acquaintance, but the pressure of my duties didn't quite allow. I'm John Degnan, Governor."

"Glad to know you, Mr. Degnan,"

Skeffington said. "As you say, it's a sad occasion. I'm happy to see you've done your best by it, however. I've been admiring your handiwork with the deceased."

"Thank you, Governor. Thank you very much. That's nice to hear. I did my best," the undertaker said modestly. "I don't mind telling you, Governor, that Mr. Minihan presented a very difficult case. Because of the age and the sunken cheeks and the wrinkles. I'm sure you can appreciate the difficulty of the task, Governor. Everything had to be smoothed out delicately, the youthful contours restored, and so forth."

"Yes. Now, Mr. Degnan, only one feature of your work disturbs me and that is the probable cost. You don't mind if I say that I was rather struck by the fact that the coffin, and what might be called the general deathroom décor, seem a trifle splendid for someone who was in decidedly modest circumstances?"

The undertaker smiled; it was, Adam thought, a nervous smile. "I see what you mean, Governor," he said swiftly. "I appreciate that point of view. And yet I always think the family is more satisfied if the final homage, as I like to think of it, is really nice in its every aspect. Something that the deceased would have been proud of if he could have seen it.",

"Why, those are the feelings of an artist," Skeffington said. "They do you credit, Mr. Degnan. I presume, incidentally, that you've discussed all this with Mrs. Minihan?"

"Well, no. Not exactly, that is, Governor. I thought it best not to in her distraught condition. Just a few words here and there. I think you could say, more or less, that it was left to my discretion, as it so often is. I always believe in taking as many worries as possible from the shoulders of the family."

"That's very thoughtful of you. Now then, you're a young man, Mr. Degnan, but I understand you've had quite a bit of professional experience. As you might put it, you've been in charge of a good many final homages. Or as I might put it, you've buried a good many people. What would you say was the lowest price you've ever buried anyone for?"

"The lowest *price*, Governor?" The smile remained; it wavered uncertainly. "I don't quite understand. . . . What I mean to say is, Governor, I don't believe that's anything I've ever quite figured out."

"Try," Skeffington urged him. "Make a rough estimate. Would it be . . . oh, say thirty-five dollars?"

"Thirty-five dollars!" The gasp of astonishment and pain broke through the modulated occupational tones; the undertaker looked wildly at Skeffington and said, "You couldn't *begin* to bury anyone for that price today, Governor!"

"I'll bet you could if you really tried," Skeffington said pleasantly. "I'll bet you could both begin and end. And just to prove my confidence in your resourcefulness, Mr. Degnan, why don't you do that very thing with Mr. Minihan? Let's give it a real try. I think you can do it. I'm sure the final bill won't read over thirty-five dollars. Matter of fact, I'll instruct the widow to that effect immediately."

"But Governor, you can't be serious!" Degnan cried. The smooth round face had become agonized; the soft hands were united in front of him in a tight, beseeching clasp. He looked as if he were about to hurl himself at his persecutor's feet, and Adam, who had not until a moment ago realized just what it was that his uncle was doing, now felt a sudden pity as well as disgust for this abject little profiteer. "The costs alone, Governor," Degnan moaned. "They're going up every day. I couldn't possibly do it. It's all *arranged—*"

"Fine," Skeffington said. "Then let it go through as arranged. But for thirty-five dollars."

"But, *Governor* . . ."

Skeffington pulled his watch from a vest pocket and examined it with apparent surprise. "It's later than I thought," he said. "Well, then, Mr. Degnan, it's all settled. I'll leave the details to you. A suitable funeral conducted for thirty-five dolars, with no cutting of corners. All the normal courtesies extended, the usual paraphernalia available. I'll have a few men on hand just to see that everything goes along well. I know you'll do a grand job. In any event, I'll be sure to hear about it: my observers will give me a full report."

The undertaker's face, which for some moments had been the color of putty, now had turned a vivid red. "But Governor! I hope you know how eager I am to co-operate in anything you suggest. How eager I *always* am. But what you're asking is *impossible. . . .*"

"Why, that's one of the words that doesn't belong to the bright lexicon of youth," Skeffington said reprovingly. "I've always believed that nothing is impossible when one has youth and ambition. I hope you won't be the one to shake this treasured belief. Because if you do," he said, regarding Degnan with a stare which its recipient suddenly found to be as unpleasant as anything he had ever experienced, "you might shake my confidence in you. What's worse, you might even begin to shake public confidence in you. That is a bad thing to have happen to a young undertaker with dreams, Mr. Degnan. You never can tell how far it might reach. It might even reach the members of the licensing board for your profession. You never know. But we mustn't keep you from your labors any longer. I suppose you have many things to do at a time like this. Possibly even more than you'd anticipated. Good night, Mr. Degnan. Glad you introduced yourself."

They went out the door and down the steps; Degnan's anguished voice trailed them to their car. "Thirty-five dollars!" it wailed. "Governor, I *appeal* to you . . ."

Then, because there was much he was still curious about, and because a note of comradeship, almost of complicity, seemed to have been established between them on this ride home, [Adam] decided to move into more doubtful waters. He said, "Actually, he didn't talk much about himself at all. He talked mostly about you, Uncle Frank. About you and the wake."

"Reasonable enough, under the circumstances. The wake was there, and so was I."

"Yes. The thing was that he seemed to be saying that the conjunction had a

rather peculiar effect on the wake, that it changed its character pretty drastically."

Skeffington nodded. "From the funereal to the political," he said. "And what did you think of that?" Adam hesitated again, and Skeffington gave him a look of pleasant inquiry. "Go ahead," he invited. "I'll probably be able to bear it."

"Well," Adam said reluctantly, "to be honest, I had something of the same thought myself a little earlier, before Charlie arrived. I had quite a talk with Mr. Gorman about it." Now that he had gone this far, further frankness seemed unavoidable: somewhat uneasily he gave his uncle the full account of what had passed between Gorman and himself. Was it a mistake? he wondered. Probably not; it occurred to him that Gorman would himself unquestionably have mentioned it in due course.

As he talked, he kept his eyes on his uncle's face: the scrutiny proved remarkably unfruitful. The heavy features registered nothing more than a polite, unchanging interest; it was impossible for Adam to tell whether his uncle was indignant, whether he was outraged, whether he was totally unaffected. Or—in a sense, even worse—whether he was simply amused. It was most disquieting . . .

He completed his explanation. Skeffington said, "I've seldom heard of John's being so eloquent; it stands as a great tribute to your qualities as a listener. I must say he put the case for me rather well; I couldn't have done better myself. Charlie's approach, on the other hand, must have been considerably different. I imagine he probably said something to this effect." And then, while Adam stared at him, he proceeded to duplicate Charlie's speech in astonishing detail; it seemed to Adam, remembering the original, that the reproduction was virtually word for word. Finishing, Skeffington said, "Close enough?"

"Close enough," Adam agreed, bewildered. "The question is: How? You couldn't have heard it from where you were."

"Extrasensory perception," Skeffington said gravely. "A man can't go far without it today." Once again, Adam heard the familiar deep chuckle. "Of course, there is the additional fact that Charlie's principal addresses don't change very much over the years. He has the unwillingness of the artist to tamper with the perfect production. This is one of his best, a regular party piece. Or wake piece, if you prefer. I must have heard it a hundred times. It's extremely entertaining. In addition to which," he said casually, "it contains more than a little truth."

Adam looked up sharply, but his uncle seemed preoccupied in withdrawing a cigar from his vest pocket. It was long, fat, dull-greenish in color. It did not appear to be at all the same grade of cigar that had been provided in quantities for the wake.

"One over the limit," he said cheerfully, lighting it. "A happy shortcut to the Dark Encounter. Well, you see me refusing to be less than candid with you. I don't want to give you a misleading impression. I should add that while Charlie was telling the truth, up to a point, so was John Gorman. Actually, they were both right: Knocko's wake was and it wasn't a political rally. Given the circum-

stances, and," he added, with a faintly deprecatory wave of the cigar, "given myself, it could hardly have been anything else. You see, what you're up against here is the special local situation. To understand what happened tonight, you have to understand a little bit about that situation, and just a little bit more about my own rather peculiar position in it." . . .

"You see," he said, "my position is slightly complicated because I'm not just an elected official of the city; I'm a tribal chieftain as well. It's a necessary kind of dual officeholding, you might say; without the second, I wouldn't be the first."

"The tribe," said Adam, "being the Irish?"

"Exactly. I have heard them called by less winning names: minority pressure group (even though they've been the majority for half a century), immigrant voting bloc (even though many of the said immigrants have been over here for three generations). Still, I don't suppose it makes much difference what you call them; the net result's the same. I won't insult your intelligence by explaining that they're the people who put me in the mayor's chair and keep me there; I think you realize that the body of my support doesn't come from the American Indian. But as a member—at least by birth—of the tribe, you might give a thought to some of the tribal customs. They don't chew betel nut, and as far as I know the women don't beautify themselves by placing saucers in their lower lips. Although now that I come to think of it," he said, "that might not be a bad idea. It might reduce the potential for conversation. However, they do other things, and among them they go to wakes. And so do I."

"Which are and are not political rallies?" Adam asked. "Or was Knocko's case a special one?"

"Not at all special, except that the guest of honor was somewhat less popular than many of his predecessors. But of course when you speak about wakes as being political rallies, that's a little strong. You have to remember something about the history of the wake around here. When I was a boy in this city, a wake was a big occasion, and by no means a sad one. Unless, of course, it was a member of your own family that had died. Otherwise it was a social event. Some of my most vivid memories are of wakes. I remember my poor mother taking me to old Nappy Coughlin's wake. We went into the tenement, and there was Nappy, all laid out in a little coffin which was kept on ice. Embalming was a rather uncertain science in those days. It was a hot day in July and there were no screens on the parlor windows; there were flies in the room. I can still hear the ice dripping into the pans underneath the coffin, and I can still see Nappy. He had one of the old-fashioned shrouds on, and he lay stretched out stiff as a ramrod. And on his head he wore a greasy black cap, which his good wife had lovingly adjusted so that the peak was pulled down over one eye. It gave him a rather challenging look; you had the feeling that at any moment he might spring out of the coffin and offer to go four fast rounds with you. My mother was horrified at the sight, and I remember that she went directly over to the widow and told her she ought to be

ashamed of herself, putting her husband in the coffin with his hat on. Whereupon the widow simply said that he'd never had it off; he'd worn it for thirty years, day and night, in bed and out. So naturally she left it on, not wanting to say good-by to a stranger. However, when Father Conroy came in, the hat was whisked off fast enough. I can remember—it was my first wake, by the way—going into the kitchen, where somebody gave me a glass of milk and a piece of cake. And while my mother was in the parlor talking with the other women, I was out there with the men, just sitting around, eating cake, and listening to them talk. I hadn't the faintest notion of what they were talking about, but it didn't matter much. I was in seventh heaven. Everybody seemed to be enjoying themselves, and I knew I was. When my mother came to get me and take me home, I left with the greatest regret; I decided I'd never had a better time. Well," he said, "so much for memories of happy days. I wouldn't imagine it would sound like very much to anyone who'd been brought up today."

Adam smiled. "It sounded like a little boy having a wonderful time for himself. Although I must say that it didn't sound very much like death. Or even a political rally, for that matter."

"Matter of fact, it was the first political rally I'd ever been to," Skeffington said. "I was just too young to know it. You see, that's what all the men were talking about: politics. There was even a moment, just before I left, when Charlie McCooey himself came in: a fat man with a red face and handlebar mustache. He was the ward boss. I didn't know what that was, at the time, but I did know that the name of Charlie McCooey commanded respect and awe. I thought he must have been some kind of god. Twenty years later this childhood illusion was blasted. I gave him the beating of his life in a fight for the leadership of the ward; the vote was four to one. In the process of doing so I discovered that the god was nothing more than a dull bullyboy with no imagination and just enough intelligence to read his way through the daily adventures of Happy Hooligan. . . ."

. . . [Adam] had suddenly remembered, while Skeffington was talking, that once, years ago, and from a source he could not now place, he had heard a series of quite different stories about the old wakes; in these, the cake-and-milk had not figured largely. He said, "But I had the idea from somewhere, Uncle Frank, that many of these wakes got to be pretty violent affairs. I know there was always a certain amount of drinking, but didn't some of them actually become brawls?"

Skeffington's heavy face assumed a mildly shocked expression. "Why, I hardly know what to say," he murmured. "I have heard that drinking men occasionally forced their way into these gatherings, but I like to believe that they were instantly sobered by the sight of decent men and women shrinking from them in revulsion." He glanced at his nephew, and his lips twitched just slightly. "No," he said, "of course you're right. There was drinking and sometimes things got a little rough. You might not have enjoyed it

very much. But it's all gone by the boards long ago, and it was the exception rather than the rule; while it may seem terrible enough from your point of view today, you might reflect on the fact that there just might have been some excuse for it. I think what you have to do," he said, "is to see the wakes and everything that happened to them in the light of the times. I mentioned to you the other afternoon that life wasn't exactly a picnic for our people in those days. They were a sociable people but they didn't get much chance for sociability. They were poor, they worked hard, and they didn't have much in the way of diversion. Actually, the only place people got together was at the wake. Everybody knew everybody else; when somebody died, the others went to pay their respects and also to see and talk to each other. It was all part of the pattern. They were sorry for the family of the deceased, to be sure, but while they were being sorry they took advantage of the opportunity to have a drink and a chat with the others who were being sorry, too. It was a change, an outlet for people who led back-breaking, dreary, and monotonous lives. And if, once in a while, someone took a few too many and wanted to set fire to the widow or play steamroller in the kitchen, it was possibly deplorable but it was also slightly understandable. All in all, I've always thought the wake was a grand custom, and I still do."

"Yes," Adam said slowly. "I hadn't thought of it in that light—I mean, I hadn't thought of the wake as being a kind of *relief* from grimness. And yet I guess it must have been, all right. But what about *now*, Uncle Frank? Those same conditions don't exist, do they?"

"No," said Skeffington, "and neither does the wake. Not in the same way, that is. It's a disappearing phenomenon, like the derby hat. As the younger people grow up, the wakes are more and more changing their character: for example, they're being held now in funeral parlors rather than in the homes. The wake will still continue in some form; after all, it takes a long time to get rid of old tribal customs. And Knocko's was a bit like some of the old wakes; that's why I wanted you to see it. And as for the political discussion, that was in the grand tradition, too. By the way, did you happen to wonder why they might have been talking politics tonight?"

"Well, I naturally thought it was because you were there. But—"

"But," Skeffington said, interrupting with a look of some amusement, "was I there because they were going to talk politics? Right?" It was all too remarkably right; Adam flushed and began to protest, but Skeffington said, "A perfectly natural question. I'd be astonished if it hadn't occurred to you. The answer, by the way, is a little bit of both. I suppose I went at least partly because it was one more opportunity to keep the ball rolling. It's almost impossible for an old campaigner to avoid the occasions of sin. But whether I'd been there or not, they would have talked politics anyway. It's what interests them most. It ought to: it gave most of them everything they have. I mentioned to you the other day that the main reason I went into politics was because it was the quickest way out

of the cellar and up the ladder. A good many others felt the same way. A lot of the younger men wanted a nice new dark serge suit that didn't necessarily come equipped with a chauffeur's cap. And the only way out was through politics; it was only when we gained a measure of political control that our people were able to come up for a little fresh air. They know that; they think of it as the big salvation for them; that's why they talk about it when they all get together. It's a very serious part of the business of living. And when I'm around, naturally I'm expected to talk it with them. And I do. I may add," he said, "that I don't find it a hardship."

Adam thought of one more question. "And the family?" he said. "The family of the deceased, I mean. Like Mrs. Minihan tonight. How do they feel while all this is going on? Don't they sometimes mind, Uncle Frank?"

"I know what you mean," Skeffington said, "but I think you're a bit wrong there. I don't think they mind a bit. There is a contrary opinion, however. Every once in a while I see where some advanced young public servant, who still had the ring of the pot on his seat while all this was going on, publicly applauds the passing of 'that cruel and barbarous custom, the wake.' Whenever I see that I take down my little book and chalk up a new name in the boob section. The man who said it obviously hasn't the faintest notion of what he's talking about. He hasn't the remotest understanding of the times, the circumstances, of our people, the way they feel and the way they regard death. I've seen a good many people die around here and I'll probably see a good many more. Unless, of course," he added, in another of those detached and faintly chilling parentheses which never failed to jolt Adam, "I beat them to it; there's always that possibility. But I've never seen the family that thought the wake was cruel and barbarous. They expected it. They wanted it. More than that, it was good for them: it was a useful distraction, it kept them occupied, and it gave them the feeling that they weren't alone, that they had a few neighbors who cared enough to come in and see them through a bad time. And you could say, too, it was a mark of respect for the deceased: rest assured that *he* wanted his wake. I remember what happened when the Honorable Hugh Archer died. The Honorable Hugh was considerably before your time; I don't imagine you'd have heard much about him."

"No, nothing."

"He was a prominent Republican attorney who once refused ten thousand dollars offered to him if he'd defend a notorious criminal. The noble gesture was unprecedented in Republican circles, and immediately he became known as the Honorable. It wasn't until much later that it was discovered he had asked for twenty thousand. Well, eventually he died. He was a huge man: six foot four and weighing nearly three hundred pounds. At that time, cremation was just coming into fashion, following closely upon Mahjongg, and they whipped the Honorable Hugh out to the incinerator on the very day he died. Old Martin Canady went to the ceremony, out of a curiosity to see how the other half died, and when he came running back to me he was literally popeyed with shock. 'By God, Frank!' he said. 'They took the big elephant before he stopped breathin' almost and what the hell d'ye think they did with him? They put him in the oven and burned him up with the Sunday papers! When the poor man finished cookin' ye could have buried him in an ash tray! By God, Frank, I wouldn't want nothin' like that to happen to me! When I go I'm damned sure I mean to stay around the house a few days and nights so's some of the old pals can come in and have a drink and the last look! What the hell's wrong with that, now?' And," Skeffington said, "to save my soul, I couldn't think of a blessed thing wrong with it. It's the way I want to go myself. . . ."

WHEN
THE IRISH RAN NEW YORK

Daniel P. Moynihan

New York used to be an Irish town. Or so it seemed. New York, to be sure, has never been anyone's town, but there were sixty or seventy years when the Irish seemed to be everywhere. *They* felt it was their town. It is no longer, and they know it. That is one of the things that are bothering them.

It is not hard to date the Irish era. It begins in the early 1870's: about the time Charles O'Conor, whom the *Dictionary of American Biography* calls "the ablest member of the New York bar," began the prosecution of the Honorable William Marcy Tweed. It ends some sixty years later: a good point would be the day Jimmy Walker sailed for Europe and exile with his beloved, but unwed, Betty.

Boss Tweed was the last vulgar white Protestant to win a place in the city's life. There have been Protestants since who have served the city with distinction, but

always as representatives of "the better element." Tweed was hardly that: he was a roughneck, a ward heeler, a man of the people at a time when the people still contained a large body of native-born Protestant workers of Scotch and English antecedents. By the time of his death in the Ludlow Street Jail, this had all but completely changed. The New York working class had become predominantly Catholic. The Irish promptly assumed the leadership of this class. "Honest John" Kelly succeeded Tweed as leader of Tammany Hall, and in 1880 Kelly elected the city's first Irish Catholic mayor, William R. Grace of the shipping line. This ascendancy persisted for another half century, reaching a kind of apogee toward the end of the 1920's when Al Smith ran for President and Jimmy Walker "wore New York in his buttonhole."

New York was perhaps the first great city in history to be ruled by men of the people, not as an isolated phenomenon of the Gracchi or the Commune but as a persisting, established pattern. To this day the men who run New York talk out of the side of their mouths: they may be millionaires, but they are no less representative of the people. The intermittent discovery that New York does have representative government leads to periodic reform movements. But the reformers come and go, the party remains. The secret lies in the structure of the Democratic party bureaucracy, which perpetuates itself. The measure of its success is that it works with almost undiminished effectiveness long after the Irish, who created it, have moved on to other things.

In their politics as in their race and religion, the Irish brought many of their traits from the Old Country. The machine governments which the Irish established in New York (as in many Northern cities) show three distinct features of early nineteenth-century Ireland.

First, a considerable indifference to Yankee proprieties. The Irish managed to make it somehow charming to steal an election—scoundrelish, rascally, surely not to be approved, but neither to be abhorred. This, it must be insisted, is something they learned from the English. Eighteenth-century English politics in Ireland was as corrupt—in Yankee terms—as is to be imagined. George Potter has written in *To the Golden Door:* "The great and the wealthy ran Ireland politically like Tammany Hall in its worst days. Had they not sold their own country for money and titles in the Act of Union with England and, as one rogue said, thanked God they had a country to sell? ... A gentleman was thought no less a gentleman because he dealt, like merchan-

dise, with the votes of his tenants or purchased his parliamentary seat as he would a horse or a new wing for his big house." The Irish added to this, from their own social structure, a personal concept of government action. Describing the early period of Irish self-government, Conrad H. Arensberg relates, in *The Irish Countryman:* "At first, geese and country produce besieged the new officers and magistrates: a favourable decision or a necessary public work performed was interpreted as a favour given. It demanded a direct and personal return. 'Influence' to the countryman was and is a direct personal relationship, like the friendship of the countryside along which his own life moves."

The Irish also brought to America a settled tradition of regarding the formal government as illegitimate and the informal one as bearing the true impress of popular sovereignty. The brutality of the English landlords in eighteenth-century Ireland gave rise to secret societies that fought back by terrorism. An English observer described the results: "There are in fact two codes of law in force and in antogonism—one the statute law enforced by judges and jurors, in which the people do not yet trust—the other a secret law, enforced by themselves. . . ." This habit of mind pervaded the atmosphere of Tammany at its height: City Hall, like Dublin Castle, was not to be trusted. If you need help, see The McManus. The fact that the McMani were like as not running City Hall, as well as the Tuscarora Regular Democratic Organization of the Second Assembly District South, only strengthened this habit.

119

Finally, most of the Irish arrived in America fresh from the momentous experience of the Catholic Emancipation movement. The Catholic Association, which the Irish leader Daniel O'Connell established in 1823 for this purpose, has been called the "first fully fledged democratic political party known to the world." "Daniel O'Connell," Potter writes, "was the first modern man to use the mass of a people as a democratic instrument for revolutionary changes by peaceful constitutional methods. He anticipated the coming into power of the people as the decisive political element in modern democratic society." The Irish peasants, who had taken little part in Gaelic Ireland's resistance to the English—that had been a matter for the warrior class of an aristocratic society—appear to have been quite transformed by O'Connell. They arrived in America thoroughly alive to the possibilities of politics and they brought with them the phenomenally effective technique of political bureaucracy.

More has been written against Tammany Hall than about it. With little evidence, it is difficult to speculate on the nature of the system during the Irish era, but some patterns can be discerned, particularly those which persist in the present Democratic party organization. Foremost is the pattern of bureaucracy. Politics in a "natural" state is pre-eminently a personal affair—a matter of whom you know and who knows you; whom you like and trust; who you think likes and trusts you; whom you can intimidate and vice versa. The personal nature of such relations makes for a fluctuating, confused, perilous enterprise. Thus politics, business, and war have ever been the affairs of adventurers and risk takers. These are anything but peasant qualities. Certainly not those of Irish peasants, who, collectively, yielded to none in the rigidity of their social structure and their disinclination to adventure. Instead of letting politics transform them, they transformed politics, establishing a political system in New York City that from a distance seems like nothing so much as the social system of an Irish village writ large. Village life was characterized by the pre-eminence of formal family relations under the dominance of the stern father. Substituting "party" for "family" and "leader" for "father," the Irish created the political machine.

According to Roy V. Peel, *The Political Clubs of New York City*, Irish Catholics achieved a position of predominance within Tammany Hall by 1817. Working from the original Tammany ward committees, they established a vast hierarchy of party positions descending from the county leader at the top down to the block captain and beyond even to building captains. Each position had rights and responsibilities which had to be observed. The result was a massive party bureaucracy, which rivaled the medieval Catholic Church in the proportion of the citizenry involved. The county committees of the five boroughs came to number more than thirty-two thousand persons. It became necessary to hire Madison Square Garden for their meetings—and to hope not much more than half the number would show up as there wouldn't be room. The system itself was remarkably stable. "Honest John" Kelly, Richard Croker, and Charles Murphy in succession ran Tammany for half a century. Across the river Hugh McLaughlin ran the Brooklyn Democratic Party and fought off Tammany for better than forty years, from 1862 to 1903. He was followed shortly by John H. McCooey, who ruled from 1909 until his death a quarter of a century later. Ed Flynn ran the Bronx from 1922 until his death in 1953.

There is no greater nonsense than the stereotype of the Irish politician as a beer-guzzling back-slapper. Croker, McLaughlin, *Mister* Murphy were the least affable of men. Their task was not to charm but to administer with firmness and predictability a political bureaucracy in which rights appertained not to individuals but to the positions they occupied. "Have you seen your block captain?" It did not matter that your captain was an idiot or a drunk or a devout churchgoer who would be alarmed by the request at hand; the block captain had to be seen first. Then the election district captain. Then the district leader. The hierarchy had to be recognized. For the group as a whole, this served to take the risks out of politics. Each would get his deserts—in time.

At the moment no one characteristic divides the "regular" party men in New York City from the "reform" group more than the matter of taking pride in following the chain of command. The "reform" group is composed principally of educated, middle-class career people quite hardened to the struggle for advancement in their professions. Waiting in line to see one's leader seems to such persons slavish and unmanly, the kind of conduct that could only be imposed by a boss. By contrast, the "organization" regulars regard it as proper and well-behaved conduct. The reformers, who have a tendency to feel superior, would be surprised, perhaps, to learn that among the regulars they are widely regarded as rude, unethical people.

It would also seem that the term "boss," and the persistent attacks on "boss rule," have misrepresented the nature of power in the old machine system. Tammany was not simply a concentrated version of the familiar American municipal power structure in which an informal circle of more or less equally powerful men—the heads of the two richest banks, the three best law firms, four largest factories, and the chancellor of the local Methodist university—run things. Power was hierarchical in the machine, diffused in the way it is diffused in an army. Because the commanding general was powerful, it did not follow that the division generals were powerless—anything but. In just this way Tammany district leaders were important men; and, right down to the block captain, all had rights.

At the risk of exaggerating, it is possible to point out any number of parallels between the political machine and rural Irish society. For example, the incredible capacity of the rural Irish to remain celibate—i.e., to wait their turn—in order to earn the reward of inheriting the farm is well known. Even after an Irish son has taken over direction of the farm, he will go each morning to his father to ask what to do that day. So with the "boss," whose essential demand often seemed only that he be consulted. There is a story that one day a fellow leader of Sheriff and Sachem Thomas J. Dunn confided that he was about to be married. "Have you seen Croker?" asked Dunn. In 1913, when Governor William Sulzer refused to consult the "ahrganization" on appointments, Murphy did not argue; he impeached and removed him. Doubtless the most painful onus of the current Tammany organizations that have been overthrown by reform clubs is to hear themselves called "insurgents"!

It seems evident that the principle of boss rule was not that of tyranny but of order. When Lincoln Steffens asked Croker, "Why must there be a boss, when we've got a mayor and—a council?" "That's why," Croker broke in. "It's because there's a mayor *and* a council *and* judges—*and*—a hundred other men to deal with."

The narrow boundaries of the peasant world were ideally adapted to the preoccupations of precinct politics. The parallel role of the saloonkeeper is striking. Arensberg writes:

"The shopkeeper-publican-politician was a very effective instrument, both for the country side and for himself. He might perhaps exact buying at his shop in return for the performance of his elective duties, as his enemies charge: but he also saw to it that those duties were performed for the very people who wished to see them done. Through him, as through no other possible channel, Ireland reached political maturity and effective national strength."

So with the New York Irish. "The saloons were the nodal points of district organizations," Peel points out. It used to be said the only way to break up a meeting of the Tammany Executive Committee was to open the door and yell, "Your saloon's on fire!" At the same time a mark of the successful leader, as of the successful saloonkeeper, was sobriety. George Washington Plunkitt related with glee the events of the election night in 1897 when Tammany had just elected—against considerable odds—the first mayor of the consolidated City of New York (Croker had slyly chosen for his candidate an inoffensive Old-Dutch-Family gentleman named Van Wyck):

"Up to 10 P.M. Croker, John F. Carroll, Tim Sullivan, Charlie Murphy, and myself sat in the committee-room receivin' returns. When nearly all the city was heard from and we saw that Van Wyck was elected by a big majority, I invited the crowd to go across the street for a little celebration. A lot of small politicians followed us, expectin' to see magnums of champagne opened. The waiters in the restaurant expected it, too, and you never saw a more disgusted lot of waiters when they got our orders. Here's the orders: Croker, vichy and bicarbonate of soda; Carroll, seltzer lemonade; Sullivan, apollinaris; Murphy, vichy; Plunkitt, ditto. Before midnight we were all in bed, and next mornin' we were up bright and early attendin' to business, while other men were nursin' swelled heads. Is there anything the matter with temperance as a pure business proposition?"

As a business proposition it all worked very well. The Irish habit of dealing with an informal government, combined with the establishment of an elaborate bureaucracy for that government, proved enormously effective in electoral politics. The "organization" spread to the darkest reaches of the city, places the middle-class reformers never lived in and rarely visited. Reform would come and go, but the organization remained, co-opting its members, getting out the vote, winning two elections in three, and quite able to sit out the third.

But that is about as far as it went. The Irish were immensely successful in politics. They ran the city. But the very parochialism and bureaucracy that enabled them to succeed in local politics prevented them from doing much else. In all these sixty or seventy years in which they could have done almost anything they wanted in politics, they did very little. Of all those candidates and all those campaigns, what remains? The names of two or three men: Al Smith principally, and his career went sour before it ever quite came to glory.

In a sense, the Irish didn't know what to do with power once they got it. Steffens was surely exaggerating when he suggested the political bosses only kept power on the sufferance of the business community. The two groups worked in harmony, but it was a symbiotic, not an agency, relationship. The Irish leaders did for the Protestant establishment what it could not do for itself, and could not do without. But the Irish just didn't know what to do with their opportunity. They never thought of politics as an instrument of social change—their kind of politics involved the processes of a society that was not changing. Croker alone solved the problem. Having become rich, he did the thing rich people in Ireland did: he bought a manor house in England, bred horses, and won the Derby. The king did not ask him to the Derby dinner.

BOSSES, MACHINES, AND ETHNIC GROUPS

Elmer E. Cornwell, Jr.

Though the direction of the causal relationship may be difficult to establish, the classic urban machine and the century of immigration which ended in the 1920s were intimately intertwined phenomena. This fact is not always recognized as fully as it should be. Much of the literature on bosses and machines, beginning with the muckrakers, but not excluding more recent studies with less overt moralistic flavor, carries the implication that such factors as the dispersal of power in urban government—under weak mayor charters and through rivalries among state, county, city and special district authorities, all plowing the same field but none with full responsibility for its cultivation—invited the machine's extralegal reconcentration of power. It is also true that attitudes engendered by a busi-

Reprinted from "Bosses, Machines, and Ethnic Groups" by Elmer E. Cornwell, Jr., in vol. 353 of *The Annals* of the American Academy of Political and Social Science, © 1964, by the American Academy of Political and Social Science.

ness society whose prime movers characteristically had their eye on the "main chance"—and specifically on traction franchises and the like—also fostered the growth of the essentially entrepreneurial role and amoral attitude of the boss.

RELATION OF MACHINE TO IMMIGRATION

When all this has been said, however, the fact still remains that the classic machine would probably not have been possible, and certainly would not have been so prominent a feature of the American political landscape, without the immigrant. Essentially, any disciplined grassroots political organization rests upon a docile mass base which has in some manner been rendered dependable, predictable, and manipulable. The rank and file of the Soviet Communist party is disciplined by a combination of ideological allegiance, fear, and hope of reward. The average party supporter in a liberal-democratic society cannot be so disciplined under ordinary circumstances, at least not for long. The newly arrived immigrant was a special case, however, He was characteristically insecure, culturally and often linguistically alien, confused, and often in actual want. Thus, even if he had valued the franchise thrust upon him by his new political mentors, its careful exercise would have taken a low priority in his daily struggle for existence. In most cases, he did not value or even understand the political role into which he was being pushed.

Thus, it was the succeeding waves of immigrants that gave the urban political organizations the manipulable mass bases without which they could not have functioned as they did. And, until immigration dried up to a trickle in the 1920s, as one generation of newcomers began to espouse traditional American values of political independence, there was always a new group, often from a different country of origin, to which the machine could turn. As long as this continued to be possible, machines persisted, and once the immigrant base finally began to disappear, so did most of the bosses of the classic model. In a very real sense, then, the one phenomenon was dependent on the other.

The argument can be made that there were other machines that clearly were not immigrant-based in this sense. All generalizations, especially those in the social sciences, are but proximate truths. At the same time, machines based on white, Protestant, "old stock" clienteles were not wholly unrelated in their motivation and operation to the factor of immigra-

tion. Platt's smooth-functioning organization in New York State[1] and Blind Boss Brayton's contemporary operation in Rhode Island[2] were both based, in the immediate sense, on what Lincoln Steffens called "the good old American stock out in the country."[3] And yet recall that both of these states were highly urbanized even in the 1890s and early 1900s when these two worthies flourished and had ingested disproportionate numbers of immigrants. As of 1920, when 38 per cent of the total United States population was foreign born or of foreign parentage, the corresponding percentages for New York and Rhode Island were 64 and 71.[4] These facts alone suggest what the political history of both makes clear: these rural "old stock" machines existed largely as means of political defense against the newcomers and doubtless would not have existed had there been no immigrants.

The point, then, is that, whereas in the cities the immigrants sold their political independence for the familiar currency of favors and aid, their rural native cousins were sometimes prompted to do the same, in part out of desire for cultural-religious as well as political, and perhaps at times economic, self-protection. Recollection of the Know-Nothing era of militant nativist activity a half-century earlier suggests that this kind of cultural-religious antagonism can be a very potent political force indeed. An analogous explanation could even be offered for the existence of machines in the South like that of Harry Byrd in Virginia, by simply substituting the perceived Negro threat for the danger of engulfment by foreigners in the North. And, curiously enough, the two examples of reasonably thoroughgoing machine-like organizations that flourished in the otherwise inhospitable English soil—Joseph Chamberlain's Birmingham caucus[5] and Archibald Salvidge's "machine" in Liverpool[6]—also were at least indirectly related to the problem of Irish home rule, and, in Liverpool, to actual rivalry with Irish immigrants over religion and jobs.

In short, whatever else may be said about the conditions and forces that spawned the classic machine, this kind of disciplined political entity must rest at bottom on a clientele which has felt it necessary to exchange political independence—its votes, in a word—for something seen as more essential to its well-being and security. In general, such a group will be the product of some kind of socioeconomic disequilibrium or cultural tension which finds its members in an insecure or seriously disadvantaged situation. Thus, the immigrant was willing to submit to the boss in exchange for aid—real or imagined—in gaining his foothold in the new environment, and the old-stock machine supporters, North or South, submitted in part for protection against swarming aliens or a potential Negro threat to white dominance.

THE CLASSIC MACHINE IN OPERATION

It cannot be assumed that the process of machine exploitation of succeeding groups of newcomers was a smooth and simple operation. Any formal organization, political or otherwise, must maintain a continuing balance among a series of often contradictory forces.[7] Its very existence rests on the success with which it achieves its objective—in the case of a political party, the winning of elections and, thus, power. In the long run, this success depends on the organization's continuing ability to tap fresh sources of support as time goes on and old reliances dwindle and may at times depend on keeping newly available resources away from its rival or rivals. For the machine, this has meant wooing each new ethnic contingent. Yet this process of growth and renewal will inevitably threaten the very position of many of the proprietors of the organization itself by recruiting rivals for their roles. Any organizational entity must not only achieve its corporate goals but, to survive, it must also satisfy the needs and desires of its members as individuals. If it fails in this, its supporters will vanish and its own objectives remain unattainable. Specifically, for the machine, this fact of organizational life often tempered missionary zeal and tempted its members to protect even an eroding *status quo*.

Usually the machine did yield in the long run to the political imperative that all groups of potential supporters must be wooed, if for no other reason than to keep them from the enemy. The short-term risk to the present leadership often must have appeared minimal. The plight of the newcomers was so pitiful, their needs so elemental, and their prospects of achieving security and independence so problematical in the foreseeable future that they must have appeared like a windfall to the machine proprietors. Thus, after initial hesitancy, the Irish were tak-

126

en into Tammany and found their way into the ranks of the clientele of other big city party organizations.

The ways in which immigrant political support was purchased are familiar and need no elaborate review here. They had at least three kinds of needs which the ward heeler could fill on behalf of the party leadership. Above all, they needed the means of physical existence: jobs, loans, rent money, contributions of food or fuel to tide them over, and the like. Secondly, they needed a buffer against an unfamiliar state and its legal minions: help when they or their offspring got in trouble with the police, help in dealing with inspectors, in seeking pushcart licenses, or in other relations with the public bureaucracy. Finally, they needed the intangibles of friendship, sympathy, and social intercourse. These were available, variously, through contact with the precinct captain, the hospitality of the political clubhouse, the attendance of the neighborhood boss at wakes and weddings, and the annual ward outing.[8]

As has often been noted, these kinds of services were not available, as they are today, at the hands of "United Fund" agencies, city welfare departments with their platoons of social workers, or through federal social security legislation. The sporadic and quite inadequate aid rendered by the boss and his lieutenants thus filled a vacuum. Their only rivals were the self-help associations which did spring up within each ethnic group as soon as available resources allowed a meager surplus to support burial societies and the like. The fact that the politicians acted from self-serving motives in distributing their largess, expecting and receiving a *quid pro quo*, is obvious but not wholly relevant. At least it was not relevant in judging the social importance of the services rendered. It was highly relevant, of course, in terms of the political power base thus acquired.

Some of the later arrivals following the pioneering Irish were in at least as great need of aid. The Irish did speak English and had had some experience with political action and representative institutions at home. This, plus the fact that they got here first, doubtless accounts for their rapid rise in their chosen party, the Democracy. The groups that followed, however, usually did not know English and bore the additional burden of a cultural heritage that had less in common with the American patterns they encountered than had been the case with the Irish. And, too, almost all groups, the Sons of Erin included, differed religiously from the basic Protestant consensus of their Anglo-Saxon predecessors.

As group followed group—not only into the country but into the rickety tenements and "river wards" reserved, as it were, for the latest arrivals—the processes of absorption became more complex. The Irish ward politicians doubtless had, if anything, more difficulty bridging the cultural and language gap to meet the newcomers than the "Yankees" had had in dealing with themselves some decades earlier. Also, while it may well be that the Yankees gave up their party committee posts fairly willingly to the Irish, because politics was not essential to their well-being either economically or psychologically, the Irish were in a rather different position when their turn came to move over and make room.[9] They had not fully outgrown their dependence on politics for financial and psychic security. Thus, the conflicting demands of the machine for new sources of support versus the reluctance of the incumbents to encourage rivalry for their own positions, produced tension. In the long run, however, most of the new ethnic groups found their place in the party system. In some cases, as with the Italians, the Republicans, generally less skillful in these arts, won support by default when the Irish were especially inhospitable.

THE MACHINE AS SOCIAL INTEGRATOR

There is another side to the coin of machine dependence on the continuing flow of immigrants. The "invisible hand"—to use an analogy with Adam Smith's economics—which operated to produce social benefits out of the *quid pro quo* which the ward heelers exchanged for votes was at work in other ways, too. Henry Jones Ford noted in the 1890's, while discussing the role of party:[10]

This nationalizing influence continues to produce results of the greatest social value, for in co-ordinating the various elements of the population for political purposes, party organization at the same time tends to fuse them into one mass of citizenship, pervaded by a common order of ideas and sentiments, and actuated by the same class of motives. This is probably the secret of the powerful solvent influence which American civilization

exerts upon the enormous deposits of alien population thrown upon this country by the torrent of emigration.

Again, in other words, the selfish quest by the politician for electoral support and power was transmuted by the "invisible hand" into the major force integrating the immigrant into the community.

This process has had several facets. In the first place, the mere seeking out of the immigrants in quest of their support, the assistance rendered in getting them naturalized (when it was necessary to observe these legal niceties), and so forth were of considerable importance in laying the foundation for their more meaningful political participation later. In addition, the parties have progressively drawn into their own hierarchies and committee offices representatives of the various ethnic groups. The mechanics of this process were varied. In some cases, there doubtless emerged leaders of a particular group in one ward or neighborhood who, if given official party status, would automatically bring their followings along with them.[11] On other occasions, new ethnic enclaves may have sought or even demanded representation in exchange for support. Perhaps prior to either of these, the machine sought to co-opt individuals who could speak the language and act as a cultural bridge between the party and the newcomers. Depending on the situation, it probably was essential to do this and impossible for precinct captains of a different background to develop adequate rapport. It is as this point that ethnic group rivalry in the organization becomes difficult. Gratitude to the boss for initial admission into the lower ranks of the hierarchy would be bound to change in time into demands, of growing insistence, for further recognition of the individual and his group.

These general patterns can to some extent be documented, at least illustratively. The tendency for the urban machines to reap the Irish vote and later much of the vote of more recent arrivals is well known. The process of infiltration by group representatives into party structure is harder to identify precisely. With this in mind, the author did a study of the members of party ward committees in Providence, Rhode Island, the findings of which may reflect trends elsewhere.[12] Analysis of committee membership lists or their equivalent going back to the 1860s and 1870s showed initial overwhelming Anglo-Saxon majorities. For the Democrats, however, this majority gave way, between the 1880s and 1900, to a roughly 75 per cent Irish preponderance, while the Republican committees stayed "Yankee" until after the First World War. Then, in the 1920s, both parties simultaneously recruited Italian committeemen to replace some of the Irish and white Protestants, respectively. Today, both have varied, and roughly similar, proportions of all major groups in the city population. In other cities, the timing of shifts and the ethnic groups involved will have differed, but the general process and its relation to local patterns of immigration were doubtless similar.

It is incredible, viewed now with hindsight, how reckless the American republic was in its unpremeditated policy of the open door and the implied assumption that somehow, without any governmental or even organized private assistance, hundreds of thousands of immigrants from dozens of diverse cultures would fit themselves smoothly and automatically into a native culture which had its own share of ethnocentrism. The fact of the matter was that the process did not operate smoothly or particularly effectively. There were tensions and incidents which accentuated cultural differences and engendered bitterness. These ranged, chronologically, all the way from the abuses of the more militant Know-Nothings to the Ku Klux Klan activity of the 1920s.

Economically, most occupational doors that did not lead to manual labor jobs were closed to the Irish and later arrivals and were only gradually pried open after much time had passed and many lasting intergroup enmities had been engendered. Here again, the party organizations represented one of the few mechanisms, public or private, that lubricated a process of integration which, in its very nature, was bound to generate enormous amounts of friction. Besides drawing group representatives into its councils, party work also was one of the few career ladders available to the immigrant and his ambitious sons. Here, status could be achieved, as well as a comfortable income, one way or another, when few other routes were open. This became not just status for the individual but a measure of recognition and acceptance for the group as a whole through the individual's success. In fact, not only did the newcomer use this alternative career ladder, but he carried over into the political sphere some of the "Horatio Alger" quest for success and other aspects of an essentially pragmatic, materialistic American culture as well.

Politics for the machine politician never was an ideological enterprise or a matter of beliefs and principles. As someone once said, the boss had only seven principles, five loaves and two fishes. Rather, politics was an entrepreneurial vocation like any other business. Banfield and Wilson have written: "A political machine is a business organization in a particular field of business—getting votes and winning elections. As a Chicago machine boss once said . . . it is 'just like any sales organization trying to sell its product.' " [13] The politician's aim was and is so to invest his supply of capital—jobs, favors, and the like—as to earn a profit, some of which he will take as "income" and the rest reinvest in quest of larger returns. In other words, the immigrant political leader took the one vocation open to him, politics, and made it into as close an approximation as he could of the more valued business callings in the society, from which he was effectively barred. He acted out the American success story in the only way open to him.

Obviously, the foregoing is not designed to portray the machine as a knight-errant rescuing American society from its willful folly. In the first place, the folly was not willful, and perhaps not folly. In the second, the boss's contribution toward making the melting pot melt should not be overrated. At the same time, many have testified—as does the record itself—to the almost unique ability

of party as organization to bring people together across cultural and similar barriers. As Glazer and Moynihan have written of New York City: [14]

. . . political life itself emphasizes the ethnic character of the city, with its balanced tickets and its special appeals. . . . For those in the field itself, there is more contact across the ethnic lines, and the ethnic lines themselves mean less, than in other areas of the city's life.

Ticket-balancing, or United Nations politics, as it is sometimes called, is perhaps symbolic of the ultimate step in the process of granting group recognition and confirming the fact that something approaching intergroup equality has been achieved. Either, as with the Manhattan Borough presidency and the Negro group, certain prescriptive rights become established to a particular office or to one place on a city-wide ticket or ethnic allocation is made using the background of the head of the ticket as point of departure.

In short, the classic urban machine rested upon the immigrants, while at the same time it fostered their integration into American life. It also made, in the process, a major contribution to the over-all American political style. It is true that politics as a pragmatic entrepreneurial vocation owes much in America to the contributions of Burr, Van Buren, Weed, Marcy (to the victor belong the spoils), and, in a sense, to Andrew Jackson himself. Thus, Richard Hofstadter's attribution of one of the two central systems of political ethics in America to the immigrants is only partially valid.[15] He is clearly correct, however, in suggesting that a political style which stressed "personal obligations, and placed strong personal loyalties above allegiance to abstract codes of law or morals"[16] was congenial to the machine politicians and their followers, and they made it their own, developing its full implications in the process. At the same time, the immigrant versus old stock cultural cleavage prompted the latter to espouse the more vigorously the typically middle-class, reformist style which stresses honesty, impartiality, and efficiency. These two styles or ethics, since the late nineteenth century, have, by their interaction, shaped both the evolution of urban politics and the machinery of urban government.

THE DECLINE OF THE MACHINE

The decline and fall of the boss as a political phenomenon has often been chronicled and explained. It is argued, *inter alia*, that reforms like the direct primary, nonpartisan systems of election, voting machines and tightened registration requirements, and city-manager schemes often dealt crippling blows. In the aggregate, they doubtless did, though many exceptions can be found to prove the rule. One particular contribution of the reformers which has had unquestioned importance—though circumvention has not proven impossible—was the elimination of patronage with the installation of civil service based on the merit principle. And, generally, educational

levels have risen, and occupational levels and incomes have risen as well. Even where patronage remains available, the latter development has rendered it less attractive, and to fewer people. Finally, and most often cited, there was the impact of the New Deal. Its installation of publicly sponsored welfare programs eliminated many of the rough-and-ready welfare functions of the precinct captain, though the more imaginative recouped part of their loss by helping to steer constituents through the bureaucratic maze, claiming credit for the benefits thus obtained.

Granting the importance of all of these developments, in the long run, the decline of immigration doubtless proved the most important blow to the traditional machine operation. New arrivals had been entering the country at a rate in excess of four million each half decade up to the First World War. The rate averaged barely more than one third of that between 1915 and 1930 and dropped to a mere trickle for most of the period down to the present. Sharply restrictive legislation passed in 1921 and 1924 was responsible. Obviously, the impact on the machines came in the form of a delayed reaction, but most of them gradually withered. The few that survived did so through shrewd adaptation to changed conditions, specifically through judicious self-administered doses of reformism, as, for example, with the Daley organization in Chicago.

Thus ended an era. Immigration may not have called the boss into being, but the two in most cases were closely linked. Two questions remain to be dealt with. What contemporary counterparts are there, if any, of the immigrant influx of yesteryear and how are the parties dealing with them? And what can be said of the current political behavior of the children and grandchildren of the former immigrants?

THE PARTIES AND THE NEW IMMIGRATION

There are, of course, two major groups that do represent close parallels with the earlier influx and at the same time carry important differences. These are the Negroes who have been migrating in increasing numbers from the South to northern urban centers since the First World War and the Puerto Ricans who began coming to New York City, for the most part, after the Second World War.[17] Both resemble their alien predecessors in the magnitude of their numbers, their basic and important cultural differences from the population into whose midst they are moving, an almost invariable need of assistance in adjusting to a new environment, and their potential impact on the political balance of forces.

The major points of difference are also worth noting. Both come bearing the credentials of American citizenship, which was not the case with the earlier groups. Though this factor should make for easier adjustment, other group characteristics operate to make acceptance more difficult. For the Negro, there is the fundamental problem of color, coupled with cultural characteristics which, though acquired ostensibly in the American environment, operate to make assimilation

more difficult. These include all the long deposit of servitude and enforced inferior status: loose marital ties and correspondingly weak family ties generally, a poverty of leadership potential, low literacy and skill levels, and the like. For the Puerto Ricans, there is language, plus differences of culture, and a partial color barrier which operates to cause at least some Spanish Americans to be classified—against their will—as Negroes. On balance, it is probably true that, so far as these two groups are concerned as groups, they face higher barriers to integration into American life than almost any earlier group save, possibly, the orientals.

But the society itself has changed enormously from the society to which the Irish, Italians, and Jews sought entrance. Urban areas are now equipped with facilities to which the newcomer can turn for aid that counterbalance to some degree the particular hostilities which members of these two groups arouse. There are now elaborate public welfare programs, there is Aid to Dependent Children for the many fatherless families, there are numerous private agencies and charities which stand ready to help, and, in the case of the Puerto Ricans, their land of origin has taken a unique interest in the welfare of its emigrants. There have even been legislative efforts to ban the discrimination in housing or employment which they encounter.

Though these facilities stand ready to ease aspects of the economic and social integration of these latest immigrants, there still remains the question of political absorption. Here, too, the situation today sharply differs from the past. The political parties now have neither the incentive nor the means with which to perform the functions they performed for the earlier immigrants. The machine in most affected areas is gone beyond recall, and there remain in its place party organizations that are hollow shells of their former strength and vigor. Party in general, given the proliferation of both public bureaucracies and the mass entertainment industry, has been pushed to the fringes of the average citizen's attention span and often to the fringes of the governing process itself. The debilitating impact of reform legislation contributed to the same end, needless to say. Thus, in general, the new immigrants can look to the parties for little of the former assistance they once provided in gaining entrance and leverage in the political processes of their new homes.

There are partial exceptions here, as there are to all the foregoing generalizations. Mayor Daley's modern Chicago version of the old-style machine has been mentioned earlier. Within his over-all Cook County Democratic organization, there is the "sub-machine" comprising the Negro followers of Representative William E. Dawson.[18] Dawson, a former maverick Republican, shifted parties in 1939 and joined forces with Mayor-boss Kelly. Some twenty years later, he had put together a combination, under his leadership, of five or six Negro wards. This "organization within an organization" appears to bargain as a unit through Dawson and his lieutenants for patronage and other kinds of preferment in the gift of Mayor Daley and in turn tends to exert a moderating influence on the more aggressive elements in the Negro community. Trends suggest that this is not destined to be a permanent arrangement. The population of the Dawson-controlled wards has been declining as the more prosperous Negroes manage to settle in more desirable locations, and, as Dawson and his associates grow older, they become more conservative. Whether or not this latter is partly an illusion produced by the rapid rise in Negro militancy since 1954 would be hard to say. It is probably true that leaders of the Dawson type will get more "out of phase" with the civil rights movement as that movement gains further momentum.

New York City, almost by traditional right, is *the* locale for the study of the behavior of American parties in relation to the immigrant. The 1960 census reported just over a million Negroes in New York City and somewhat more than 600,000 Puerto Ricans. In broad terms, it can be said that since the days of Al Smith and Boss Murphy, New York politics have been long on confusion and fragmentation and short on centralized, disciplined organization. There was, therefore, little possibility that a relationship such as Representative Dawson worked out with his Negro clientele on the one hand and the leaders of the Cook County Democracy on the other could be developed in New York. Especially in Manhattan—which we shall take for analysis—one finds exemplified the more typical contemporary party situation: no dominating borough-wide authority save that in the hands of the mayor himself, hence a series of local feudal chiefs who are rarely

willing to exchange their relative independence for the rather meager supplies of
patronage available, and the whole system
wracked periodically by factional feud-
ing.

The Negro in New York, in apparent
contrast to the Chicago situation, has
been more fragmented in his political
organization, has found little borough-
wide structure with which to associate,
but has made more spectacular symbolic
gains in the party and city government.
Representative Adam Clayton Powell, the
rather erratic champion of the city's non-
whites, reaps vastly more national publicity for his espoused cause than the pub-
licity-shy Congressman Dawson.[19] How
much this means in concrete benefits
would be hard to determine. More significant is the fact that in 1953 a Negro,
Hulan Jack, was elected for the first time
to a major office in the city, that of
Borough President of Manhattan. Powell
had a major role in this, though he later
broke with Jack. Since then, this position
has become an accepted Negro preroga-
tive. Other high positions have been filled
by Negroes in the city administration in
recent years.

REPRESENTATION ON
PARTY COMMITTEES

A somewhat more useful basis for judging
the reality of ethnic or racial group political absorption and power position than
possession of some of these "commanding heights" (in Lenin's phrase) would be
an analysis of the extent to which they
had gained footholds in the lower and
intermediate levels of the party organiza-

tion. The ethnic proportions among Providence ward committee members cited
above are a relatively accurate reflection
of the nationality power relationships in
city politics. For example, the fact that
the Irish Democrats have held onto about
half of the ward committee seats after
yielding some places to Italians reflects
the fact that they still have the dominant
voice in the party. The rise of the Italians
on the Republican side to the status of
the largest single ethnic group also reflects their growing power.[20]

Table 1 shows the approximate percentages of ethnic/racial representation in
the total New York City population and,
in the second column, the background of
the Manhattan Democratic Assembly district leaders and coleaders insofar as these
could be determined.[21]

There are sixteen Assembly districts, but
most are divided into two or three parts
with a leader and coleader for each. There
were some vacancies at the time the data
were obtained. It can be seen that the
Negro has done quite well by this measure of political integration in that the
group has considerably more than the
share of district leadership positions it
would be entitled to on a strict population basis. The bulk of these Negroes
preside over districts in or around Harlem, as might be expected—the 11th,
12th, 13th, 14th, and 16th Assembly
districts. Of the eighteen occupied positions in these five Assembly districts,
they hold twelve. There are two Negroes,
one each in the 5th and 10th, to the west
and east of Central Park, respectively, but
none to the south of the Park at all.

In passing it might be noted that the

TABLE 1.
COMPARISON OF ETHNIC PROPORTIONS
IN POPULATION WITH DEMOCRATIC
DISTRICT LEADERS IN MANHATTAN

	Approximate Percentage of New York City 1960 Population[a]	Percentage of Democratic Assembly District Leaders (N = 66)
Negroes	14	21
Puerto Ricans	8	6
Jews	25±	38
Italians	17±	11
Irish	10±	9
Others	26±	15[b]
	100	100

[a]Population percentage estimates are from Nathan Glazer and D. P. Moynihan, *Beyond the Melting Pot* (Cambridge: M.I.T. and Harvard Press, 1963). Only figures for Negroes and Puerto Ricans were given in the 1960 census. It was impossible to get ethnic group percentages for Manhattan alone.

[b]Includes Anglo-Saxon Protestants and others of unidentified background.

other groups on the Table each have something approximating their proportionate share of the leaderships. The Jewish contingent is disproportionately large, due in considerable measure to the fact that three-fifths of all the anti-Tammany "reform" leaders come from that part of the city population. True to what one knows about their situation in other cities, the Italians appear to be underrepresented. The Irish, however, even in view of the extreme difficulty in guessing their share of the city population, have far fewer positions than the prevailing myth of continuing Irish dominance of urban Democratic politics would suggest.

Turning now to the Puerto Ricans, they offer the best opportunity for assessing the ability of at least the Manhattan Democratic organization to absorb a genuinely new ethnic group. In Table 2, the backgrounds of the district leaders in the areas of heaviest Puerto Rican population are tabulated. Also included, in the last two columns, are figures on the personnel of the lowest level of "grass-roots" party organization, the election district captains. Out of the twelve district leader positions occupied at the time the data were obtained, four were held by Puerto

Elmer E. Cornwell, Jr.

TABLE 2.
AREAS OF HEAVY PUERTO RICAN POPULATION[a]

| Area | Assembly District | District Leaders | ELECTION DISTRICT CAPTAIN | |
			Total	Puerto Ricans
Lower East Side	4th, South	2 Jewish	29	7
East Harlem	10th, North	1 Puerto Rican and 1 Negro	16	9
	14th, South	2 Puerto Ricans	17	8
	14th, North	2 Negroes	_[b]	_[b]
	16th, South	1 Italian and 1 Puerto Rican	_[b]	_[b]
Upper West Side	13th, South	1 Italian and 1 Negro	52	23

[a]Puerto Rican population location was determined by plotting location of census tracts with at least 15 per cent Puerto Ricans and coloring these in according to density. There are scatterings in a few other parts of Manhattan as well.
[b]Data could not be obtained.

Ricans, giving that group representation in three of the six most heavily Puerto Rican districts. Though only firsthand knowledge would indicate how effective these individuals are in representing their ethnic group and bargaining on its behalf, there is indication here of rather significant infiltration into the party structure. The figures for election district captains, where these could be obtained, point to the same conclusion. Except for the lower east side, where the proportion is smaller, roughly half of these captains are also Puerto Rican, casting further doubt on common assumptions that the party in Manhattan is lagging seriously in making room for this latest group to arrive.

In general, both Table 1 and Table 2 suggest that the Puerto Ricans have secured, in the relatively short time since their arrival in large numbers, party of-

fices roughly commensurate with their share of the population over-all in areas of high concentration. In addition, there are three state assemblymen from this group (two from East Harlem and one from the Bronx) and four or five with high positions in the city administration.[22]

These achievements, obviously, as well as the district leaderships themselves and election district captaincies, can only be taken as rough indicators of the political progress of the group as a whole and are doubtless far less significant than they could have been viewed in the political setting of forty or fifty years ago when parties were central to the governing process and urban life generally. At the same time, they must be evaluated in light of the fact that New York State will not accept literacy in a language other than English (such as Spanish) as qualification

136

to vote, and, thus, only some 150,000 to 175,000 of the total Puerto Rican group are on the rolls.

Returning for a moment to the current status of descendants of earlier immigrants, the assumption that significant cultural distinctions and tendencies toward common political attitude and behavior would disappear in two or three generations has proven erroneous. Ticket-balancing, for example, in ethnic or religious terms is as prevalent, perhaps, as it ever was and shows few signs of disappearing in the immediate future. The election of an Irish Catholic President in 1960, if anything, enhanced the importance of such balancing tactics, as the discussion in early 1964 of Democratic vice-presidential candidates indicated. In psychoanalysis, it is well recognized that problems have to be clearly recognized and frankly made explicit before they can be eliminated. The same may in a sense be true of ethnic factors in American politics. Only the frank recognition of the once-potent barrier to a Catholic in the White House paved the way for the Kennedy election. At the state and local level, it is probably also true that only after various groups have achieved and enjoyed the recognition they feel they are entitled to and have done so for a long enough period to transform a privilege into a quasi right will it become possible, gradually, to choose candidates without these criteria in mind. The unfortunate thing is that American parties have decayed as organizations to the point that they can make far less contribution to this process of adjustment than they could and did in the past.

NOTES

1. See Harold F. Gosnell, *Boss Platt and His New York Machine* (Chicago: University of Chicago Press, 1924).
2. See Lincoln Steffens, "Rhode Island: A State for Sale," *McClure's Magazine*, vol. 24 (February 1905), pp. 337-353.
3. Lincoln Steffens, *Autobiography* (New York: Literary Guild, 1931), p. 367.
4. E. P. Hutchinson, *Immigrants and Their Children* (New York: John Wiley, 1956), p. 27.
5. See J. L. Garvin, *The Life of Joseph Chamberlain* (3 vols.; London: Macmillan, 1932-34).
6. Stanley Salvidge, *Salvidge of Liverpool* (London: Hodder and Stoughton, 1934).
7. For an elaboration of this approach to the internal dynamics of the machine, see James Q. Wilson, "The Economy of Patronage," *Journal of Political Economy*, vol. 69, pp. 369-380.
8. One of the most readable depictions of these machine functions is to be found in Edwin O'Connor's novel *The Last Hurrah* (Boston: Little, Brown, 1956).
9. See the author's "Some Occupational Patterns in Party Committee Membership," *Rhode Island History*, vol. 20 (July 1961), pp. 87-96.
10. *The Rise and Growth of American Politics* (New York: Macmillan, 1911), p. 306.
11. *Ibid.*, p. 307.
12. "Party Absorption of Ethnic Groups," *Social Forces*, vol. 38 (March 1960), pp. 205-210.
13. Edward Banfield and James Q. Wilson, *City Politics* (Cambridge: Harvard and M.I.T. Presses, 1963), p. 115.
14. Nathan Glazer and Daniel Patrick Moynihan, *Beyond the Melting Pot* (Cambridge: Harvard and M.I.T. Presses, 1963), p. 20.
15. Richard Hofstadter, *The Age of Reform* (New York: Knopf, 1955), pp. 8 ff.
16. *Ibid.*, p. 9.
17. Two recent books are especially useful discussions of these groups: Glazer and Moynihan, *op. cit.;* and Oscar Handlin, *The Newcomers: Negroes and Puerto Ricans in a Changing Metropolis* (Cambridge: Harvard Press, 1959).

18. This discussion of the Dawson organization draws particularly on James Q. Wilson, *Negro Politics* (Glencoe, Ill.: Free Press, 1960), pp. 50 ff. and *passim*.

19. A useful source on Powell is David Hapgood, *The Purge That Failed: Tammany v. Powell* (New York: Holt, 1959).

20. "Party Absorption of Ethnic Groups," *op. cit.*

21. Thanks are due the author's former student, Edwin Cohen, now active in Manhattan politics, and to George Osborne, himself a district leader, for tracking down the leadership data used.

22. Layhmond Robinson, "Voting Gain Made by Puerto Ricans," *New York Times*, November 23, 1963.

~❦ FOUR ❦~
Bosses and Boodle

⚘ COMMENTARY ⚘

Graft is the common cold of politics. The Dutch called it *boedel*. The Americans corrupted the word into boodle, and for generations it remained the favorite nickname for graft. For generations, too, bosses and boodle seemed synonymous. Cities appeared to have a monopoly on sin. New York was characterized as "an underground rapid transit railroad to hell." Pittsburgh was compared to the Biblical hellholes Sodom and Gomorrah. Philadelphia was called "The City of Brotherly Loot"; and Chicago was so tough and wicked "that even the canaries sang bass." But the city had no monopoly on political corruption. At one time or another it was rampant in every form of human settlement—the farm, the village, the small town—manipulated by railroad magnates, courthouse gangs, and land speculators. It permeated every level of government, not only city hall but county administration, state legislature, Capitol Hill, and the White House. The Grant Administration was fouled by the Credit Mobilier. Harding had his Teapot Dome. And then there was Watergate. An Illinois poll watcher summed it up: "I've learned that nothing crooked is done in the river wards of Chicago that is not done more effectively by the Downstate Republicans."

Yet the city and the city boss have traditionally received most of the attention and bad publicity concerning political sin, partly because of the deep strain of anti-urbanism in American thought, partly because city hall represents the government closest to the people. Local government is the testing ground for self-government. Rascals might be expected in the Sacramento capitol or in the U. S. Congress, but dishonesty in local government comes terribly close to violating the institutions that most directly concern the people.

Graft is a word to conjure with. Americans have viewed it with both
indignation and cynicism. They have fought it, tolerated it, rationalized it,
ignored it. In the first essay of the present chapter, a classic of a kind,
George Washington Plunkitt "explains" it: You see, there are actually two
kinds of graft, honest and dishonest. Now, we all know what dishonest
graft is, but the honest variety can be a mind-boggler—though it need not.
Honest graft is simply an honorarium for services rendered. It is the fee
the boss exacts for building, rebuilding, and patching the city. It explains
the politicians's fascination for, say, real estate. Thus, for example, the
boss is privy to the "inside" information that State Street is to be
widened. He invests in the property along that street and thereby executes
a brilliant coup in business practice, since real estate values are most assur-
edly due to rise.

A city might reek of corruption, but the city boss and his machine still
could manage to pave its streets, provide services, build schools, and keep
its citizens safe. For example, Tom Pendergast's "Kansas City Ten-Year
Plan" provided for a huge public-works program: a towering new city hall,
a large public auditorium, a courthouse, police station, a multitude of
parks and playgrounds, and significant improvements to hospitals and
sewer and road systems. Of course, this meant that Pendergast would
never have to go on welfare (though he did land in jail). It is conceivable
that these projects might not have been realized without large-scale graft,
honest or dishonest. Indeed, Seymour Mandelbaum, in his book, *Boss
Tweed's New York*, suggested that in the fragmented metropolis of the
Tweed era, the "big payoff" was an essential if not the most efficient way
of getting things done, considering the problems of New York at that
time. After all, the city boss as the entrepreneur-politician was not in the
game for his health. In view of the role and aspirations of the city boss,
the influence of entrenched special-interest groups, and the rapid urbanization of the American city, corruption was almost, if not completely,
inevitable.

Graft, in Robert Merton's phrase, was a "latent function of the machine." It served a number of purposes. It was at once compensation for
the boss and fuel to keep the machine running, paying for its "overhead,"
financing the election campaigns. It was a function of political power, a
decision-maker, if you will—a promise of special privilege to powerful
groups who could serve the boss. It was as well, as Richard Sennett has
suggested, a means to "cut in" the poor on the profits, however meager. It

was an instrument of discipline, a means to reward the faithful and punish the unworthy. In a free-wheeling free-enterprise system, where certain goods are limited, the competition is keen, the stakes are high, there will be those who seek special advantage. When society slams the door on the *two* oldest professions, prostitution and gambling, and when, as in the 1920s, ardent spirits such as the Prohibitionists got between a man and his beer, graft is inevitable.

This is not to suggest that *all* city bosses in America, past and present, were corrupt. Power can be as mighty an inducement as profit. There is no solid evidence for adjudging Victor L. Berger of Milwaukee, or Edward Flynn of the Bronx, or Richard J. Daley of Chicago personally dishonest. Personal virtue, however, does not ensure that honest politicians won't ignore graft in the lower orders of the machine's organization for bone-hard political reasons. It is a good question whether Mayor Daley could mount an all-out crusade against graft in Chicago and still have an effective machine. Indeed, when questioned about the presence of organized crime in Chicago, Daley was capable of a dumbfounding evasiveness.

Q. Is there any organized crime remaining?

A. Well, you have crime always, whether it's the large city or the village or the neighborhood.

Q. But what about the Syndicates, like the Capone gang—do they exist?

A. Well, whether it's organized or unorganized, it's still crime and it has to be met on all the various levels by very rigid law enforcement.[1]

Throughout all of this, it may have struck anyone of sensitivity about morality in politics that it is rather easy to rationalize graft on the part of the city boss and his machine. One might say that, the latent functions and inevitability of graft, the facts of political life to the contrary notwithstanding, the question—a good one and a big one—is begged. Graft is still wrong. No matter which way you explain it, graft of whatever variety has always been and certainly still is considered immoral in American politics. Like Gertrude Stein's famous rose, graft is graft is graft. One difficulty in defining graft is that it is often measured by the intensity of one's

1. William Gleason, *Daley of Chicago: The Man, the Mayor, and the Limits of Conventional Politics* (1970), p. 20.

own political persuasion.[2] Some Democrats dismissed the antics of Bobby Baker, just as some Republicans shrugged off Watergate ("The Democrats do it, don't they?").

There is also the problem of perspective. Present-day urban historians tend to minimize corruption, in the belief that excessive emphasis on it in the past has obscured the facts on how the machine's worked, and the point that the boss's contribution to the social mobility of the poor may have outweighed his alleged misdeeds. And there is the problem of a change in social mores. Today violations involving prostitution, gambling, and, in some quarters, drugs, are considered "victimless" crimes or "workingmen's vices," and so provoke much less outrage than they did in the past. But the question is still begged. Graft is still graft. Perhaps the heart of the issue is not the kind of graft or who perpetrates it or even its magnitude but rather its impact upon the democratic process. Graft of any kind breeds distrust. Distrust breeds cynicism. Cynicism is the most powerful enemy of the democratic/representative process. When people lose faith in their institutions and their politicians, the political system is ripe for collapse.

Both the extent and the methods of graft varied over time with changes in the economic and social system. The profits were highest, the restrictions least, the opportunities greatest, and the methods flashiest in the high day of the old-fashioned boss—the period of massive city-building. As Chris Buckley said, "I had opportunities—certainties, I might say." In his 1930 study of the old-fashioned boss, Harold Zink found that, of the twenty bosses he discussed, eighteen left estates that can be discreetly described as ample. Still, considering the stakes, the risks were relatively modest. While only eight of the twenty escaped prison, trial, or indictment (for crimes ranging from malfeasance, perjury, and grand theft to murder), only two—Tweed and Ruef—went to jail. There were some narrow escapes—which might lead one to feel that God looked after not only drunks and children but city bosses as well.

Graft was possible in any area touched by political power. It was limited only by the imagination of the boodlers or an outraged reform move-

2. On the ambiguities of corruption, see Arnold J. Heidenheimer, ed., *Political Corruption: Readings in Comparative Analysis,* (1970), pp. 3-9; Colin Leys, "What Is the Problem about Corruption?" *Journal of Modern African Studies* (August 1965), pp. 217-24; and probably the best overall treatment, John A. Gardiner and David J. Olson, eds., *Theft of the City: Readings on Corruption in Urban America* (1974).

ment. For a powerful city boss there were three primary sources of graft: the city, the state, and the business community. There were four broad categories yielding booty: franchises, public contracts, public funds, and vice. A strong boss sought to control the key legislative and financial officials—from supervisors and aldermen to comptroller and mayor. This allowed him to manipulate warrants charged against the city treasury. Every program for city improvement, be it new streets, public buildings and parks, mass transit, or sewers, had to be financed from the city treasury, and contracts could be awarded to favorite businessmen who were expected in turn to pad their bills and pass back to the boss sizable portions of their profit via the "kickback."

Every charter and franchise for a new business had to meet the approval of the city legislature and usually the Mayor, and many a company had to pay the tribute of a bribe to win approval. All the city's sources of revenue, such as bond issue, income tax, rental on city properties, tax assessment, were opportunities for graft. If a boss was strong enough to spread his tentacles to the state legislature, he could gain control of the State Finance Committee and committees on municipal affairs, and thus be in a position to influence tax levies, bond issues, and special projects for the city—all sources of graft. Often the boss operated as lobby broker for businessmen seeking to pass or kill legislation vital to their interests. The "cinch" bill, legislative extortion threatening business firms and individuals, was a common tactic.

Most boss-ridden cities paid the price of political sin: massive, shocking investigations into municipal corruption. Fittingly enough, the greatest city, New York, was the scene of some of the most spectacular of such inquiries, from the Lexow, Mazet, and Fassett investigations of the late-nineteenth and early-twentieth centuries to the Seabury investigations of the early 1930s, and most recently, in the 1970s, those of the Knapp Commission. Their probing questions elicited some interesting responses: e.g., Richard Croker, "I work for my pocket all the time"; or William Devery, "Touchin' on and appertainin' to that matter, I disremember." Of all the old-time machines, the most gifted, audacious, and notorious practitioners of the art of graft belonged to the Tweed Ring of Tammany Hall. The second essay of this chapter, "The House That Tweed Built," shows the Tweed Ring in action, performing one of the most stunning feats of corruption in the robust history of urban graft.

The next essay, "Vote Early and Often," illustrates another form of corruption that for many cities was a common occurrence—cheating, violence, even slaughter, at the polls on election day. After all, winning elections was the business of the city boss; his survival depended upon it, and often the ends justified the means. This essay discusses the many tactics used by the boss to influence the voice of the people, and some of these tactics were ingenious to the point of brilliance. It is mistaken, however, to think that the boss *always* relied on election fraud. Party partisanship was a staunch buttress of power. People voted for their party through idealism, habit, apathy, or the feeling that the enemy party should be kept out regardless of corruption within. Small shopkeepers, big businessmen, lawyers, and judges, some of whom had no love for the boss, believed nonetheless that they could enhance their own interests by exploiting the boss's favors; and others, in the same group, hated the boss but were terrified of his power of retaliation and did not dare vote against him.

By present-day standards, old-fashioned graft by old-fashioned bosses was a swaggering, raucous, ugly, outrageously blatant bawd. Today she is more sly, more sophisticated—the highly complicated dummy corporation, the undercover payoff via the "respectable" attorney, the campaign contribution—and she has a prettier face. Just as political, social, and economic changes have affected the city boss and his machine, his ethnic following, and the city itself, so too have such changes affected the methods, magnitude, and location of corruption.[3] The familiar alliance between certain members of the business community and the boss publicized by Lincoln Steffens, the energetic journalist with a muckrake, has changed character. The outright bribe given by large, long-established corporation and business is becoming rarer, occurring usually when new firms are trying to break into already pre-empted areas. As Harvard political scientists Edward C. Banfield and James Q. Wilson explain:

> These latter—businessmen who are "on the make"—are viewed with pain and disgust (as of course they should be) by the owners and managers of businesses that were created in exactly the same way not many years ago.
>
> Today the respectable (established) businessman is likely to use political influence for purely private purposes only in what may be called defensive actions. He may try his best to prevent some disturbance to the *status quo* that would affect his company adversely, but he is not at all likely to try to upset the *status quo* in

3. On municipal corruption, see the above-recommended Gardiner and Olson, eds., *Theft of the City: Readings on Corruption in Urban America* (1974).

order to get a windfall for himself. For example, he may pull wires at City Hall
to block a change of assessment practices that would hurt his company but he
would not think of soliciting a change to benefit the company. The reason he
behaves as he does is perhaps not hard to find. Not being willing to resort to
bribery, and dealing with an officialdom that is too large and too professionalized to be bribed, he must limit himself to demands which are in some sense
legitimate. In short, defensive action, being easier to justify, is more likely to
succeed.[4]

Another more recent development has been the growth of organized
crime, especially via "fat cat" campaign contributions such as, for example, Al Capone's $250,000 donation to the mayoralty campaign of
Chicago's William "Big Bill" Thompson in 1927; the thousands of dollars
Thomas "Three-Finger Brown" Luchese added to the campaign fund of
William O'Dwyer of New York twenty-two years later; and the money and
political influence of the racketeer Frank Costello that controlled a working majority in Tammany's Executive Committee during the 1940s. A
study made in November of 1973 by the National Advisory Commission
on Criminal Justice Standards and Goals estimated that some 15 per cent
of the money contributed to municipal and state election campaigns—
roughly $20 million—comes from organized crime.

What is striking about corruption in modern times, the so-called age of
megamuck, is that graft has been prevalent in cities that do not have a
strong political machine or, in some cases, like that of Los Angeles, have
never had a tradition of machine politics. This suggests a new locus of
corruption in the cities—and a delicious irony to boot. In the last selection
in this chapter Edward N. Costikyan argues that the contribution is no
longer funneled to the traditional, stereotyped bad guy, the party leader,
or a Tammany Hall. It goes to where the power is: to the bureaucrat—the
civil servant, the career government officer—the elected public official
who was never associated with the machine. The irony is that the new
corrupters are creatures of a reform movement dating from the Progressive
period, a movement claiming that clean government was government free
of professional politicians. Nor does corruption always revolve around
cash, as Costikyan makes clear in his discussion of influence-peddling in
any area from the urban renewal project to the location of fireplugs. As a
former Tammany leader, Costikyan is a realist. Graft, he says, will never

4. *City Politics* (1963), p. 266.

be completely eliminated, it can only be minimized: first, by identifying the new locus of corruption; second, by scotching discretionary distribution of governmental privilege—in Title I housing projects, urban renewal sponsorships, public architectural contracts—to cite a few that have been given without competition for either quality or quantity. Finally, and perhaps most importantly, we must shatter the myth of the nefarious professional politician. Costikyan poses this question: Are politicians, *as a profession*, any more corrupt than civil servants, lawyers, businessmen, doctors, or even advertising men? After Watergate, it is a question that deserves some thought.

To many Americans today, however, what has changed is not quality but quantity. At this writing, corruption seems to have hit the nation like a plague. Scandals have struck a score of cities, among them Miami, Philadelphia, New Orleans, Baltimore, New York, Albany, Cleveland, and Los Angeles. There have been three hundred indictments in twenty cities. The State of New Jersey alone is becoming a kind of superrogue. In the last three years, thirty-five municipal and state officials, a motley crew ranging from mayors, state legislators, and a Congressman to judges, highway officials, and postmasters, have been convicted of corruption, and sixty-seven have been indicted. Police graft has fouled New York, Houston, Chicago, Cleveland, Philadelphia, and Indianapolis. And then there was Watergate, which would probably have stunned Boss Tweed. Corruption, then, seems epidemic. The political system is ravaged by cynicism. The old joke about politics never changes: politics *is* a dirty business. As a *Time* magazine writer put it recently, the national motto appears to have changed from *E Pluribus Unum* to *Omnes Idem Faciunt*—"Everybody's doing it."

Are they? Is graft on the rise, or has the chemistry of corruption changed? Students of political malfeasance argue there is no hard evidence to prove either that corruption is increasing or that all politicians are boodlers. They say that what has changed is not the appetite for corruption but the appetite of the public for the prosecution of corruption. What is new is not graft but the public's increasing indignation, its rising sensitivity to corruption. In the large view, what is striking is that not *more* of the hundreds of thousands of municipal officials and the hundred Senators and four hundred-odd Representatives in the Congress cannot say with George Washington Plunkitt, "I saw my opportunities—and took 'em."

HONEST GRAFT
AND
DISHONEST GRAFT

George Washington Plunkitt

Everybody is talkin' these days about Tammany men growin' rich on graft, but nobody thinks of drawin' the distinction between honest graft and dishonest graft. There's all the difference in the world between the two. Yes, many of our men have grown rich in politics. I have myself. I've made a big fortune out of the game, and I'm gettin' richer every day, but I've not gone in for dishonest graft—blackmailin' gamblers, saloon-keepers, disorderly people, etc.—and neither has any of the men who have made big fortunes in politics.

There's an honest graft, and I'm an example of how it works. I might sum up the whole thing by sayin': "I seen my opportunities and I took 'em."

Just let me explain by examples. My party's in power in the city, and it's goin' to undertake a lot of public improvements. Well, I'm tipped off, say, that

From William L. Riordon, *Plunkitt of Tammany Hall* (New York: Alfred A. Knopf, 1948), pp. 3-8.

they're going to lay out a new park at a certain place.

I see my opportunity and I take it. I go to that place and I buy up all the land I can in the neighborhood. Then the board of this or that makes its plan public, and there is a rush to get my land, which nobody cared particular for before.

Ain't it perfectly honest to charge a good price and make a profit on my investment and foresight? Of course, it is. Well, that's honest graft.

Or, supposin' it's a new bridge they're goin' to build. I get tipped off and I buy as much property as I can that has to be taken for approaches. I sell at my own price later on and drop some more money in the bank.

Wouldn't you? It's just like lookin' ahead in Wall Street or in the coffee or cotton market. It's honest graft, and I'm lookin' for it every day in the year. I will tell you frankly that I've got a good lot of it, too.

I'll tell you of one case. They were goin' to fix up a big park, no matter where. I got on to it, and went lookin' about for land in that neighborhood.

I could get nothin' at a bargain but a big piece of swamp, but I took it fast enough and held on to it. What turned out was just what I counted on. They couldn't make the park complete without Plunkitt's swamp, and they had to pay a good price for it. Anything dishonest in that?

Up in the watershed I made some money, too. I bought up several bits of land there some years ago and made a pretty good guess that they would be bought up for water purposes later by the city.

Somehow, I always guessed about right, and shouldn't I enjoy the profit of my foresight? It was rather amusin' when the condemnation commissioners came along and found piece after piece of the land in the name of George Plunkitt of the Fifteenth Assembly District, New York City. They wondered how I knew just what to buy. The answer is—I seen my opportunity and I took it. I haven't confined myself to land; anything that pays is in my line.

For instance, the city is repavin' a street and has several hundred thousand old granite blocks to sell. I am on hand to buy, and I know just what they are worth.

How? Never mind that. I had a sort of monopoly of this business for a while, but once a newspaper tried to do me. It got some outside men to come over from Brooklyn and New Jersey to bid against me.

Was I done? Not much. I went to each of the men and said: "How many of these 250,000 stones do you want?" One said 20,000, and another wanted 15,000, and another wanted 10,000. I said: "All right, let me bid for the lot, and I'll give each of you all you want for nothin'.

They agreed, of course. Then the auctioneer yelled: "How much am I bid for these 250,000 fine pavin' stones?"

"Two dollars and fifty cents," says I.

"Two dollars and fifty cents!" screamed the auctioneer. "Oh, that's a joke! Give me a real bid."

He found the bid was real enough. My rivals stood silent. I got the lot for $2.50 and gave them their share. That's how the attempt to do Plunkitt ended, and that's how all such attempts end.

I've told you how I got rich by honest graft. Now, let me tell you that most politicians who are accused of robbin' the city get rich the same way.

They didn't steal a dollar from the city treasury. They just seen their opportunities and took them. That is why, when a reform administration comes in and spends a half million dollars in tryin' to find the public robberies they talked about in the campaign, they don't find them.

The books are always all right. The money in the city treasury is all right. Everything is all right. All they can show is that the Tammany heads of departments looked after their friends, within the law, and gave them what opportunities they could to make honest graft. Now, let me tell you that's never goin' to hurt Tammany with the people. Every good man looks after his friends, and any man who doesn't isn't likely to be popular. If I have a good thing to hand out in private life, I give it to a friend. Why shouldn't I do the same in public life?

Another kind of honest graft. Tammany has raised a good many salaries. There was an awful howl by the reformers, but don't you know that Tammany gains ten votes for every one it lost by salary raisin'?

The Wall Street banker thinks it shameful to raise a department clerk's salary from $1500 to $1800 a year, but every man who draws a salary himself says: "That's all right. I wish it was me." And he feels very much like votin' the Tammany ticket on election day, just out of sympathy.

Tammany was beat in 1901 because the people were deceived into believin' that it worked dishonest graft. They didn't draw a distinction between dishonest and honest graft, but they saw that some Tammany men grew rich, and supposed they had been robbin' the city treasury or levyin' blackmail on disorderly houses, or workin' in with the gamblers and lawbreakers.

As a matter of policy, if nothing else, why should the Tammany leaders go into such dirty business, when there is so much honest graft lyin' around when they are in power? Did you ever consider that?

Now, in conclusion, I want to say that I don't own a dishonest dollar. If my worst enemy was given the job of writin' my epitaph when I'm gone, he couldn't do more than write:

"George W. Plunkitt. He Seen His Opportunities, and He Took 'Em."

THE HOUSE
THAT TWEED BUILT

Alexander B. Callow, Jr.

This is
BOSS TWEED
The Tammany Atlas who all sustains,
(A Tammany Samson perhaps for his pains),
Who rules the City where Oakey reigns,
The master of Woodward and Ingersoll
And all of the gang on the City Roll,
And formerly lord of "slippery Dick,"
Who *con*troll'd the plastering laid on so
   thick
By the comptroller's plasterer, Garvey by
   name,
The Garvey whose fame is the little game
Of laying on plaster and knowing the trick
Of charging as if he himself were a brick
        Of the well-plaster'd House
        That TWEED built.

      "The House That Tweed Built"

Today among the sleek, soaring municipal buildings of downtown Manhattan huddles a shabby, squat pile of Massachusetts

From *The Tweed Ring* by Alexander B. Callow, Jr. Copyright © 1966 by Alexander B. Callow, Jr. Reprinted by permission, Oxford University Press, Inc.

marble. It is the old County Courthouse, a sad, forlorn, almost forgotten little building. A small, chunky, three-story structure, barely reaching a hundred feet, it is dwarfed by surrounding buildings and shunted aside from the main legal traffic in New York. Behind its dirty gray walls only a few offices are now used. There is nothing in this ancient and rather grotesque relic of little old New York to suggest a raucous past, or even the slightest hint of scandal. But in its old rooms and long corridors there is a whisper of history, like the sound of the sea in shells.

The courthouse was designed with great expectations. By the time the Tweed Ring finished with it, however, it looked more like a cross between Middle Tweed and Late Sweeny. It exceeded by more than four times the cost for the Houses of Parliament. It cost nearly twice as much as the whole of Alaska.

The house that Tweed built was actually begun years before the Tweed Ring was formed. In 1858, the distinguished architect John Kellum (who had designed

the *New York Herald* building) completed the designs for the new Courthouse. Here was to be a Corinthian marvel signifying the greatness of New York
and the sanctity of the law. Except for
providing for the site in City Hall Park,
little was done until 1862 when, by no
coincidence, William Tweed became president of the Board of Supervisors. There
had been a legal wrangle over who should
appropriate funds for the new building:
the State, by a Board of Commissioners,
or the City, by the Board of Supervisors.
It was Tweed's artful persuasion that won
the case for the City. Thereafter appropriations became particularly brisk.

The enactment law of 1858 stated
specifically that the building, with all its
furnishings, should not cost more that
$250,000. But this was hardly enough,
argued Tweed, to build a fitting tribute to
the city and to the law. The city fathers
complied, and $1,000,000 more was
authorized. In 1864 an additional
$800,000 was granted. But even this was
not enough. In 1865, $300,000 more was
appropriated, yet the very next year still
more money was needed, and Tweed lob-
bied successfully for an additional
$300,000.

When a further half million dollars was
granted in 1866, a reform group became
suspicious. It seemed a bit odd that
millions of the taxpayers' dollars had produced a courthouse that was still not finished, except for one corner occupied for
only a few weeks during the year by the
Court of Appeals. The reformers indig-
nantly demanded an investigation. The
statesmen of the City and County of New
York were obliging, but their feelings

were somewhat ruffled. They pointed out
that the Board of Supervisors had already
set up a committee to investigate the
courthouse contracts. Nevertheless, to
serve justice, they established another
committee, christening it the Special
Committee to Investigate the Courthouse.
This committee was to investigate the
investigating Committee of Supervisors
who were investigating the courthouse.

The Special Committee took a remarkably short time to declare that the investigating committee, the contracts, and the
courthouse were free from fraud. The reformers were appalled, but what was
acutely exasperating was that the Special
Committee had taken this opportunity to
investigate its own chances for graft. For
just *twelve* days' work, the Special Committee submitted this bill of expenses:
$2938 for a clerk and stenographer; $900
for legal counsel; $6389 to the *Transcript*
(a journal owned by Boss Tweed) for
publishing the report of the original investigating committee, the Committee on
Investigation; $205 to one George W.
Roome, for "meals furnished"; and
$7718.75 to the New York Printing Com-
pany (owned by Boss Tweed) for printing
5000 copies of its own investigation report, making a grand total, for what was
now called the Notorious Investigating
Committee, of $18,460.35. The Mayor of
New York, John Hoffman, had little to
say. After this slight interruption, business went on as usual.

The tempo now increased as the
Tweed Ring expanded its power in the
city and state. The State legislature authorized the Board of Superivisors to
spend more money. But this was not

153

enough, and the City donated $6,967,893.24 more. "Just imagine," said a newspaper, "the untiring industry, the wear and tear of muscle, the anxiety of mind, the weary days and sleepless nights, that it must have cost the 'Boss' to procure all these sums of money." Thus from 1858 to 1871 the courthouse had suffered awesome growing pains. In thirteen years, more than $13 million had been spent—and it still was not finished.

When New Yorkers realized in 1871 that their courthouse had been the instrument for graft, one of their first questions was, how was this incredible swindle managed? What astonished, angered, and perhaps embarrassed New Yorkers was that the Ring, confident of its power, contemptuous of detection, had employed tactics so simple that they were conspicuously brazen.

The scheme hinged upon each Ringman's playing his role according to his particular talent and position. Boss Tweed was left free of dreary administrative detail to operate on the higher levels of decision-making and to exercise his charm—always enhanced by a bulging pocketbook—among his colleagues in the city and in the State legislature. To assist him in the subtle art of political persuasion, Tweed, like most successful executives, was able to call upon a resourceful and imaginative aid—Peter Barr Sweeny.

The scheme was launched when Tweed and Sweeny made arrangements with businessmen of easy conscience, the contractors of the courthouse. The operation then swung into the bailiwick of Richard Connolly, the City Comptroller, and his right-hand man, the ex-convict James

Watson, the County Auditor. It was Connolly's job as the Ring's bookkeeper and financial expert to supervise the assault on the soft underbelly of the city treasury.

The contractor submitted a bill for his work, so ill-disguised that the most untutored could recognize it as being padded to its final decimal point. Connolly made sure that the Ring received 65 per cent as its commission, with 35 per cent going to the contractor. He then drew up payments, or warrants, which he and Watson approved. Boss Tweed, in turn, "persuaded" the Board of Supervisors to give its official approval to the warrants. When in 1870 this authority was shifted to a Board of Courthouse Commissioners as a reform move, the Boss was equal to the occasion. Using his position in the State legislature, Tweed made sure that appointive power lay with the Mayor, and the congenial Oakey Hall thereby packed the Board with four Tammany buffs: Mike Norton, James Ingersoll, Thomas Coman, and John J. Walsh. At first there was unexpected trouble. The Commissioners were not agreeable to certifying bills for the current courthouse appropriation of $600,000. Watson, the paymaster, was as canny as Connolly was slippery. He immediately made up $600,000 worth of vouchers and expedited them before the Commissioners took office. It was not long before two of the Commissioners—Walsh and Norton—changed their minds and agreed to take a cut of 5 per cent.

The operation then reached its final stage, as the fraudulent warrants were placed under the authority of the Mayor of New York, Abraham Oakey Hall. When he, as the highest officer in city government, signed the padded courthouse warrants, the deed was done.

What made the building of the County Courthouse a classic in the annals of American graft was the way in which money was spent. As Robert Roosevelt, one of the reformers, put it, the bills rendered by the Ring's contractors were "not merely monstrous, they are manifestly fabulous." For example, for just three tables and forty chairs, the city paid to the penny, $179,729.60. Roscoe Conkling, a Republican leader in New York state, complained that more money was spent for furnishings than it cost the Grant Administration to run the United States mail service, as much as the yearly cost of collecting the customs revenue, and nearly three times as much as the entire diplomatic expenses for two years. Conkling was referring to expenses for furniture, carpets, and shades supplied by the James Ingersoll Company, a faithful tool of the Tweed Ring. The total expense was "the rather startling sum" of $5,691,144.26. Fascinated by the charge of $350,000 for carpets alone, the *New York Times* asked Ingersoll for an explanation. "There is one thing you people down in the *Times* don't seem to take into account," was the angry reply, "the carpets in these public buildings need to be changed a great deal oftener than in private houses." The *Times* concluded that the city had been overcharged $336,821.31.

John Keyser, the plumber, surpassed the fees of even his highly paid colleagues of today. He received nearly a million and

a half dollars for "plumbing and gas light fixtures." It was estimated that in one year alone, Keyser made over a million dollars.

Compared to Ingersoll and Keyser, Tweed's carpenter, "Lucky" George S. Miller, submitted puny expenses. Lumber not worth more than $48,000 cost the city $460,000. Miller, who kept a fine, large lithograph of Boss Tweed in his office, was apparently a fast worker. He was paid $360,747.61 for one month's work. All this was rather odd because little carpentry was needed, as the building was made primarily of iron and marble. As for the marble, it was supplied by a quarry owned by the Boss, and the *New York Times* claimed it cost more to quarry marble than it cost to build the entire courthouse in Brooklyn.

Thy prices for safes and awnings suggested an obsession with security and shade. J. McBride Davidson, who maintained a private bar in his office for select politicians, charged over $400,000 for safes (door locks cost $2676.75). James W. Smith charged $150 apiece for 160 awnings. Considering this, plus the charge for carpentry, a newspaper calculated each courthouse window was costing an astounding $8000. Smith defended himself by saying his charge for awnings including taking them down in the fall, putting them up again in the summer, and repairing them, and therefore he was entitled to every cent he charged. Another manufacturer said, however, the awnings were worth not more than $12.50 apiece.

When a person is building a house he does not expect the architect to send him a huge bill for repairs. Yet the house that

Tweed built cost the taxpayers of New York nearly two million dollars in repairs before the building was ever finished. In one year Garvey, the "Prince of Plasterers," charged the city $500,000 for plastering, and a million dollars for repairing the same work. His bill for a three-year plastering job on an iron and marble building was $2,870,464.06—the *Times* suggested the six cents be donated to charity—and of this $1,294,685.13 went for repairs! It was estimated that an honest plasterer could have done the job for $20,000. For "repairing and altering wood work," Tweed's carpenter George Miller was paid nearly $800,000.

For all the shocking displays of greed, there was sprinkled throughout the Ring's secret account books evidence of good humor, a certain dash, a feeling that here were men who really enjoyed their work. For example, two checks dated December 28, 1869, and December 31, 1869, were made out to Fillippo Donaruma. The first check was endorsed by "Philip F. Dummey," the second by "Fillip Dummin." Together the checks amounted to over $66,000. Another check was made out to T. C. Cash for $64,000. And wedged in among columns of massive figures was this masterpiece of understatement: "Brooms, etc., . . .$41,190.95." A devil-may-care attitude, or just plain sloppiness, was displayed when in no less than thirteen instances the day upon which large fraudulent payments were made was Sunday.

Then there was the astonishing charge for thermometers. Tweed bought eleven thermometers for the new courthouse, each five feet in length and one foot in breadth and encased in heavily carved frames. The faces were made of inexpensive paper, highly varnished and badly painted. Everything about them was cheap. The taxpayers paid for those eleven thermometers exactly $7500. A reporter asked a reputable thermometer manufacturer what he could supply with this amount. "For $7500," he said, "I could line the courthouse."

The New York Printing Company's charge of $186,000 for stationery was unique. Since it included the printing of all the reams of contractors' bills—and repair bills—it does have a ring of honesty to it.

While the Boss busily built and rebuilt New York's Corinthian marvel, he did not overlook the opportunity to use the courthouse as a rich patronage mine. The courthouse became another way to woo the immigrant by giving him a job as well as to reward the political faithful. Thus Jim "Maneater" Cusick, a prize-fighter, was graduated from Sing Sing to become a Court Clerk. William Long, alias Pudding Long, was made a court "Interpreter." He could neither read nor write. But no one seemed to mind. He spent most of his time looking after Boss Tweed's valuable kennel. M. E. Flanagan, Thomas Connor, James Carty, Thomas Pender, and William Runnett were on the payroll. They were all dead—but mysteriously their pay went on. As the *New York Times* said, "What's in a name?"

The basement of the new courthouse was so crowded with political appointees that it must have resembled the Black Hole of Calcutta. For just one job, the maintenance of the heating apparatus, thirty-two men were employed as engineers, firemen, secretaries, clerks, messengers, and inspectors. For this the city paid $42,000 in wages. But even this veritable army could not do the job. A basement engineer complained to Tweed that his contractors were sending him boilers of such poor quality that not one could produce more than 50 pounds of pressure!

When the Tweed Ring was exposed in 1871, it became a game to calculate how far, placed end to end, the chairs, carpets, awnings, shades, etc., would reach. An historian of Tammany Hall said that some mathematicians got as far as China before they finished. One newspaper reckoned that the 122,222 square yards of carpeting would reach nearly from New York to New Haven, or halfway to Albany, or from Albany to Oswego, or four times from the Battery to Yonkers.

The exposure also inspired several New Yorkers to visit their new courthouse. Although they realized that corruption had been at work, they expected to see some kind of magnificence for their thirteen million dollars. Instead they found a waste of masonry, a gloomy maze of dirty rooms, dark halls, and ugly walls, resembling more an ancient ruin than a new, unfinished building. In 1871, after thirteen years of construction work, one of the largest rooms, the Bureau of Arrears of Taxes, had no roof. The County Clerk's office, Sheriff's office, and office of the Surrogate were not carpeted but were covered with oilcloth and grimy matting. The walls were filthy, and in many places large chunks of plaster had peeled off, leaving ugly blotches—a fitting tribute to Garvey and his repair bills. The *New York Times* concluded that a stranger visiting the courthouse would think the city officials were the

most economical, indeed, the most miserly of men. Charles Nordhoff expected to find something of a mansion, since he had heard that Ingersoll had made Tweed's stable a marvel of fine wood and expensive furniture and that the mighty plasterer, Andrew Garvey, had once worked on Vassar College. Instead, he found that only the old City Hall was dirtier and more dilapidated than the new courthouse.

The prominent reformer George C. Barrett made his pilgrimage and came away shocked. His impression left no doubt that the city must long endure a reminder of the most audacious swindle in its history. "It might be considered," he said, "that the cornerstone of the temple was conceived in sin, and its dome, if ever finished, will be glazed all over with iniquity. The whole atmosphere is corrupt. You look up at its ceilings and find gaudy decorations; you wonder which is the greatest, the vulgarity or the corruptness of the place."

A few months after Barrett made his observation, the Tweed Ring was smashed, and Tammany braves scattered. But the courthouse remained. As the years went by, the scandals of the Tweed Ring softened into just another memory of old New York, but this was one which Tweed had made certain would not be forgotten. The shabby little building in City Hall Park, the house that Tweed built, was as unforgettable a memorial as a statue in Times Square. And Tweed had provided his own epitaph. When he arrived at prison to begin his sentence, the warden asked him what his profession was. The Boss, in a clear, strong voice, answered, "Statesman!"

VOTE
EARLY AND OFTEN

Alexander B. Callow, Jr.

When Americans go to the polls these days, Election Day will probably be a quiet one. But in the days of the city boss, from the Civil War to well into the 20th century, elections were riotous affairs in which brawls, bribery and intimidation of voters were common practices throughout the country, but especially in the big cities.

In times of crises, when an election promised to be close, or the city machine was challenged by a reform movement, political bosses of both parties acted accordingly. From South of the Slot in San Francisco to the Strip in Pittsburgh, from the North Side in Kansas City to the South Side in Chicago, they mustered an army from the saloons, flophouses and gambling dens and sent them to the polls to vote early and often, stuff ballot boxes, destroy rival voting booths—and each other.

From *The New York Times Magazine* (Sept. 27, 1964), pp. 60-66. © 1964 by the New York Times Company. Reprinted by permission.

No better example of fabled American ingenuity can be found than the techniques used in cheating at the polls. The first trick in any wholesale election fraud was for ward heelers and corrupt election officials to pad the registration lists with phony names and addresses. They did so with an imagination that was breathtaking. Names of persons in jail, in the hospitals, in the cemeteries or simply nonexistent were added with cavalier abandon.

An angry Philadelphia newspaper once printed the pictures of a dog and a 4-year-old boy listed on the registry. Lincoln Steffens recalled a campaigning Philadelphia politician who, after reminding his audience that Independence Hall was in his ward, went on to name the signers of the Declaration of Independence. "These men," he said, "the fathers of American liberty, voted down here once. And," he added with a sly grin, "they vote here yet."

The next step in rigging elections was to recruit men, known as "repeaters," to vote the fraudulent names. Particularly resourceful were the tiny, flinty-eyed saloonkeeper, Hinky Dink Kenna, and Bathhouse John Coughlin, lords of Chicago's wicked First Ward, the best of all possible wards—for vice and corruption. They brought in voters from the Hospital for the Insane at Dunning. It was said that Hinky Dink, a Democrat, found the Dunning inmates more astute politically than the most erudite of Republicans.

Hinky Dink and Bathhouse John also took advantage of woman suffrage. On election day their lieutenants, Make-a-Fuss Wilson and John (Mushmouth) Johnson, recruited hordes of ladies of joy still in their working clothes from such places as the Bucket of Blood, Black May's, the House of All Nations and a place whimsically called "Why Not?"

Immigrants proved ready recruits for the bosses' election armies, because the bosses played like virtuosos on their ignorance of political issues and on their old world prejudices. In New York City Tim Campbell, an old Tammany leader, made this clear in a classic speech in his Irish district (his opponent was an Italian named Rinaldo).

"There is two bills before the country—the Mills bill and the McKinley bill," Campbell declared. "The Mills bill is for free trade with everything free; the McKinley bill is for protection with nothing free. Do you want everything free or do you want to pay for everything?

"Having thus disposed of the national issue, I will now devote myself to the local issue, which is the Dago Rinaldo. He is from Italy. I am from Ireland. Are you in favor of Italy or Ireland?

"Having thus disposed of the local issue and thanking you for your attention, I will now retire."

Big Tim Sullivan, a tough Tammany Hall buff alias Dry Dollar Sullivan (he was once found drying off a revenue stamp from a brewery keg under the impression it was a dollar), argued that repeaters had to have whiskers:

"When you've voted 'em with their whiskers on, you take 'em to a barber and scrape off the chin fringe. Then you vote 'em again with the side lilacs and a mustache. Then to a barber again, off comes the sides and you vote 'em a third time with the mustache. If that ain't enough and the box can stand a few more ballots, clean off the mustache and vote 'em plain face. That makes every one of 'em good for four votes."

Often repeaters voted under bona fide names and legitimate voters arrived at the polls to be greeted with "Mr. ——, you've already voted."

One election official told the story of a repeater who, when asked his name at one polling place, identified himself as "William Croswell Doane," a prominent Episcopal clergyman.

"Come off," said the official. "You're not Bishop Doane."

"The hell I ain't, you bastard!" said the voter.

Another weapon in the bosses' arsenal of fraud was the gangs of barroom gladiators hired to intimidate and terrorize the legitimate voter. Thus a respectable citizen who seemed likely to vote the "wrong" ticket might find himself slugged and thrown into the street, where, as one observer reported, "He would meditate on the beauties of our free institutions for a few moments, and depart, a sadder if not wiser man."

At least this was better than what happened to a voter in a wild election in 1856 in New York City. When he voted against Tammany, his nose was shot off. (It was reported that he was consoled by an onlooker who told him that his face was less ugly now.)

And then there were the ladies. Gallus Mag, Sadie the Goat and Euchre Kate Burns, the champion heavyweight female brick hurler of New York, were specialists in election-day mayhem. Hell-Cat Maggie filed her front teeth to points and wore long artificial nails made of brass on her fingers. When she unleashed her battle cry and dashed biting and clawing into a polling place, even the bravest of men lost their poise. The huge and violent Battle Annie, the sweetheart of Hell's Kitchen, was a terrifying bully. She commanded a gang of blood-thirsty females called the Battle Row Ladies' Social and Athletic Club.

The bosses' control over repeaters, the courts, the police and organized crime often led to the ultimate form of intimidation: the election-day massacre. The bloodiest of them all occurred in the present century and has gone down in Kansas City history as Bloody Tuesday.

When the polls closed on March 27, 1934, machine-gunnings, pistol-whippings and blackjackings added up to four murders, eleven cases of critical injuries, more than 200 cases of assault and Tom Pendergast's machine ticket returned to

office by a margin of 59,000 votes. Boss Buckley of San Francisco put it well: "The game of politics is not a branch of the Sunday school business."

Fraud during election hours was one thing, but it did not end with the closing of the polls. When election officials counted the votes, the laws of mathematics were subject to political necessity. The bosses nominated election officials more for their party loyalty than for their devotion to civic duty, like the Philadelphia official who returned 252 votes from a precinct which had only 100 registered voters. Perhaps anticipating accusations of fraud, election officers appointed by Boss Tweed of New York protected themselves morally by being sworn in not upon the Bible but on Ollendorf's "New Method of Learning to Read, Write and Speak French."

Election officials had an imaginative repertory of tricks. Ballots were switched. In one New York election, an official simply dropped ballots on the floor, substituting for them a pile of previously marked tickets he had beside him. When a voter protested, the official threatened him, a man kicked him, another punched him in the mouth and a policeman arrested him.

Ballot boxes in New York were often stuffed with additional ballots. A Boston politician was once asked if any such thing went on in his home town. He answered with an emphatic "No! Ballot boxes are never stuffed unless it's absolutely necessary!"

Ballots were also invalidated. In Chicago, deft fellows known as "short-pencil men" palmed pencil stubs in their hands. As they counted the votes, they added a cross mark to each opposition ballot; such ballots, with both candidates marked, were thus invalid.

In the rogues gallery of American city bosses, there was one rascal endowed with such infinite guile that he did not always have to resort to such crudities as repeaters or crooked election officials. He was the charming, quick-witted James Michael Curley of Boston.

When he was running against Thomas M. Joyce for Congress, Boss Curley performed an election masterpiece. Curley sent his supporters out in the very early hours of election day with instructions to ring doorbells. When the enraged citizen, groggy with sleep, stumbled out of bed, opened the door and asked why in the hell he was being awakened at this unholy hour, Curley's boys merely said they wanted to be sure he was going to vote for Thomas Joyce. The usual response was something to the effect that "I wouldn't vote for that son-of-a-bitch if he were . . ." As Curley said, "Do others or they will do you."

Fraud still plays a part in the American way of voting. In recent years, "irregularities" at the polls were reported in Chicago, New York and Philadelphia. Indeed, it is not unlikely that some may occur in a Presidential election. Nevertheless, the days of the massive, wholesale election fraud are gone forever. The secret ballot, the voting machine and permanent registration have not eliminated fraud, but they have tamed the wild and sly ways of the old-fashioned city boss.

One ancient relic from the good old days was sorry to see them go. "Elections nowadays are sissy affairs," he wrote. "Nobody gets killed anymore and the ambulances and patrol wagons stay in their garages. . . . It was wonderful to see how my men slugged the opposition to preserve the sanctity of the ballot and stop the corruption of Tammany Hall."

THE NEW LOCUS
OF CORRUPTION

Edward N. Costikyan

Just as our ideas about good city government are largely the product of confusing a symptom of bad government with its cause, so our defenses against the symptom of bad government—corruption—are the product of the same confusion. In narrow obedience to our tradition, the principal defense against corruption continues to be an attempt to keep political leaders out of the government process. Nothing more is thought necessary to mind the store.

This defense presupposes that political leaders as a group are less honest and more likely to engage in nefarious conduct than other groups such as lawyers, businessmen, and civil servants. The evidence to support this assumption is flimsy at best. I do not have the statistics, but I suspect that the percentage of political leaders convicted of crime is far less than the percentage of political leaders in the population. It is not, for example,

unusual to read in the press of businessmen or lawyers of doctors convicted of income-tax evasion or some other crime of corruption. The back pages usually suffice to carry this not unusual news. But let a charge of corruption be even leveled at a political leader and it is front-page news. Even the prominence accorded to such news is not sufficient in itself to justify the assumption that underlies our defenses against government corruption: that the political leaders are the likeliest causes of the disease.

I reject this assumption.

In my experience it is not true.

That is not to say that all political leaders are honest and incorruptible. They are not, and I know they are not, but I reject the popular assumption about the frail honesty of political leaders, even though I acknowledge that they, like all human beings, are corruptible and from time to time are corrupted.

Indeed, the last thing a serious practitioner of the political process can afford is to be naïve about the possibility of corruption. There is nothing worse than having your own people stealing behind your back. If they do steal, the defect, while hardly yours at law, does not make them less your people in the public's eye. And the public—though it may forget and forgive—will not be wrong. They were your people. You put them there. That you called the police, and they were fined and their offices cleaned out as soon as possible, does not quite take the smell out of the air. For his own effectiveness, then, as well as for his own self-respect, the politician may never forget that men and women who can be corrupted are always in sufficient supply.

A serious politician allows his power to be exercised by subordinates only so long as he trusts them. The flow of power to a subordinate responds with the utmost delicacy to the eddies of disquiet which corruption—or the suspicion of it—inevitably sets in motion.

It is not a particular group of people that is the magnet which attracts corrupters. Power, and power alone, attracts. The natural locus of corruption is *always* where the discretionary power resides. It follows that in an era when political leaders exercised basic power over the government officials whom they controlled, the locus of corruption was in the offices of the political bosses—Tweed, Croker, Kelly, and the rest. But as power has shifted from the political leader to the civil servant and the public office-holder, so the locus of corruptibility and of corruption has shifted. The evidence demonstrates this clearly, and yet little attention is paid to the evidence, because the old myths and preconceptions are too strong.

Let us first put aside the few cases that

invite public attention because the items involved are so easily understood. For example, an Oriental rug given to a political official is something the ordinary voter comprehends. Many millions of dollars in a Dixon-Yates contract (involving no political leaders) is not. A bathtub given to a political leader is understood. A television-antenna franchise awarded to businessmen is not. A deep-freeze given to a political leader is understood. Stocking a substantial part of a retired general's farm with cattle from wealthy friends is not. But the deep-freezes and the vicuna coats and the bathtubs and the Oriental rugs are not the great danger to honest government. It is the relationship reflected by these gifts that causes the problem.

The question of whether Sherman Adams used his public power to help his friend Bernard Goldfine is more disturbing than the hospitality enjoyed and gifts received by Adams. Indeed, these gifts are neither the stuff with which corruption is accomplished, nor the subject matter of political deals. The real corrupters rarely leave tangible evidence of where they have been and what they have sought.

Those who seek the benefit of licit and illicit government favors are nothing if not perfectly attuned to shifts in power, and they instinctively go where the power is. What needs to be made clear is that the power is no longer in the hands of political leaders. It has been transferred to the hands of public officials and civil servants long since.

So why deal through a political leader when you can go direct to the source of power? Why contribute to the party when you get more consideration by making your contribution to the candidate himself? Why deal with secondary sources when the primary source is an independent, uncontrolled civil servant?

When a parking-meter company's public relations expert sought to create a "bribe plot," in order, as it later developed, to pocket the bribe himself, the person whose name he invoked as the recipient of the bribe was a former career civil servant, then high in the city government, not a political leader. In 1961, one newspaper, intent upon attempting to discredit the Wagner administration, ran a box-score of "scandals" day after day; I remember that it got as high as twenty-one or twenty-two "scandals." With *one* exception, every one of the "scandals" involved civil servants, not political leaders or appointees. By the same token, Republican strategists, in early 1965, before Congressman John Lindsay decided to run for mayor, were reported to be disheartened at the prospects of "fusion" because fusion had never succeeded in the absence of wide-spread *political* scandals.

Does the absence of political scandal mean there is no corruption? Of course not. It means that corruption has taken new forms and found a new locus.

By "corruption" I mean not only the use of a consideration such as money to persuade government to do something it shouldn't, although that is one form of corruption. There are other forms: the exercise of discretion to award a government privilege to an old friend as against an equally or better qualified applicant is a form of corruption. The tender treatment of a regulated industry by a regula-

tory commission whose members look to an ultimate future in private industry is a form of it. In short, corruption is the exercise of governmental power to achieve nongovernmental objectives.

From the point of view of the public and competing aspirants, what difference does it make whether the consideration for such an exercise of power is cash, or friendship, or future campaign contributions, or a future job, or nothing?

For example, since World War II a massive government-sponsored housing program has been carried on almost continuously in one form or another. The essence of the slum-clearance program has been to encourage private enterprise by almost guaranteeing builders a substantial profit and perhaps a windfall. The essence of the program—"Title I" or "urban renewal"—is for government to acquire slum properties at market value and resell them (or make them available) to private builders or sponsors at a lower cost. The subsidy is supposed to permit the construction of housing that will rent—or in the case of co-operatives, sell—at lower prices than would otherwise obtain.

The rule is that the sponsor is selected through the exercise of discretion among a host of applicants who are for all measurable purposes equally qualified. Why is A selected, instead of B or C, to sponsor or build such a development? There is no public bidding; no objective measure of who ought to be selected is applied.

Under current practices a "project" for a given area is developed by government officials and approved. A "sponsor" of the development, who is in charge of carrying it out and controls it, is then selected by government officials. The sponsor selects a builder, an architect, a lawyer, an accountant, insurance broker, and all of the rest of the retinue needed to build a complex of buildings, hires them through a corporation organized to build the project, secures financing, and sees that the development is created.

The power to designate these participants is a valuable one. The architect, the lawyer, the insurance broker, may be prepared to share their profits with the source of business. The possibilities for profit to the sponsor are substantial. Certainly the builder, the lawyers, the architect, and the insurance broker are all well compensated.

"Title I," urban renewal's predecessor, was administered by Robert Moses, that conspicuous agent of good government. He and his varied Public Authorities, accountable to no one ("since there are no politicians involved, it must be honest, so why should it have to account?") are a monument to the anti-political good-government tradition of "keep the politicians out and it will be okay."

Moses' administration of Title I was so unsatisfactory that the program was killed. If a political leader had made one-tenth of the mistakes Moses made in that program alone, he would have been destroyed, defeated, out of business. Arbitrariness; designation of favored associates for choice patronage, high salaries, limousines, and chauffeurs; and invulnerability to any requirement of public accountability or auditing of accounts are the earmarks of an entrenched machine. Moses' Public Authorities have them all.

Moses' reward for so directing his many enterprises has been continuing editorial adulation, new jobs, constant praise, and finally the opportunity to run the greatest boondoggle of them all, the 1964–65 New York World's Fair—again, because he is politically pure and deemed to be "efficient."

The potential for abuse in such a setup could not have escaped the attention of those who seek the pleasures of governmental favor. Who would not prefer the favors of an anonymous Public Authority, which is not subject to public accountability, to the friendship of a political boss. (Moses' critics have repeatedly suggested that his authorities should be subjected to methodical public examination. All to no avail.)

Probably the reason is Moses' accepted and undisputed personal honesty in money matters. But this begs the question. Personal honesty is the *first* requirement for public service, not the only one. And, as noted above, corruption as I have used the term does not require cash as a consideration. There are subtler and more utilitarian forms—future support, campaign contributions, honorific appointments, even ill-defined debts and obligations available for later redemption, or merely old friendships—or whim!

The irregularities in the Moses operation of Title I are well documented elsewhere. Their significance, however, as a demonstration of the new locus of corruption has been generally disregarded—except, I suspect, by the corrupters.

What of the Title I's successor—urban renewal? Here again a sponsorship is a valuable asset. Anyone schooled in traditional notions about good government would expect to find the politician's heavy hand allocating sponsorships and designating builders, architects, and the like.

There were political leaders involved in the process, but as supplicants for favors, not dispensers of them. My successor as county leader, J. Raymond Jones, a Harlem political leader, was the most notable of these. Jones's dealings in urban renewal projects—he became a sponsor of at least one major project—came to light when he and Congressman Adam Clayton Powell had a falling out about one project, and a lawsuit was started in which Powell claimed that a sponsorship which was to have been awarded to a company in which they were both interested was at the last moment awarded to a company in which Jones was interested but Powell was not.

Decisions on sponsorships of these projects were made on the very highest level of city government—not by any political leaders. The political leaders, except occasionally as supplicants, played no role in the process. But I cannot believe that their absence rendered the projects 99 44/100 per cent pure. For the discretionary power to designate sponsors carries with it all the conditions that inevitably lead to "influence" and influence-peddling. If indeed these sponsorships have value, why shouldn't they be *sold* by government to the highest bidder, instead of given away? If an FCC license to operate a television station is of great value, why not have the government *sell* it, instead of giving it to one of half a dozen equally qualified applicants?

The gift of public privileges by government officials on a discretionary basis in the absence of public bidding is the greatest source of corruption, quasi-corruption, influenced-peddling, and demeaning of the governmental process in America today. That distribution of public largess is more and more nonpolitical does not make it any better. Indeed, as in so many other cases, the division of power between political leaders and public officeholders might tend to diminish the opportunities for overt corruption in the dispensation of such government favors. But the greatest preventive would be to charge for the value of the government privileges being dispensed.

A classic example of the whole problem is the tale of the television-antenna franchise in New York City, which briefly attracted public attention in the spring of 1965. Six applicants sought the privilege of running master television antennas beneath New York City's streets, and charging residents at stipulated rates for connecting into the master antenna and thus securing first-rate reception. In some areas of the city where high buildings block reception (especially public housing projects), such a service was badly needed.

The proposed charges and rates varied from a $60 connection charge to $19.95, and from $20 a month service fee to $4.50. Some of the applicants had had extensive prior experience in operating such systems and some had not. Lo and behold, the two approved franchisers had the least experience and the highest charges of all the applicants. According to the New York *World-Telegram and Sun*, one of the two successful applicants had some unexplained connection with a former legislative representative and close confidant of the mayor. This mayoral friend had been involved in the process of securing the franchise. The other successful applicant was a firm headed by another old mayoral friend. Both had cut their proposed fees (although they were still well above those of the other applicants). What is more, according to the New York *World-Telegram and Sun*, the cuts had been made by the head of the Bureau of Franchises at the *mayor's* suggestion. No political leaders were involved in any way with the successful applicants (what a departure from the days of Boss Tweed!), so it was okay. One unsuccessful applicant was represented by the law firm to which New York County's former law chairman belonged. And one of my partners—by then I had retired as a political leader—represented another unsuccessful applicant.

If the myths were true, should not the ex-Tammany law chairman's client and the ex-county-leader's partner's client have triumphed—especially since their rates were lowest and their experience greatest?

The point, it seems to me, is clear. The pathway to government preference no longer passes through Tammany Hall or the internal political leader's office. It goes direct to the source. This phenomenon of modern urban government has hardly been noted by the theorists or the specialists in good government. They seem to be so convinced that civil service and grwoth of the public officeholder's independence have created such impregnable fortresses of rectitude that they have devoted all their attention when discussing corruption to looking for political

leaders in the governmental process. Noting their absence, the good-government forces viewing a veritable parade of nude emperors have been satisfied that corruption has disappeared.

Indeed, not long ago this preconception so dominated the thinking of those investigating the city government that they laid a colossal egg. In 1959 the state legislature created a "Little Hoover Commission" to investigate New York City. The commission's activities were supposed to expose enough political corruption to lay the basis for a 1961 fusion movement to defeat Mayor Wagner. The Commission and its staff honestly believed, I think, that New York City was beset by the same conditions of political corruption that had laid the basis for the 1933 election of La Guardia. The staff apparently immersed itself in the literature of corruption, particularly that revealed by the Seabury Commission, which uncovered and documented the shenanigans of the political leaders of the 1930s. They had fixed judges and commissioners, sold contracts, and generally operated the city through the public officeholder nominees they controlled. (When one of their designees, Mayor O'Brien, was asked in 1933 who his police commissioner would be, he replied: "I don't know. They haven't told me yet." And he was telling the truth!) But thirty years later, the pattern wasn't there. The corruption was among civil servants—usually lowly ones—and it was minor nickels-and-dimes stuff, not the classic corruption of the Tweed era.

Yet, obsessed by their preconceptions about what *ought* to be wrong (i.e., crooked politicians, not dishonest civil servants), the investigators never realized that what had been established was a shift in the nature and locus of corruption from the socially despicable politician middleman to the socially acceptable reform product—the civil servant, the career government servant, the elected public official who was free of domination by the machine. What had happened was that the corrupters, like water, had found their own level—underpaid and frustrated civil servants who yearned for a more affluent life, or ambitious public office-holders hoping to make affluent friends upon whom they could call when campaign funds were needed.

The frustrated civil servants do not represent any real threat to government. Their number is low and the graft is comparatively small, and no serious student of government would attribute to this kind of activity the manifold faults of modern urban misgovernment.

Of course, petty corruption remains a heavy burden to the person who must endure it. The construction of buildings in New York, for example, is still reported to involve substantial amounts in ten- and twenty-dollar payments to inspectors. How much of this gets to the inspector and how much is an excuse for the builder to get a little tax-free income ("petty cash" in his books) is anyone's guess.

But several things are clear. First, the supposition that such bribery exists, whether the supposition is true or not, saps popular confidence in government. Second, none of the principal defenses built up to protect government from corruption—the isolation and elimination of the politician from government—have had any success in eliminating the occasional bribery of civil servants.

My own belief is that the amount of such corruption is exaggerated, that the overwhelming bulk of civil servants are honest and that, like politicians, they have about the same percentage of corruptible people as the population at large—or less.

The real threat posed by corruption to good government is the fact that, as the form and locus of corruption has shifted from the middleman politician to the civil servant or elected official, so has the technique of receiving discretionary governmental largess.

The corrupter seeking to lease the Brooklyn Bridge for a dollar a year in exchange for $100,000 in cash, or engaged in an effort to accomplish such misbehavior, is a political and governmental joke. Nobody pays any attention to him. Moreover, the political graft of the Tweed and post-Tweed eras—liquor, prostitution, police protection and the like—is simply nonexistent (unless it is a direct deal between criminal and civil-servant policeman).

"Graft" today, if it can be called that, is the kind described by George Washington Plunkitt as "honest graft"—only now it is more "honest" by far. In short, the political plums today are nonpolitical: urban-renewal projects, contracts to build schools and public buildings and roads and sewers, franchises to install community television antenna systems, and what have you—all involving government funds or privileges, with contracts given for value received with built-in profit of varying amounts, and all disbursed on a *discretionary* basis.

When the time comes to raise funds for the public officeholder who dispensed that favor, or this sponsorship, he has a ready-made list of potential contributors, just as Charles Murphy and Boss Tweed and their predecessors did—the recipients of discretionary public largess.

Should a portrait be painted and presented to the city? Run down the list! And before you know it a patron has hired a portraitist. The patron, moreover, has a tax-deduction. He is, of course, a public benefactor, not a political wheeler-dealer.

Sometimes the cloak of purity achieved through association with public officeholders instead of dirty political leaders reaches ridiculous proportions. For example, one prominent citizen, who, unlike the late Vice-President Alben Barkley, would far rather "sit at the feet of the mighty" than be a "servant of the Lord" is famed for his ability to move fireplugs on Park Avenue. The basis of his celebrity arises from the desire of Park Avenue building managements to have a "no parking" area near their front doors, so that tenants don't have to crawl between parked cars as they come and go. The best way to achieve this is to have a fire hydrant right next to the awning—that guarantees twelve feet of "no parking" on each side of it.

And so this scion of civic virtue specializes in securing fireplug movements in exchange for long-term retainers. He accomplishes these results (and Park Avenue's fireplugs have seen a fair amount of movement lately) not because of any relation with political leaders, but because of his nonpolitical, good-government status and his close friendships with significant public officeholders.

The locus of corruption is always where unrestrained power exists. The political leader's present function in the scheme of corruption is to be a scapegoat, who shields the self-styled public vindicator of political morality from public scrutiny. After all, so long as the "bosses" exist, their opponents, being saints, should be protected. So long as the political leaders are excluded from the process, why is it necessary to inquire why fire hydrants are moved or how urban-renewal-project sponsorships are allocated?

Of course, I am sufficiently skeptical to be unable to believe that corruption will be eliminated from the conduct of human affairs, either by eliminating the power of political leaders or by restoring their power to what it once was. But I do believe there are ways to minimize the improper exercise of governmental power—ways that would make it more difficult for the corrupter to corrupt and easier to uncover him and his activities.

The first step is to realize that the locus of corruption is where the power is. The second is to destroy the stereotypes that brand the political leader as thief and the public official as saint. The third is to eliminate the discretionary distribution of governmental privileges—Title I housing projects, urban-renewal sponsorships (and construction contracts), public architecture contracts, and so on—without competition for either quality (where the arts are involved) or quantity (where money is involved).

Is there any good reason why every architect who wants to should not submit a design for a school or a courthouse and have the winning design selected on the basis of merit, utility, and decent cost ratios of the design, and not because of the name attached to it? Why should not an urban-renewal sponsorship, worth a million dollars to the sponsor, be awarded on the basis of price paid to the city, instead of unexplained "discretion"?

The reason why such discretion is granted to public officials—especially the "nonpolitical" ones—is the public supposition that since they are outside the traditional political structure, they, rather than the politician, should have power—and by some magic, rectitude will be achieved.

What has happened is that a new politics has been created, certainly no better and in some ways worse that the politics this "nonpolitical" politics has replaced. It is indeed time to re-examine the post-Tweed-era assumptions which have led to this new form of urban mismanagement.

The ideas I am suggesting seem at first blush to be radical, perhaps half-baked, certainly unusual. But it seems clear to me that in a city where the power is in the bureaucracy, the locus of corruption must also be there. And the discretionary exercise of power by bureaucrats is to be feared and needs to be dealt with at least as much as—probably far more than—the venality of Boss Tweed's successors.

❧ FIVE ❧
The Boss and the Reformer

❧ COMMENTARY ❧

The boss and the reformer are inseparable.

Without the reformer, the saga of the city boss in America is only half-told, and vice versa. Their confrontation exposed the raw sores of urban problems. Together they solved some of those problems as each sought the advantage over the other. Together they learned from each other, each borrowing his rival's strategy, tactics—and purple prose. In the war of words and the thunder of campaigns, the quality of urban government improved, the number of municipal services increased, and the question of how best to govern was revived. Together they helped build the city.

The American imagination has shaped the reformer, like the boss, into a stereotype, part fact, part fancy. Compared to his roly-poly, plug-ugly enemy, the reformer is envisaged as tall but trim, elegant but severe, with starched lips, soaring forehead, and chilly eyes—a tidy man with high-collar attitudes, indulging in souffléd political polemics. One might laugh at the Tammany chieftain John O'Brien, his aldermanic belly flopping as he took his daily jogging exercises in a gymsuit weighted down with religious medals. Reformers were not amusing. Paragons of self-righteousness solemnly preening their virtue, they may command respect but seldom affection.

In the confrontation between boss and reformer there was something majestic about the roar of rhetoric, and this helped considerably to create the stereotype of both the boss and the reformer. Listen to Dr. Charles Parkhurst, high on moral pepper, take on Tammany Hall: [they are] "a lying, perjured, rum soaked, and libidinous lot . . . polluted harpies that under the pretense of governing this city, are feeding day and night on its

quivering vitals." Alfred Steinberg, in *The Bosses*, describes how Boss
Crump of Memphis regarded the reformers. He described one as an "insipid ass, moron, unworthy, despicable, low filthy scoundrel, pervert, degenerate, . . . with the brains of a quagga" (an African wild donkey) . . . who
wrote "just as one would expect of a wanderoo" (a purple-faced ape).
"Now we come to that slimy rat, Joe Hatcher . . . a low, filthy, diseased
mind full of ululation" (a loud and shrill wailing). When some Boston
Brahmins labeled Boss Curley a thief, Curley countered with, "The term
'codfish aristocracy' is a reflection on the fish." For every variation on the
word "crook" hurled at the boss by the reformer, the boss replied with
"Goo-Goos," "Simon Pures," "Gold-plated Holies," or "YMCA Types"
for the reformer. "Silk hats and silk socks and nothing in between," as
Tim Sullivan called them.

If there is one critic in the literature of machine politics who best expresses the old-time politicians' contempt for the reformer, it is George
Washington Plunkitt, whose essay, "Reformers Only Mornin' Glories," is
the first selection of this chapter. Plunkitt quickly establishes his theme in
his second paragraph: "They were mornin' glories—looked lovely in the
mornin' and withered up in a short time, while the regular machines went
on flourishin' forever, like fine old oaks. Say, that's the first poetry I
ever worked off. Ain't it great?"

Just as the first step in understanding the boss was to shatter the myth
about him, this is necessary as well for his arch-rival. It is true that many
reformers were pompous, pretentious, humorless, naïve, rigidly inflexible,
and suffocatingly holier-than-thou. One thinks of Samuel Tilden, cool,
austere, aloof, the ice man in the Prince Albert coat. If Seth Low was
humorless and naïve ("A politician can say "no" and make a friend," Lincoln Steffens wrote, "where Mr. Low will lose one by saying "yes".), Jane
Addams, the grand lady of American urban reform, was warm and knowledgeable. If Charles Eliot Norton was the haughty American version of an
aristocrat, distrustful of the masses, disenchanted with democracy, there
were earthy, compassionate reformers alive to the aspirations of the working class, committed to the democratic process, like Samuel M. "Golden
Rule" Jones of Toledo, and Tom Johnson of Cleveland. No one could ever
accuse Hazen S. Pingree of political naïveté. He incorporated the tactics
and techniques of machine politics in his reform administration in Detroit
in the 1890s. Fiorello La Guardia was no "morning glory." Tough and
street-wise, he beat Tammany at its own game.

It is one thing to repair the stereotype of the reformer, and quite another to make sense of urban reform itself. The subject of intensive research in recent years, especially concerning the Progressive era, it has so far defied consensus among historians. Urban reform is an intellectual problem of immense complexity, snarled in its own variety, contradictions, and shifting moods. Historians are firing the right questions but getting different answers. If reform implies social, economic, and political change—it is change to what, by whom and for what purpose? To capture a more perfect past or to cope with a better future? Reform for the "people"?—But what people? the businessman? the middle class? the poor? the workingman? the rich? Was it a success or a failure? Was it liberal or conservative? Searching questions all, provoking furious debate.

According to Richard Hofstadter, the movement was led by fairly affluent and well-educated members of the middle class who were tormented by "status anxieties." Inspired by the so-called "Protestant ethic," they sought to turn back to an older America, an imagined era of golden yesteryears, unrelated to the realities of a modern urban age. Samuel P. Hays challenged this "status revolution" theory, to argue that reform was in fact led by an upper-class group who, far from alienated by society, were experts in the techniques of business management and the newer technological procedures and sought to introduce them into city government. Then J. Joseph Hutchmacher and John D. Buenker countered with the thesis that the movement was led by liberal elements of the immigrant working-class. Gabriel Kolko struck back with the notion that reform was actually profoundly conservative, a triumph for the business community, whose members captured the movement to serve their own interests. Where Hofstadter saw reformers as naïve, and Samuel Hays found sharp anti-democratic overtones, Otis A. Pease argued that reformers were politically more astute and democratic than certain recent historians have given them credit for.[1]

As controversial and divergent as these interpretations are, a number of

1. See Richard Hofstadter, *The Age of Reform* (1955); Samuel P. Hays, "The Politics of Reform in Municipal Government in the Progressive Era," *Pacific Northwest Quarterly* (October 1964); J. Joseph Hutchmacher, "Urban Liberalism and the Age of Reform," *Mississippi Valley Historical Review* (September 1962); John D. Buenker, *Urban Liberalism and Progressive Reform* (1973); Gabriel Kolko, *The Triumph of Conservatism: A Re-Interpretation of American History, 1900-1916* (1963); Otis A. Pease, "Urban Reformers in the Progressive Era," *Pacific Northwest Quarterly* (April 1971).

points became clear in the debate. First, historians no longer view the re-former-boss confrontation as a simple morality play of the virtuous reformer, as David, battling the terrible Goliath. Indeed, some historians are wondering who *does* represent Goliath. Secondly, urban reform was diverse, reflecting the rich pluralism of American society. Over time, from the post-Civil War era to the present, there were all kinds of reformers with all kinds of reform, with a variety of platforms, values, tactics, and aspirations. The profusion and heterogeneity was a response to the chang-ing problems of the city, be it the flood of immigrants, the city's growing pains, the rise of industry, or the new instruments of technology. The confusion was intensified because reformers joined changing coalitions, depending upon the issues of the day.

In this seeming anarchy of diversity, there do emerge among reform movements certain similarities that suggest a kind of unity. Thus, while the reformers' motivation, tactics, and ideals might differ, there was a broad commonality in their goals. Most reformers sought, in one degree or another, more honesty, more efficiency, more democracy, and more and better municipal services. Above all, they shared a common target. In the jargon of our own time, they sought to make the boss and his machine inoperative.

To clarify the problem further, each of the remaining selections in this chapter was chosen to illustrate an event, or period, or turning point in the evolution of reform in the American city. "The Crusade Against the Tweed Ring," describes the attitudes of the genteel post-Civil War re-formers toward the boss, machine politics, corruption, the poor, and urban institutions. This essay analyses the crusade against one of the most notorious city machines in American urban history, a crusade ended in one of the most dramatic and ironic elections in New York City's history.

With the late 1880s, following the Tweed era, reform took on a new intensity and complexity, exploding like a skyrocket in all directions, re-flecting at once the growing demands of rapid urbanization, the new con-ditions calling for technological innovation, and awareness of the need to improve the quality of urban life. Political rhetoric remained the same—deep purple laced with inspirational messages concerning good *vs.* evil and the traditional cry of "bossism." But it became apparent to many that it was no longer enough to rely on putting "decent" men in office, or re-turning to the glories of the Old Republic, or placing all bets on morality to roust the rascals. Many businessmen who had earlier acquiesced in or

benefited from machine politics rallied to reform, either to protect interests now entrenched or to exploit new opportunities. Political involvement through reform seemed essential to control the functions of the
city and bring about better streets, deeper harbors, increasing municipal
services, technological advances in mass transit, lighting, water, and sewer
systems. More and more businessmen supported reform because machine
politics seemed bad for business. Concerned less about the long-term ideological aspirations of reform, and more about real or fancied deterioration
of services, local firms such as retail shops and department stores, banks,
and utilities sought a better business environment to attract customers
through cleaner streets, more efficient police, less restrictive ordinances,
and a municipal bureaucracy geared to serving the happy combination of
civic pride and self-interest. On the other hand, there were those who
were less concerned with the commercial advantages of urban life, and
more with its social injustices, perpetuated and exploited, it was thought,
by boss rule. There were still others such as the Prohibitionists who
doggedly clung to the one-issue panacea which would at a stroke shatter
the boss and purify the city.

As a result, there was not one reform movement but several. Reform
wings of the major parties became rambunctious, some taking on the
"regulars," others splitting off to form fusion groups. Third parties appeared. Most significant were the private voluntary associations that multiplied with astonishing fertility. New York alone spawned a host of good-
government clubs. The movement spread to most cities of any size. There
were the Detroit Citizens' League, the Pennsylvania Economy League, the
Seattle Municipal League, and the Boston Municipal Research Bureau. The
scandals of the 1890s led to the creation of the Chicago Civic Federation,
which became a model for a national organization of reform, the National
Civic Federation, founded in 1900.

The latter organization typified many of the volunteer citizens' associations. Elitist, conservative, endowed with the spirit of city-boosterism,
dedicated not to the interests of the "little people" but to those of bank-
ing, industrial, and insurance firms, and department stores, largely through
taxing and charter reforms beneficial to the business community. Consequently, it never attracted wide-spread popular support. Labor flirted with
it, felt uncomfortable, and quit.

From the plethora of such movements came a barrage of reforms—
reforms calling for the Australian (or secret) ballot, the short ballot, recall

and referendum, a civil service system, nonpartisan elections, proportional representation, independent audits of city accounts, fact-finding bureaus, and the commission and city manager movement—all having one common denominator: the purpose of creating an organizational revolution that would in fact produce a viable alternative of government to boss rule and machine politics.

Common denominator or not, reform during the Progressive period was riddled with contradictions and divergences in ideology and tactics. In the next essay, "Social and Structural Reform," Melvin Holli attempts to put the Humpty Dumpty back together again by posing questions that tended to separate reformers into two camps: What is the proper role of government? and, Whose interests shall it serve? Response to these questions delineates two kinds of urban reformers, the structural reformers (the right wing of the movement), and the social reformers (the liberal element).

The structural reformers held that the proper role of government was to serve business. Men like Grover Cleveland of Buffalo, Seth Low, John Purroy Mitchel, and William F. Havemeyer of New York, and San Francisco's reform mayor, James D. Phelan, believed that government should serve not the interests of the "people," but the "right" people, respectable people—the middle and patrician classes—who would substitute business for political practices. Their rhetoric, persuasive to a business-oriented society, echoed with calls for efficiency, economy, responsibility, and clean government. Their strategy called for reform in structural terms: revising city charters, hacking budgets to the bone, drastically reducing municipal services. Like the genteel reformers before them, they mounted crusades for the moral uplift of the "other half" and attacks upon the vices of the working class—drinking, gambling, and prostitution. Moral reform was aimed at changing the behavior of the lower and lower-middle classes, rather than, as Andy Logan has written, "improving the morality of the financial and industrial trusts whose dividends made it possible for them to practice their civic philanthropy." The saloon was viewed with more moral indignation than the absence of good parks and schools. As M. R. Werner described the noisy New York reformer Theodore Roosevelt, "He became a terror to pinochle players in the back rooms of saloons. The small joys began to disappear from daily life, and their place was taken by that abstract ghost, The Law, which could neither see, taste, nor touch."

In the name of efficiency and low-cost economy, the structural reform-

178

ers single-mindedly pursued special tax advantages, leaving the "people" burdened with outrageous if not fraudulent franchise contracts, bloated light and gas rates and streetcar fares. Services for the working and lower class were ignored.[2] Mayor Phelan, for example, suspended vital health services, allowed police to protect strike-breakers, and authorized such a low tax rate that the city had to withhold teachers' salaries.

The structural reformers wrought a significant change in urban politics. Before the Progressive era the tone of reform was set by a slogan of *Harper's Weekly*, "United good men" must replace "combined bad men." The structural reformers were less interested in decent men and more in how efficient men could govern. They were in fact administrative innovators, seeking new devices to manage authority in order to replace those "combined bad men." Like the bosses, they sought to centralize political power—a far cry from Samuel Tilden with his horror of centralization in the 1870s. Unlike the "genteel" reformers, they depended less on virtue than on the more sophisticated methods of business enterprise to govern the city. While their voice was moral, their attack was empirical. As Charles Glaab has suggested, the city was no long considered merely a place of pathology, but a place to study.[3]

Unlike the structural reformers, the social reformers felt that the business of government was not business but people. Men like Hazen S. Pingree of Detroit, Samuel M. "Golden Rule" Jones of Toledo, Thomas L. Johnson, Brand Whitlock, and Newton D. Baker of Cleveland, Mark Fagan of Jersey City—humane and practical—deliberately avoided legislating the morals of the workingmen. They believed that the spoilsport Blue Laws regarding drinking, gambling, and prostitution were only symptoms that

2. For a tightly argued and persuasive essay showing that the structural reformers were by no means more "efficient" than the machine politician, see Monte A. Calvert, "The Manifest Functions of the Machine," in Bruce M. Stave, ed., *Urban Bosses, Machines, and Progressive Reformers*, pp. 45-55.

3. Augustus Cerillo, Jr., gives us an excellent example of this in his "The Reform of Municipal Government in New York City: From Seth Low to John Purroy Mitchel," *New-York Historical Society Quarterly* (January 1973). The ground was sowed in 1907 with the creation of the Bureau of Municipal Research, dedicated to fact-finding and the principles of structural reform. With the advent of Mitchel's administration (1914–17), he was prepared through intensive research to modernize the city's bureaucracy. His work on budgets, accounting systems, efficiency commissions, and his professionalization of municipal departments led to a centralization of both purchasing and payroll, consolidation of functions previously fragmented, such as licensing and inspection, among other things.

diverted attention from the real causes, an unhealthy urban environment and the boss system. To enhance the quality of urban life, they promoted public baths, schools, parks and playgrounds, and public welfare programs. To ease the plight of the poor, they regulated franchises, gas, water, and street-railway rates, and tried to equalize tax rates. To eliminate graft, they attacked the special-privilege groups such as the public service corporations, and real estate interests, many of which sponsored the structural reformers. The settlement-house movement sought to rejuvenate the neighborhood. A more radical group, raucously labeled "sewer socialists," called for municipal ownership of water, light, mass transit, and, of course, sewer systems.

The Progressive era gave another twist to the road of urban reform. Changing urban conditions blurred the gap and muddied the distinction between boss and reformer. Each learned from and often copied the other, although this trend varied in degree and quality from city to city. The reformer became more realistic and tough-minded, alert to the benefits of centralized authority and the necessity of "delivering the goods." Some reformers, like Tom Johnson, Hazen Pingree, and the socialist mayor of Milwaukee, Victor Berger, deliberately adopted the techniques of machine politics in order to make reform work. In fact Berger has been called by David Shannon "one of the bossiest 'bosses.' " If some reformers found in machine politics a means of survival, the city boss, always confronted with survival, found in reform the techniques to cope with new urban conditions. The city was becoming infinitely more complex: special interest groups multiplied and scrambled for political recognition, old constituencies became restless, and new ones, such as the growing suburbs, became particularly active for reform. The boss was forced to broaden his power base. Stealing the thunder of the reformers was an effective device to woo new supporters and console the faithful.

It wasn't easy. It pushed the boss to his limits as a power broker. It demanded an artful performance of balancing a variety of groups—women's clubs, labor leaders, civic associations, social workers, downtown business elites, the state legislature, and his own party officials. Some groups demanded changes of significant social value, others were patently self-serving; some wanted to cut costs, others wanted to raise them. No matter what he did, one group would benefit at the expense of the other. The boss was often like a circus juggler with nine balls in the air. Cincinnati's George Cox, for example, had to satisfy his party followers and the poor of the inner city with patronage and favors. At the same time he responded to reformers in the business community and the suburbs by supporting the secret ballot, changes in voter registration, and a crackdown on vice and minor graft. On his record of reforms, he helped modernize city government, professionalize the police and fire departments, and build a large and expensive waterworks.

Indeed, one of the major themes in the current literature on urban politics is the notion of the boss as reformer.[4] Tom Pendergast of Kansas City and Robert W. Speer of Denver sponsored important civic improvements in the City Beautiful movement. Two Tammany warhorses, Charles Murphy and Alfred E. Smith, supported major social reform in New York. James Curley of Boston, who campaigned as "Curley the Builder," was responsible for one of the most extensive public works programs in the history of that venerable town. Martin Behrman of New Orleans was awarded a loving cup from the Mothers Club for his efforts toward civic improvement. Several bosses identified themselves as upholders of law and order. In Chicago, Anton J. Cermak made war on criminal elements; and Frank Hague attacked narcotic peddling and prostitution. "Jersey City," Hague said, "is the most moralest [sic] city in America." In fact, Hague's Jersey City had an astonishing low crime rate, in part because of Hague's sense of semantics: thus, e.g., he refused to define bookmaking as a crime, and he interpreted all domestic killings as manslaughter. "When a man kills his wife," he explained, "that's not murder, that's manslaughter."

Thus the interpretive pendulum, in some quarters at least, has swung from defining the city boss as rogue to placing him firmly in the reform tradition. Balance and perspective suggest, however, that if the gap between reformer and boss narrowed, it did not, in most cases, mesh. There were still enough distinctions in organization, tactics, aspirations, and ideology to keep the two traditions intact, even though they did borrow from each other. The tradition of the boss, from Vare to Daley, of

4. See Lyle W. Dorsett, "The City Boss and the Reformer: A Reappraisal," *Pacific Northwest Quarterly* (October 1972), and his *The Pendergast Machine* (1968); Zane Miller, *Boss Cox's Cincinnati* (1968); Nancy Joan Weiss, *Charles Francis Murphy, 1858-1924: Respectability and Responsibility in Tammany Politics* (1968); Otis A. Pease, "Urban Reformers in the Progressive Era," *Pacific Northwest Quarterly* (April 1971); J. Paul Mitchell, "Boss Speer and the City Functional," *Pacific Northwest Quarterly* (October 1972); Mark Foster, "Frank Hague of Jersey City: The Boss as Reformer," *New Jersey History* (Summer 1968); William D. Miller, *Mr. Crump of Memphis* (1964); John D. Buenker, *Urban Liberalism and Progressive Reform* (1973); J. Joseph Hutchmacher, *Senator Robert F. Wagner and the Rise of Urban Liberalism* (1968).

"giving the people something they can see," was an important lesson seized on by some reformers, but even here there was a distinction. As Monte A. Calvert has ruefully noted, the bosses' motto was "Give people what they want," while the reformers impulse was to "give people what we think they should have." Expediency and motivation were other distinctions. Donning the mantle of Progressivism was a key device in Hague's road to power, but when elected mayor in 1917 and firmly in power, he abandoned it. J. Joseph Hutchmacher pointed out that reform proposals did not originate with Charles Murphy of Tammany Hall, but came instead from reform-minded organizations and newspapers. "When the selfish and altruistic motives of two or more of these elements corresponded, they collaborated and worked together for adoption of their common end."[5]

The concept of boss as reformer begs the question, What kind of reformer? Many of the reforms backed by bosses from the Progressive period to the present have been structural reforms, which aided rather than endangered vested interests and allowed the boss to work both sides of the street.[6] Beautifying the city certainly led to civic improvement, but it also gained new allies in the business community, gave the people something to see, and led to more jobs, patronage, and profit for the machine. Efficiency did indeed help to modernize municipal government, but it usually did not lead to significant social reforms that either challenged special interest groups or ameliorated the condition of the poor. While the favors and jobs provided by the boss helped the downtrodden and the immigrant, in the long run they were ploys that never significantly changed the social system. Indeed, it can be argued that if the boss had instituted a thorough-going program of social reform, he would have changed the very conditions that made his machine possible and, in effect, reformed himself out of existence.

This is not to invalidate the notion of boss as reformer, it is rather to adjust its balance and qualify its perspective. Historians must become, one man suggested, "the 'however' boys." Thus Hague, Crump, and Pendergast championed the reform city-manager movement; *however,* they captured and dominated it. Tammany Hall may have embraced important Progres-

5. "Charles Evans Hughes and Charles Frances Murphy: The Metamorphosis of Progressivism," *New York History* (January 1965), p. 33.
6. See note 25 in "Social and Structural Reform," for Melvin Holli's spirited delineation of this point.

sive measures; *however*, Chicago politicians in the same period were custodians of the status quo, battling Progressives as a threat to the machine. Frank Hague may have built one of the finest medical centers in the country; *however*, he opposed Social Security because "it would take the romance out of old age." Crump, Pendergast, and Hague provided services for the workingman; *however*, they were virulently anti-labor, realizing that organized labor was a keen competitor to the machine, since it had its own inducements, sociability, and commitments. Over time, then, the city boss deserves neither the epithet of "bad guy" nor the hurrah of "good guy." Like Moby Dick he was a bit of both.

The boss seemed more adept at applying the tactics of reform than the reformer was at using the devices of machine politics. There were exceptions, of course, in the reigns of Pingree, Berger, and Johnson. As Augustus Cerillo, Jr., has noted, the structural reforms of John Purroy Mitchell were not scotched by Tammany Hall when it returned to power. In the main, however, as George Washington Plunkitt would say, the reformers "saw their opportunities but didn't take 'em." Cities dethroned their bosses—Tweed, Butler, Ruef, Ames, Curley, Hague, and Crump—but the reform administrations that followed never seemed to live up to their aspirations. Crucial to the understanding of both the confrontation of boss and reformer and the nature of urban reform itself is the question raised by this remark of a machine politician: "These reform movements are like queen hornets. They sting you once, and then they die."

The explanation is that many reform movements contained the seeds of their own disintegration. The heart of the matter was their underlying philosophy, destructive in itself, because it was essentially anti-political. It was based on the proposition that good government could be achieved not only by taking the boss and his machine out of politics but also by taking politics itself out of politics. This could be done by replacing professional politicians with professional administrators; the neighborhood expert replaced by the efficiency expert; nonpartisanship prevailing over partisanship. The art of business, it was thought, and not the art of politics, was the secret of good, clean, honest government.

This concept appealed enormously to those millions of Americans who felt that politics was bad and politicians were venal and nonpolitical experts were not only good but right. The hard fact is, however, that governing a city, especially the larger city, depends upon the management of conflict, which is a way of defining politics. To balance, satisfy, control, and lead the many disparate urban interest groups—ethnic, financial, class—requires the skills of politics, not the precision of budget balancing. The boss ran the city with party government, offering material and psychological inducements, intent upon capturing as many offices as possible. The reformer ran an organization based largely upon volunteers, offering ideological inducements, intent upon capturing only the prestigious higher offices. The result was that the reformer failed to establish a permanent organization based upon the political skills necessary to survive the moral trauma of winning one election after another. Ideological inducements could not compete over time with the attractions of jobs, prestige, and fellowship.

Burning issues had two results, both destructive to political success. They either fizzled out—since it was difficult to keep ideological fires lighted long enough to guarantee the intensity of commitment necessary to win in the rough-and-tumble of urban politics—or they became bones of contention among the reformers themselves. The very lack of ideological commitment allowed the boss flexibility, room for maneuvering, compromise, and bargaining—the instruments of managing conflict. But only a cad compromises his "principles"; indeed, how do you bargain with "values"? To be flexible about right and wrong is to behave just like the enemy, the ward-heeling politician. Moreover, just which ideological values should predominate? Reform organizations were usually a coalition of several ideological positions, often at variance with if not sometimes contradictory to each other. Consensus was difficult, dissent was common. If thieves fall out, so do saints. It was not unusual to see a reform movement disintegrate, the reformers (almost literally) scratching each other's eyes out.

And there was another problem. To paraphrase Daniel Moynihan: "Urban politics is a neighborhood business"—and reformers were not neighborhood people. Granted that in some cities working- and lower-class men and women participated in reform movements; most reform efforts, however, were dominated by the middle and upper classes, holding to values that often ignored or were hostile to the needs of the "other half." The boss cultivated the neighborhood. The reformer either challenged it or patronized it. A major theme running through the history of urban reform, with variations seen even today, was the nativist and racist assumption that the less affluent were basket cases, morally crippled and politically unable to participate responsibly in self-government. You win elections by flattering your supporters. You don't woo a girl by telling her how ugly she is.

Revolutions may fail, but they do leave monuments. In their search for an alternative method of managing municipal government, reformers were inspired by the commission system of government which arose from the wreckage wrought by the Galveston hurricane in 1900. When the regular government was unable to manage the city's reconstruction, the state legislature appointed a commission of five successful businessmen, four to manage each a specific area of city government, and the fifth to act as a quasi-mayor. It was a smashing success. Other communities followed suit, and by 1917 over five hundred cities had incorporated the commission system in their city charters. After that date, however, the commission system skidded in popularity, in part because it did not eliminate politics or increase efficiency enough, and in part because it could not cope with the requirement in many state constitutions that cities must be represented by councils and mayors. Primarily it slipped because it could not compete with another new system, one that promised to solve all these difficulties, the council manager or city manager form of government.

This plan was put forth in 1911 by an important reform association, the National Short Ballot Organization (whose president was Woodrow Wilson), and effectively promoted by the secretary of that group, Richard S. Childs, an advertising man with great gifts of persuasion. As Childs and others argued, it was an improvement over the commission system in that it eliminated politics by a sharp delineation between decision-making and the implementation of those decisions: the council would initiate policies; the city manager would administer them. The first city of any size to try it was Dayton (Ohio) in 1914, like Galveston, a victim of the elements—in this case a disastrous flood. Success in Dayton led the National Municipal League to sponsor it as a godsend to the woes of urban America.

The city manager movement became at once a turning point in American urban reform and one of the most enduring legacies of the Progressive period. At a time when the Progressive movement was dissipating on the national level, the city manager movement enjoyed an astonishing growth on the local level. Between 1918 and 1923, 153 cities adopted the plan, and between 1923 and 1928, 84 more cities followed. It continued to flower during the Depression and spurted after World War II, when 75 cities opted for it. By the 1960s more than 1,700 communities had the plan. Today either the commission or the council manager form of government prevails in almost half the cities in the United States.

The city manager plan, usually offered as a package deal with other Progressive reforms—recall, referendum, the initiative, elections-at-large, and civil service reform—institutionalized one of the chief thrusts of the Progressive movement. Here was the alternative to boss rule. It was the triumph of the expert-technician over the city boss, administrator over district the leader, nonpartisanship over partisanship, efficiency over waste; honesty, impartiality, and the public interest, over graft, patronage, and ethnic lower-class recognition. At-large elections would replace the ward system, and recall, referendum and the initiative would return power to the people. It heralded a new set of philosopher kings to govern urban America—the businessman, the engineer, the professional man. Above all, it took politics out of politics.

The city manager plan was both a triumph of strucural reform and of the ethos of the business-oriented Protestant middle and upper classes. Business and municipal government were considered the warp and woof of local politics. The city manager was likened to a corporation president; the council was his board of directors. "A city," as one buff put it, "is a great business enterprise whose stockholders are the people."

Reform via the city manager plan wasn't as simple as that. At first blush a new reform program is usually rosy, overstated, and unqualified. Over the years proponents of the city manager plan have made extravagant claims, but the results are mixed. True, in many cities the plan has helped enormously in rationalizing and modernizing municipal government, slashing waste, cutting cost, increasing and improving services, and creating permanent civic improvements. In other cases, however, services have been cut back and taxes raised. The claim that the city manager form of government has replaced the boss and the machine is open to question. The plan has been most effective in middle-sized and small cities, cities-on-the-make, engaged in rapid growth and seeking more urban amenities, and, importantly, cities more or less homogeneous in character, without deep class and economic cleavages. Many of these cities—San Diego, for example—never had boss rule or a history of party government in the first place. Only 1,110 communities of the 1,756 that had the plan in 1961 had a population over 5,000. It was a notable failure in the large, complex, heterogeneous cities.[7] Despite its success during the immediate years after

---

7. Only four cities with more than a half-million population have the plan: Dallas, Cincinnati, San Antonio, and San Diego. Only twelve cities with populations ranging from 250,000 to 500,000

World War II, the movement has faltered appreciably except in the small cities.[8]

The city manager form's claim of broadening the democratic base by returning government to the people is highly suspect. It raises that old question, Which people? If representation is any measure of the prevalence of democracy, then the city manager plan is conspicuously inadequate. The old ward system, for all its vulnerability to machine rule, at least allowed representation for most groups, from the poor of the inner city to the affluent of the silk-stocking suburbs. The city manager plan has retained the ward system in only a few cities. The majority have adopted the election at-large system which drastically reduced representation from working and lower-class groups. One looks long and hard to find blacks, Mexican-Americans, Puerto Ricans, carpenters, electricians, bartenders, or labor leaders in city manager organizations. One finds instead the Anglo-Saxon Protestant merchant, big businessman, engineer, or lawyer. In 1938, for instance, when Jackson (Michigan) adopted the plan, after a celebration in the Masonic Temple the new council proceeded to eliminate most of the Catholics who worked for the city and replace them with good Protestants. Nonpartisan at-large elections switched the election machinery from party management to the use of the media and thereby gave the advantage to the well-heeled, well-known man, and not the obscure truck driver of modest income.

Moreover, because a candidate had to appeal to a large, diverse electorate, he tended to shun controversial issues and, instead, engaged in pedestrian generalities. Reliance upon the media enhanced the importance of one's public image. The result in such cases was a politics of personality, the pitching of epithets to smear an opponent's character. Furthermore, the city manager system tended to produce men of conservative hue, men who sought efficiency in administration, efficiency in low-cost govern-

---

have it: Oakland, Oklahoma City, Norfolk, Dayton, Miami, Phoenix, Long Beach, Fort Worth, Kansas City, Wichita, Toledo, and Rochester. As Edward C. Banfield and James Q. Wilson point out, "The number of large cities having the plan has increased in the last ten years, but not because large cities have adopted it; rather, because cities having it have grown." *City Politics* (1963), p. 169.

8. While sixteen cities with more than 250,000 population adopted the plan, only San Antonio did so before 1933. Of the thirty-nine city manager cities with 100,000 to a quarter-million population, seventeen adopted it before 1933, but only five after 1952. In the three years between 1958 to 1961, only two cities of more than 100,000 incorporated the plan, of those between 50,000 and 100,000 only four did so, and only twenty between 25,000 and 50,000.

ment, not efficiency in human relations or in solving the personal problems of the city dweller.

When the city manager plan did take over in a city that had known boss rule, its victory was not always clear-cut. For example, when the plan was adopted in Cincinnati, a reform administration was already in control of local politics. In Kansas City the victory of the city manager plan was in fact a triumph for Boss Tom Pendergast, who immediately controlled the council and thereby was able to elect his own city manager, the obliging Henry "Old Turkey-neck" McElroy. For Boss Pendergast it was business as usual.

In the next selection of this chapter, "The Politics of Urban Change," Peter A. Lupsha surveys the city manager plan from the Progressive era to the present. He concludes that, far from constituting a viable alternative to the city boss, the movement "has perhaps done more damage to the political life of our cities than all the ill-gotten gains of the city boss."

Since World War II, urban reform, in some cities at least, has taken another turn in the road, with the appearance of a new breed of reformer armed with a new strategy. Until that time, most urban reformers operated outside the major party system—i.e., through civic organizations, private reform associations, research bureaus, and local parties independently organized. Largely eschewing lower-class support, these organizations and the elites dominating them, were wealthy (with few exceptions) and dedicated to nonpartisanship on the local level to the Republican party in national politics.

With the failure of fusion and extraparty politics, there was a shift from the volunteer association to intraparty activity, and with that came a new generation of do-gooders, liberal in ideology, Democratic in party allegiance, similar to their predecessors in their dislike of machine politics, but different in tactics. Instead of battling the party from outside, they sought to unseat the "regulars" from inside. Intraparty reform had the significant advantage of the stability and prestige of a permanent and established organization as a power base. Interestingly if not ironically, intraparty reform involved the tactics and other requirements of party politics, certainly not unlike those employed by the machine politician himself.

Political commitment was no longer limited to a financial contribution, membership on a blue-ribbon committee or on a high-minded volunteer association. Intraparty politics required neighborhood politics, the bone-hard, tedious, menial, unromantic day-to-day chores of grass roots politics: pounding sidewalks, ringing doorbells, circulating petitions, passing out leaflets, making street-corner speeches, and mixing with the common folk, tasks not always congenial to the sensibilities of middle-class people. The terms of survival were similar to those of the old-fashioned machine: compromise, inducements, wooing diverse groups, and winning elections—requirements that made painful demands upon the reform style. Like the old reformers, the new breed found it difficult to compromise on principles. Patronage reeked of machine politics, but ideological inducements did not fill bellies. Winning Democratic primaries in their own liberal bailiwicks was one thing, but success in a general election was quite another. Election success meant support from groups either hostile to the liberalism of the reformers, or rejected for their conservatism by the reformers.

Perhaps the best illustration of this intraparty phase of reform is provided by the period 1949-61 in New York. The creation of the Lexington Democratic Club in 1949 initiated numbers of liberal reform clubs, which, with the old battle cries of "bossism" and "roust the rascals," worked within the Democratic Party to wrench control from the Tammany Hall regulars. Their victory in 1961 was more apparent than real. A one-two punch ousted Carmino DeSapio from his Greenwich Village district, ending hope of leadership of Tammany, and Robert Wagner was re-elected Mayor of New York. But as James Q. Wilson has dryly noted, the reformers had "lost a valuable enemy and gained a reluctant friend," and the road has been rocky ever since.[9]

Any assessment, then, of the progress of urban reform in the twentieth century must begin with the premise that the reformer did not realize his aspirations. He called for more democracy, honesty, and efficiency. Urban government since (roughly) 1920 has improved appreciably in all those categories, but reform has fallen short of its goals. Reform launched the middle and upper classes back to dominance in urban affairs, but at the expense of the lower and working classes. Even the most highly vaunted instrument of change—the civil service system—fell short of the mark. It discriminated against those with modest educational backgrounds. It did not insure appointments based on merit and nonpartisanship. For exam-

9. "Politics and Reform in American Cities," from Ivan Hinderaker, ed., *American Government Annual, 1961-1962*, p. 49. This is an extremely valuable essay on recent urban politics.

ple, loopholes made way for temporary appointments which were promptly filled by the party faithful, and were regularly renewed—to become, for all practical purposes, permanent. Civil service boards were captured by party partisans who could cancel the list of eligible persons, and order new examinations not distinguished for their intellectual demands. Civil service reform, like other reforms, tended also to bring about the opposite effect of its intention, often creating a bureaucracy neither efficient nor responsive to the needs of the people.

Nor did reform always bring honesty in government. Boston, the first large city to incorporate nonpartisan government, was struck by corruption involving contract awards, building inspections, highway development, housing projects, and the enforcement of gambling regulations. Reform administrations in New York, Philadelphia, and the most pristine of nonpartisanship cities, Los Angeles, have been embarrassed by both "honest" and "dishonest" graft. Above all, reform did not bring a workable substitute for machine politics. Government remained inefficiently decentralized, grass-roots neighborhood politics was covered with weeds as lines to decision-making bodies were clogged, and significant groups lost effective representation.

This rather bleak conclusion is modified somewhat by developments in our own time, when reform elements established direct contact with the urban poor. In the last selection of this chapter, "Reformers, Machines, and the War on Poverty," J. David Greenstone and Paul E. Peterson have analyzed the responses to the war on poverty in the 1960s by both machine and reform cities. Their conclusions suggest that reform may have taken yet another turn in the road, one that may augur more effective portents for the future. But this will depend upon an awareness of, and a dedication to, the problems of urban poverty. At this writing, however, the war on poverty has fizzled to hardly a skirmish, and our conclusion still seems intact. Reform has not "gone to hell", but it hasn't unlocked those pearly gates either. Whatever changes have occurred in machine politics during the last generation, have come about less through the efforts of reformers and more through changes in urban life beyond the control of reform, as we shall see in the last chapter.

REFORMERS
ONLY MORNIN' GLORIES

George Washington Plunkitt

College professors and philosophers who go up in a balloon to think are always discussin' the question: "Why Reform Administrations Never Succeed Themselves!" The reason is plain to anybody who has learned the a, b, c of politics.

I can't tell just how many of these movements I've seen started in New York during my forty years in politics, but I can tell you how many have lasted more than a few years—none. There have been reform committees of fifty, of sixty, of seventy, of one hundred and all sorts of numbers that started out to do up the regular political organizations. They were mornin' glories—looked lovely in the mornin' and withered up in a short time, while the regular machines went on flourishin' forever, like fine old oaks. Say, that's the first poetry I ever worked off. Ain't it great?

Just look back a few years. You re-

From William L. Riordon, *Plunkitt of Tammany Hall* (New York: Alfred A. Knopf, 1948), pp. 22-27.

member the People's Municipal League that nominated Frank Scott for mayor in 1890? Do you remember the reformers that got up that league? Have you ever heard of them since? I haven't. Scott himself survived because he had always been a first-rate politician, but you'd have to look in the newspaper almanacs of 1891 to find out who made up the People's Municipal League. Oh, yes! I remember one name: Ollie Teall; dear, pretty Ollie and his big dog. They're about all that's left of the League.

Now take the reform movement of 1894. A lot of good politicians joined in that—the Republicans, the State Democrats, the Stecklerites and the O'Brienites, and they gave us a lickin', but the real reform part of the affair, the Committee of Seventy that started the thing goin', what's become of those reformers? What's become of Charles Stewart Smith? Where's Bangs? Do you ever hear of Cornell, the iron man, in politics now? Could a search party find R. W. G. Welling? Have you seen the name of Fulton

McMahon or McMahon Fulton—I ain't sure which—in the papers lately? Or Preble Tucker? Or—but it's no use to go through the list of the reformers who said they sounded in the death knell of Tammany in 1894. They're gone for good, and Tammany's pretty well, thank you. They did the talkin' and posin', and the politicians in the movement got all the plums. It's always the case.

The Citizens' Union has lasted a little bit longer than the reform crowd that went before them, but that's because they learned a thing or two from us. They learned how to put up a pretty good bluff—and bluff counts a lot in politics. With only a few thousand members, they had the nerve to run the whole Fusion movement, make the Republicans and other organizations come to their headquarters to select a ticket and dictate what every candidate must do or not do. I love nerve, and I've had a sort of respect for the Citizens' Union lately, but the Union can't last. Its people haven't been trained to politics, and whenever Tammany calls their bluff they lay right down. You'll never hear of the Union again after a year or two.

And, by the way, what's become of the good government clubs, the political nurseries of a few years ago? Do you ever hear of Good Government Club D and P and Q and Z any more? What's become of the infants who were to grow up and show us how to govern the city? I know what's become of the nursery that was started in my district. You can find pretty much the whole outfit over in my headquarters, Washington Hall.

The fact is that a reformer can't last in politics. He can make a show for a while, but he always comes down like a rocket. Politics is as much a regular business as the grocery or the dry-goods or the drug business. You've got to be trained up to it or you're sure to fall. Suppose a man who knew nothing about the grocery trade suddenly went into the business and tried to conduct it according to his own ideas. Wouldn't he make a mess of it? He might make a splurge for a while, as long as his money lasted, but his store would soon be empty. It's just the same with a reformer. He hasn't been brought up in the difficult business of politics and he makes a mess of it every time.

I've been studyin' the political game for forty-five years, and I don't know it all yet. I'm learnin' somethin' all the time. How, then, can you expect what they call "business men" to turn into politics all at once and make a success of it? It is just as if I went up to Columbia University and started to teach Greek. They usually last about as long in politics as I would last at Columbia.

You can't begin too early in politics if you want to succeed at the game. I began several years before I could vote, and so did every successful leader in Tammany Hall. When I was twelve years old I made myself useful around the district headquarters and did work at all the polls on election day. Later on, I hustled about gettin' out voters who had jags on or who were too lazy to come to the polls. There's a hundred ways that boys can help, and they get an experience that's the first real step in statesmanship. Show me a boy that hustles for the organization on election day, and I'll show you a comin' statesman.

That's the a, b, c of politics. It ain't easy work to get up to y and z. You have to give nearly all your time and attention to it. Of course, you may have some business or occupation on the side, but the great business of your life must be politics if you want to succeed in it. A few years ago Tammany tried to mix politics and business in equal quantities, by havin' two leaders for each district, a politician and a business man. They wouldn't mix. They were like oil and water. The politician looked after the politics of his district; the business man looked over his grocery store or his milk route, and whenever he appeared at an executive meeting, it was only to make trouble. The whole scheme turned out to be a farce and was abandoned mighty quick.

Do you understand now, why it is that a reformer goes down and out in the first or second round, while a politician answers to the gong every time? It is because the one has gone into the fight without trainin', while the other trains all the time and knows every fine point of the game.

THE CRUSADE
AGAINST THE TWEED RING

Alexander B. Callow, Jr.

I thank my God the sun and moon
Are both stuck up so high
That no presumptuous hand can stretch
And pluck them from the sky.
If they were not, I do believe
That some reforming ass
Would recommend to take them down
And light the world with gas.
Judge James T. Brady

For five years the Tweed Ring had led a
great treasury raid. The power of the
Ring, like the tentacles of an octopus,
encircled city government, the courts, the
police, the underworld, and the State legislature. The command centers of political power from the Governor to the
Board of Aldermen were controlled by
the Ring and its lieutenants. The Ring
ruled over an empire of patronage with
thousands of the faithful on the city pay-

From *The Tweed Ring* by Alexander B. Callow,
Jr. Copyright © 1966 by Alexander B. Callow,
Jr. Reprinted by permission, Oxford University
Press, Inc.

rolls. Tammany Hall had been remodeled
into an awesome political machine, supported by the immigrant and the native
poor, and sustained on election day by a
horde of Tammany warriors, repeaters,
and corrupt election officials who made a
mockery out of the ballot. No wonder
Boss Tweed could ask the reformer,
"What are you going to do about it?"

Seldom have the forces of "good" government faced such a formidable opponent as they did in July 1871. Yet five
months later the Tweed Ring was destroyed. Most accounts of this campaign
emphasize the Ring's sensational thefts.
But few questions have been raised about
the crusade itself; few attempts have been
made to understand the anatomy of a
reform movement on a local, grass-roots
level. For example, how was the crusade
conducted? What was the impact of the
Tweed Ring upon the reformer's imagination and in what way did the Ring reveal
his attitudes toward reform, corruption,
and political institutions? If the rascals

were such capital rogues, why did it take so long to destroy them?

By the fall of 1871, when damning evidence was being unearthed and New York echoed from the cries of one reform rally after another, most of the press, a multitude of reform groups, and politicians from both parties were noisily scrambling after the scalps of the Tammany Ring braves. Now that the Ring was disintegrating, all vied for the heroic role of redeemer. Samuel Tilden almost reached the Presidency on the claim that he destroyed the Ring. But Tilden was a hero of last moments. A skillful general when the enemy was in retreat, he was the soul of indecision, procrastination, and lost opportunities when the Ring was in power. In those quiet days before the great uprising, only two led the crusade against the Tweed Ring: Thomas Nast of *Harper's Weekly*, and the *New York Times*. *Harper's Weekly* began in 1868 to print Thomas Nast's brilliant political cartoons, and his talent with the poisoned-pen portrait, which could at once inspire fear and ridicule, has led many to think he was the chief wrecker of the Ring. Tweed himself thoroughly recognized Nast's artistry in making a cartoon a deadly political weapon. "I don't care a straw for your newspaper articles, my constituents don't know how to read, but they can't help seeing them damned pictures."[1]

A picture may say a thousand words, but it still took many a thousand words to excite and motivate the indignation of New Yorkers. It was the *New York Times* which published the first evidence of corruption, helped to raise the crusade to the heights of near hysteria, and therefore deserves the mantle of champion opponent of the Tweed Ring. The role played by the *Times* is a kind of case study of the enormous difficulties and stubborn persistence involved in arousing a sometimes confused and often apathetic public.

Prior to September 1870, the fight against corruption was represented by a series of angry but irregular outbursts from reform groups and newspapers. These in turn were thwarted by grand juries vulnerable to the persuasion of hard cash and lack of evidence. The Citizens' Association and the Union League, both eminent bodies of "respectabilities," had long fished in the murky waters of New York politics with only occasional luck.[2] While the reformers suspected that something was desperately wrong, the rub was in proving it. Although the Ring was organized as early as 1866, there was little awareness by reformers of either a centralized city machine or of how politics operated at the level of the ward and precinct. Instead, there was talk of a host of "rings" but uncertainty as to who were the ringleaders.

Apathy, a lack of civic conscience, and fear—which permeated every level of society—also accounted for the reformers' failure to get an audience. An absence of consensus, generated by party partisanship, divided the press and the gentry, the two groups who might have sounded the alarm and carried the fight. While the business community furnished several

195

Alexander B. Callow, Jr.

leaders to the reform groups, other businessmen were either afraid of the retaliatory power of Tammany Hall or they benefited from the Ring's operations, while others, too interested in making money, simply did not care.

The Tweed Ring exploited these conditions and reinforced complacency by giving something to everyone: city advertising to the press, special favors to businessmen, state aid to charitable and religious organizations, jobs and food to the poor. Tweed through his business connections and Hall through his clubs ingratiated themselves in the upper branches of society, while Sweeny and Connolly, seasoned ward leaders, were effective in the rank and file. And then there was the Astor Committee and its whitewash of the Comptroller's records, which contributed as much as any event to creating complacency.

Into this atmosphere, the champion of reform, the *New York Times*, made its "auspicious" beginning in the winter of 1870, by announcing that Messrs. Sweeny, Hall, and Hoffman were busily engaged in bringing good government to New York![3] One delicious irony was topped by another when the *Times* gave its first (and last) cheer for the Boss himself.

Senator Tweed is in a fair way to distinguish himself as a reformer. . . . From beginning to end the Tweed party has not manifested the slightest disposition to evade or prevaricate. . . . As a whole, the appointments of the heads of the various departments of the City Government . . . are far above the average ·in point of personal fitness, and should be satisfactory.[4]

The *Times*'s course, however, was radically altered by the summer of 1870. Ugly rumors of corruption were once again abroad, and George Jones, the *Times* publisher, apparently feeling hoodwinked and humiliated, angrily turned on the charter and its creators. An Englishman, Louis Jennings, was imported as editor. Jenning's zest for a good fight, his acerbic prose, coupled with Nast's cartoons in *Harper's Weekly*, infused the campaign with a pitch and tempo of almost evangelical fervor. For over a year, from September 20, 1870, on, there was not a day that the *Times* did not, with furious and heroic invective, assault the Tweed Ring, its organization, and allies. The *Times* begged, cajoled, scolded, and demanded that the electorate rout the rascals; nevertheless, the public, including some of the "best people," seemed to sink deeper in its apathy, and the Ring got stronger. What was wrong? Was it entirely public indifference, the usual scapegoat for corruption, or did the trouble lay partly in the nature of the crusade itself?

Two elements are necessary in any successful campaign against civil corruption: moral indignation and facts. Until July 1871, the *Times*'s attack was a grand crusade conducted without fear and without facts; it was long on denunciation, short on documentation. The slack in legal evidence was taken up in an amazing exercise of invective, the central theme of which was the wickedness of the Tweed Ring, a theme with a hundred variations on the words "thief," "rogue," and "scamp." The crusade had persistence. It had gusto. It had all the subtlety of a

196

sledge hammer. It was literary alchemy using the crudest of alloys. There was none of the humor or painful ridicule of a Nast cartoon, none of the dash of the *New York Herald* or the deft sarcasm of Dana's *Sun* when those two papers finally joined the bandwagon later in 1871. It was just a juggernaut of epithets, taking the edge off the crusade by dulling the reader's senses with a repetitive cry of "wolf." E. L. Godkin of *The Nation*, although admiring the newspaper's spirit, found its denunciation "tiresome."[5] Even the *Times* admitted that its readers were probably bone-tired from the constant accusations.[6] And while the *Times* spewed platitudes about political sin, the elegant Mayor of New York quipped, "Who's going to sue?"[7]

Nor was abuse heaped solely on the Ring, for the public in general, and the rich, the workingman, and the church in particular, came within the *Times*'s range as it sharpened its aim at iniquity. One major strategic device of the crusade was to arouse a feeling of guilt and shame. The public had failed its civic responsibilities. There should be a moment of self-castigation coupled with redeeming political New Year's resolutions to sweep away the apathy that allowed the monstrosities of the Tweed Ring. The rich were scorned for their complacency, hypocrisy, and lack of action.[8] They were "cowardly and effeminate," refusing to leave the comfort of their libraries for the "unpleasant smells" of the political arena.

The policy of the Ring, in fact, was to drive the honest, decent middle class out of the city and leave it to the very rich and the very poor—"the one too lazy to oppose them, and the other too ignorant."[9] It the workingman understood the elementary principles of political economy, he would not be grateful for the jobs the Ring gave him on the streets and in the parks. He should realize that the robbery of the rich was the robbery of the poor. Labor actually took the full brunt of the Ring's adventures in graft through raised rents, increased taxes, and higher priced goods.[10] As for the church, the *Times* said, at most it applauds while others fight. If only the church acted with responsibility, the public conscience would be inflamed, and the sores on the body politic would be burned out, "as if by fire."[11]

With these tactics of shock, blame, and invective, the *Times* seemed to be searching for some way to shatter the complacency of the public. An attempt was made, in a pedestrian Jeffersonian vein, to exploit the chasm between town and country, the fear—and fascination—of the city. The "hay-loft and cheese-press Democrats" were told of the moral quagmire of the Sodom-by-the-Hudson, its city-slicker politicians, its crime, its cancerous effect on the Democratic party.[12] The trouble with that approach was that upstate politicos well knew that the success of the party depended on the city Democrats' delivering a large bloc of votes, and the Tweed Ring had time and again shown it could deliver.

Perhaps an appeal to the citizens' pocketbook would help, for here lay men's hearts—"touch them there and they will wince and exhibit more sensitiveness than they will show to even the strongest appeals made to their sympathies," as the

Times said.[13] The newspaper became choked with figures demonstrating the Ring's damage to property owners. But most of the electorate did not own real property. Columns were devoted to an awkward analysis of city finances. But the average voter would have difficulty making sense of them. As the *Times* executed its complicated sums, apathy seemed to increase.

One reason why the crusade raged on for so long amid apparent indifference from the rest of the New York press was that the Democratic press, from the *World* on down—"or rather up, for you cannot get lower than the *World*"—(as the *Times* remarked)—were infuriated over the profound Republican partisanship of Nast and the *Times*. The *Times* was fond of repeating the adage that every Democrat was not a horse-thief, but that every horse-thief was a Democrat. Moreover, according to the *Times*, "all" Democrats were corrupt; the party had "never" undertaken a "genuine" reform.[14] Righteous moral indignation was rudely compromised when the *Times* condemned city Democrats and blithely whitewashed the Grant administration.[15]

Skepticism (and perhaps jealousy) also influenced the press. The *Times* motto should read, said one newspaper, "Print everything you please, without regard to whether it is true or false, but refuse to prove anything."[16] Horace Greeley, who puffed hot and cold throughout the campaign, even suggested that the Ring sue the *Times* for libel.[17] The *New York World*, after a brief flirtation with the Young Democracy, returned to revolve around Tammany Hall; it stoutly defended the Ring, calling the crusade as "stupid and absurd as it is wicked," and designed to introduce "a reign of anarchy."[18] Moreover, both the *Herald* and the *World* liked Oakey Hall. James Gordon Bennett of the *Herald* once said approvingly of Tweed's left-hand man, "He calls a spade a spade and Horace Greeley a humbug."[19]

Thus when Tammany wildly celebrated on July 4, 1871, it seemed that Nast's cartoons and the *Times*'s river of rhetoric had produced a crusade without followers, a cause apparently lost to corruption and apathy. All had not been lost, however, for it prepared New Yorkers for what was to follow. This was made possible not by any renewed moral gusto from Tammany's "unloyal" opposition, but by a quirk of fate and an emotion common in politics—the hankering for revenge.

The first real step in the Ring's fall to disaster came on January 21, 1871, when James Watson, the trusty County Auditor and Ring bookkeeper, was killed in a sleighing accident. The Ring was to learn how indispensable he was, for the door was now open for espionage. Matthew O'Rourke was appointed County Auditor, but was not taken into the Ring's confidence. It was a fatal appointment—"a dirty traitor and a fraud," Tammany's *Leader* cried later. O'Rourke was not a happy man. He once had a claim against the city which the Ring had seen fit not to pay. A disgruntled claim-seeker could be as vicious as a woman scorned. With the patience and accuracy of a good bookkeeper, O'Rourke copied the explosive facts and figures of corruption from the Ring's account books and passed them on to the *Times*.[20]

Acting independently, Jimmy O'Brien, one of the leaders of the rebel Young Democracy, assumed the role of a political Judas. He had managed to ingratiate himself back into the good graces of the Ring, by abandoning the Young Democracy and acting as an enthusiastic trustee for the Tweed monument association. But beneath his ruddy Irish complexion, he smouldered with resentment over the Ring's refusal to pay him $300,000 in claims he collected while Sheriff. O'Brien persuaded Connolly to give one William Copeland a job in the Comptroller's office. Copeland was, in fact, O'Brien's spy, sent to obtain information to use as blackmail to get O'Brien's claims. With Watson dead, Copeland found the voucher records loosely guarded. Lush accounts, such as "County Liabilities," furnished him with a wealth of information, which he copied for O'Brien. Confronted with this political dynamite, Tweed began to pay blackmail. He paid O'Brien over $20,000 with the promise that $130,000 would be forthcoming in mortgages on prime property. O'Brien coolly pocketed the cash and turned his information over to the *Times*.[21]

The breakthrough in the crusade had come. Publisher Jones began his attack with uncommon good sense. He bought up a large block of *Times* stock, fearful the Ring might retaliate by a stock raid. And then on Saturday, July 22, 1871, the *Times* opened up with its first front-page blast: "The Secret Accounts: Proofs of Undoubted Frauds Brought to Light." Slowly and deliciously, as if opening a long-awaited Christmas package, Jones released his figures—on the armories, the courthouse, padded payrolls, judicial indiscretion—topping one horror with another.[22] On the 29th the *Times* printed a special supplement in English and German of statistics on the armory and courthouse swindles; 200,000 copies of the first printing were quickly sold out. It was not only a sensation in New York, but it also attracted immediate national attention. For the next four months Jones never let up; front page and editorial page boiled with journalistic frenzy—and Nast drew his cartoons with even greater venom.

Now as the facts were exposed, New York stirred, rumbled, and awoke—shocked, frightened, angry. It was now time for the reformers to take more decisive action. The massive reform rally on September 4 at Cooper Union, the first of many, registered the impact of the *Times*'s exposures: the temper was explosive, the spirit was that of a back-country revival meeting. The rally was sponsored by the Committee of Seventy, whose roster bulged with some of the most distinguished names in New York, such as William F. Havemeyer, Judge James Emott, Robert Roosevelt, Charles Richard O'Conor, and Joseph H. Choate, who presented the Committee's resolutions against the Tweed Ring with the battle cry, "This is what *we* are going to do about it!"[23]

A rostrum of distinguished speakers aroused the audience to a passionate fervor: "We shall get at them. The wicked shall not always rule"; "Pitch into the boss, give it to him, he deserves it";

199

"There is no power like the power of the people armed, aroused, and kindled with the enthusiasm of a righteous wrath"; "What are we going to do about it?"—"Hang them," cried the voices from the audience.[24] The *Times* said afterward that if the Ring had heard the curses, hisses, and denunciations heaped on them they would have felt "too mean to live."[25]

It was evident that New York had awakened from its apathy. The Citizens' Association, the New York Council of Political Reform, and the Union League threw their weight into the crusade, and they were followed by a host of reform groups—the Young Men's Municipal Reform Association, the Apollo Hall Democracy, the Young Democracy, the German Reform Organization, the Democratic Reform Association, and the Ward Councils of Political Reform. The press joined the chorus. Prominent businessmen and attorneys like R. A. Hunter, Geroge W. Benster, and James Whitten met and considered forming a Vigilance Committee, but cooler heads prevailed. And Samuel Tilden entered on his somewhat gray charger. It was now expedient for him to be a reformer. The crusade reached a new dimension. It was no longer the concern of two but an issue that attracted many New Yorkers.

The impact of the Tweed Ring upon the reformer's imagination once again demonstrated the American capacity to create a morality play out of politics. Here was a drama of good versus evil. The principal characters were so wonderfully wicked that little embellishment seemed necessary. But embellished they were.

While the reformers' responses were varied and often contradictory, certain dominant themes emerged.

The beginning theme, which Thomas Nast did more than anyone else to fix, was the image of the city boss, a portrait of evil. Tweed was pictured as gross, vicious, lowborn, colossally corrupt. Sweeny was the man with the black brains; Connolly was dark and oily; and Nast's favorite target, Oakey Hall, was the buffoon. These "beastly rascals" were also seen not as indigenous product of the American urban political system, but as something sinister and alien. The corruption of the Ring was compared to the treachery of a Judas Iscariot, to the cunning of a Robespierre, the slothful greed of Oriental potentates; in tyranny and insolence they "would put their Roman predecessors to the blush."[26]

But the boss and his ministers were only mirrors in larger size and more evil proportions of those who flocked to their support—the Irish-Catholic immigrants. One of the most significant responses to the Tweed Ring, one which rounded out the image of evil by adding fear to it, was the revival of nativism in New York. On July 12, 1871, Protestant and Catholic Irish engaged in a bloody riot which shocked New York and revived the Know-Nothing attitudes of the 1850s and nativist fears of the 1863 draft riots. The Ring was vehemently denounced for trying to prevent the annual parade for the Orangemen, which precipitated the riot, as pacifying the Catholic Irish. When the parade was allowed, the Ring was accused of protecting the Catholic rioters. No other single event so well illustrated the tie betweeen Tammany Hall and the Irish-Catholic voter. The cry for "clean government" now emitted the voice of nativism. There was a papal conspiracy as "Irish Catholic despotism rules the City of New York, the Metropolis of free America."[27] Letters poured into the *Times* office calling for a revival of the Native American party.[28] The Citizens' Association announced that the city had become a "common sewer" for the "dregs" of Europe; an army of ignorance was being led to the polls by the Tweed Ring.[29]

Nativism, in turn, elicited another response. The reformers, for the most part of the middle and upper class—professional men, bankers, merchants, journalists, the "better" politicians—felt a distinct loss of status since their old position of leadership had been captured by the wicked and the mob. Prior to the reign of Fernando Wood, political factions were controlled by men belonging to the upper or middle class, to whom the emoluments of office, while desirable, were not always essential. From the days of Tweed's Forty Thieves through the Civil War, a change was occurring in New York politics, gradually, not completely, not easy to recognize; like the grin of the Cheshire Cat, sometimes it was seen, sometimes it was not. The old ruling groups, even the august Albany Regency, were being slowly displaced by a group not new, but different in numbers and the ranks from which it came—the lower-middle class, and the bottom of the social heap, the immigrant and native poor. The old ruling groups had to begin to move over and make a place for a new group,

the Irish. This change found its source in the city, its growth, the changing composition of its population, the nature of its government. But the old middle- and upper-class elite, especially the reformers, who largely came from these groups, never completely understood this change and felt only bitterness toward the new and not always "respectable" elite. Republican institutions under the Tweed Ring, the reformers declared, were safe only in the "rightful" hands of the educated, the wealthy, and the virtuous. Now power had shifted to those at the bottom of society, their morals decayed, their religion Romanist, their Alma Mater the corner saloon.[30] The *Times* echoed the reformer's fears: We exist over a volcano, a vast, explosive mass of the poor and ignorant—"the dangerous classes," who "care nothing for our liberty and civilization."[31] E. L. Godkin traced the phenomenon back to the excessive democratization of the 1846 New York State Constitution.[32] Others saw it compounded by another insidious development, the rise of a new political breed, the professional politician.

As New York itself grew, politics became more centralized, more disciplined, more professionalized. While the professional politician had long been on the scene in New York politics, the impact of the Tweed Ring seemed to wipe out that memory and fix the emergence and the novelty of the professional as coinciding with the Tweed era. The *Times*, in fact, wrote of the "new profession" as if it were just making its appearance.[33] The reformer gave the professional little credit for skill in handling

201

men or for artful political techniques at the "low" level of the ward or precinct, or for his sometimes masterful sense of organization. The reformer generally was little interested in the rude day-by-day operations of politics. His middle- and upper-class sensibilities were congenial to ideals and principles, not to the often rough, dreary, but necessary work of the primaries. The professional, in the reformer's eyes, was not a Robin Hood to the needy, but rather a Robin the Hood to the degenerate, wasting the taxpayers' money by giving jobs to the immigrant, bailing the drunkard out of jail, and corrupting the unemployed by giving them food and cigars—a parasite undermining the Protestant ethic of civic responsibility. The New York Council of Political Reform summed it all up. It was a contest between two forces: one made up of ruffians and desperadoes, and the other of "the delicately reared, the moral, humane, and the peace loving."[34]

Thus his sense of lost status, his contempt and fear of the masses, his nativism, his reaction to the city boss as rogue and professional politician—all indicate that the reformer's response to the Tweed Ring was more than simple moralizing about political sin. But if there was one response, a dynamic one which gave cohesion and direction to his other reactions and provided the most powerful stimulus to reform, it was the fear that civil liberties were in danger, which to a certain degree was true. This response finally gave to the crusade a sense of genuine crisis, its *raison d'être*. The capital crime, then, was not merely the plundering of the treasury, nor the danger to the taxpayer's pocketbook; it was something more sinister than that. It was that a gang of rogues and its vicious brood, an organization alien to American life, was threatening the very bases of republican institutions—the ballot box, the schools, the church, the freedom of speech and press. "This wholesale filching and slaughter of the suffrage is a deadly thrust at the very source and fountain of our liberties ... [we must] recover our mutilated liberties and vindicate our civil rights," shouted Joseph Choate at Cooper Union.[35] The danger to civil liberties was one of the most persistent themes of the *New York Times*.[36] Judge James Emott, Henry Clinton, Henry G. Stebbins, William Evarts, and others, all repeated the same theme: the Tweed Ring had threatened "the existence of free institutions," republicanism was "poisoned," "the glories of liberty are in danger."[37] The threat was felt even outside New York. "Democratic principles can no more carry this curse of Tammany upon them than virtue can thrive in a brothel," said the *Chicago Times*.[38]

If these fears seem exaggerated, it was because the reformers of the Tweed era were faced with their first city boss and his well-organized machine. There had been corruption in the past, but no precedent of modern city bosses to temper the reformer's idealism and sharpen his realism

Although there were differences among the reformers, and their schemes often overlapped, there were broadly two schools of thought on how best to cleanse New York City. The largest school believed that the Ring was not a natural

202

product of American municipal government but a political disease alien to New World representative democracy. The cure, therefore, was relatively simple. Rout the rascals, lance the boil on the body politic, and the organism would be healthy again. This prognosis reflected an implicit faith in the efficacy of American institutions. The defeat of the Tweed Ring meant the vindication of republicanism, not the questioning of it. There were, of course, minor wounds to be treated: the charter needed patching up, there were too many appointive offices, and a tight little bureaucracy should replace the Ring's bloated monster. If the Ring discredited any institution, it was the political party. Partisanship, therefore, should be replaced by efficiency, honesty, and the methods of business. "The government of a city," declared the Union League, "is altogether more a matter of business, than of statesmanship." The party system led only to "lawlessness, disorganization, pillage and anarchy."[39]

For these reformers, the cause of corruption could be the cure of corruption. The absence of the "best people" in government had allowed the wicked to rule. Thus the call was for the return to power of men with substantial wealth, education, and virtue. "The Ring could not keep its own for a day in the teeth of a combined and vigorous opposition from the men of large property."[40] New York was choked with foreigners, "many of them not possessed of virtue and intelligence sufficient for self-government."[41] Therefore, what was needed, said the New York City Council of Political Re-

form, under the heading of "The Effectual Remedy," was for the "right-minded" to enter "into a covenant with each other . . . and the work is done."[42] If this sounded like the voice of the happy ending, it was also the voice of elitism. By implication, the "right-minded" were always the old ruling elite. It represented government of the people, for the people, *by* the "best people."

The second group of reformers did not share the extravagant optimism of the first. Corruption had forced them to re-examine the efficacy of democratic institutions and in so doing they found them wanting. Patchwork will not answer, wrote James Parton. The ship of state needed an overhaul from keel to taffrail, and perhaps it was necessary to "abandon the vessel and build a new one."[43] There must be some "profound defect," said C. C. P. Clark, in the American system which produced the horrors of the Tweed Ring.[44] The defect these reformers saw was one of the hallowed tenets of the American dream, universal suffrage. The comments of E. L. Godkin best illustrate this position. It was nonsense to talk about the Ring as a novelty to the American scene; it was the inevitable result of a "process of evolution," and other great cities have their "mute, inglorious Tweeds" waiting for their opportunity.[45] The curse of the city, "the great city problem " *is* the "people"—or about half of them who constitute the poor, "that huge body of ignorant and corrupt voters." The poor have no conception of self-government and choose only to live off the rich. The blight of universal suffrage is the secret of the Ring's power because it gave them an army. There can be, then, only two cures: first, suffrage should be limited, because only the propertied class, those who have a stake in society, should rule, for "we must somehow put the government into the hands of men who pay taxes." And second, the municipality should be converted into a business, stripped of political influence.[46] This program did not go far enough for Francis Lieber, James Parton, and Isaac Butts. They wanted to impose a literacy test on all New York voters.[47] It was a fine irony that those who felt their civil liberties in danger should seek to curtail the liberties of others.

From whence had come these dreams for a reformed New York? Not from the reformer's own time, for which he expressed a withering indictment. The reformer turned away from his own era, which spawned chaos and upheaval, looked back over his shoulder and found his solutions in a remembrance of things past—or what he *thought* had passed. He reached back for a lost innocence, the simplicity of an older era, the chaste republican order of a golden yesteryear. When he called for the return of the "best people," he thought of past mighties—James Kent, De Witt Clinton, Edward Livingston. His plan for a small, simplified government was the vision of the clean, honest symmetry of the town meeting, which James Welsh fondly recalled as the "natural school of American statesmanship."[48] The concept of limited suffrage, that ideological dog which had had its day, was an image of Order, a responsible aristocracy balancing a rapacious mob. The warmth of reminiscence, however, was an anesthetic to the

reformer's memory. For him the Tweed era dated the decline of political virtue. Before that ranged the long years of a paradise to be found again. Forgotten were the gentlemen rogues, Fernando Wood, the Forty Thieves, and Samuel Swartwout. Nostalgia even led the reformer to tidy up the Albany Regency. Now it was remembered as an organization of "culture, integrity, and character."[49] And Thurlow Weed, an able opponent of the old, honest Regency, apparently with straight face, testified that "formerly the *suspicion* of corruption in a member [of the State legislature] would have put him 'into Coventry.'"[50] As one reform pamphlet said, "Pause here, Reader, sadly to drop a tear on the grave of departed Patriotism."[51]

As the crusade accelerated and unified both reformers and the press by early fall of 1871, the Ring, realizing it was in deep trouble, fought back like a trapped tiger and made some clumsy but typical maneuvers. George Jones was offered a bribe of $500,000 to silence the *Times*. He turned it down saying, "I don't think that the devil will ever bid higher for me than that."[52] Perhaps Thomas Nast needed a rest. He was promised $500,000 if he would leave the country and study art in Europe. "Well, I don't think I'll do it," Nast said. "I made up my mind not long ago to put some of those fellows behind the bars, *and I'm going to put them there!*"[53]

For a while Tweed remained cool and calm. A reporter for the *Missouri Republican* asked him if it were true that he had stolen money. Tweed thought a while and said, "This is not a question one gentleman ought to put to another."[54] George Templeton Strong said: "Tweed's impudent serenity is sublime. Were he not a supreme scoundrel, he would be a great man."[55] Finally, on September 8 he lost his composure and declared to a *Sun* reporter:

The *Times* has been saying all the time I have no brains. Well, I'll show Jones that I have brains. . . . I tell you, sir, if this man Jones had said the things he has said about me, twenty-five years ago, he wouldn't be alive now. But, you see, when a man has a wife and children, he can't do such a thing (clenching his fists). I would have killed him.

Nor did Mayor Hall help matters. He became ensnarled in his own contradictory statements and succeeded only in deepening the Ring's guilt. At first Hall cried innocent. The disclosures of the *Times* were "a tempest of ciphers and calumny . . . a second-hand roar about the accounts of the Supervisors and the salaries of extinct sinecures." Then he admitted some frauds were committed by the "old" Supervisors, but not by the Ring. This was interesting, because Tweed was president of the old Board of Supervisors. He said he never signed the alleged fraudulent warrants, and blamed Watson. He retracted this and admitted signing them, but only as a "ministerial act." He then claimed the signatures were forged; then retracted again and said he had signed but had been "hoodwinked." He tried sonorous prose: "When at last the smoke shall clear away, it will be seen where the political sun will clearly shine, that the proudest flag of them all, waving

untorn from the highest staff of the victorious army, is that which shall never cease to be borne by Tammany Hall."[56]

And naturally Hall attempted humor. "We are likely to have what befell Adam—an early Fall."[57] In an interview with a newspaper, he showed what the *Times* called "cheek."

Reporter: "You are looking very well."

Mayor: "Oh yes, I am always cheerful. You know the true philosophy of life is to take things just as they come. How was the clever definition—let me see, I forget his name—of life? What is mind? No matter. What is matter? Never mind. That's my philosophy."[58]

Once more cupidity came to the aid of the reformers. The Committee of Seventy as well as the Citizens' Committee, composed of private citizens and Aldermen, made plans to examine Comptroller Connelly's books for further proofs of the Ring's misdeeds. On Sunday, September 10, the day before this was to happen, Connolly's office was broken into. From three small cupboards more than 3500 vouchers were stolen. It became a sensation. The Ring had panicked. The *Times* asked sarcastically why the city had spent $404,347.72 on safes and had not given one to the Comptroller. At the same time news came from Washington that Mrs. Connolly had just put one and a half million dollars into government bonds. No longer could the *World, Sun,* and *Herald* spoof the *Times* on its crusade. Even Horace Greeley overcame his jealousy of the *Times* and admitted that a crusade was in order. The theft only intensified Tilden's efforts—he had now committed himself completely to the crusade—to find more proof, which he did when he investigated the accounts at the Ring's Braodway Bank. So careless was the Ring that duplicates of the stolen vouchers were found by Tilden at the bank.

The Ring at best had been untidy. Now all became a shambles. The pressure of the crusade was more than the Ring could endure. The thieves who had traveled so far and so long together quarreled and split into enemy camps. Hall and Sweeny, joining forces against Tweed and Connolly, saw a chance for survival with the voucher disaster. On September 12, 1871, Hall asked Connolly to resign. Connolly, with some logic, replied to Hall that such a step would be equal to a confession, and added: "My official acts have been supervised and approved by your superior vigilance. So far as my administration is questioned equal responsibility attaches to yourself."[59]

It was now, as George Templeton Strong put it, "skunk vs. rattlesnake." Connolly, caring little for the role of sacrificial skunk, fled to the reformers. Tilden then performed a master stroke. He persuaded Connolly to step aside for four months, naming in his place Andrew Green as Acting Comptroller. Green was a distinguished public servant, and by no coincidence, a member of the Committee of Seventy.[60] Hall had made himself ridiculous by demanding Connolly's resignation, which he had no authority to do; Connolly refused and imported some of his toughs from the lower wards to guard his office. It was now skunk vs. *coiled rattlesnake*. Hall asked former General George McClellan to take Connolly's post, but McClellan, cautious in peace and war, refused. The press hooted that Hall had failed. In an interview, Hall told reporters, "Gentlemen, some of you yesterday said that I had received a severe check, and *in testimonium veritatis*, I have, so as you see, put on a check suit."[61] Connolly did deputize Green, and so one of the principal bastions of the Ring's stronghold, the Comptroller's office, was captured.

In the meantime, treason developed on the general staff. John Foley, president of one of the ward reform clubs, applied to George Barnard for an injunction to stop the Ring from paying or raising money in any way in the name of or on the credit of the County and City. Barnard, sensing the coming debacle of the Ring, responded with all the agility of a rat leaping from a sinking ship and granted the injunction. The reformers, never expecting this boon, were elated. As Tweed explained it:

So he put the injunction upon us, and in the straitened condition of our credit, which was so extended on every side, broke us. You see our patronage had become so enormous and so costly that the injunction, which might not have troubled us at any other time, destroyed all our power to raise money from the banks or elsewhere and left us trapped.[62]

Although the injunction was later modified, government was temporarily brought to a standstill. With the city treasury nearly empty, and no recourse to raise money, city employees went for weeks without wages. Tweed gave $50,000 from his own pocket to help laborers and their families, and the *Star*, one of a few remaining journals kind to the Ring, called on the laborers to start a bread riot.[63] New Yorkers, remembering the horror of the draft riots of 1863, and the bloody Orange Parade riot of July 12, 1870, redoubled their efforts to oust the Ring.

The injunction accomplished its purpose. The main arteries of political power, money, and patronage were suddenly dried up. The thieves were fighting among themselves. With Green ruthlessly chopping off sinecure appointments, the shiny hats, stripped of place and status, were losing faith in their chiefs. With an election coming up, *Harper's* and the *Times* were joined by the rest of the New York press, and the crusade reached fever pitch. The public was daily reminded of Tweed's arrogant, "What are you going to do about it?" The Tweed Ring seemed on the threshold of disaster. But the reformers underestimated the talents of the Boss.

For the leaders of the anti-Tammany Democracy it seemed that victory was in easy grasp. All that was necessary was to control the State nominating convention at Rochester. This did not appear difficult in light of the disasters that had befallen Tweed and company. Then the reformers could elect a reform platform, reveal the further evidence compiled by the investigations of the Committee of Seventy, campaign against the horrors of the Tweed Ring, and ride to victory in the November election. Tilden made elaborate preparations to capture the convention by sending out 26,000 letters to Democratic politicos asking for support with a one-two punch: he put the name of Charles O'Conor in nomination for the attorney-generalship, and disputed the right of the regular Tammany delegates to represent the city in the convention. Thus with belated courage, Tilden arose, rallied the reformers, and denounced the Ring. He realized the Ring's only chance of survival lay in renominating its henchmen for city and state offices, and helping the election of Republicans who had worked with it in past legislatures—but so did the Boss.

The reformers lost some of their confidence when Tweed and his entourage, gangs of New York toughs, arrived in Rochester. Threats of violence were made against anyone who should interfere with the Ring; delegates were warned that the convention would be broken up by force if anti-Tammany delegates were admitted to the floor. The reformers found themselves reliving an old story: once again they were outmaneuvered and outwitted. Crafty as usual, Tweed moved among the delegates and argued that the recent exposures were merely a local issue and that an all-out fight in the convention would undoubtedly split the party and allow the Republicans an easy victory in November. For the sake of party unity he was willing to compromise. If the reform representatives were omitted from the roll of delegates, he would omit the Tammany representatives.

207

Alexander B. Callow, Jr.

What appeared as a compromise was actually a victory. Even with the Tammany delegation missing, Tweed was able to control the convention, through lack of opposition from the reformers, and with the help of friends won by bribery. Charles O'Conor, who would never have hesitated to throw the entire machinery of the state against the Ring, was defeated for the attorney-generalship by a large majority. A state ticket bulging with names of the Ring's minions was nominated. Tweed turned against the reformers with arrogance. He called Tilden, Horatio Seymour, and Francis Kernan "three troublesome old fools."[64]

Tweed had good reason to gloat. A few days before the convention he was re-elected chairman of the Tammany General Committee, and at the convention he was renominated for State Senator. He returned to New York in triumph. At Walton House he took the platform, removed a little Scotch tweed cap, and told a boisterous audience:

The newspapers have already indicted, tried, convicted and sentenced and sentenced (roars of laughter), but I feel perfectly free to appeal to a higher tribunal, and have no fear of the result (cheers). I do not come to you, my fellow citizens, in a circuitous way, indicative of the possession of the thought of the necessity of caution engendered by fear, but directly, openly, squarely, as a man to men, and without an appeal for your sympathy other than so far as my family have suffered from the cruel indignities that have been heaped upon them for my political actions (sensation). But asking at your hands the justice and fair play that have

been denied me by bitter, unrelenting, unscrupulous, prejudiced and ambitious partisan foes (deafening shouts of approval). . . .[65]

The reformers, who had once gloated, returned to New York shaken and sober. The glitter of their confidence was dulled, but their resolution was firm—even firmer. Tweed's victory at Rochester had robbed them of a valuable tactical weapon, the opportunity to proclaim themselves the regular Democratic organization. The Ring, even though quarreling among themselves, still commanded a powerful election-day army. But failure only reinforced the reformers' determination. What had seemed after the exposures to be an easy victory was now an uphill fight. The reformers were forced to be a rival of the regular organization, and hence a third-party group, with all the difficulties a third party faced. Many of the reformers' leaders were political prima donnas—O'Conor was known for his irascibility, Tilden could be exasperatingly aloof. If thieves fell out, reformers seemed to delight in dissension and to fragment into splinter groups. If the reformers were going to battle the Tweed Ring, they needed unity, organization, and outside support. But the Republicans were notoriously weak and inept. Then, as now, thousands of eligible voters never bothered to go to the polls. There was the danger that the none-too-reputable groups, like Mozart Hall and the Young Democracy, posing as reformers now that the Ring was embarrassed, might capture leadership from the reformers.

If the odds were formidable, the re-

208

formers were driven to work together if for no other reason than the fact that election day might be the last chance to destroy the Ring. Public indignation could not be sustained at a high pitch forever. Six days before the election, the Committee of Seventy released the evidence they unearthed from the Broadway Bank accounts. Important Republicans were persuaded to unite in a common cause by voting a straight reform ticket and not to present a separate Republican ticket to complicate matters. Young Men's Reform Associations were organized. The students of New York University, to whom Hall had recently lectured with applause, tore down the Mayor's portrait from their walls. The newspapers maintained a heavy barrage, exhorting voters to register, publicizing the facts behind the Ring's schemes, and explaining all the tactics Tammany might use to defraud the public on election day. Huge express wagons, drawn by six horses, stood ready to convey a reserve police force to any scene of disorder. Plans were made to take detected repeaters to the armories for custody to avoid the sure chance of their discharge by the courts. With a burst of excitement and energy, the reformers invaded the lower wards, the central nervous system of Tammany Hall, posting signs, passing out pamphlets, haranguing the native and immigrant poor with sidewalk speeches.

The tempo increased as the clergy of New York, pounding their pulpits, spoke out against the Tweed Ring for the first time. Dr. Henry D. Northrup of the Presbyterian Church echoed a common theme: there were but two parties, he roared, God's and the devil's. Election day "is a time when every citizen should show himself to be a man and not a sneak."[66]

The reformers, who now thought they could win, called several rallies to keep things going at a white heat. On November 2, a rally was held to receive the report of the Committee of Seventy. The motto over the president's chair read: "What are we going to do about it?" George Templeton Strong, pessimistic as usual, did not think they were going to do anything. "The disease of this community," he wrote in his diary, "lies too deep to be cured by meetings, resolutions, and committees. We the people are a low set, without moral virility. Our rulers, Tweed and Company, are about good enough for us."[67]

But Strong's pessimism seemed to be shared by few. The cadence of protest from the reformers, the press, the clergy, was picked up in the saloons, the restaurants, the clubs. Apathy had vanished. New York was agog with one topic of conversation, not the recent Chicago fire, not the visit of the Grand Duke Alexis, but the chance—the bare chance, that the reformers might beat the Tweed Ring on November 7th. On the eve of election day, New Yorkers waited with apprehension, and prepared themselves for one of the most important and exciting elections ever held in New York City.

Much to their own astonishment, the reformers gave Tammany Hall one of the worst defeats in its history up to that time. The scandals had finally roused New Yorkers into action. There was an unusually large turnout, and many who previously had been apathetic, went to the polls and registered their indignation with Tammany. The reformers guarded the polling places well, and were successful in protecting themselves against excessive fraud and repeating. Moreover, several of the repeater gangs sensed the fall of the Ring and withdrew their support. The reformers elected all fifteen Aldermen, thirteen Assistant Aldermen out of twenty-one, and carried fourteen of the twenty Assembly districts. Prominent among the new Assemblymen were ex-Mayor Daniel E. Tiemann and Samuel Tilden. General Franz Siegel effectively wooed the Germans and became State Register. There were impressive upstate gains. The reformers captured four out of five Senatorial seats. The one they failed to win was the sour note. O'Donovan Rossa had once led the Irish against the British but could not do the same against Tweed in New York. The people of the Seventh District stood by the man who had served them so well with patronage and charity, and Tweed won over Rossa by over 10,000 votes. The reformers' broom swept out many of the Ring's important lieutenants. Henry Woltman was defeated by Augustus Weismann, the first German-born man to be elected to the State Senate. Timothy Campbell, Henry Genet, James Irving, and Michael Norton were all defeated. Alexander Frear and Thomas Fields were prevented from taking their seats because of election fraud. The full measure of defeat was revealed a few days later. It was announced that the annual Americus Club ball was postponed.

Once again the *Times* reported a quiet election day. It was a moot point, the newspaper said, whether this resulted from the precautions taken by the reformers or that Tammany was cowed. Of course there were some "altercations and word-combats," and, "heads punched in the good old fashion so dear to the Democracy." Compared to the previous year, the reformers had won away from the regular Democrats almost 75,000 votes in the city and state, "one of the most remarkable political revolutions in the history of the country," said a contemporary, with some exaggeration.[68] The *Times* maintained that the election was won by the strong vote of the so-called neutral population, who seldom voted— "the gentlemen and quiet citizens."[69] But while there was a large registration, there were not enough neutrals to decide the election. Ironically, it was the very people the reformers despised the most, the immigrants and the native poor, who, because of their great numbers, put the reformers into office by splitting their vote between Tammany and the men running on the Democratic reform ticket.[70]

The victory over Tammany was seen as the end of a great crusade. There was much excitement. For most it meant the vindication of popular government, the triumph of the people's voice, a moral struggle where good overwhelmed evil. Under a huge headline, "New York Redeemed," the *Times* said:

The victory we have won is priceless, not only from what it gives us now, but because it will revive every man's faith in the ultimate triumph of truth and justice—because it will teach scheming poli-

210

ticians that the voice of the people is supreme, and that immortal principles on which this Government is founded, although they may be momentarily stifled by dishonest factions, will constantly rise triumphant, while the men who assailed them will pass away to everlasting infamy.[71]

The reformer George C. Barrett, a successful candidate, said the victory was an answer to those who had scoffed at the success of a republican form of government.[72] *Harper's Weekly* said it was one of the most significant events in the history of free governments.[73]

Only E. L. Godkin pondered whether the great "uprising" was the final and complete triumph over political corruption, whether routing the rascals was only the beginning of reform—real reform. . . .[74]

What, then, was the final reckoning of the Tweed Ring? Although Judges Barnard and McCunn were impeached, and removed from office, and Cardozo resigned but continued to practice law, none of the three were criminally prosecuted. With two exceptions, none of the Ring and its many partners in graft were ever caught or punished. Only Tweed and Ingersoll went to jail. From 1871 to 1878, Tweed spent less than half of that time in prison. Ingersoll who turned himself in, hoping for a light sentence, was sentenced to five years and seven months, but served only a few months of his term before he was pardoned by Tilden for turning State's evidence and promising to become a witness in any forthcoming Ring trials. At the time of Tweed's death

sixteen suits were pending against various members of the Tweed Ring organization.[75] None came to trial. Garvey was granted immunity to appear as a witness at the Tweed and Hall trials. Although a millionaire, he never returned any of the money he made. Woodward was granted immunity for returning $155,000, although he had stolen over a million. John Keyser had the delightful gall to claim that is was the city who owed him, and he was almost successful in being awarded a $33,000 claim based on a fraudulent contract![76] Of the twenty to two hundred million dollars estimated to have been stolen by the Ring, it cost the city $257,848.34 to recover $894,525.44, most of which came from the estates of two dead men, James Watson and James Sweeny.

The ethos of reform however, was essentially moralistic and conservative. For some the issue was a total commitment to punishing bad men, not the examination of the institutions and conditions that made it possible for bad men to exist and thrive. To them, the cause of corruption was the work of evil men. Their optimism blinded them to the realities of a rapidly growing society, the massive growth of a great city and the effects it would have on political life. For those who questioned institutions, the answer lay not in adaptation but in a return to the good old days of rule by gentry, suffrage restrictions, tight economy, and a tiny bureaucracy. In the months, years, and decades following the Ring's fall, the reformer, imprisoned by his own social philosophy, continued to alienate the immigrant newcomer. What could have been a source of

Alexander B. Callow, Jr.

power for the reformer remained the strength of later city bosses. As the city grew and its problems multiplied, the reformer continued to turn back to that Promised Land of the good old days for his solutions to corruption, patching the charter here, passing a resolution there, always haunted by his failure to restore the profession of politics to the nobility of the Old Republic. Exposure of the Tweed Ring had given him a glimpse into the hard realities of big-city politics. But he continued to be an innocent abroad in the strange land of the professional politician and practical politics, preferring the platitude to the free cigar. He never understood the politicians who made politics their business, their appeal to the masses, their attention to the plight of the immigrant, nor, indeed, the kind of world they were living in. Thus the rascals were routed, but their supreme achievement, the city machine itself, remained essentially intact, to become a model, a legacy, to be improved upon by succeeding monarchs of New York, the Kellys, the Crokers, and the Murphys.

After all was said and done, the crusade against the Tweed Ring won the battle but lost the war. In a real sense, William Marcy Tweed had the last word, when he asked, "Well, what are you going to do about it?"

NOTES

1. Wingate, "Episode in Municipal Government," July 1875, p. 150.
2. See Citizens' Association, "An Appeal by the Citizens' Association of New York against the Abuses in the Local Government to the Legislature of the State of New York, and to the Public" (New York, 1866); "Items of Abuse in the Government of the City of New York" (New York, 1866); "Report of the Executive Council to the Honorary Council of the Citizens' Association" (New York, 1866); "Wholesale Corruption! Sale of Situations in Fourth Ward Schools" (New York, 1864); Union League Club, "Report on Cities" (New York, 1867); "The Report of the Committee on Municipal Reform" (New York, 1867).
3. Jan. 24-25, Feb. 15, 1870. The *Times* also reported on Mar. 9, 1870, that Richard Connolly was fighting the Ring.
4. Apr. 8, 13, 1870. See also Apr. 6, 12, and May 1, 1870.
5. July 13, 1871, quoted in the *Times*, July 14, 1871.
6. Apr. 3, 1872.
7. J. D. Townsend, *New York in Bondage* (1901), p. 73.
8. Nov. 3, 1870.
9. Ibid.
10. Ibid.; Sept. 16, 1871.
11. Dec. 4, 1870. When the celebrated Henry Ward Beecher said he pitied wicked men because their consciences would surely suffer, the *Times* replied in a blistering attack, saying Beecher's pity was "morbid, unwholesome, sentimental." Oct. 24, 1871.
12. Oct. 3, 1870.
13. Sept. 13, 1870.
14. Feb. 26, May 1, 1870; Oct. 3, 1870.
15. "The great strength of General Grant's Administration . . . lies in the fact that he is believed to be honest himself, and disposed to enforce honesty and fidelity in all departments of the Government under his control." *New York Times*, Sept. 21, 1871.
16. Unidentified newspaper, *Scrapbooks of Clippings Relating to the Career of A. Oakey Hall* (New York Public Library), Vol. iv, p. 113.
17. *New York Times*, Jan. 25, 1873.
18. July 28, 31, 1871. See also *New York World*, Aug. 2, 7, 10, 1871. The *New York Sun* and *New York Evening Post* also criticized the *Times*. Bowen, *The Elegant Oakey*, p. 99. Moreover, Charles Nordhoff, the managing editor

of the *Evening Post,* was fired for attacking Tweed. Lynch, *Boss Tweed*, p. 355.

19. Bowen, *The Elegant Oakey*, p. 106. See also Allan Nevins and Thomas Milton Halsey, *The Diary of George Templeton Strong*, III (4 vols.), pp. 376, 383, 385-6.

20. Genung, *Frauds of New York*, pp. 9-13.

21. *Tweed Investigation*, pp. 50-55; Hirsch, "More Light on Boss Tweed," p. 272.

22. For a compilation of the *Times's* evidence, see *New York Times*, "How New York is Governed. Frauds of the Tammany Democrats," 1871.

23. Breen, *Thirty Years of New York Politics*, p. 337.

24. *New York Times*, Sept. 5, 1871.

25. Oct. 2, 1871.

26. *New York Times*, Oct. 10, 1870; Jan. 20, Mar. 6, 1871.

27. *New York Times*, July 12, 1871.

28. Ibid. July 16, 1871.

29. "Report of the Executive Council to the Honarary Council of the Citizens' Association" (New York, 1866), p. 21. See also "Civil Rights: A History of the New York Riot of 1871" (1871), p. 20; Nevins and Halsey, *Diary of Strong*, iv, p. 352; Thomas Nast, *Miss Columbia's School, or Will It Blow Over?*, 1871, p. 71, *passim; Harper's Weekly*, July 29, 1871. For other examples of the nativist impulse, see *The Nation*, July 20, 1871. p. 36; *New York Times*, Mar. 18, Apr. 7, July 17-18, 21, 24, Aug. 17, 1871; Wingate, "Episode in Municipal Government," Oct. 1874, pp. 378-9; Townsend, *New York in Bondage*, p. 186; Nevins, *Diary of Strong*, iv, p. 317.

While nativism was widespread in the reformers' camp, some were anti-nativist. See A. R. Lawrence, "The Government of Cities" (New York, 1868), pp. 4-5, 11.

30. *New York Times*, Sept. 17, 1869; Jan. 7, Nov. 30, 1870; Mar. 19, 26, July 16, Sept. 17, 1871. Otto Kempner, "Boss Croker's Career," p. 6.

31. July 16, 1871. See also Sept. 17, 1869; Oct. 17, 1870; Feb. 2, Mar. 19, 1871.

32. *The Nation*, Nov. 16, 1871, p. 316.

33. Jan. 25, 1871. See also *New York Times*, Jan. 24, 1870; *New York Star*, Mar. 25, 1870; Wingate, "Episode in Municipal Government," cxix (Oct. 1874), p. 379.

34. "Statement and Plea of the New York City Council of Political Reform," p. 34.

35. *American Addresses*, pp. 61-2, 72; *New York Times*, Sept. 18, 1871; (Anon.) "Why Vote at All in '72," p. 37. Robert Roosevelt declared that the Ring "pulled away the very keystone of the arch of liberty." If the public money is stolen, wrote another reformer, "why not the public liberties too?"

36. Feb. 8, April 3, Oct. 12, 17, Nov. 3-4, 1870; Jan. 24, Feb. 24-25, Apr. 7, May 1, July 16, Sept. 5, 26-27, Oct. 27, Nov. 3, 1871.

37. Jones, *Fisk*, p. 226; *New York Times*, Sept. 4, Nov. 3, 1871. See also Abram Genung, *The Frauds of the New York City Government Exposed*, p. 41; Gustav Lening. *The Dark Side of New York*, p. 694; James Welsh, "The Root of the Municipal Evil," p. 7; Nast, *Miss Columbia's School*, pp. 39, 71; New York Council of Political Reform, "Statement and Plea," p. 40.

38. Sept. 29, 1871.

39. "Report on Municipal Reform," pp. 17-18; see also "Why Vote at All in '72," p. 72; Welsh, "Root of the Municipal Evil," p. 5.

40. *New York Times,* Jan. 23, 1871.

41. New York City Council of Political Reform, "Report of the New York City Council of Political Reform," p. 3.

42. "Statement and Plea," p. 28. See also "Report of the New York City Council of Political Reform," pp. 4-11; The Citizens' Association, "Report of the Executive Council to the Honarary Council," p. 22; Wilson, *Memorial History*, iii, p. 562; Bryce, *American Commonwealth* (1889 ed.), ii, p. 353, (1895 ed.), ii, pp. 391, 403.

For an interesting criticism of the "best people" theory, see *The Nation*, Aug. 24, 1871, p. 125.

43. "The Government of New York," p. 451.

44. "The Commonwealth Reconstructed," p. 26.

45. *The Nation*, Apr. 18, 1878, p. 257; Nov. 9, 1871, p. 300; Nov. 27, 1873, p. 350.

46. Ibid. Nov. 4, 1875, p. 288; Oct. 18, 1877,

p. 238; Nov. 27, 1873, p. 350; Apr. 18, 1878, p. 257; Oct. 12, 1871, p. 237; Nov. 4, 1875, p. 289. See also Union League, "Report on Municipal Reform," pp. 19-20, 76-7, 88; Parton, "Government of New York," p. 463.

For an attack on this position, see Charles Nordhoff, "The Mis-Government of New York, a Remedy Suggested," *North American Review*, ccxxxiii (Oct. 1871), pp. 321-43, *passim*.

47. Francis Lieber, "Reflections on the Changes Which May Seem Necessary in the Present Constitution of the State of New York," p. 4; Parton, "Government of New York," p. 460; *Rochester Union and Advertiser*, Oct. 3, 1871.

48. "Root of Municipal Evil," p. 19.

49. *New York Times*, Sept. 11, 1869.

50. Parton, "Government of New York," p. 457.

51. (Anon.), "Why Vote at All in '72," p. 29.

52. Werner, *Tammany Hall*, p. 210.

53. Albert Paine, *Thomas Nast*, 1904, p. 182.

54. *New York Times*, Aug. 24, 1871.

55. Nevins and Thomas, *Diary of Strong*, Vol. iv, p. 394.

56. For Hall's excuses, see *New York Times*, July 12, 29, Aug. 12, Sept. 11, Oct. 10, 13; *The Leader*, Aug. 19, 1871.

57. Flick, *Tilden*, p. 213; see also *New York Times*, Aug. 29, 1871.

58. *New York Times*, Sept. 22, 1871.

59. Ibid. Sept. 17, 1871.

60. Green had served thirteen years on the Park Commission, helped to plan Central Park, suggested Riverside Drive and many of the smaller parks, established the American Scenic and Historic Preservation Society, and did much to effect the merger of the Tilden, Astor, and Lenox foundations in the New York Public Library.

61. Wingate, "Episode in Municipal Government," Oct. 1876, p. 379.

62. Lynch, *Boss Tweed*, p. 375.

63. Sept. 27, 1871.

64. Flick, *Tilden*, p. 219.

65. *New York Times*, Nov. 5, 1871.

66. Ibid. Nov. 6, 1871.

67. Nevins and Thomas, *Diary of Strong*, Vol. iv, p. 382.

68. Wingate, "Episode in Municipal Government," Oct. 1876, p. 389.

69. Nov. 11, 1871.

70. O'Connor, *Hell's Kitchen*, p. 50; Lynch, *Boss Tweed*, pp. 383-4.

71. Nov. 8, 1871.

72. Ibid.

73. Cited with no date in *New York Times*, July 12, 1872.

74. *The Nation*, Nov. 9, 1871, p. 300.

75. *Tweed Investigations*, pp. 841-45.

76. Ibid. pp. 601-85.

SOCIAL
AND STRUCTURAL REFORM

Melvin Holli

Pingree's brand of social reform—whose objective was to lower utility rates for the consumer and which attempted to place a larger share of the municipal tax burden on large corporations—was not the prevailing mood of urban reform in late-nineteenth and early-twentieth-century America. Far more prevalent in the programs of large-city mayors who earned the epithet "reformer" was the effort to change the structure of municipal government, to eliminate petty crime and vice, and to introduce the business system of the contemporary corporation into municipal government. Charter tinkering, elaborate audit procedures, and the drive to impose businesslike efficiency upon city government were the stock-in-trade of this type of urban executive. Mayors of this kind of reform persuasion could be found in New York, Brooklyn, Buffalo, San Francisco, and countless other cities.

From *Reform in Detroit: Hazen S. Pingree and Urban Politics* by Melvin G. Holli. Copyright © 1969 by Oxford University Press, Inc. Reprinted by permission.

Although most of these structural reformers did not articulate their positions as eloquently as Seth Low or attempt to install business methods as ruthlessly as John Purroy Mitchel, they all shared a certain style, a number of common assumptions about the cause of municipal misgovernment, and, in some instances, a conviction about which class was best fitted to rule the city. Few of them were as blatantly outspoken in their view of democracy as Samuel S. McClure, the publisher of the leading muckrake journal. He instructed Lincoln Steffens to prove that popular rule was a failure and that cities should be run by a dictatorship of wise and strong men, such as Samuel S. McClure or Judge Elbert Gary. Similarly New York's former reform mayor Abram Hewitt asserted in 1901 that "ignorance should be excluded from control, [and] the city business should be carried on by trained experts selected upon some other principle than popular suffrage."[1]

None of the structural reformers had the unqualified faith in the ability of the masses to rule themselves intelligently that social reformers Hazen S. Pingree, Samuel "Golden Rule" Jones, or Tom L. Johnson did. "I have come to lean upon the common people as the real foundation upon which good government must rest," Pingree told the Nineteenth Century Club in 1897. In a statement that represented more than a rhetorical flourish, "Golden Rule" Jones chastised Reverend Josiah Strong for his distrust of the masses and told him that the "voice of the people is the voice of God." Tom Johnson, asserted Brand Whitlock, knew that "the cure for the ills of democracy was not less democracy, as so many people were always preaching, but more democracy." When Johnson was defeated by the Cleveland electorate at the very pinnacle of one of the most productive urban reform careers in the nation, he told Whitlock, "The people are probably right."[2]

The structural reform movement was in sharp contrast to the democratic mood of such a statement. It represented instead the first wave of prescriptive municipal government which placed its faith in rule by educated, upper class Americans and, later, by municipal experts rather than the lower classes. The installation in office of men of character, substance, and integrity was an attempt to impose middle class and patrician ideals upon the urban masses. The movement reached its height in the second and third decades of the twentieth century with the city-manager and city-commissioner forms of government, which called for the hiring of nonpartisan experts to decide questions hitherto viewed as resolvable only by the political process. Like the structural reform movement of the late-nineteenth-century, the city-manager movement reflected an implicit distrust of popular democracy.[3]

New York's Mayor William F. Havemeyer was a prototype of the twentieth-century structural reformers. Having inherited a substantial fortune, he retired from the sugar refining business at the age of forty and devoted most of his career to public service. Elected mayor in 1872 during the public exposure of the Tweed Ring, Havemeyer was a reformer who championed "clean government," "economy," and the business class point of view. Obsessed with tax cuts and retrenchment, he and his fiscal watchdog, city Treasurer Andrew H. Green, cut wages on public works and demanded elaborate procedures to account for all petty expenditures of public funds. Green's painstaking scrutiny of every claim snarled the payroll so badly that the city's laborers rioted when their pay checks got lost in an administrative tangle.[4]

To practice economy, Havemeyer sacrificed important public services and, in the process, "crippled downtown development." During a three-month period in 1874 the Mayor vetoed more than 250 bills related to street grading, paving, and widening, board of education contracts, and appropriations intended for public charities. In justifying his liquidation of work relief, Havemeyer told the Harvard Association that contributions of private individuals and Christian and charitable associations were generous enough to meet the needs of the poor. According to

Seymour Mandelbaum, the lower classes and the promoters of new areas of the city suffered most from Havemeyer's policies.[5]

During his second year in office, the aging Mayor fought with the city council and accomplished nothing of lasting importance. Havemeyer and the New York Council of Political Reform were so obsessed with "honest, efficient and economical government" that they indicted every public improvement as a "job" and labeled every politician who supported such measures as an "exponent of the class against which society is organized to protect itself." The Mayor's death in 1874 mercifully ended the agony of a reform administration which was strangling the city with red tape generated by its own economy programs. Ironically, Havemeyer helped to perpetuate the widespread belief that reformers were meddling, ineffectual reactionaries, or, as George Washington Plunkitt charged, "morning glories" who wilted in the heat of urban politics.[6]

Buffalo's "fighting mayor," Grover Cleveland, 1882, was another one of the progenitors of the structural reform tradition. Preoccupied as much as Havemeyer with cutting taxes and municipal expenditures, Cleveland had no positive programs to offer, with one notable exception: he fought and won authorization for a massive interceptor sewer system to diminish the dumping of refuse into the Erie Canal. He made his mark in Buffalo by the veto of a corrupt street-cleaning contract, the "most spectacular single event" of his administration in Allan Nevins's view. In addition, Cleveland fought to stop the constant proliferation of city jobs, exercised a Havemeyer-type of vigilance over all claims made against the city treasury, and directed city employees to stop closing their offices at 4:00 P.M. and to perform a full day's work. His inflexible drive for economy and efficiency and his contempt for the dishonesty of city machines won him a reputation as a rugged veto and reform mayor.[7]

Seth Low, a wealthy merchant, philanthropist, and univeristy president, was mayor of Brooklyn (1882-85) and later of New York (1902-03). Perhaps more than any other American mayor, he possessed the qualities of a high-minded, nonpartisan structural reformer who attempted to infuse a large dose of businesslike efficiency into municipal government. He was widely recognized by his generation as one of the most prominent practicing reformers on the urban scene, but he also built a considerable reputation as a scholar of municipal affairs. In countless addresses, Low argued that the answer to urban problems was charter reform to bring nonpartisanship and a centralized administration into city government. Reform of this sort would arouse a new civic consciousness and create a cohesive corporate government that could be run along business lines, free from outside influences.[8]

Under the aegis of a silk-stocking Citizens' Committee, Low, with his refined eloquence and business support, had waged an effective campaign against political spoilsmanship and partisanship and won Brooklyn's mayoralty election in 1881. Low disregarded political affiliation and based his appointments on ability and merit. Although his two terms proved to be unspectacular, Low had advanced what he considered the cardinal principles of municipal reform: he had reduced the city's debt, tightened up the tax system and conducted a vigorous campaign at Albany to stop special state legislation from interfering in Brooklyn's affairs. Such social questions as tenement house reform and aid to the aged, the poor, or workingmen were for Seth Low but special benefits which could not be considered until local partisanship had been wiped out and municipal government had been reorganized along the lines of authority and responsibility. Low's name had become synonymous with efficiency, responsibility, and clean government.[9]

After a particularly flagrant period of municipal corruption under Tammany Hall, a reform-minded Citizens' Union, which counted J. Pierpont Morgan and Elihu Root among its founders, asked Seth Low to enter the lists as an independent candidate for mayor of New York against the Tammany favorite in 1901. Low ran on a platform of home rule and nonpartisanship, avoided the social-welfare planks endorsed by the Citizens' Union, and discussed honesty, economy, and responsibility in his speeches. Low was known to the voters because he had assisted in drafting the first charter for Greater New York, which consolidated hundreds of small towns and three large cities into one unit. Low's victory in 1901 was probably less an endorsement of his brand of reform than a public reaction against the excesses of Tammany.[10]

As New York's mayor, Low brought in

experts to operate the various departments, pared away Tammany's payroll padding, and set himself up as the businessman in office. He cut salaries, increased the length of the working day for municipal employees, and reduced the city's annual budget by $1,500,000. In the public transit and utility field, Low saw to it that franchises were carefully drafted to safeguard the city's interests and to provide for additional revenue. He failed to press for lower rates, to agitate for a public rate-making body, or to instruct his district attorney to investigate the corrupt alliances between private business and politicians. He balked at appointing one of the best-qualified housing reformers, Lawrence Veiller, to head the tenement house commission, apparently because Low did not wish to disturb the conservative real estate interests. Low was willing, however, to use the full force of law against Sunday drinking, petty gambling, and prostitution, which were commonly found in the immigrant and lower class sections of the city. The Bureau of Licenses also cracked down on the city's 6,000 pushcart peddlers who were operating without licenses, and the Department of Law prosecuted residents whose tax payments were delinquent. With similiar zeal, the Department of Water raised nearly $1,000,000 in income from overdue water bills.[11]

Low's tinkering with the machinery of government, his charter revision and rewriting, his regularization of tax collections, his enforcement of the city statutes, his appointment of men of merit, and his reduction of city expenditures were laudable actions by almost anybody's test of good government. Unfortunately, these measures bore most severely upon the lower classes. Low's structural reforms were also very impolitic, as his defeat in the election of 1903 demonstrated. Low never seemed to realize that his municipal reform had nothing to offer the voters but sterile, mechanical changes and that fundamental social and economic conditions which pressed upon the vast urban masses of immigrants and poor could not be changed by rewriting charters or enforcing laws.[12]

San Francisco's reform mayor James D. Phelan, a wealthy banker and anti-Bryan Democrat who held office from 1897 to 1902, was also a structural reformer like his model, Seth Low, whom Phelan frequently quoted. Phelan's program for reform included the introduction of efficiency and economy to ensure "scientific, systematic and responsible government," which was also the goal of the San Francisco Merchants' Association. Franchise regulation, lower traction rates, municipal ownership, and equal taxation were not part of Phelan's design for a better San Francisco. The distinguishing mark of the Phelan administration was its sponsorship of a strong mayor, and a short ballot charter that provided rigid fiscal controls over expenditures, city-wide elections for the council, and a merit system. Known as a "watchdog of the treasury," Mayor Phelan supported a low tax rate that forced the city to withhold schoolteachers' salaries, suspend many of the essential functions of the city health department, subject patients at the city hos-

pital to inadequate care, and turn off the street lights at midnight. Phelan crippled his administration when he permitted the president of the police commissioners (who was also president of the Chamber of Commerce) to protect strikebreakers and club pickets during a teamsters' and a dock-workers' strike against the open shop. Although the 18 unions lost their strike, they retaliated by forming their own political party and defeating the reformers in 1901. In the famous graft prosecutions after 1901, Phelan continued to act like a "member of his class" or, as Fremont Older put it, "a rich man toward a great business in which he is interested."[13] Like Low, Phelan failed to attack what social reformers recognized as the basic problems confronting the city.

Equally ineffectual in his attempt to make New York the best governed city in the nation was Mayor John Purroy Mitchel, who served from 1914 to 1917. He was an "oddly puritanical Catholic" who represented the foibles and virtues of patrician class reform. Mitchel's election in 1913 was the result of voter reaction to a decade of brazen looting by Tammany Hall. Like his reform predecessors, Mitchel was responsible for little of lasting importance and did not generate enthusiasm among the large mass of voters with his structural reforms.[14]

Mitchel's failure was due to his misconception that city government could be conducted by the "ledger book ethics of the corporation accountant." So dedicated was Mitchel to budgetary cutbacks that he adopted the Gary Plan of education, which enabled New York City to cram more children into the existing schools. He decreased appropriations for the city's night schools, thus seriously hampering the entire program; for the summer program, Mitchel asked the teachers to volunteer their services without remuneration. Mitchel also appointed cost-cutting charity agents who began either to return feeble-minded children to their parents or to threaten to charge the often hard-pressed parents if their children were kept in public supported institutions. In addition, he instituted an investigation of the city's religious child-care organizations, hoping thus to cut the city subsidy; but this action brought the wrath of the Catholic church down upon him.[15] Mitchel, although well-intentioned, had a kind of King Midas touch in reverse: everything he touched seemed to turn to ashes.

Robert Moses dismissed the Mitchel administration's efficiency drives as "saving rubber bands" and "using both ends of the pencil," but its flaws were much greater. The Mitchel administration and the structural reform movement were not only captives of a modern business mentality but sought to impress middle and upper class social values upon the urban community and to redistribute political power to the patrician class.[16]

Built upon a narrow middle and patrician class base and a business concept of social responsibility, the structural reform movement, with its zeal for efficiency and economy, usually lacked staying power. As George Washington Plunkitt pointed out, such crusaders were usually repudiated by lower class voters after a brief tenure in office. Unlike the social

reformers, who were also interested in economy, the structural reformers had a blind spot when it came to weighing the human cost of their programs. They failed to recognize that a dose of something as astringent as wage-cutting and payroll audits had to be counterbalanced with social welfare programs if the public were to be served effectively. Too often they blamed the immigrant for the city's shortcomings or directed much of the force of their administrations to exterminating lower-class vices, which they saw as the underlying causes of municipal problems.[17]

Unlike the structural reformers, social reform mayers such as Hazen S. Pingree (1890-97), "Golden Rule" Jones (1897-1904), Tom Johnson (1901-09), Mark Fagan (1901-07), Brand Whitlock (1906-13), and Newton D. Baker (1912-16) began with a different set of assumptions about the basic causes of misgovernment in the cities. They shared the view, which Lincoln Steffens later publicized, that big business and its quest for preferential treatment and special privileges had corrupted municipal government. The public service corporations, the utilities, the real estate interests, and the large industrial concerns all had vested interests in urban America. They sought special tax advantages, franchises which eliminated competition, and other municipal concessions. They bought aldermen, councilmen, and mayors to protect these interests and, in the process, demoralized urban politics and city government. Mayor Tom Johnson's aide Frederic C. Howe was shocked when he was berated by his upper class friends for opposing a franchise steal; they explained that the public utilities have "millions of dollars invested" and had to "protect their investments." "But I do say emphatically," declared Mayor Pingree in 1895, ". . . better take [the utilities] out of private hands than allow them to stand as the greatest corruptors of public morals that ever blackened the pages of history."[18]

The programs of the social reform mayors aimed at lower gas, light, telephone, and street railway rates for the community and higher taxes for railroads and business corporations. When they were unable to obtain the regulation of public utilities, these mayors fought for municipal ownership, the only technique to redistribute economic power available to them as urban executives. Establishment of free public baths, expansion of parks, schools, and public relief were similarly attempts to distribute the amenities of middle class life to the masses. The social reformers recognized that the fight against crime in its commonly understood sense (i.e., rooting out gambling, drinking, and prostitution) was an attempt to treat the symptoms rather than the disease itself and that such campaigns would burn out the energies of a reform administration and leave the fundamental problems of the urban masses untouched. Pingree, like Jones and Johnson, believed that such binges of "Comstockery" were irrelevant to municipal reform. "The good people are always insisting upon 'moral' issues," asserted Toledo Mayor Brand Whitlock, "urging us to turn aside from our large immediate purpose, and concentrate our official attention on the

'bad' people—and wreck our movement."[19]

The saloons where drinking, gambling, and other vices flourished, Pingree, Jones, and Johnson agreed, were but poor men's clubs and offered the workers but a few of the comforts that most rich men enjoyed. "The most dangerous enemies to good government are not the saloons, the dives, the dens of iniquity and the criminals," Pingree told the Springfield, Massachusetts, Board of Trade. "Most of our troubles can be traced to the temptations which are offered to city officials when franchises are sought by wealthy corporations, or contracts are to be let for public works." For refusing to divert public attention from the "larger and more complex immoralities" of the "privileged" interests, as Brand Whitlock put it, to the more familiar vices, the social reformers earned the bitter censure of the ministerial and "uplift" groups.[20]

The whole tone of the social reform movement was humanistic and empirical. It did not attempt to prescribe standards of personal morality nor did it attempt to draft social blueprints or city charters which had as their goals the imposition of middle class morality and patrician values upon the masses. Instead, it sought to find the basic causes of municipal misgovernment. Pingree, the first of the broad-gauged social reformers, discovered the sources of municipal corruption in his day-to-day battle with the light, gas, telephone, and traction interests, the latter represented at the time by Tom Johnson. Johnson, like Mayor Newton D. Baker, knew from his own experience as a utility magnate why municipal government had been demoralized. Mayor Mark Fagan discovered that Jersey City could neither regulate nor tax the utilities and the railroads because both parties were dominated by these interests.[21]

In attempting to reform the city, Pingree, Jones, Johnson, and Whitlock lost upper class and business support and were forced to rely upon the lower classes for political power. The structural reformers, on the other hand, were frequently members of and sponsored by the very social and economic classes which most vehemently opposed social reform. "If we had to depend upon these classes for reforms," Pingree told the *Outlook* in 1897, "they could never have been brought about." "It is not so much the undercrust as the upper crust," asserted Professor Edward Bemis, who served as a Pingree aide, "that threatens the interests of the people."[22]

The inability of the structural reformers to pursue positive programs to alter the existing social and economic order was probably a reflection of their own business and class backgrounds. Their high regard for the sacrosanct nature of private property, even if obtained illegally, limited them to treating but one aspect of the municipal malaise, and then only when corruption by urban machines reached an intolerable point. This halfway attempt at urban reform prompted Brand Whitlock to observe in 1914: "The word 'reformer' like the word 'politician' had degenerated, and, in the mind of the common man, come to connote something very disagreeable. In four terms as mayor I came to know both species pretty well, and, in the latter connotations of the term, I prefer politician. He, at least, is human."[23]

The structural reform tradition drew much of its strength from a diverse group of theorists composed of good government people, spokesmen for the business community, civic uplifters, representatives of taxpayers' associations, editors, and college professors. The most prominent and influential spokesmen of this persuasion were the Englishman James Bryce, college professors Frank J. Goodnow and William B. Munro, and the editor and scholar Albert Shaw. These theorists diagnosed problems of the city differently from the social reformers. Of fundamental importance to the models they formulated to bring about better city government was their view of the basic causes of the urban malaise. New York's problems, according to Professor Frank Goodnow, had begun in 1857, when the "middle classes, which had thus far controlled the municipal government, were displaced by an ignorant proletariat, mostly foreign born." Three decades later, James Bryce, who dealt with the problems of the city in one of the most influential books of his age, observed that the same "droves of squalid men, who looked as if they had just emerged from an emigrant ship" were herded by urban bosses before magistrates to be enrolled as voters. Such men, said Bryce, were "not fit for suffrage" and "incompetent to give an intelligent vote." Furthermore, their odious habits and demeanor had driven "cultivated" and "sensitive" men out of political life and discouraged the business classes from assuming their share of civic responsibility. One of the most able students of comparative municipal government, Albert Shaw, agreed with Bryce and Goodnow and concluded that the foreign-born had provided the opportunities for the "corruptionist and the demagogue,"[24] who had demoralized city government and lowered the tone of civic responsibility. The immigrant was central to the analyses of the theorists: although a few of them admitted other contributing factors, it is doubtful that any of them believed that the quality of civic responsibility, the level of public morality, and the honesty of urban administrations could have sunk as low had not the immigrant been present in overwhelming numbers in American cities.

Unlike the immigration restrictionists, the theorists did not distinguish between the new and old immigrants but lumped them together with the urban lower classes and attacked the political agencies that had facilitated the rise to power of these new groups. Even the newcomers from Northern Europe "know nothing of the institutions of the country, of its statesmen, of its political issues," Bryce argued. "Neither from German nor from Ireland do they bring much knowledge of the methods of free government." Lower class representatives from the wards were not welcome in municipal circles, for presumably the district system produced "inferior men" of "narrowed horizons," or as Alfred Conkling put it, permitted the balance of power to be held by the "worst class of men." "Wards largely controlled by thieves and robbers," Cornell's Andrew D. White warned, ". . . can control the city." Harvard's Professor Munro

argued that the ward system elected councils that only wasted time and money in "fruitless debate" and sent to councils men "whose standing in the community is negligible." The ward system of representation was denounced by Professors Goodnow and Munro and Delos F. Wilcox for producing the worst representatives in the city. The National Municipal League's model charter called upon municipalities to abolish local representation. In Goodnow's view there were no local interests worthy of political representation anyway.[25]

In building their case against the ability of a mass urban electorate to rule itself, the theorists also drew upon psychology and history. The "craving for excitement" and the "nervous tension" of the city had a degenerative effect, Delos F. Wilcox argued, for "urban life tends to endanger the popular fitness for political power and responsibility." City populations were "radical rather than conservative," and "impulsive rather than reflective," asserted Goodnow, and far less inclined than rural populations to have "regard for the rights of private property." This was caused in part by the fact, Goodnow continued, that urban residents, unlike rural, had "no historical associations" with the cities in which they lived and thus had a poorly developed "neighborhood feeling." The elective system that depended upon familiar relationships and a cohesive community for its success was thus a failure in the city. Goodnow was also disturbed by his study of the larger contours of Western municipal history which convinced him that when city populations

Melvin Holli

had been permitted to develop free of outside control, they evinced an "almost irresistible tendency to establish oligarchical or despotic government." American cities that were under Boss rule, in his opinion, showed similar tendencies.[26]

The first solutions proposed by many spokesmen of reform were hardly original. Outright disfranchisement had been suggested frequently since the end of the Civil War. Some cities had enacted stiffer registration requirements to pare down the vote of the unwashed, and some states had followed the pattern of Michigan, which revoked the alien franchise in 1894. Just as effective, although less direct, was the 1876 recommendation of the New York commissioners for the creation of an upper house with control over money bills in New York City, which was to be elected by propertied voters.[27]

The theorists, however, appear to have been inspired by a contemporary historical event. Drawing upon the Southern experience of disfranchising the Negro, Albert Shaw and Frank Goodnow suggested that such a measure might be applied to Northern cities. The "grandfather clause" apparently convinced Goodnow that the nation was not irrevocably committed to universal suffrage: once the people became convinced that "universal suffrage inevitably must result in inefficient and corrupt government, it will be abandoned," he predicted. The safeguards of suffrage, Fourteenth and Fifteenth Amendments, did not pose insurmountable obstacles, argued Goodnow. He dismissed the Fourteenth Amendment as merely an appeal to Congress, and he pointed out that the Fifteenth left room for educational and property qualifications.[28]

Accepting the Southern solution as reasonable, Shaw argued that the franchise in the North should be "absolutely" restricted to those who could read English, and "in the case of the foreign-born, to those showing positive fitness for participation in our political and governmental life." Furthermore, Shaw argued that European immigrants should be directed southward where they would provide competition for Negroes which would result in a beneficial "survival of the fittest." In order to upgrade the quality of the urban electorate, Professor Munro recommended that the literacy test for the franchise should be extended throughout the nation. Universal suffrage was a "sacrifice of common sense to abstract principles," Bryce asserted. "Nobody pretends that such persons [immigrant voters] are fit for civic duty, or will be dangerous if kept for a time in pupilage, but neither party will incur the odium of proposing to exclude them."[29]

Although demands to purge the unfit elements from urban voting lists were often voiced during the 1890's, it became apparent that such a solution was too drastic. Few civic federations and even fewer politicians picked up the suggestion. Despite the prestige and influence of the theorists, it was evident that disfranchisement was unacceptable to the American public as a way to solve its urban problems. Clearly, less abrasive and more refined techniques would have to be found.

The theorists often spoke of installing into office the "better" classes, the

224

"best" citizens and civic patriots. Excluded were labor, ethnic, or lower class representatives. As Goodnow put it, their choice was "men engaged in active business" or professionals, presumably associated with the business community. The theorists did not distinguish between big and small businessmen, or between entrepreneurs and financiers. What they wanted, as Conkling expressed it, was "any business or professional man ... who has been successful in private life" and who was reasonably honest. As Richard T. Ely observed, the battle cries of the good government crowd in the 1890's had been: "Municipal government is business not politics." "Wanted, A municipal administration on purely business principles." If one accepted the premise it followed logically, as Ely noted, that businessmen were the "natural and inevitable directors of local affairs."[30]

The theorists argued that the business of city government was business and not politics. The "purely administrative functions—that is to say business functions— outweighed the political functions nine to one," declared Walter Arndt. They extensively used the modern business corporation as a model in their discussions of city government; some called the citizens "stockholders," and others referred to the council as the "board of directors" and the mayor as the "chairman of the board." They spoke of the pressing need for efficiency, the complexity of urban problems, and favored the use of experts to replace elected amateurs. Goodnow argued that a clear distinction must be drawn between legislative and administrative duties and that municipal departments must be staffed by experts. Munro warned that public opinion was the "worst" enemy of the expert and therefore should be rendered less influential in municipal decision-making. In short, the theorists were arguing that the role of public opinion and political expression should be substantially reduced in governing the modern city.[31]

In urging the reconstruction of city government, the theorists called for far-reaching changes in city charters. They advocated a strong mayor system, which accorded with what most of them knew about New York City politics: at least once during each decade since the end of the Civil War, "reformers" had been able to win the mayoralty, although they repeatedly failed to control the city council. The theorists also recommended that the mayor be given complete authority to appoint members to the various municipal boards. Board members, they argued, should serve without pay since this would remove the mercenary motive that prompted professional politicians to serve and, incidentally, would eliminate most of those without substantial wealth as well. If those who got their "living out of their salaries" could be excluded from municipal office, Goodnow argued, the way would be open for the "business and professional classes" to assume control of the city.[32] At the lower levels of municipal administration, Shaw, Goodnow, and Munro recommended a thoroughgoing application of the civil-service system, which also tended to eliminate ethnic and lower class representatives. A professional civil service at the lower grades, the theorists argued, would create a good technical and supportive staff and, as Goodnow put it, "make it possible for the business and professional classes of the community to assume the care of public business without making too great personal sacrifices."[33]

The recommendations of the theorists aimed at weakening popular control over the legislative arm of government, the city council. Goodnow was convinced that the council system, since it provided so many "incompetent if not corrupt men," should not be a powerful force in municipal government. Goodnow was more favorably impressed by municipal arrangements in Berlin, Germany, where a propertied electorate comprising less than 10 per cent of the voters elected two-thirds of the city council. "This gives to the wealthier class the directing voice in municipal affairs," commented Professor Leo S. Rowe with approval. Andrew D. White argued that men of property should be represented by a board of control, "without whose permission no franchise should be granted and no expenditure should be made." The English system which in effect disfranchised most lower class slum residents also met with Goodnow's favor. Councils elected by a nonpropertied franchise disturbed Goodnow, for such bodies often prodded cities into "undertakings which are in excess of the city's economic resources." Evidently pessimistic about changing the basis of municipal suffrage to one of property, Goodnow reversed the formula and suggested that to extend the tax-paying obligation to more citizens might produce better councils. That failing, he supported

state intervention to limit taxing and spending of municipal governments. "The trouble with leaving our cities to govern themselves, at least along purely democratic lines," argued C. E. Pickard, is "that they are utterly unworthy of trust."[34]

The theorists also argued for fewer elective offices and smaller city councils. "Men of little experience and less capacity have found it easy to get themselves elected to membership in large city councils," asserted Munro. Smaller councils would presumably concentrate responsibility and produce better men. The at-large election was a favorite device of the theorists and one of the most important structural changes they proposed. City-wide elections to the council, in their opinion, could be won only by men of commanding presence and city-wide prominence. Obviously the lower class politician or the ethnic representative who served his ward well would come out second best if pitted against a prominent businessman or professional. Not until late in the Progressive period, after the at-large system began to elect the "better classes" into office, did the theorists return to decentralizing authority and to expanding the powers of councilmen who then would be known as city commissioners. The ideas of the theorists make it difficult to quibble with Frederic C. Howe's observation: "Distrust of democracy has inspired much of the literature on the city."[35]

Agencies to regulate utility rates, to investigate tax inequities, or to foster and advance social reform were not on the drawing boards of the theorists. Few of them focused their wrath and moral indignation upon the corrupting influence of privately owned utilities and the real estate interests on city councils. They were less bothered by the businessman who bribed the city council than by the machine politician who accepted the bribe. Yerkes and Whitney seldom warranted their attention in the way that Tweed did. They chose instead to focus responsibility upon the individuals who sat on councils and the political systems that elected them rather than upon the business interests that sought favorable franchises, tax favoritism, and city services, such as paving, sewers, and water, which enhanced the value of their enterprises.

The ideas of the theorists were not lost upon the practitioners and designers of good city government. The structural reformers began to design new forms of urban organization and to codify the ideas of the theorists into new city charters. Two decades of searching and theorizing produced the city commissioner and later the city manager systems.

The theorists provided the rationale for the most radical departure the American city took in all its history. The widespread adoption of the commissioner and manager systems late in the Progressive period brought about what one scholar called a "revolution in the theory and practice of city government." Although the commissioner system had its origins in an accident of nature, it and the manager plan soon became the favored devices for achieving what the old political system could not—namely, the large-scale movement of businessmen and business-minded representatives into public office. Both systems were patterned after the modern business corporation and rapidly adopted its ideals. Henry Bruère, a director of the New York Bureau of Municipal Research, boasted that commission governments were often made a "part of the progressive programs of 'boosting' commercial organizations." "Money saving and efficiency" were pursued as key objectives under the manager plan. The "Godfather of City Managerism," Richard S. Childs, observed that the city managers at their fourth annual conference could "unblushingly point with pride" to an average savings of 10 per cent in tax levies in the cities under his brain child. The first city manager of the publicized "Dayton Plan," Henry M. Waite, admitted that the "main thing" the nation's fifty manager towns had accomplished up to 1917 was a "financial saving." "Economy, not service," James Weinstein correctly asserted, was the "basic principle" of both the commissioner and manager systems. As Harold A. Stone has suggested, and Weinstein has demonstrated, no important reform movement of the Progressive period was more peculiarly the captive of organized business than the commissioner and manager movements.[36]

Although the commissioner and manager systems achieved their greatest success in middle-sized and smaller cities, they represented the ultimate ideal of the earlier theorists (whose major concern had been large American cities). Commissioner and manager reorganization brought about in its finished form the structural arrangements that facilitated the movement into office of that class of people whom Bryce, Goodnow, Munro, and Shaw believed best fitted and qualified to rule the city. Chambers of commerce and the dominant business groups were the main force behind the movement, and, as James Weinstein and Samuel P. Hays have demonstrated, these new forms facilitated the inflow of the commercial and upper class elements into the centers of municipal power at the price of ethnic and lower class representation.[37] The business model of municipal government would eventually spread to nearly one-half of our cities, and the structural-reform persuasion would dominate the main stream of urban reform thought in the twentieth century.[38] This extension of the instruments and the ideology of the business world would help to return to power men with the temperaments of Havemeyer, Cleveland, and Low and considerably diminish the electoral prospects for men like Pingree, Jones, and Johnson—as well as like Tweed.

The conservative revolution in city government would also help to end the process whereby astute politicians and socially-conscious reformers used the political system to ease the shock of assimilation for newcomers into American life. The political machine may have been one of the most important institutions not only for acknowledging the immigrant's existence but for interpreting a new environment to him and helping him to adjust to a bewildering new society.

By concentrating on the mechanistic and bureaucratic aspects of city government and by throwing the weight of their influence behind the election of business-men, the theorists grossly oversimplified the problems of the city. Wiping out lower-class and foreign-born corruption unfortunately took precedence in their minds over the social needs of the city. The theorists confined themselves to dealing with the plumbing and hardware of city government and finally became narrow administrative reformers. In the process, they deceived themselves and helped to mislead a generation of reformers into thinking that they were dealing with the fundamental problems of the city, when in reality they were retooling the machinery of urban government to fit the needs of the business world.

Characteristically, the manager and commissioner movement, which represented the greatest achievement of the structural-reform tradition, experienced its greatest success during the twilight of the Progressive period and during the nineteen twenties,[39] when great expectations for social reform were withering and receding. This late triumph of good government reform was not an accident of historical timing. It was not a case of cultural lag, nor can it be attributed to a late blooming of the urban Progressive spirit. If anything, new concepts and systems of organization usually appeared sooner at the urban level than at the national. The victory of the manager-commissioner system during the age of Harding and Coolidge was an historical acknowledgement of the basically conservative nature of the structural-reform tradition. The nation had finally tailored the urban political organization and molded reform thought to respond to the most powerful economic forces in the city. In this instance it was not free silver but the chamber of commerce that became the cowbird of reform. This should not be surprising, for the chamber of commerce and its affiliates had also proved to be the greatest obstacle to social reform in Pingree's Detroit.

NOTES

1. Lincoln Steffens, *The Autobiography of Lincoln Steffens* (New York, 1931), pp. 374-75; Hewitt quoted in *Pilgrim* iii (December, 1901), 4.
2. Hazen S. Pingree, "Address to the Nineteenth Century Club of New York," November 11, 1897, p. 7; S. M. Jones to Josiah Strong, November 15, 1898, Jones Papers; Brand Whitlock, *Forty Years of It* (New York, 1914), pp. 172-74.
3. Frederic C. Howe, *The City: The Hope of Democracy* (New York, 1913), pp. 1, 2. For the elitist views of reformers who overthrew Boss Tweed, see Alexander B. Callow, Jr., *The Tweed Ring* (New York, 1966), pp. 69-71, 265-67. Charles R. Adrian, "Some General Characteristics of Nonpartisan Elections," Robert C. Wood, "Nonpartisanship in Suburbia," both in *Democracy in Urban America*, ed. Oliver P. Williams and Charles Press (Chicago, 1964), pp. 251-66. For an exposition of the views regarding municipal government of one of the most prominent twentieth-century "structural" reformers, see Richard S. Childs, "The Faith of a Civic Reformer," *ibid.*, pp. 222-24. The "elitist commitments" of the city manager system (as prescribed in city government textbooks) can also be seen in Lawrence J. R. Herson, "The Lost World of Municipal Government," *American Political Science Review*, LI (June, 1957), 330-45.
4. Howard B. Furer, *William Frederick Havemeyer: A Political Biography* (New York, 1965), pp. 14, 144-54, 160; Seymour J. Mandelbaum, *Boss Tweed's New York* (New York,

1965), pp. 91, 97, 108, 111; Callow, *The Tweed Ring*, p. 253-86.
5. Mandelbaum, *Boss Tweed's New York*, pp. 97-100, 111; Furer, *William F. Havemeyer*, pp. 156, 158, 160-61, 169.
6. *Ibid.*, p. 161; Mandelbaum, *Boss Tweed's New York*, pp. 112-13; William L. Riordon, *Plunkitt of Tammany Hall* (New York, 1963), p. 17.
7. Allan Nevins, *Grover Cleveland, A Study in Courage* (New York, 1941), pp. 61-62, 83-94.
8. Harold Coffin Syrett, *The City of Brooklyn 1865-1898, A Political History* (New York, 1944), p. 134; Steven C. Swett, "The Test of a Reformer A Study of Seth Low," *New-York Historical Society Quarterly*, XLIV (January, 1960), pp. 8, 9; Lincoln Steffens, *The Shame of the Cities* (New York, 1966), p. 201.
9. Syrett, *Brooklyn*, pp. 104-6, 109-19, 134; Swett, "Test of a Reformer," pp. 7-9.
10. Albert Fein, "New York City Politics From 1897-1903; A Study in Political Party Leadership" (M.A. thesis, Columbia University, 1954), pp. 19-20; Swett, "Test of a Reformer," pp. 10-14, 16-18.
11. *Ibid.*, pp. 21-23, 26-31, 35-36; Roy Lubove, *The Progressives and the Slums, Tenement House Reform in New York City, 1890-1917* (Pittsburgh, 1962), pp. 153-54.
12. Swett, "Test of a Reformer," pp. 6, 32, 35-36, 38-41; Wallace S. Sayre and Herbert Kaufman, *Governing New York City Politics in the Metropolis* (New York, 1960), p. 695.
13. James D. Phelan, "Municipal Conditions and the New Charter," *Overland Monthly*, XXVIII (no. 163, 2nd series), pp. 104-11; Roy Swanstrom, "Reform Administration of James D. Phelan, Mayor of San Francisco, 1897-1902," (M.A. thesis, University of California-Berkeley, 1949), pp. 77-79, 80, 83, 85, 86; Walton Bean, *Boss Ruef's San Francisco: The Story of the Union Labor Party, Big Business, and the Graft Prosecution* (Berkeley, 1952), pp. 8, 9, 16, 17, 23; George E. Mowry, *The California Progressives* (Chicago, 1963), pp. 23-25; Fremont Older, *My Own Story* (San Francisco, 1919), pp. 27, 31, 65.
14. William E. Leuchtenburg, Preface to Edwin

R. Lewinson, *John Purroy Mitchel: The Boy Mayor of New York* (New York, 1965), pp. 11-13; Lewinson, *Boy Mayor*, pp. 93, 95, 100, 102, 117, 124.

15. Leuchtenburg, *ibid.*, p. 12; Lewinson, *ibid.*, pp. 18, 151-69, 175-88.

16. Leuchtenburg, *ibid.*, pp. 11-13; Samuel P. Hayes, "The Politics of Reform in Municipal Government," *Pacific Northwest Quarterly*, LV (October, 1964), pp. 157-69.

17. Lewinson, *Boy Mayor*, pp. 11-13; 18, 93, 95, 102; Riordon, *George Washington Plunkitt*, pp. 17-20; Swett, "Seth Low," pp. 8, 9; Allan Nevins, *Abram S. Hewitt: With Some Account of Peter Cooper* (New York, 1935), pp. 515-16, 529-30; Seth Low, "An American View of Municipal Government in the United States," in James Bryce, *The American Commonwealth* (New York, 1893), I, 651, 665.

18. Hoyt Landon Warner, *Progressivism in Ohio 1897-1917* (Columbus, 1964), pp. 32, 70-72; Whitlock, *Forty Years of It*, pp. 211, 252; Clarence H. Cramer, *Newton D. Baker: A Biography* (Cleveland, 1961), pp. 46-47; Steffens, *Autobiography of Lincoln Steffens*, pp. 447, 492-93; Frederic C. Howe, *The Confessions of a Reformer* (New York, 1925), pp. 98, 102-8; Pingree, *Facts and Opinions*, p. 196. For Mark Fagan, see Lincoln Steffens, *Upbuilders* (New York, 1909), pp. 28, 30, 33, 35, and Ransom E. Noble, Jr., *New Jersey Progressivism before Wilson* (Princeton, 1946), pp. 13-42. St. Louis Circuit Attorney Joseph W. Folk (1901-04), who began his career by investigating and prosecuting franchise "grabs," discovered that the real despoilers of municipal government were not minor city officials but promoters, bankers, and corporation directors who profited by misgovernment. After he became governor he dropped his crime-busting and supported progressive and urban reforms. Louis G. Geiger, *Joseph W. Folk of Missouri* (Columbia, 1953), pp. 32, 41, 81, 88, 93, 99-117. Robert Wiebe's assertion that the "typical business ally of the boss, moreover, was a rather marginal operator, anathema to the chamber of commerce" is at variance with what is known about the political influence wielded in Detroit by urban capitalists such as the Hendries, McMillans and Johnson or for that matter with the role played by Yerkes and Insull in Chicago, Mark Hanna in Cleveland and the Huntington interests in Los Angeles, just to cite a few examples. *The Search for Order, 1877-1920* (New York, 1967), p. 167.

19. Steffens, *Upbuilders*, p. 3-45; Warner, *Progressivism in Ohio, 1897-1917*, pp. 71, 74; Cramer, *Newton D. Baker*, pp. 50-52; Howe, *Confessions of a Reformer*, pp. 90-93, 108-9; Carl Lorenz, *Tom L. Johnson, Mayor of Cleveland* (New York, 1911), p. 152; Steffens, *Autobiography of Lincoln Steffens*, p. 480; Detroit *Free Press*, March 14, 1896, P.S.; Samuel M. Jones to Henry D. Lloyd, April 16, 1897, Lloyd Papers; Samuel M. Jones to James L. Cowes, April 27, 1897; Tom L. Johnson to S. M. Jones, May 3, 1902, Jones Papers; Harvey S. Ford, "The Life and Times of Golden Rule Jones" (Ph.D. thesis, University of Michigan, 1953), pp. 185, 284-85, 330; Whitlock, *Forty Years of It*, p. 212. William D. Miller has argued that "Boss" Edward H. Crump, who was Memphis mayor from 1910 to 1916, stands with "Golden Rule" Jones and Tom L. Johnson as a typical progressive of the period, but an examination of Miller's book raises serious doubts about that judgment. Although Crump occasionally employed reform rhetoric, established a few milk stations for the poor, and put screens on public school windows, he used most of the energy of his administration to enforce the laws and instill efficiency into the municipal government in the structural-reform tradition. Crump wiped out "policy" playing by Negroes, eliminated loafing by the garbage collectors and street pavers, forced the railroads to construct eleven underpasses, lowered city taxes, reduced waste in municipal government by extending audit procedures even to the purchase of postage stamps, and increased city income by selling empty bottles, feed sacks, and scrap. William D. Miller, *Mr. Crump of Memphis* (Baton Rouge, 1964), pp. 79-113. Brooklyn's Mayor Charles A. Schieren (1894-95), who gained some stature as a reformer by defeating a venal Democratic machine, also followed a well-trodden path of

cleaning out "deceit and corruption" and installing "integrity, nonpartisanship, and routine efficiency." Like most of the reform mayors of his period, Schieren failed to advance or support social reform programs. Harold C. Syrett, *The City of Brooklyn, 1865-1898, A Political History* (New York, 1944), pp. 218-32. Geoffrey Blodgett has tried to show that Boston became for "a brief time the cutting edge of urban reform in America" under Mayor Josiah Quincy (1896-1900), who established a publicly owned printing plant and expanded the city's playgrounds. Although the Dover Street Bath House may have been a "monument to municipal socialism" as Blodgett contends, Mayor Quincy stopped his programs short of anything that would have threatened the vested interests in the traction and utility business. Geoffrey Blodgett, *The Gentle Reformers: Massachusetts Democrats in the Cleveland Era* (Cambridge, 1966), pp. 240-61. For Quincy's absurd notion that regular bathing would cause the "filthy tenement house" to disappear, crime and drunkenness to decrease and the death rate to drop, see Josiah Quincy, "Municipal Progress in Boston," *Independent*, LII (February 15, 1900), 424. Henry Demarest Lloyd was critical of Mayor Quincy's failure to resist the traction interests and referred to the Mayor's public baths as Quincy's "little sops." H. D. Lloyd to Samuel Bowles, December 13, 1898, Lloyd Papers.

20. Ford, "Golden Rule Jones," pp. 151, 166, 339; Samuel M. Jones to Dr. [Graham] Taylor, October 5, 1897; S. M. Jones to L. L. Dagett, April 17, 1899, Jones Papers; Hazen S. Pingree address to Springfield, Massachusetts, Board of Trade, March 3, 1894, Ralph Stone Scrapbook; Whitlock, *Forty Years of It*, pp. 252, 254.

21. Robert H. Bremner, "The Civic Revival in Ohio: The Fight Against Privilege in Cleveland and Toledo, 1890-1912," (Ph.D. thesis, Ohio State University, 1943), p. 25; Hazen S. Pingree, "The Problem of Municipal Reform. Contract by Referendum," *Arena*, XVII (April, 1897), 707-10; Cramer, *Newton D. Baker*, p. 46; Steffens, *Upbuilders*, pp. 28-30, 33, 35; Noble, *New Jersey Progressivism before Wilson*, pp. 25-26, 35, 38.

22. Tom L. Johnson, *My Story* (New York, 1911), p. 113; Ford, "Golden Rule Jones," pp. 136-37, 170, 339; Hazen S. Pingree, "Detroit: A Municipal Study," *Outlook*, LV (February 6, 1897), 437; Bemis quoted in Detroit *Evening News*: June 21, 1899, Stone Scrapbook; Whitlock, *Forty Years of It*, p. 221.

23. Whitlock, *Forty Years of It*, p. 221.

24. Frank J. Goodnow, "The Tweed Ring in New York City," in James Bryce's *The American Commonwealth* (London, 1888), II, 335; Bryce, *ibid.*, p. 67; Bryce, *ibid.*, I, 613; Albert Shaw, *Political Problems of American Development* (New York, 1907), p. 66. According to Edwin L. Godkin, New York City's problems began with the establishment of universal suffrage in 1846 which coincided with the beginning of the great Irish migration. Edwin L. Godkin, *Problems of Modern Democracy*, ed. Morton Keller (New York, 1896, Cambridge, 1966), p. 133.

25. Bryce, *American Commonwealth*, II, 67; William B. Munro, *The Government of American Cities* (New York, 1913), pp. 308-9, 310, 312; Andrew D. White, "The Government of American Cities," *Forum*, X (December, 1890), 369; Alfred R. Conkling, *City Government in the United States* (New York, 1899), p. 49; Frank J. Goodnow, *Municipal Problems* (New York, 1897), pp. 150-53; Delos F. Wilcox, *The Study of City Government* (New York, 1897), p. 151; "Report of the Committee on Municipal Program," *Proceedings* of the Indianapolis Conference for Good City Government and Fourth Annual Meeting of the National Municipal League (Philadelphia, 1898), p. 11 (hereafter cited *Proceedings for Good City Government*).

26. Wilcox, *The Study of City Government*, pp. 237-38; Frank J. Goodnow, *Municipal Government* (New York, 1910), pp. 39, 149, 378-79; James T. Young, *Proceedings for Good City Government*, 1901, p. 230.

27. *Michigan Legislative Manual and Official Directory 1899-1900* (Lansing, 1899), p. 322; *Report of the Commission to Devise a Plan for the Government of Cities in the State of New York* (New York, 1877), pp. 35-36.

28. Goodnow, *Municipal Problems*, pp. 148-49.

29. Shaw, *Political Problems of American Development*, p. 65-67, 82, 125; Munro, *Government of American Cities*, p. 120-21; Bryce, *American Commonwealth*, II, 67.

30. Goodnow, *Municipal Problems*, p. 278; Conkling, *City Government in the United States*, p. 34; Richard T. Ely, *The Coming City* (New York, 1902), p. 29.

31. Walter T. Arndt, *The Emancipation of the American City* (New York, 1917), p. 12; Frank M. Sparks, *Government As a Business* (Chicago, 1916), pp. 1, 7; Goodnow, *Municipal Government*, pp. 150, 381-82; Munro, *Government of American Cities*, p. 306; William H. Tolman, *Municipal Reform Movements in the United States* (New York, 1895), p. 34.

32. Conkling, *City Government in the United States*, pp. 6, 32; Goodnow, *Municipal Problems*, pp. 262-65.

33. *Ibid.*, pp. 204-5, 265; Munro, *Government of American Cities*, p. 241, 279-80; Albert Shaw, "Civil Service Reform and Municipal Government," in *Civil Service Reform and Municipal Government* (New York, 1897), pp. 3-7.

34. Goodnow, *Municipal Government*, pp. 142-46, 385-86, and *Municipal Problems*, pp. 66-67; Leo S. Rowe, "City Government As It Should Be And May Become," *Proceedings for Good City Government, 1894*, p. 115; White, "The Government of American Cities," p. 370; John Agar, "Shall American Cities Municipalize?" *Municipal Affairs*, IV (March, 1900), 14-20; C. E. Pickard, "Great Cities and Democratic Institutions," *American Journal of Politics*, IV (April, 1894), 385. The Boston mayor Nathan Mathews, Jr., asserted that the proposal to restrict municipal suffrage to the propertied classes was one of the most common remedies for the evils of city government of his age. Nathan Mathews, Jr., *The City Government of Boston* (Boston, 1895), p. 176.

35. Munro, *Government of American Cities*, pp. 294, 308-10; Goodnow, *Municipal Problems*, pp. 150-53; Leo S. Rowe, "American Political Ideas and Institutions in Their Relation to the Problem of the City," *Proceedings for Good City Government, 1897*, p. 77; William Dudley Foulke, *ibid.,* 1898, p. 137; Frederic C. Howe, *The City, The Hope of Democracy* (New York, 1913), p. 1.

36. Henry Bruère, "Efficiency in City Government," *Annals* of the American Academy of Political and Social Science, XLI (May, 1912), 19; Richard S. Childs, "Now That We Have the City Manager Plan, What Are We Going To Do With It," *Fourth Yearbook of the City Managers' Association* (Auburn, 1918), pp. 82-83; Henry M. Waite, *ibid.*, pp. 88-89; Harold A. Stone, Don K. Price and Kathryn H. Stone, *City Manager Government in the United States* (Chicago, 1940), pp. 25-27; James Weinstein, "Organized Business and the City Commissioner and Manager Movements," *Journal of Southern History*, XXVIII (May, 1962), 166, 179.

37. *Ibid.*, p. 173; Samuel P. Hays, "The Politics of Reform in Municipal Governmnet in the Progressive Era," *Pacific Northwest Quarterly*, LV (October, 1964), 157-69.

38. Edward C. Banfield and James Q. Wilson, *City Politics* (New York, 1963), p. 148.

39. The peak period for the spread of the city commissioner and the city manager system was 1917-27. Leonard D. White, *The City Manager* (Chicago, 1927), p. 317; Harold Zink, *Government of Cities in the United States* (New York, 1939), p. 301.

THE POLITICS
OF URBAN CHANGE

Peter A. Lupsha

SHIFTING POLITICAL STYLES

... The development of urban political organizations in many respects parallels the development of national politics. The political parties in the cities began as coteries of notables, members of the social and economic élites meeting together to seek solutions to community problems, to select candidates and develop issues. While these cohort groups formed the nucleus of political organization, the extension of suffrage by the 1830's required that this élite seek a broad base of popular support. In some cities, this simply meant passing the trappings of power over to the lower-middle-class; in others it meant the demise of patrician politics and the rise of ethnic political organizations.

The latter half of the nineteenth century saw the zenith of ethnic machine politics in the United States.[1] For ethnic politics provided the immigrant—often

registered to vote as he stepped off the boat—with an avenue of upward mobility, just as the ethnic ghetto provided him with a base of support. City politics of this era is usually remembered for graft, vote fraud, nepotism, vice and civic corruption and, from the perspective of the reform movement that followed, this corruption seemed boundless. Yet from current perspective, it may have been the only assurance of constructive change in the city.

What is usually forgotten about this period of the nineteenth century is that it was one of rapid urban growth and industrial expansion. Then, as now, the cities were faced with an urban crisis. Hordes of immigrants clogged many neighborhoods, living in miserable housing and unsanitary conditions. They needed jobs, food, shelter and education—for often all they brought with them besides the clothes on

From *Current History* 55 (December 1968): 329-32. Reprinted with permission of the publisher.

1. For further discussion of this topic, see Allan Sindler, "Negroes, Ethnic Groups and American Politics," *Current History*, 55 October 1968, p. 207.

their backs were their foreign politics and ideologies. At the same time, the economy was rocketing through cycles of boom and bust expansion, with the urban economic élites seeing fortunes and speculation in every type of venture. The element holding this hyperactive community together was the political boss. He bridged the chasm between the immigrants and the élite, providing money, jobs and welfare to the immigrants, and servicing the avaricious appetites of the élites through municipal expansion. Through the retrospective lenses of middle-class morality the fees of the party boss might seem high, yet he fostered stability in a period of flux and change.

During the decades at the turn of the twentieth century, a reaction to the personal politics of the boss and the ethnic machine took place in many cities, and this style of politics was replaced by the efficiency and administrative politics of the reform movement. This movement, for all its good intentions, has perhaps done more damage to the political life of our cities than all the ill-gotten gain of the city bosses. The reform movement was the only social movement consciously directed at depoliticizing the political, and while it was not the only factor in fostering the notion of political consumership, it played an important part in that trend.

One of the reformers' first goals was to take partisan politics out of city hall. For partisanship, they believed, lay at the root of patronage and bossism in city government. The tool the reformers designed for this task was the non-partisan election. A candidate should stand, they

argued, not on the political record of his party or its registration on the rolls, but on his own merits. While the intention of this reform was to get the best men in office, it had a number of side effects. First, by removing the party label, this reform often took away the one cue a voter had to a candidate's policy orientation. Second, by removing in an overt way the political party's role in city politics, this reform took away the best mobilizing force for informing and involving the electorate. Third, in placing the responsibility for discovering a candidate's merits squarely on the individual citizen, this reform greatly raised the time and information costs of participation, especially for the poorer and less well-educated members of the polity.

A second tool for depoliticizing the city was the at-large election. This reform made office holders responsible to a diffuse, general electorate covering the entire city, rather than to a specific geographic area, district or ward. A side effect of this reform was to make it more difficult for the voter to know exactly who was responsible for actions taken. A second side effect was to make the officeholder less willing to undertake any specific action in one area since this might alienate or anger another section of the city. In the long run, this reform also increased the hold of the better educated middle-class, business and economic élite on city hall, while weakening the impact of poorer, less well educated minority enclaves.

Another major goal of the reform movement was to decentralize the decision-making structure of the city. Power, the reformers noted, had often been capriciously and inefficiently used when centralized in a boss. By separating policy-formation from policy-administration the reformers felt they could bring greater checks and balances into the system, while at the same time increasing the efficiency and professionalization of city administration. The means to this goal was the council-manager system, in which a professional manager ran the city administration, while a non-partisan, at-large council initiated policy. All too often, however, the professional manager in daily contact with the city system and with more complete information than the council both administered and initiated policy, while the council simply ratified it. This reform helped bring efficiency and professionalism to the city, but it also aided the decline of political citizenship. People as individuals no longer needed to be so vigilant or responsible, for the running of the city was now in the hands of a professional. Now, expertise rather than political utility, reality, or compromise could be used to justify decisions.

Still another goal of the reformers was to stop the capricious use of municipal revenue and bonding for public projects which had been used by the machine bosses to provide patronage and opportunities for personal aggrandizement. The reformers accomplished this goal by passing legislation requiring public approval with a two-thirds majority for all revenue bond measures. The effect of this reform was to limit municipal effectiveness, for it enshrined negative politics; a relatively small minority could continually thwart the wishes of a considerable majority. This reform helped also further remove responsibility from the people, for it often forced urban decision-makers to seek less publicly visible means of funding at the state and federal level rather than to seek voter consent.

In some large cities, especially in the East, the reform effort was transitory. It left its impact on administration through civil service reforms, but the party organizations were often able either to coopt the reformers or sabotage them and regain control. In other cities, the ethnic organizations were strong enough to withstand many of the initial onslaughts of reform. Yet even in those cities the reform ethic and the ethnic machine's intransigence helped increase the consumer philosophy.

The reform ethic with its emphasis on professionalism, efficiency and rationality, assisted by the rising social welfare movement, undercut the machine's ability to reward the faithful. Welfare benefits, jobs and aid were less available to the party, for increasingly these benefits could be obtained from public agencies. The public could consume services without being concerned about politics and the parties, with a lessened ability to engage in direct-benefits politics, had to turn to symbolic politics for mobilizing the electorate. Urban politics would no longer be dominated by bread and butter politics; now the stress would be laid on personality politics emphasizing candidates, style issues and symbolic appeals to past identifications.

It must be noted that other factors in the urban society were simultaneously working to support reform by weakening the old-style machines. First, many of the ethnic supporters of the old machine were moving up the class ladder; and with jobs and education they were less dependent on machine rewards. Second, many of the ethnic groups with increased money and status were leaving the ethnic ghettos of the central cities and settling in the suburban fringe. Third, the machine supporters were being replaced in the central city by newcomers the machine was either unwilling or unable to accept.

In sum, it can be said that the reform movement helped bring middle-class values and middle-class politics to the operation and administration of many of our cities. Ironically, this was happening at the same time the cities were beginning to be drained of their middle classes, and were left with a population of the aged, the poor, and the new migrants, many of whom needed the personal politics that had been so efficiently supplied by the machine.

The urban political machines in most cities were, however, both unwilling and unable, for a variety of reasons, to bring the new migrants, the blacks, into active participation in the organization. A handful of black leaders were coopted, and the black voters were dutifully marched to the polls on election day, but the machine failed to capture the interest of the black masses. There are many reasons for this, but one of the more salient is that—to continue the irony—the blacks arrived in the city at a time when the machines were losing their reward structure. The aging political organizations also denied internal mobility to the blacks because of prejudice, black visibility, and

the blacks' numerical minority status. Thus, black citizens were shunted out of partisan politics, where power and political skills could be learned, to the administrative politics of the public agencies where one was rarely considered a participant or citizen, but was usually viewed as a client or a consumer. Many aspects of the current urban malaise can perhaps be traced to this sad juxtaposition of circumstances.

THE NEW POLITICS AND TECHNOLOGY

The politics of our cities has shifted from the patronage and voter-reward politics of the machine period, to the candidate-appeal personality politics of the post-reform period, to the "new" politics of the present period. This "new" politics is the politics of image, the politics of the electronic media. Today it is the image and the packaging of images that are stressed by party organizations. A candidate must not only have personality and appeal; he must have the ability to project an image of dynamism, sincerity and warmth to the viewing audience. Furthermore, the candidate must often accomplish this feat within the limited space of the 60-second television spot announcement. It is not just happenstance, therefore, that we are witnessing a rather startling increase in the number of professional actors seeking and often winning political office. This is simply an outgrowth of the "new" politics and the new technology of campaigning.

Colorful personalities have often dominated urban political campaigns but, in the main, the old politics operated in a world of print. There was time to read over statements, to analyze their content, and even to seek alternative perspectives from a variety of dailies. Print provided a neutral distance between politician and citizen. Today, most Americans derive the bulk of their news and political information from the images of the electronic media, where there is no time or opportunity to separate statement from personality, no chance for re-viewing, and little hope for in-depth analysis or alternative perspective. Thus, the image has become the end of campaigning, rather than the means to the end of a better informed and knowledgeable electorate. The medium, in Marshall McLuhan's terms, has become the message, and the passive viewer consumes political images just as he consumes political services.

This new technology has reinforced the decline of urban commitment for, as a medium, it is geared to a national constituency rather than a local one. Also, the costs involved in its use make it an expensive means of reaching a geographically-confined urban electorate. In spite of these factors, television is being increasingly used in urban campaigning, encouraging the passive consumption of politics without the necessary active interaction of citizenship. . . .

From another perspective, there is at least one ray of hope for our cities. Local concern and participation may be aroused through local control: through the neighborhood corporation. This issue of local control, just coming to the fore, arises primarily from the black community, which has been so effectively shunted from political decision-making and power. A logical outgrowth of the civil rights movement, the desire for manhood and equality of opportunity and control, it is likely to be the most important urban political question of the next decade. If local control, participation, and the neighborhood corporation can gain a foothold in our cities, then there is hope for a revival of commitment, of political citizenship, and a rebirth of our cities. If the movement fails, the logical—although not presently politically feasible—alternative may be slowly to abandon our present cities, permitting them to continue to decay, for even now they are technologically obsolete.

In the past, men came to cities because they served a number of purposes— defense, the easier exchange of economic goods and social services, the rapid communication of messages and ideas, preservation of societal trends, culture and heritage. Technological developments, high speed transit, television, computers and cheap long-distance telephone communication have made it possible to diffuse the traditional activities and purposes of the city, just as they have aided the diffusion of population across the nearby landscape. In addition, the development of atomic bombs and missiles have made concentrated cities prime targets and liabilities on the war maps of tomorrow.

If the demands and desires for active citizenship in the processes and policies of our cities do not successfully arise to make the effort and risk of rebuilding our present cities worthwhile, perhaps it would be better to bend with the winds of technological change, and diffuse our population across the land.

237

REFORMERS, MACHINES, AND THE WAR ON POVERTY

J. David Greenstone and Paul E. Peterson

Scholars of American politics have been notably solicitous about the interests of the urban lower classes. In particular, this concern has focused on the class bias of machine and reform politics. The resulting analyses, however, have produced conflicting interpretations. While political scientists of an earlier generation believed political reforms weakening urban machines would benefit the poor, some contemporary scholars have taken an opposite view. Nevertheless, these two perspectives share certain common insights which we propose to apply in examining four local community action programs of the Economic Opportunity Act of 1964. Specifically, we seek to explain the variation in the initial implementation of the poverty program among the nation's four largest cities—New York, Chicago, Los Angeles, and Philadelphia.[1] We shall argue that in its first two years (1964 to

1966) the war on poverty pursued two goals which were not entirely compatible: (1) to end economic poverty by distributing various material perquisites, and (2) to end the virtual exclusion of low-income groups from political life by distributing power. Consistent with their historical backgrounds, reform cities were generally more successful at distributing power, while machine cities were more adept at distributing material perquisites.

MACHINES AND REFORMERS IN CITY POLITICS

S. M. Lipset has observed that:

... the political intellectual, the man of ideas, is nowhere very interested in

1. The authors wish to express their appreciation to the Russell Sage Foundation for making possible this research. Mr. Peterson would like to express similar appreciation to the Woodrow Wilson Foundation.

238

defending inconsistencies, and every *status quo* is full of inconsistencies. Only by attacking the limitations of his political and social order can he feel he is playing a fruitful creative role.[2]

Accordingly, scholarly analyses of city politics have varied inversely with the changes in the political life of American cities. From the late nineteenth century to World War II, political scientists viewed with alarm the concentration of power achieved by organized political parties.

While relying on the votes of the poor, the machine cooperated in their exploitation by more privileged groups. As Ostrogorski said, machines only insured "the power of plutocracy . . . in the political sphere."[3] Machines often provided large personal profits to individual racketeers, speculators, and businessmen. Basing their power on control of lower-class voters, the most successful members of the machine emulated their robber baron contemporaries in accumulating personal fortunes. The motto of George Washington Plunkitt of Tammany Hall, a master at procuring "honest graft," was "I seen my opportunities and I took 'em."[4] Merton, himself a sympathetic interpreter of the machine, observed that one of the machines' "latent functions" was to provide a locus of political power with which the business community could negotiate.[5] At the height of their power, moreover, machines were not noted for instituting massive new government services that redistributed wealth collectively to the urban lower classes.

Throughout the twentieth century,

however, the machine's power has declined, partly in response to rising education and income levels, the greater political influence of the news media, and increasing bureaucratization of welfare programs. Of equal importance, the reform movement, adopting the views of Ostrogorski and others, weakened or destroyed party machines by transforming the politics of many American cities. Reform innovations, such as nonpartisan elections and a civil service merit system, often eliminated patronage and reduced graft, two bulwarks of machine power.

As the power of the machine declined, new scholars, in keeping with Lipset's observation, began to depict favorably the political machine as the articulator of the wants of the immigrant, working-class population. They have cited the views of machine politicians such as Plunkitt himself:

If a family is burned out I don't ask whether they are Republicans or Democrats, and I don't refer them to the Charity Organization Society which would investigate their case in a month or two and decide they were worthy of help about the time they are dead from starvation. I just get quarters for them, buy clothes for them if their clothes were burned up, and fix them up till they get things runnin' again. . . . The consequence is that the poor look up to George W. Plunkitt as a father, come to him in trouble and don't forget him on election day.[6]

Simultaneously these contemporary scholars saw reform innovations favoring more privileged groups in the community, and they began to view this movement

239

with increasing suspicion.[7] Hofstadter's influential analysis of *The Age of Reform* spelled out the middle-class, Protestant basis of the Progressive movement as a reaction to the value system of lower-class, Catholic immigrants. Hofstadter argued that:

On one side [the reformers] feared the power of the plutocracy, on the other the poverty and restlessness of the masses. But if political leadership could be firmly restored to the responsible middle classes who were neither ultra-reactionary nor, in T. R.'s phrase, "wild radicals," both of these problems could be met.[8]

Political scientists have added that the reformers' structural changes contributed to middle-class domination of city politics. In nonpartisan elections the lower-class voters, lacking a middle-class sense of civic duty, stayed at home, for there was no organization to stir them to political action.[9] Business-oriented civic associations and daily newspapers became the bulwark for many office-seekers.[10] City-wide elections favored politicians with independent sources of income.[11] The new city manager, with an invariably middle-class background, found himself most at home with leaders in the business community.[12] Finally, these new scholars have suggested, the declining strength of party organizations encouraged an interest group politics, often favorable to large corporations and businessmen's associations.

In our view this critique of the reform movement overlooks several of its important attributes. Certainly the reformers initially attacked both the machine's ac-

cumulation of power and its defense of privilege. Social workers such as Jane Addams and muckrakers such as Lincoln Steffens called for public policies which would improve the position of the entire lower class.[13] Earning the enmity of businessmen, they advocated better schools, garbage collection, and other services in poor areas, as well as the abolition of sweatshops and child labor. The comparatively progressive policies of Theodore Roosevelt and Woodrow Wilson were in many ways the product of the reform movement.

Nevertheless, the reformers' paternalistic attitude toward the lower classes, their reluctance at times to engage in ethnic politics, and their indifference to the immediate material needs of individual immigrants prevented them from developing a reliable lower-class constituency. Following World War I, the social conscience of the reform movement was conspicuously absent; as the entire political system became more conservative, reform focused more on corruption than on general social ills. Reformers were more successful in altering political structures than in redistributing wealth to the poor.

We conclude that each scholarly tradition was more accurate in its critique than in its defense, since both the machine and the reform movement had conservative consequences. For businessmen "on the make," machine politics provided franchises and special privileges. For their better established successors good government seemed both efficient and morally praiseworthy.[14] The machine *controlled* the lower-class vote, while somewhat later the reformers' structures *reduced* it. By drastically reducing party competition each protected vital business interests from significant political interference. Their consequences were similar to those of the one-party system of 1896, which, as Burnham shows, dramatically reduced and disoriented the electorate in national and state party politics from 1900 to the New Deal.[15]

Indeed, once the question of favoritism for particular classes is set aside, the two scholarly traditions actually agreed on certain differences between machine and reform politics in the allocation of political values. Machines directly tied their governmental outputs to the maintenance of their organization. The machine was willing and able to distribute governmental resources to individuals, but the criterion of distribution was not whether the individual was deserving or fell within the category prescribed by the relevant law but whether the individual contributed to the political success of the organization. For rich and poor alike, partisan political criteria were the universal standards for distributing values. At the same time, the patronage system meant that party campaign workers staffed the city's administrative bureaucracy. Both policy and personnel practices, then, served to obliterate the distinction between input and output structures. The early scholarly tradition condemned these practices of the machine as an abuse of governmental power for partisan aggrandizement. Modern revisionists have noticed the importance of these practices in serving the individual wants of an immigrant, working-class population.

The reformers, on the other hand, have studiously tried to separate the input and output structures. By eliminating patronage, exposing graft and corruption, and rigorously adhering to the letter of the law, reformers have consciously conformed to explicit legal criteria in distributing government outputs.[16] These steps, Ostrogorski believed, would mean the reinvigoration of democratic processes. More recent scholars, however, have emphasized the advantages such changes confer on the middle and upper classes in urban politics.

These differences in style had important consequences for urban political systems as such. Whereas the machine centralized political power in its own hands, the reformers overtly attempted to disperse this power to "better government" civic associations, the civil service, the press, and (through the initiative, referendum, and recall) to individual voters. Many reformers did centralize formal *authority* in the hands of the mayor or city manager, but these steps by no means fully offset the over-all dispersion of power.[17] In sum, the machine concentrated power among a few of its own leaders, while the reform movement dispersed power to a wide range of individuals, groups, and agencies.

But this very dispersion of power produced latent consequences unforeseen by reformers. The centralization of political power by the machine enabled city officials to move quickly and decisively in obtaining and distributing material resources. The machine's distribution system may not have followed Weberian bureaucratic norms, but its cohesive, centralized structure of power enabled it to

241

move efficiently in overcoming political barriers to the establishment of governmental programs. Once a program was established, a reform administration could employ a bureaucracy committed to principles of scientific and efficient management. But these more pluralistic reform regimes found it exceedingly difficult to secure agreement among all the centers of power who could veto their suggestions. The dispersal of power, in other words, made the rapid distribution of resources more difficult.

Both the upper-class bias common to reformers and machines and the scholarly consensus on the different political processes characteristic of machine and reform politics suggest that the real dispute between the two scholarly perspectives reflects an underlying clash of political values. Defenders of reform voiced a nineteenth-century Jeffersonian optimism: widespread political participation meant good citizenship, vigorous republican government, and sound public policies.[18] The vote buying, vote stealing, and sheer organizational strength of the machine led Ostrogoski to argue that:

Where the Machine is supreme, republican institutions are in truth but an idle form, a plaything wherewith to beguile children. . . . It is no longer "a government of the people, by the people, and for the people."[19]

Reflecting the pessimistic theories of mass society characteristic of the twentieth century, critics of reform believed the public interest is better served by limiting direct mass participation in policy making. This theory argues that such

direct participation as that currently generated by interracial tension too often leads to confrontations that not only make compromise of diverse interests difficult but also prevent political leaders from disregarding "public opinion at crucial moments when public opinion, or intensely moved parts of it, is out of line with long-term national interests."[20] By contrast, machine control of the electorate through ethnically balanced tickets and material payoffs to individual voters reduces the accessibility of city officials to mass pressures and any temptation to demagoguery.[21]

We contend that these three considerations—the upper-class bias of both reform and machine politics, the different approaches of machines and reform to distributing power and perquisites, and the scholarly disagreement on the proper political role of the mass population—are all relevant for analyzing the intercity variation in the administration of community action programs.

COMMUNITY ACTION PROGRAMS: MATERIAL PERQUISITIES OR POLITICAL POWER?

The war on poverty is one of the clearest examples of a post-New Deal welfare state program designed to redistribute material perquisites to lower-class citizens. Community Action Programs were expected by law to give "promise of progress toward elimination poverty . . . through developing employment opportunities, improving human performance, motivation, and productivity, or bettering the conditions under which people live, learn, and work."[22] But the legislation conceived of poverty as a political as well as an economic condition. In a celebrated phrase it required that Community Action Programs be "developed, conducted and administered with the maximum feasible participation of residents of the areas and members of the groups served."[23] While some personnel in the federal Office of Economic Opportunity (OEO) were concerned only with finding more jobs and better services for the poor, other officials, together with certain civil rights organizations, saw this "maximum feasible participation" phrase as an opportunity to increase the political power of the Negroes and other disadvantaged citizens. According to the OEO's Community Action Workbook, for example, a "promising method" of implementing "maximum feasible participation" was "to assist the poor in developing autonomous and self-managed organizations which are competent to exert political influence on behalf of their own self-interest."[24]

According to the view that poverty was a political as well as an economic condition, low-income groups lacked financial resources, social prestige, and easy access to decision makers. Such groups continue to be known for low voter turnout where parties are weak and for the ease with which their vote can be "controlled" by strong party organizations. Most important of all, the poor have had few autonomous organizations which articulate their collective demands and maximize their electoral influence—requisites for becoming more than a "po-

tential group" in urban politics.[25] "Maximum feasible participation" was thus interpreted as the organized and active pursuit of political power.

In practice, the OEO was constrained by the decentralized American political system to administer the "war on poverty" through local community action agencies, keeping for itself only the power to choose among the proposals submitted for its approval. Consequently, its attempt to disperse political power to the poor was confined to the formalistic requirement that representatives of the poor—chosen "whenever feasible" in accord with "traditional democratic approaches and techniques"—comprise approximately one-third of the policy-making body for local Community Action Agencies.[26] Although its actual effectiveness is far from clear, presumably this requirement would stimulate the growth of indigenous organizations, increasing the political power of the poor. In any case all the major political actors—the OEO, the big city mayors, reform and civil rights leaders, interested Republicans, congressmen, and articulate members of neighborhood groups—regarded the question of representation as potentially significant.

The duality of viewpoints within the OEO was reflected in the pattern of cleavage in all four cities. In 1964 and 1965 the four incumbent mayors regarded poverty as an economic condition and resisted those in OEO who sought to disperse political power. Initially, the mayors each formed a committee to centralize decision-making among key members of their administrations.[27] When

OEO sought to disperse political power by including representatives of the poor on the policy-making body, Wagner of New York articulated the common mayoral reaction in testimony before a congressional committee.

When I testified a year ago, I urged that the local governing bodies, through their chief executives or otherwise, should have the ultimate authority, as they have the ultimate responsibility, for ... the conduct and operation of the anti-poverty program.[28]

Similarly, the executive committee of the U.S. Conference of Mayors resolved:

Whereas, no responsible mayor can accept the implications in the Office for Economic Opportunity Workbook that the goals of this program can only be achieved by creating tensions between the poor and existing agencies and by fostering class struggle; ... NOW THEREFORE BE IT RESOLVED that the Administration be urged to assure that any policy ... assure the continuing control of local expenditures relative to this program by the fiscally responsible local officials.

The mayors had sound political reasons for viewing poverty as an economic condition. An antiquated tax structure had created severe financial burdens for city administrations. Demands of the poor and minority groups for costly changes in education, for expansion of hospitals and public health services, expensive vest pocket parks, and improved welfare services obviously strained local budgets.[29] Mayors, therefore, welcomed federal aid designed to alleviate the eco-nomic plight of slum residents who might resort to direct action and even violence. To be sure, the Community Action Program was far from a complete answer to these problems; the resources available were both too few and too restricted.[30] As practical politicians, however, the mayors regarded any program alleviating economic poverty as better than none; besides, the accompanying publicity would give at least the appearance of action.

By contrast, attacking poverty as a political condition appeared exceedingly risky. Dispersing power to the poor would only increase their demands for more governmental services, which were already in short supply. Even worse, these demands of new autonomous organizations would inevitably antagonize other urban interests and weaken the mayor's own position. Complaints about police brutality and calls for a civilian review board had aroused the ire of police departments. Public housing authorities had often objected to the formation of militant tenant groups demanding more responsiveness to the wishes of residents. Principals and teachers generally opposed public pressure against traditional educational practices, especially when generated by poorly educated slum dwellers. Real estate interests bitterly attacked picketing, demonstrations, and rent strikes aimed at better maintenance of tenement housing. Private welfare agencies have disliked the development of autonomous organizations that compete for clients, funds, and staff. Few mayors desired to antagonize any of these entrenched interests; independent militant groups spawned by the war on poverty might well arouse most of them.

Understandably, then, the mayors in all four cities simultaneously conceived of poverty as a purely economic condition and sought to centralize power during the initial development of the poverty program. In each case, however, the chief executive encountered opposition from those who conceived of poverty as a political condition as well. These included neighborhood organizations, certain settlement houses, the more militant civil rights groups, liberal Republicans, and, in Philadelphia, some industrial unions. When OEO revealed that it would withhold funds until the poor were represented on policy-making bodies, these groups held meetings and rallies calling for dispersal of power to the poor. Significantly, their demands were also articulated by two supporters of the reform tradition, who, as our previous analysis would suggest, favored a further dispersal of political power. Newspapers, almost everywhere a stalwart of reform, were particularly important, since one of the few weapons neighborhood groups have is the unfavorable publicity that they can create for the mayor. News stories focusing on the role of the poor and official reluctance to involve them were published in each of the four cities. The *Philadelphia Bulletin* devoted an average of eight column inches per day to the controversy in the four months before the final decision on the structure of the program. In each of the cities except Los Angeles, at least one major paper backed the critical view of the mayor expressed in news stories with editorial support of

varying enthusiasm for participation by the poor.

Favorable coverage of the demands of neighborhood groups reflected the traditional commitment of newspapers to the reform cause.[31] More specifically, in New York City, Republican Congressman John Lindsay had announced as a reform candidate for mayor. Many newspapers were preparing to support him against Democrat Paul Screvane, the man Wagner had chosen both to supervise the poverty program and to succeed him as mayor. In Philadelphia both the major newspapers were in bitter opposition to the former Democratic ward politician who had become mayor. In Chicago the Republican-oriented newspapers were willing to attack the mayor, although his formidable political strength made them hesitant and selective in their criticism.

Still more vigorous support for representation of the poor was provided by the liberal political clubs who had become the major organizational arm of the reform movement. Not only were the clubs ideologically committed to dispersion of power, but in all four cities they were to some degree antagonistic to the incumbent mayor. In both Los Angeles and New York relatively pro-reform candidates had emerged in the forthcoming mayoral election. The Independent Voters of Illinois and their one alderman on the council vigorously supported participation by the poor in Chicago's program. Philadelphia's more influential Americans for Democratic Action, which disliked Mayor Tate's ward politician image, lent the neighborhood groups office space, staff, materials, and the prestige of a middle-class, intellectual organization. Of the four Los Angeles area congressmen who opposed Mayor Yorty's efforts to assure official control of the program in early 1965, three were identified with the reform clubs in California. (The fourth represented the one Negro district in the state.)

The reformers had their greatest impact in New York City. Democratic Congressman William Fitts Ryan, a leading Manhattan reformer who had recently announced his candidacy for mayor, attacked his rival Paul Screvane for "visions of a new patronage pool." In the spring of 1965 Ryan called for representation of the poor on the policy-making body and for administration of the programs by "democratically" selected local boards. That summer, the Republican candidate, Congressman John Lindsay, adopted the campaign style of a reformer, charging that "City Hall is now setting up a structural monstrosity" and favored instead "prompt steps to increase representation of the poor on the Council."[32]

The dual commitment within the OEO to both economic and political solutions to poverty thus became a matter of open political controversy in the four cities. The mayors held to the conception of poverty as an economic condition and sought to consolidate their power over this program. By contrast, reform groups saw poverty as in part a political condition and supported the dispersal of power to representatives of the poor. Resolution of this conflict varied according to the relative strength of the combatants. This in turn led to intercity variations in the outputs of the community action program.

INTERCITY VARIATION: ATTACK ON POLITICAL POVERTY

In light of the contrasting machine-reform traditions in the four cities, we hypothesized a considerable variation in the local poverty programs funded by OEO. The federal agency would presumably be most successful in distributing power to the poor in reform cities, given the existing dispersion of power. On the other hand, machine cities would probably be more successful at distributing material resources. In order to test this hypothesis, we first assessed the city's *dispersion of political power*, which reflected the existing strength and past success of the reform movement. As an index of power dispersion, we used the strength of the dominant party organization, which in all cases was that of the Democratic party. The four cities were ranked as follows: Chicago (with the strongest organization), Philadelphia, New York, and Los Angeles.

Both qualitative and quantitative data support this rank ordering. In Chicago the mayor was also the leader of the dominant Democratic organization, whose loyal congressional delegation was noted for unrivaled cohesion. Reformers were chronically ineffective, while the Republicans had been an insignificant force in city politics since the 1930's. The Philadelphia Democratic organization also had a relatively united congressional delega-

246

tion, and in the 1963 mayoral election the organization had elected James H. J. Tate, a ward committeeman, as mayor. On the other hand, the organization lacked Chicago's extensive state and local patronage and after his election Mayor Tate and the party chairman fell into a dispute, reflecting in part the greater influence (compared to Chicago) of reform Democrats in city-wide elections. In 1965, a Republican-reform candidate was elected as the city's district attorney with the support of the Americans for Democratic Action; and in 1966 an independent gubernatorial candidate came within a few thousand votes of carrying Philadelphia in the Democratic primary.

The New York Democratic party organization had so much less cohesion than either Chicago or Philadelphia that the opposition attacked the "bosses" rather than the "boss." Not only had reformers periodically been elected mayor since 1902, but the organization was defeated in the mayoral race both in 1961 by a reform-supported coalition within the party and in 1965 by a Republican-reform opposition. Moreover, the New York Democratic congressional delegation had little unity. The Los Angeles party organization was even more feeble. The city was governed by a nonpartisan mayor who had limited formal powers and operated under a rigid merit system. Nor were state and county governments sources of significant patronage. Legally handicapped in local politics and denied all effective patronage, the formal party organization could not be meaningfully compared even to their New York counterparts. By 1964, the informal Democratic organizations, which had developed over the previous twelve years, were quarreling with each other and were themselves internally divided.

Since these factors have also affected electoral behavior, analysis of election data confirm these considerations. V. O. Key once noted that:

... among the sure districts for each party, there were many in which the organization was so strong that no aspirant dared challenge its man in the primary while in many others the organization was so weak that a primary fight could occur.[33]

Drawing on Key's insight, we examined in each city both the number of candidates per available Democratic nomination to the lower house of the state legislature and the proportion of the vote obtained by the losing candidates. We thus obtained an index of the strength of the organization by considering perhaps the very core of its political power—its ability to monopolize effectively the path to public office.[34] The calculations were based on the 1958-1964 elections—that is, the four preceding the period when major decisions affecting the poverty program were made.

Even this crude measure of organizational strength sharply differentiates the four cities, as shown in Table 1. Chicago's powerful organization so discouraged insurgent candidates that over three-fourths of the races were uncontested. The party's power to prevent contests declined somewhat in Philadelphia, fell even more

TABLE 1.
PERCENTAGE OF VOTE CAST FOR LOSING CANDIDATES IN
DEMOCRATIC PRIMARIES FOR LOWER HOUSE OF STATE
LEGISLATURE (1958-1964)

Percentage Cast for Losing Candidates[34]	Possible Contests (per cent)			
	Chicago	Philadelphia	New York	Los Angeles
No opposition	77.5	67.1	61.2	51.7
1-19	14.5	9.9	6.1	5.2
20-39	8.0	20.4	16.5	20.7
40-59[a]	0.0	2.6	16.2	12.1
60-	0.0	0.0	0.0	10.3
Total	100.0	100.0	100.0	100.0
Number of possible contests	(138)	(152)	(260)	(58)

[a]In contests involving three or more candidates, the losers together can receive more than 50 per cent of the vote.

in New York, and reached a low point in Los Angeles, where scarcely more than one-half the elections were uncontested. The impact of the regular organization's strength on the voters is further demonstrated in those elections which were contested. In only 8 per cent of all cases did opposition candidates in Chicago receive 20 per cent or more of the vote. This figure increased to 23 per cent in Philadelphia, to 33 per cent in New York and in Los Angeles to 43 per cent. Additional details in Table 1 emphasize these intercity differences still more, but it is clear that this quantitative index conforms to the qualitative data on the strength of the dominant party in the four cities.

We hypothesized that the rank order of cities on this index of power dispersion would be directly associated with the intercity variation in the distribution of

power to the poor through community action. In order to measure this power distribution through community action we constructed an index based on the following three indicators: *first*, the percentage of neighborhood and minority group representatives on the city-wide community action agencies; *second*, the relative influence of the city administration over the selection of these representatives; and *third*, the degree to which the representatives could be held accountable by an organized constituency.

Chicago officials rejected uncontrolled participation of representatives as unwarranted. By March, 1966, only 8 per cent (six of seventy-eight) of the members of the decision-making committee even formally represented the poor. Moreover, these representatives were chosen directly by the staff of the Chicago poverty program, providing only *controlled* representation. Even though OEO in the summer of 1966 insisted on twice this number of low-income representatives, no substantial change in the process of selection was implemented. The controlled selection process prevented the representatives from developing any autonomous relations with their constituency.

Direct elections were held in Philadelphia to select the representatives of the poor to twelve neighborhood committees. Each committee chose one representative to the city-wide committee, giving the poor 40 per cent representation on a thirty member body. The process of selection in Philadelphia was virtually *free of control* by either the city administration or the party organization. But it failed to encourage the *organization* of the poverty program's clients. Turnout in the first poverty election amounted to only 3 per cent of the eligible voters and the vote itself revealed a "friends-and-neighbors" pattern.[35] Without an organized constituency for whom the representatives could speak and to whom they could be held accountable, they lacked both the power and the continuing mandate to influence decisively either the poverty program or city politics in general. Developments in Los Angeles resembled the Philadelphia pattern. The poor were given 35 per cent representation on the policy-making body (seven out of twenty members). The representatives were chosen in an *uncontrolled* election but less than 1 per cent of the eligible electorate participated. The winners, once again, had only limited and *unorganized* contact with their constituents.

In New York under the Wagner administration, client representatives were entitled to thirty-two out of one hundred seats on the policy-making body and another ten seats were awarded to such neighborhood nonprofit organizations as Haryou-Act and Mobilization for Youth. But before the poor filled all these seats, which would have given them 42 per cent representation, the Lindsay administration in the summer of 1966 created a new structure which gave 50 per cent representation to neighborhood organizations. Community conventions attended by delegates of neighborhood organizations were used to select the representatives of the poor; since the process was relatively free of official control, it encouraged *uncontrolled, yet organized* representation. While this process in some cases enabled established agencies and churches to influence the selection of representatives, more often it brought out leaders interested in developing new organizations with a protest orientation and militancy unrivalled in other cities. The leaders were at once free of official control yet capable to speak for a fairly well organized body of constituents.

Thus, Table 2 shows the New York program most fully realized the uncontrolled, but organized, representation of the poor. The greatest control over the representation occurred in Chicago, while Philadelphia and Los Angeles fell in between these two extremes.[36]

When we cross-tabulated the index of party strength against the propensity of community action to distribute power, the curvilinear relationship presented in Figure 1 emerged. Since we hypothesized

TABLE 2.
PERCENTAGE AND TYPE OF REPRESENTATION
OF LOW-INCOME GROUPS
ON COMMUNITY ACTION AGENCIES'
POLICY-MAKING COMMITTEES

City	Percentage Representation	Type of Representation
Chicago	8	City controlled
Los Angeles	35	Uncontrolled, but disorganized
Philadelphia	40	Uncontrolled, but disorganized
New York	50	Uncontrolled and organized

a direct or linear relationship, this finding forced us to reconsider the intervening political processes in the four cities. As we shall show, this curvilinear relationship was produced by the unexpectedly complex effect of power dispersion on *the mayor's resources, the mayor's intersts,* and *the flow of demand inputs.*

The stronger the party organization, the greater the resources of the mayor in bargaining with other political actors. The relations between the mayor and OEO provide a particularly graphic example. Chicago's Mayor Daley, through his unified congressional delegation, could force OEO to withdraw suggestions that the poor be given meaningful representation. But in cities where power was more dispersed, the mayor had fewer resources in his negotiations with Washington. In New York and Los Angeles, where reform had been most successful, several congressmen publicly opposed the mayor's attempt to centralize power over the program. Thus, the mayor's political *resources* were a critical intervening variable. The relationship between power dispersion and the

political *interests* of the mayor was more complicated. Where power was centralized, as in Chicago, the mayor's primary goal was to maintain the party organization which kept him in power. His machine, which had been the sole significant political force in low-income areas, did not welcome the growth of independent neighborhood organizations. Once such groups received federal poverty funds, they would have an interest in acquiring the political power to assure additional funding later. Thus politicized, they might begin to campaign for their friends and against their enemies, eventually entering their own candidates and threatening traditional party bastions. Saul Alinsky, a militant organizer of the poor, has argued that "City Hall obviously won't finance a group dedicated to fierce political independence and to the servicing of its own self-interests as it defines them."[37] Such considerations, while most prominent in Chicago, also affected the interests of Mayor Tate in Philadelphia and, to a lesser extent, Wagner in New York.

250

But with the election in New York of Republican-reform Mayor John Lindsay, the political interests of the city administration there were significantly altered. In fact, new community organizations in low-income neighborhoods are probably least threatening to reform mayors such as Lindsay, *who are elected over the opposition of a political machine that has* *not been completely destroyed*. Such mayors have depended largely on the newspapers, the prestigious civic associations, and middle-class reform clubs for support against the hostile party organizations. But they have lacked a stable organization to mobilize voters in low-income areas where a weakened but potentially troublesome party organization has ex-

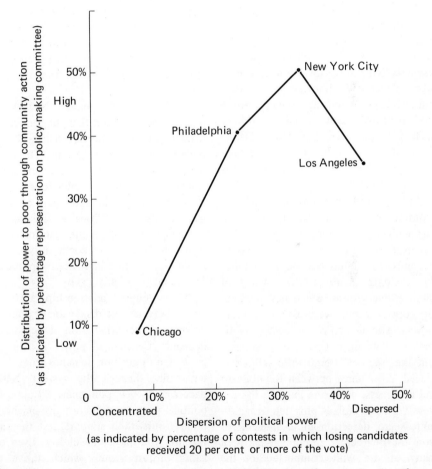

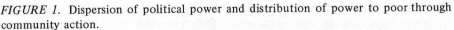

FIGURE 1. Dispersion of political power and distribution of power to poor through community action.

251

isted and, as in St. Louis, may regain power. By supporting funds for community groups in low-income areas and listening to the demands they make for better services, reform mayors may well have been able to expand their own voting constituencies. At least they created new problems for hostile party organizations.

All of this seemed to apply with particular force if the reform mayor supporting participation of the poor was also a Republican, as was John Lindsay. The Democratic Negro or Spanish-speaking residents living in the lowest-income areas often demanded desegregated housing and education as well as more opportunities for employment as skilled workers. Such policies often threatened Democratic Italian, Polish, and Irish groups more than Republicans in silk-stocking neighborhoods.[38]

At least until 1966, the machine's distribution of material benefits to particular individuals enabled the Democratic leaders to ignore some of the Negroes' demands for improved public service, thus helping maintain the loyalty of white ethnic groups. But if new community organizations were to make more universalistic demands for better public services, it would not be as easy to maintain the Negroes' Democratic solidarity. Indeed, an alliance between Republicans and reformers, occurring in 1965 in both New York and Philadelphia, led to significant Negro defection in local elections from the Democrats. In comparison with many of the white supporters of the Democratic regular party organizations, reform groups have an ideological commitment to the goals of integration and dispersal of political power to the poor. A further political link between the well-to-do and the poorest voting groups may lie in their "public-regarding" values toward major civic expenditures, as distinguished from the more "private-regarding" values held by Catholic ethnic groups.[39] Indeed, this coalition would parallel the tacit partnership between big business and Negro groups in many southern cities. In New York City the extensive but far from total dispersion of political power induced the mayor to encourage a program aimed at the political conditions of poverty.

In Los Angeles, unlike New York, power is so dispersed that the mayor has little to gain by a further distribution of power to low-income groups. The city's nonpartisan elections and utter organizational fluidity have so destroyed party structures as to eliminate them as political threats. No political considerations, in other words, offset the manifold ways in which autonomous community groups could create new administrative problems for the mayor of a large city.[40]

A curvilinear relationship also obtained between the dispersion of political power and the articulation of opposition demands. Centralized power in Chicago prevented opposition demands from flowing easily through the system. Newspapers and even politicians of opposite political persuasion did not give neighborhood groups their support, lest they antagonize the mayor needlessly. Even existing protest groups which thrive on public controversy had to concentrate their attention on one or two issues—

education and housing—lest they over-committed their limited resources. As Bachrach and Baratz have argued, this "other face of power" prevented controversial issues from arising.[41] In Philadelphia, and still more in New York, less concentrated political power enabled private welfare agencies, Republicans, reformers, and leading newspapers to support neighborhood groups seeking power for themselves. Encouraged by such support, the neighborhood groups formed city-wide *ad hoc* committees which gave organization and focus to the scattered demands of neighborhood groups. As the level of controversy rose, the mayors were forced to concede substantial representation to the poor, particularly in New York City.

In Los Angeles, on the other hand, the extreme dispersal of political power actually handicapped the demands of neighborhood groups for more power. The reform clubs had no local bosses to attack, which weakened their interest in stimulating competing community organizations. Their candidate for mayor, James Roosevelt, gave significantly less support to representation of the poor than Ryan and Lindsay had in New York City. Similarly, with no machine left to reform, Los Angeles newspapers had little incentive to encourage participation. Consequently, they supported the incumbent mayor and opposed the neighborhood groups in the controversy. As a result, disorganization of the city's political and social structures left the opposition with few channels through which their demands could flow. More successful than their eastern counterparts, Los Angeles reformers so indi-

vidualized power that, like Humpty Dumpty, it could not readily be put back together again—even to achieve reform purposes.

To summarize, in Chicago the confluence of three factors—the mayor's resources, his interests, and the flow of demands—all acted to reduce the distribution of power in the community action program. The mayor had both the interests and the resources to minimize representation for minority groups. Meanwhile, the opposition found it difficult to enlist political support for its demands. In New York City, power was distributed in the community action programs under Lindsay because the mayor's interests coincided with this policy. Even under Wagner the mayor's resources were so limited that demands for representation of the poor, which flowed easily through the political system, could not be ignored. Intermediate levels of power dispersion in the community action structures appeared in both Philadelphia and Los Angeles but for very different reasons. Although both mayors opposed extensive representation of the poor by autonomous organized groups, Mayor Tate in Philadelphia had far more resources than Mayor Yorty of Los Angeles with which to resist these demands. On the other hand, the availability of important allies provided protest groups in Philadelphia with channels for making their demands felt. In Los Angeles, these channels were unavailable. It is this *varying* combination of mayoral resources and interests together with the flow of political demands which produced the curvilinear relationship between existing power dispersion and the further distribution of power in the community action program.

INTERCITY VARIATION: ATTACK ON ECONOMIC POVERTY

Our second hypothesis was that machine cities would obtain and expend community action dollars more quickly than reform cities. To test this hypothesis we again used party strength as our index of the dispersion of political power, cross-tabulating it this time against the community action dollars per poor family granted to the city by the OEO during the first two years of the program.[42] The relationship is presented in Figure 2. The per capita grant to each city at least provides a good measure of the speed with which each city initiated a relatively sizable attack on poverty as an economic condition through OEO's program.[43]

Significantly enough, this quantitative measure correlates with the more qualitative and impressionistic data on the four local programs, particularly the speed and efficiency with which the community action activities were inaugurated. Thus Chicago, which received the highest amount per poor family—$211—was able

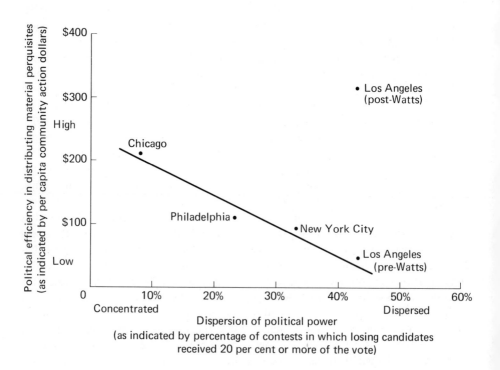

FIGURE 2. Dispersion of political power and political efficiency in distributing material perquisites.

to put its neighborhood centers, the main focus of its program, into operation as early as March, 1965. Philadelphia, which secured only $112 in federal funds per low-income family, did not select an executive director until April, 1965, and the program did not begin until the following summer. Even then most money was channeled through other agencies, such as the schools and the recreation department, because the poverty agency was not able to establish its own program quickly. New York acted still more slowly since it received only $101 per poor family and used this amount only haphazardly and after long delays. Its first Progress Center was not opened until March, 1966—one year later than the Chicago center. At the end of the 1965-1966 fiscal year, $12 million remained undistributed. The most spectacular delays occurred in Los Angeles which, at the end of the first fiscal year, did even more poorly, having been granted less than half as much per poor family as any of the other three cities—only $25 per poor family (calculated at the two-year rate of $50 in Figure 2). During this period the community action program barely got under way in the face of the many-sided and complicated conflict that pervaded the first year of the program.

But this linear relationship between centralized political power and the distribution of material perquisites was dramatically altered by the social explosion in Los Angeles at the beginning of the second fiscal year of the program. During the second year the city became the most favored of the four, receiving $158 per poor family (calculated on the graph at the two year rate of $316). The Watts

riots, the most violent of all Negro outbursts, so disturbed OEO officials that comparatively vast sums of money were allocated to the city. But in light of the poverty program's expressed goal of reducing urban violence, through the elimination of economic poverty, the disruption of the usual operation of structural variables, such as the dispersion of political power, was scarcely surprising.

But with this exception, the linear relationship did obtain between the centralization of political power in the city and the capacity of the authorities to secure and distribute material perquisites through the community action program. The intervening variables seem fairly clear. All mayors felt it was in their *interest* to obtain as much money as possible and to spend it as quickly as possible. In this way favorable publicity would replace carping criticism. The key variable thus became the resources of the mayor to attain this goal, which, as we have seen, depended directly on the dispersion of political power within the city. With centralized political power, the mayor could bargain effectively with OEO officials. In particular, Mayor Daley's cohesive congressional delegation placed him in an enviable position in comparison to his New York or Los Angeles counterpart. But of equal and perhaps greater importance, the mayor needed power to still internal dissent so that he could quickly establish this new program. One potential source of dissent was the demand for the representation of the poor on the board; where this controversy flourished, it delayed the implementation of the program. But other factors contributed to program delay as well. In

Philadelphia, Mayor Tate delayed selecting his executive director because he was unable or unwilling to choose between competing Negro factions. In New York City, the opening of neighborhood centers and sites for Head Start, the educational program for preschool children, was delayed by other city bureaucracies too entrenched to be forced to cooperate by a politically weak mayor. The Los Angeles conflict combined tensions among competing governmental jurisdictions with the struggle between neighborhood organizations and the mayor.

In summary, the strength of party organization affected both the amount of federal funding and the speed and efficiency with which local agencies were established to disburse the funds. Since machines were historically dependent on the efficient payment of material benefits to their various supporters, it is not surprising to find that greater organizational strength increases the mayor's ability to obtain and distribute poverty funds. By contrast, the far greater concern of reform movements for "democracy" and "honesty" in political processes and structures, as opposed to the distribution of material outputs, explains the less effective distribution of funds by poverty agencies in cities with strong reform traditions.

DEMOCRACY IN URBAN AMERICA: POWER, PERQUISITES, AND "CLASS BIAS"

This investigation of the community action program sustains the points of agreement between the early critics of machine politics and its more recent scholarly defenders. The tendency of machine cities to use material perquisites to concentrate power (condemned by the early and heralded by the later scholarly tradition) directed the program toward solving the economic dimension of poverty. For the most part, the stronger the machine, the greater the tendency toward distributing material perquisites rather than power. The reform tradition's propensity to disperse power even at the cost of rapid implementation of governmental programs (endorsed by the early scholars but criticized by recent social scientists) led reform cities to concentrate their attack on the political conditions associated with poverty. For the most part, the stronger the reform movement, the easier it was for neighborhood groups to gain political influence but the harder for the city to inaugurate programs intended to alleviate the economic plight of the poor. It is worth emphasizing, however, that in Los Angeles—before the Watts riots— neither the political nor the economic conditions of poverty were significantly alleviated by the program. The complete triumph of reform seems to have reduced the political system's capacity to achieve even reformist goals.

If our empirical investigation validates the consensus of the two scholarly traditions on the different political processes of reform and machine politics, it remains to assess the class bias of these two structures with regard to the community action program. In fact, community action within the war on poverty provides a case where both reform and machine administrations were explicitly directing benefits to the poor. Their common pattern of upper-class bias, in other words, was measurably reduced. This relatively greater concern for the lower classes than in the past reflects the New Deal revolution in the American party system which made the dominant national party, the Democrats, responsive to the disadvantaged urban masses. Specifically, the Johnson administration provided that federal funds be explicitly directed *by law* to a low-income clientele. Moreover, the 90 per cent federal share of the cost spared substantial expense for local taxpayers, minimizing much potential community opposition. This trend has been reinforced by the growing numbers and sophistication of urban Negro and Spanish-speaking voters. Far more than earlier urban immigrants, these groups have begun to demand political solutions for their economic and social problems. But because of the present differences in the class biases of machine and reform politics, this change has not occurred to the same extent or in the same way in all four of our cities.

As an autonomous political organization determined to maintain its centralized power, pre-New Deal machines were reluctant to become too dependent on any one social stratum—even the politically powerful business class. They balanced upper-class money against lower-class votes. By contrast, the reformers, simply by dividing and distributing power among various social groups, produced a political process which more nearly reflected the general upper-class dominance of the social system. Unlike the lower classes in machine cities, those experiencing reform rule received less in the way of both psychic rewards (such as ethnic balance on electoral slates) and particularistic material benefits. But in this post-New Deal period, the machine's same concern to maintain its independence leads it to oppose an independent position of political power for minority and low-income groups despite the rise of the welfare state. As a result, low-income groups in reform cities may eventually use their greater power to secure more far-reaching collective material rewards, such as substantial increases in city service. Just as reform politics was *relatively* more favorable to upper classes in the past, it may now—at least potentially—be *relatively* more favorable than machine politics to low-income groups.

Admittedly, the significant participation of the poor requires an extreme effort on the part of poverty officials and neighborhood leaders. Even in New York City, participation of community groups was only beginning in 1966. Yet the city's program at times neared the point of complete administrative breakdown. At least in the short run, maximizing the value of participation appeared to come only at considerable cost to alleviating economic poverty. On the other hand, the long-run solutions to economic poverty may depend on increased political power of precisely these presently disorganized and politically unsophisticated low-income neighborhood groups. Rather than limited economic assistance over the short run, it may be more beneficial for the lower classes to stimulate neighborhood and minority groups to demand future economic assistance on a far massive scale.

Finally, the varied experience of the community action program in the four cities shows that the conflict of basic political values between the two scolarly traditions over mass participation in political action parallels a continuing conflict within the American political system. As we have seen, this conflict produced a critical ambiguity in OEO's own goals. In Kornhauser's terms, the pessimistic adherents of contemporary pluralism within OEO sought to reduce the vulnerability of existing political and social elites to mass discontent and pressure by attacking the economic basis of poverty.[44] The more optimistic adherents of Jeffersonian participatory democracy sought to incorporate these same masses as effective actors in the political community by providing for the "maximum feasible participation" of the program's clientele.

We have tried to show that this ambivalence within OEO was substantially magnified by the differences imposed by the reform and machine traditions in the different cities. In a manner typical of federal programs in the decentralized American political system, OEO policies conformed to and thus reinforced the prevailing political pattern in each local community. Where the dominant party machine still had centralized political power, OEO concentrated on its goal of restraining and pacifying the lower class by improving its economic condition. In cities where an historically successful reform tradition had dispersed power, federal administrators partially realized their

Jeffersonian goal of increasing citizen participation in political life.

The continuing impact of these historical differences on contemporary efforts to end urban poverty suggest how deeply rooted has been the fear of the democratic masses in a large and necessarily impersonal republic. This presumably modern issue was not only raised by de Tocqueville in the age of Jackson, but it was also debated (although less explicitly) by the Hamiltonians and Jeffersonians of the preceding generation. Moreover, as our analysis point out, the issue of mass participation in political life was also a covert but perhaps the critical issue between machines and reformers in American urban politics even before it emerged as the mass society theory of many modern political philosophers in Europe and the United States. We have argued here that this theoretical question has reemerged as a significant political issue in contemporary American politics.

NOTES

2. S. M. Lipset, *Political Man* (Garden City, New York: Doubleday, 1963), p. 345.

3. M. Ostrogorski, *Democracy and the Organization of Political Parties*, II (Garden City, New York: Doubleday, 1964), p. 299. Ostrogorski was far from alone in his bitter attack on the "machine." Other critics include James Bryce, *The American Commonwealth II* (New York: Macmillan, 1895), and Roy V. Pell, *The Political Clubs of New York City* (New York: G. P. Putnam's Son, 1935). Of great influence in this generally critical attitude toward the party organization was Robert Michels' *Political Parties* (New York: Collier Books, 1962), which docu-

mented the oligarchical tendencies within the Social Democratic parties in Europe.

4. William L. Riordon, *Plunkitt of Tammany Hall* (New York: E. P. Dutton, 1963), p. 3.

5. Robert K. Merton, *Social Theory and Social Structure* (Glencoe, Ill.: Free Press, 1957), pp. 75-76.

6. Riordon, pp. 27-28.

7. For example, see Eugene C. Lee, *The Politics of Nonpartisanship* (Berkeley: University of California Press, 1960).

8. Richard Hofstadter, *The Age of Reform* (New York: Alfred A. Knopf, 1959), p. 238.

9. Lee, pp. 139-140. Also, Oliver P. Williams and Charles R. Adrian, "The Insulation of Local Politics under the Nonpartisan Ballot," *American Political Science Review*, LIII (December, 1959), pp. 1059-61.

10. Edward C. Banfield and James Q. Wilson, *City Politics* (Cambridge: Harvard University Press, 1963), chap. 21.

11. Lee, pp. 76-84.

12. See John Bartlow Martin, "The Town That Tried Good Government," in Edward C. Banfield, ed., *Urban Government* (New York: Free Press of Glencoe, 1961), pp. 276-84. Reprinted from *Saturday Evening Post*, October 1, 1955.

13. The best source for the views of the muckrakers is in Lincoln Steffens, *The Autobiography of Lincoln Steffens* (New York: Harcourt, Brace & World, 1931).

14. Banfield and Wilson, p. 265. For an illuminating discussion of the transformation of American reform, see Michael Rogin, *The Intellectuals and McCarthy: The Radical Spectre* (Cambridge, Mass.: MIT Press, 1967), chap. 7, especially pp. 202-7.

15. Walter Dean Burnham, "The Changing Shape of the American Political Universe," *American Political Science Review*, LIX (March, 1965), pp. 7-28.

16. An excellent discussion of the goals of these municipal reformers can be found in Banfield and Wilson, pp. 138-86.

17. Banfield and Wilson, pp. 101-11.

18. An excellent statement of the views of nineteenth-century theorists on democracy as distinguished from the pluralist viewpoint is given in Jack L. Walker, "A Critique of the Elitist Theory of Democracy," *American Political Science Review*, LX (June, 1966), pp. 285-96).

19. Ostrogorski, p. 300.

20. Banfield and Wilson, p. 345.

21. Edward C. Banfield, *Political Influence* (New York: Free Press of Glencoe, 1961), pp. 260-262.

22. U.S. Congress, *An Act to Mobilize the Human and Financial Resources of the Nation to Combat Poverty in the United States*, Public Law 88-452, 88th Cong., 2nd Sess., 1964, p. 9.

23. *Ibid.*

24. Office of Economic Opportunity, *Community Action Workbook* (Washington, D.C., 1965), III. A. 7.

25. This term is drawn from David Truman, *The Governmental Process* (New York: Alfred A. Knopf, 1965), pp. 511-516.

26. Office of Economic Opportunity, *Community Action Program Guide* (Washington, D.C., 1965), I, p. 18.

27. Characteristically, the extreme decentralization in Los Angeles required the participation of other governmental units even at the beginning.

28. U.S. Congress House Committee on Education and Labor, *Hearings, Examination of the War on Poverty Program*, 89th Cong., 1st Sess., 1965, p. 483.

29. For an interesting discussion of needs, plans, and possibilities in New York City, see Thomas P. F. Hoving, "Think Big About Small Parks," *New York Times Magazine* (April, 1966), pp. 12-13, 68-72. Changes in welfare policies—and their costs—are discussed by Richard A. Cloward and Frances Fox Piven, "The Weight of the Poor: A Strategy to End Poverty," *The Nation*, CCII (May, 1966), pp. 510-17.

30. The legislation forbade use of poverty funds for primary or secondary education and limited OEO's educational activities largely to Head Start programs.

31. Another motive may have been the penchant of newspapers for controversial issues which boost circulation. But since any number of problems can be made controversial and interesting to newspaper readers, this goal is not a sufficient explanation for newspaper focus on this particular issue.

32. A third Congressman from New York City who contributed to the debate on the poverty program was Adam Clayton Powell. While he cannot be considered part of the reform movement, his political style (which relies on issues rather than on patronage for support) resembles that of the reform clubs. See James Q. Wilson, "Two Negro Politicians: An Interpretation," *Midwest Journal of Political Science*, IV (November, 1960), pp. 349-69.

33. V. O. Key, Jr., *American State Politics* (New York: Alfred A. Knopf, 1963), p. 181. Wilson, too, has noted, "The absence of real primary contests is probably as good an indication as any of the power—both actual and imputed—of the machine." James Q. Wilson, *Negro Politics* (New York: Free Press of Glencoe, 1960), p. 45.

34. The number of candidates aspiring for political office is, to be sure, related to the probability of the party's winning the general election. Where the party has little chance, there may be only one candidate, however weak the organization. But here we are comparing the dominant party organization in each city. Since the Democratic party does well in all four cities in general elections, there are few "safe" Republican seats; thus, this factor should not pose a problem for our intercity comparison.

Special calculations were required in the multimember districts in Philadelphia and Chicago. Here the number of candidates running was calculated in terms of the available Democratic nominations. If three candidates ran in a two-member district, only one race was said to be contested. If four or more ran, both seats were considered contested. In calculating the percentage vote for losing candidates in these two-member districts, the procedures were as follows. Where three candidates ran, the opposition's percentage was calculated by taking the

vote of the losing candidate as a percentage of the combined vote of this losing candidate and the weakest winning candidate. Where four or more candidates ran, the percentage for one race was calculated by dividing the vote of the strongest losing candidate by his vote *plus* the vote of the weakest winning candidate. The opposition's percentage in the contest for the second seat was the following ratio: the total vote of all losing candidates, except the strongest, over this numerator plus the vote of the strongest winning candidate. In this way, contests in multimember districts were compared to those in single-member districts.

35. The term is taken from V. O. Key, Jr., *Southern Politics* (New York: Alfred A. Knopf, 1949). Analysis of election data on Philadelphia's poverty election discloses the same tendency to vote for one's neighbor when organization is lacking that Key found in many southern states.

36. Work is now in progress on more precise indicators of the increase in the political power of the poor due to the community action program tentatively suggests that in fact there was more participation in Los Angeles than in Philadelphia. The less refined indicators of formal participation presented here were unable to distinguish between the two cities.

37. Steven M. Loveday, *Wall Street Journal*, February 18, 1966.

38. Because of this tension between low income whites and Negroes, Samuel Lubell argued in 1964 that "for some years to come the likely pattern of political conflict promises to be stormier at the local and state levels than at the presidential level." Samuel Lubell, *White and Black: Test of a Nation* (New York: Harper & Row, 1964), p. 160.

39. James Q. Wilson and Edward C. Banfield, "Public-Regardingness as a Value Premise in Voting Behavior," *American Political Science Review*, LVIII (December, 1964), pp. 876-87.

40. *Supra*, pp. 275-76.

41. Peter Bachrach and Morton S. Baratz, "Two Faces of Power," *American Political Science Review*, LVI (December, 1962), pp. 947-952.

42. The amount of community action dollars granted to each city for the fiscal years 1964-1965 and 1965-1966 were obtained directly from the OEO. The number of poor families in each city is the number of families with incomes of less than $3000 per year given in the 1960 census.

43. These figures by themselves do not directly support the contention that a particular city distributed more material services to the poor than any others. The city that received the most money per low income family may have spent a much higher percentage for the benefit of relatively advantaged rather than poor citizens. But since there was no persuasive evidence for this contention, it was more reasonable to assume that approximately the same per cent of poverty funds actually benefited the poor in all four cities. If this is so, then we may conclude that those cities that obtained more money from Washington did do more to ameliorate the *economic* needs of the poor.

44. William Kornhauser, *The Politics of Mass Society* (New York: Free Press of Glencoe, 1959).

⇜ SIX ⇝
The Modern Machine: Decline or Change?

⊰ COMMENTARY ⊱

The incumbency of Franklin D. Roosevelt as President in 1933 seemingly triggered a chain reaction that signaled the last hurrah for that peculiar American institution, the city boss. Here at last was a new deal offering an effective alternative to machine politics. A quantity of social legislation poured from Washington, dangling services and benefits that the boss could not hope to match. Apparently outmoded, the wheezing political machines began to run out of gas. By 1950, after a world war and years of the welfare state, Tammany Hall had only a shadow of its former power, and the machines of Pendergast, Curley, Hague, and Crump were in shambles. It was the end of an era.

Or was it? Many students of urban affairs have proclaimed the decline and fall of the city boss and his machine. The downfall of machine politics, it was argued, was the New Deal. Public welfare programs, social security, workmen's compensation, collective bargaining, the rise of organized labor—added to legacies of the Progressive era such as nonpartisanship and civil service reform—all conspired to create a competing network of services and inducements that both crippled the boss's power and wooed away his traditional bases of support. The first two essays of this chapter review the decline of the machine, one in broad, general terms ("The Changing Pattern of Urban Party Politics," by Fred I. Greenstein), the other on the specific problem of patronage, so vital to the health of bossism ("The Silent Revolution in Patronage," by Frank J. Sorauf).

Recently, however, scholars have questioned the impact of the New Deal on two counts: (1) its effect has been overstated; (2) the ability of the boss to adapt has been underestimated. Urban historians like Bruce Stave and Lyle Dorsett have shown that in Pittsburgh and Kansas City, rather than destroy the boss, the New Deal invigorated and strengthened him.[1] A two-way street opened between New Dealers and the local machines. Roosevelt needed the disciplined vote-getting services of the big-city bosses, and the bosses needed and got federal funds, patronage, and control of the relief services in their respective cities. As early as October 1934, the Pittsburgh machine placed five hundred jobs in Washington itself, eight to ten times that number in Pennsylvania—and most of the jobs were exempt from civil service requirements. The machine prospered from a host of available federal positions, among them those of U.S. marshals and attorneys, internal revenue collectors, and a number of postmasterships. If the New Deal made the Christmas turkey giveaway an ancient relic from the gaslight era, in Kansas City it more than compensated by providing a harvest of federal jobs and a bountiful purse of federal funds. A Pendergast newspaper bragged, with perhaps a little exaggeration, that the machine captured federal 200,000 jobs. While Tom Pendergast went to jail in 1939 for tax evasion, he was destroyed by his own greed and election scandals, not by the New Deal.

Other boss-ruled cities also prospered from the New Deal. Crump funneled millions of federal dollars into New Deal projects in Tennessee. Frank Hague's war with the C.I.O. in particular, and with liberals in general, did not stop the flow of federal money into New Jersey. In W.P.A. funds alone, the Hague machine won control over $47 million. Boston's James Michael Curley was an ardent suitor for federal largesse. Millions poured into hospitals, parks, roads, and river and harbor improvement, creating 100,000 jobs and uncalculable goodwill for the Curley organization.

The New Deal thesis also begs this question: At a time when machines were supposedly declining, how do you account for the survival of old machines and the creation of new ones, such as those (to name a few) in Chicago, Buffalo, Pittsburgh, Philadelphia, Baltimore, Gary, the Bronx and Brooklyn organizations in New York, and that of the O'Connell brothers in Albany? The modern Democratic machine in Chicago *began* in the 1930s. In 1954, when the machine was supposedly just a fragrant memory, William Green created a most efficient organization in Phila-

1. Bruce Stave, *The New Deal and the Last Hurrah: Pittsburgh Machine Politics* (1970); Lyle Dorsett, *The Pendergast Machine* (1968).

delphia. Moreover, in the cities that had a strong tradition of party government but experienced a decline in machine politics—such, e.g., as the cities of the Northeast—there remain elements of the old politics operating in a machine-like manner. And there was the phenomenon of factionalism. The politics of faction usually occurred in cities where the machine was destroyed, or nearly destroyed, but was not replaced with alternative institutions that completely eliminated the characteristics of machine politics. It was the phenomenon of a party's being fragmented into a coalition of groups none of them strong enough to dominate the other, such as was observable in Kansas City, St. Louis, Cleveland, Cincinnati, Boston, and Jersey City. It demonstrates that while party government was down, it was not out.

This is not to suggest either that machines have continued to reflect the classic mode of the nineteenth-century boss, or that they have not declined. It is to suggest that while some machines have indeed declined and in fact vanished, others have managed to adapt to twentieth-century conditions and survived, although that survival has necessitated changes from the earlier mode. This point is demonstrated in the next two selections of this chapter. In "The New-Style Boss," Blanche Blank discusses the accommodations made by modern bosses in several cities. In "Daley of Chicago," David Halberstam, Pulitzer Prize-winning journalist, focuses on one boss—perhaps not the best and brightest, but certainly one of the most astute and adaptable of our modern urban politicians.

The problem of decline or change, then, depends in part upon what city you are talking about, and in part upon conditions that go beyond the simplistic New Deal thesis. Our argument rests upon this proposition: The very forces that helped create the city boss—urbanization, immigration, the structure of government, attitudes, the demand for municipal services, the rise of the professional politician—will themselves change. Combined with elements particularly relevant to the twentieth century—elements such as bureaucratization, mechanization, the impact of the media, demographic and class changes that sent the whites to the suburbs and former immigrants into the middle class—these forces constituted the catalysts that precipitated the decline and/or change of the city boss in America.

For example, since the early years of the twentieth century, the impact of urbanization upon urban government created new interrelations, new avenues of communication, new responsibilities, and new mechanisms for

267

distributing political influence. It made government more complex and demanded more expertise in the management of urban affairs. Its effect upon machine politics was apparent to one party official:

> The business of government is so far beyond the ward committeemen and the local political leaders that they can't cope with it. If you turn over the question of government to fifty aldermen, the city would bust within a month. They just couldn't do it. So these committeemen and the position more and more in a quiet, silent way is not what is used to be.
>
> Who can figure out the financing on a bond issue, calculate the structure or the tensile strength of a piece of steel of twenty feet? Any ward committeeman? Or the fair market value of a piece of property on condemnation? Any aldermen? The result . . . is that the influence and power of ward committeemen is on the decline. We are sacrificing the party government because government is too damned complex.[2]

Reflecting this complexity is the emergence of modern bureaucracy, creating independent agencies slow to respond to either the wile of the boss or the will of the "people."

The impact of modern technology helped to dry up the pools of semi-skilled and unskilled labor so vital as patronage to the boss, by making possible such engines of progress as, for instance, new equipment for street cleaning and garbage disposal, and machines to do much of the paper work of city government, not to mention the automated "vertical railroad," which eliminated so many elevator operators.

But if one had to single out the factor that accounted chiefly for the decline and/or change of the boss, perhaps the choice would fall to one that also constitutes a major social, political, and economic phenomenon of the twentieth century: the ascent of many of the second- and third-generation Americans into the middle class. From the World War I on, mounting prosperity, increasing opportunities, organized labor, and greater educational advantages have (despite a depression and several recessions) sent many of the immigrant siblings into the middle class, thus to change the bosses' traditional power base on one hand, and to diminish the lure of and commitment to the party machine, on the other. In the transition the symbols of prestige changed, and with them social and political aspirations. The bright, energetic young man, especially the college trained,

2. Quoted in Edward M. Levine, *The Irish and Irish Politicians* (1966), pp. 204-5.

yearned less for the congeniality of the political club and more for the security of the executive suite. The old material and psychological inducements of the machine—favors, friendship, jobs, the Christmas turkey—lost their magic when compared to the rewards of middle-class life. Greater affluence gave the "new"-middle class a higher stake in society, making its members more issue-oriented and less likely to swap a vote for a favor. Second- and third-generation Americans joined the older middle class in the scramble from inner city to suburb. For many the flight meant a loss of ethnic identity, which the old-time boss once manipulated with wondrous results. Edward M. Levine, in *The Irish and Irish Politicians,* has chronicled the "crumbling" of Irishness in Chicago. The Irish-American might still marry the nice girl next door, but her name might not be O'Leary nor her religion Catholic. And, alas, neither may known the name of the precinct captain, who just might be Polish.

Middle-class, someone has said, is drinking scotch whiskey. The exodus to the suburbs meant for many a change in political ethos: from the politics of beer to the politics of scotch, served, as it were, with the ice cubes of reform. The middle-class ethos regards with revulsion the machine commitments to immediate, personal, private, self-serving goals. More and more members of the new middle class joined in the demand for long-term goals that served the so-called "public interest" with efficiency, honesty, and impartiality. As a result, the new middle class, like the old, became anti-boss, anti-machine, anti-politician, and even anti-party. Where the grandfather might have shrugged, the grandson saw corruption as a Burning Issue.

For the new-style bosses who arose and the old-style bosses who survived, these changes required that in many areas the game be played by a different set of rules. Old-line machine inducements were still effective in lower-class neighborhoods of the inner city, but beyond that stronghold the growing power of the middle class in city hall, the state legislature, and both elective and appointive federal offices, imposed restraints not experienced by the old-fashioned boss. Even in the bailiwick of the poor, there were significant changes as the whites moved out and the blacks moved in. White precinct captains in Gary and Manhattan, for example, are not so comfortable or effective with the newer black residents as they were with the older white minorities.

There have been changes, as well, toward the style, inducements, and ideology of the city manager. Daley of Chicago, for example, campaigns snug in the robes of nonpartisanship, down-playing (if mentioning at all) his party affiliations, posing as the very model of a model administrator— the efficient, impartial, and expert manager. Forced to cope with an increasing middle class, the boss offers inducements at once more expensive and ideological, to groups that from the boss's standpoint are not always reliable. Survival necessitates the adoption, at least in part, of the middle-class ethic of serving the public interest, wooing large numbers of people to such ambitious enterprises as civil rights programs, housing projects, public welfare improvements, urban renewal undertakings, generous transportation subsidies, accomplished less through muscle and patronage than through charm and salesmanship. Thus, it is believed by some, with his tactics more fragile and his power more dissipated, the new-style boss along with the survivors from the past is living on borrowed time.

Perhaps. If all the articles and pamphlets proclaiming the downfall of Tammany Hall, written from the mid-nineteenth century to the present, were placed end to end they might reach from Manhattan's 14th Street to New Orleans's Basin Street. Tammany is staggering, but it would take an audacious soul to count her out. In the 1940s the Kelly-Nash machine was supposedly a dying shambles; yet Richard J. Daley picked up the pieces, overhauled the motor, and became a kind of wonder of urban America. When Daley goes, will he be the last of a vanishing breed? No one really knows.

Some hold that the machine is passing through yet another transitional stage, one reflecting a major transformation of the American city: the growth and maturity of the most urbanized minority in America—the black community, no longer a minority in many central cities. The profusion of black mayors, the overwhelming weight of sheer numbers, the burden of being black in American society, will, it is reasoned, produce the black city boss with a machine that will respond in much the same manner to the urban condition as the white machines of the past. One wonders, however, whether the barrier of racism will permit the same kind of assimilation as was possible for such earlier minorities as the Irish, Jews, Italians, or Poles. And there is the question of the middle class. As Banfield and Wilson remind us,

> The old-style of the boss and machine is, and no doubt will remain, highly congenial to the lower class. However, the nationally growing middle class has shown that it will use its control of state and federal governments—and partic-

ularly of law enforcement agencies and of special districts within the metropolitan areas—to withhold the patronage, protection, and other political resources that are indispensable to the growth of political machines in the central cities. This means that the lower class will have to play politics of a kind that is tolerable to the middle class or not play it at all.[3]

What, then, is the final reckoning of the city boss in America? He was both a liability and an asset. His ethical architecture was jerry-rigged. As someone once said, when one discovers a brothel one seldom finds that the madam is a virgin. Or as a parody put it:

> Tammany Hall like Robin Hood professes
> To take things from the rich to give the poor
> But Tammany Hall gets just a bit confused sometimes
> And takes from both to give to Tammany Hall.

As arbiter between power and poverty, the boss provided services for the urban poor that without his machine would not have been provided at all. Yet his tactics discredited politics—as noble a profession as any other—and his waste and corruption demoralized government. And it was the poor who bore the brunt of cynicism and misgovernment. At a time of urban confusion, his genius for the practical got things done. As Arthur Mann reminds us, however, "Men who make a profession of being practical are not necessarily the men who get the right things done." Nonetheless, by binding the neighborhood to the machine, for thousands of immigrants and native poor he opened the door to American political institutions—perhaps only a crack, but enough to get a foot in to enter the political process.

In comparison with his counterpart—the modern, nonpartisan, expert, efficient, city administrator and his "new" machine of bureaucratic agencies—the moral distinction of "better" is not clear-cut. Measuring the ward heeler as political hack against the civil servant as bureaucrat with tenure, is he any the less efficient? While the ward heeler might be cavalier about filthy streets and health inspection ordinances, he is acutely sensitive to the needs and problems of the people in his neighborhood; whereas, the civil servant remains isolated from them behind miles of bureaucratic red tape. In one sense, the ward heeler is a refreshing anti-

3. *City Politics,* p. 300.

dote to the paperbound bureaucrat, since he is gifted (as W. B. Munroe noted) at "cutting corners."

If the city boss is skewered to the interests of the lower class, the city manager serves the interests of the middle and upper classes. Like the city boss, the city manager does not always get the right things done. Studies have shown that the more middle class a citizenry, the less likely will it undertake "progressive" improvements, such as urban renewal. More efficiency and more honesty do not insure "better" government. Has non-partisan Los Angeles been more successful in solving urban problems than boss-ridden Chicago? As Alice Vandermeulen has shown, efficiency is difficult, if not impossible, to measure. The quality of municipal services varies from city to city; indeed, the needs and tastes of city dwellers are not identical in every city.[4] If the city boss has not erased the bugaboo of decentralization, modern bureaucratic agencies, self-serving and fiercely independent, have only increased it.

As for political sin, corruption is still alive and well in many non-partisan cities. In the penultimate selection, Theodore Lowi compares the defects of the old machine with those of the new machine of reform—notably its creation of a balkanized city-state, well-run but ungoverned, directed by a bureaucracy of "organized disorganization"—and the question is made even more fascinating: Which machine, old or new, is the "better"?[5] In the final selection, as though answering Boss Tweed's question, "Well, what are you going to do about it?", Edward Costikyan replies in an essay that seems controversial if not hazardous in the wake of Watergate. The answer, according to Costikyan, lies in scotching the notion of taking-politics-out-of-politics, and returning to a form of government that is in the last analysis the most responsible, humane, and representative—party government.

In the final reckoning, then, the city boss was an integral part of the urbanization process and a reflection of the growing pains of the American city. As such, he is for the past and present eminently relevant. As an urban phenomenon, the city boss is, indeed, an American original.

4. See "Guideposts for Measuring the Efficiency of Governmental Expenditure," *Public Administration Review,* Winter 1950. See also George S. Duggar, "The Relation of Local Government Structure to Urban Renewal," *Law and Contemporary Problems,* vol. 26 (1961); and Amos H. Hawley, "Community Power and Urban Renewal Success," *American Journal of Sociology,* January 1963.
5. See Robert A. Caro's brilliant epic, *The Power Broker: Robert Moses and the Fall of New York* (1974).

THE CHANGING PATTERN
OF URBAN PARTY POLITICS

Fred I. Greenstein

THE DECLINE OF OLD-STYLE
PARTY ORGANIZATION

... Although in the short run old-style party organizations were marvelously immune to the attacks of reformers, in recent decades the demise of this political form has been widely acclaimed. Because of the absence of reliable trend data, we cannot document "the decline of the machine" with precision. The decline does seem to have taken place, although only partly as a direct consequence of attempts to reform urban politics. Events have conspired to sap the traditional resources used to build voter support and to make voters less interested in these resources which the parties still command.

Reprinted from "The Changing Pattern of Urban Party Politics" by Fred I. Greenstein in vol. 353 of *The Annals* of The American Academy of Political and Social Science, © 1964 by The American Academy of Political and Social Science.

Decline in the resources of old-style urban politicians. Most obviously, job patronage is no longer available in as great a quantity as it once was. At the federal level and in a good many of the states (as well as numerous cities), the bulk of jobs are filled by civil service procedures. Under these circumstances, the most a party politician may be able to do is seek some minor form of preferment for an otherwise qualified job applicant. Furthermore, the technical requirements of many appointive positions are sufficiently complex to make it inexpedient to fill them with unqualified personnel.[1] And private concerns doing business with the cities are not as likely to be sources of patronage in a day when the franchises have been given out and the concessions granted.

Beyond this, many modern governmental techniques—accounting and auditing requirements, procedures for letting bids, purchasing procedures, even the existence of a federal income tax—restrict the opportunities for dishonest and "honest" graft. Some of these procedures were not instituted with the explicit purpose of hampering the parties. Legislation designed deliberately to weaken parties *has*, however, been enacted—for example, nomination by direct primary and nonpartisan local elections, in which party labels are not indicated on the ballot. Where other conditions are consistent with tight party organization, techniques of this sort seem not to have been especially effective; old-style parties are perfectly capable of controlling nominations in primaries, or of persisting in formally nonpartisan jurisdictions. But, together with the other party weakening factors, explicit anti-party legislation seems to have taken its toll.

Decline of voter interest in rewards available to the parties. Even today it is estimated that the mayor of Chicago has at his disposal 6,000 to 10,000 city patronage jobs. And there are many ways of circumventing good government, anti-party legislation. An additional element in the decline of old-style organization is the increasing disinterest of many citizens in the rewards at the disposal of party politicians. Once upon a time, for example, the decennial federal census was a boon to those local politicians whose party happened to be in control of the White House at census time. The temporary job of door-to-door federal census enumerator was quite a satisfactory reward for the party faithful. In 1960 in many localities, party politicians found census patronage more bother than boon; the wages for this task compared poorly with private wages, and few voters were willing to put in the time and leg work.

Other traditional patronage jobs—custodial work in city buildings, employment with departments of sanitation, street repair jobs—were becoming equally undesirable, due to rising levels of income, education, and job security.

An important watershed seems to have been the New Deal, which provided the impetus, at state and local levels as well as the federal level, for increased governmental preoccupation with citizen welfare. The welfare programs of party organizations were undercut by direct and indirect effects of social security, minimum wage legislation, relief programs, and collective bargaining. And, as often has been noted, the parties themselves, by contributing to the social rise of underprivileged groups, helped to develop the values and aspirations which were to make these citizens skeptical of the more blatant manifestations of machine politics.

VARIETIES OF CONTEMPORARY URBAN POLITICS

Nationally in 1956, the Survey Research Center found that only 10 per cent of a cross section of citizens reported being contacted personally by political party workers during that year's presidential campaign. Even if we consider only non-southern cities of over 100,000 population, the percentage is still a good bit less than 20.[2] This is a far cry from the situation which would obtain if party organizations were well developed and assiduous. But national statistics conceal a good bit of local variation. A survey of Detroit voters found that only 6 per cent of the public remembered having been approached by political party workers; in fact, less than a fifth of those interviewed even knew that there *were* party precinct officials in their district.[3] Reports from a number of other cities—for example, Seattle and Minneapolis—show a similar vacuum in party activity.[4]

In New Haven, Connecticut, in contrast, 60 per cent of the voters interviewed in a 1959 survey reported having been contacted by party workers.[5] The continuing importance of parties in the politics of this municipality has been documented at length by Robert A. Dahl and his associates.[6] New Haven's Mayor Richard C. Lee was able to obtain support for a massive urban redevelopment program, in spite of the many obstacles in the way of favorable action on such programs elsewhere, in large part because of the capacity of an old-style party organization to weld together the government of a city with an extremely "weak" formal charter. Lee commanded a substantial majority on the board of aldermen and, during the crucial period for ratification of the program, was as confident of the votes of Democratic aldermen as a British Prime Minister is of his parliamentary majority. Lee was far from being a mere creative creature of the party organization which was so helpful to him, but he also was effectively vetoed by the party when he attempted to bring about governmental reforms which would have made the mayor less dependent upon the organization to obtain positive action.[7]

Further evidence of the persistence of old-style party activities came from a number of other studies conducted in the late 1950's. For example, in 1957 party leaders from eight New Jersey counties reported performing a wide range of traditional party services, in response to an ingeniously worded questionnaire administered by Professor Richard T. Frost.[8]

SERVICES PERFORMED BY NEW JERSEY
POLITICIANS

The Service	Percentage Performing It "Often"
Helping deserving people get public jobs	72
Showing people how to get their social security benefits, welfare, unemployment compensation, etc.	54
Helping citizens who are in difficulty with the law. Do you help get them straightened out?	62

There was even some evidence in the 1950's of a rebirth of old-style urban party activities—for example, in the once Republican-dominated city of Philadelphia, where an effective Democratic old-style organization was put together. Often old-style organizations seem to exist in portions of contemporary cities, especially the low-income sections. These, like the reform groups to be described below, serve as factions in city-wide politics.[9]

Why old-style politics persists in some settings but not others is not fully clear. An impressionistic survey of the scattered evidence suggests, as might be expected, that the older pattern continues in those localities which most resemble the situa-

275

tions which originally spawned strong local parties in the nineteenth century. Eastern industrial cities, such as New Haven, Philadelphia, and many of the New Jersey cities, have sizable low-income groups in need of traditional party services. In many of these areas, the legal impediments to the party activity also are minimal: Connecticut, for example, was the last state in the union to adopt direct primary legislation, and nonpartisan local election systems are, in general, less common in industrial cities than in cities without much manufacturing activity.[10] Cities in which weak, disorganized parties are reported—like Seattle, Minneapolis, and even Detroit (which, of course, *is* a manufacturing center of some importance)—are quite often cities in which nonpartisan institutions have been adopted.

SOME NEW-STYLE URBAN POLITICAL PATTERNS

In conclusion, we may note two of the styles of politics which have been reported in contemporary localities where old-style organizations have become weak or nonexistent: the politics of nonpartisanship and the new "reform" factions within some urban Democratic parties. Both patterns are of considerable intrinsic interest to students of local government. And, as contrasting political forms, they provide us with further perspective on the strengths and weaknesses of old-style urban politics.

The politics of nonpartisanship. The nonpartisan ballot now is in force in 66 per cent of American cities over 25,000 in population. Numerous styles of politics seem to take place beneath the facade of nonpartisanship. In some communities, when party labels are eliminated from the ballot, the old parties continue to operate much as they have in the past; in other communities, new local parties spring up to contest the nonpartisan elections. Finally, nonpartisanship often takes the form intended by its founders: no organized groups contest elections; voters choose from a more or less self-selected array of candidates.

In the last of these cases, although nonpartisanship has its intended effect, it also seems to have had—a recent body of literature suggests[11]—a number of unintended side effects. One of these is voter confusion. Without the familiar device of party labels to aid in selecting candidates, voters may find it difficult to select from among the sometimes substantial list of names on the ballot. Under these circumstances, a bonus in votes often goes to candidates with a familiar sounding name—incumbents are likely to be re-elected, for example—or even candidates with a favorable position on the ballot. In addition, campaigning and other personal contacts with voters become less common, because candidates no longer have the financial resources and personnel of a party organization at their disposal and therefore are dependent upon personal financing or backing from interest groups in the community.

Nonpartisan electoral practices, where effective, also seem to increase the influence of the mass media on voters; in the absence of campaigning, party canvassing, and party labels, voters become highly dependent for information as well as advice on the press, radio, and television. Normally, mass communications have rather limited effects on people's behavior compared with face-to-face communication such as canvassing by party workers.[12] Under nonpartisan circumstances, however, he who controls the press is likely to have much more direct and substantial effect on the public.

Ironically, the "theory" of nonpartisanship argues that by eliminating parties a barrier between citizens and their officials will be removed. In fact, nonpartisanship often attentuates the citizen's connections with the political system.

The reform Democrats. The doctrine of nonpartisanship is mostly a product of the Progressive era. While nonpartisan local political systems continue to be adopted and, in fact, have become more ·common in recent decades, most of the impetus for this development results from the desire of communities to adopt city-manager systems. Nonpartisanship simply is part of the package which normally goes along with the popular city-manager system.

A newer phenomenon on the urban political scene is the development, especially since the 1952 presidential campaign, of ideologically motivated grass-roots party organizations within the Democratic party.[13] The ideology in question is liberalism: most of the reform organizations are led and staffed by college-educated intellectuals, many of whom were activated politically by the candidacy of Adlai Stevenson. In a few localities, there also have been grass-roots Republican organizations motivated by ideological considerations: in the Republican case, Goldwater conservatism.

New-style reformers differ in two major ways from old-style reformers: their ideological concerns extend beyond a preoccupation with governmental efficiency alone (they favor racial integration and improved housing and sometimes devote much of their energy to advocating "liberal" causes at the national level); secondly, their strategy is to work within and take control of the parties, rather than to reject the legitimacy of parties. They do resemble old-style reformers in their preoccupation with the evils of "bossism" and machine politics.

There also is an important resemblance between the new reform politician and the old-style organization man the reformer seeks to replace. In both cases, very much unlike the situation which seems to be stimulated by nonpartisanship, the politician emphasizes extensive face-to-face contact with voters. Where reformers have been successful, it often has been by beating the boss at his own game of canvassing the election district, registering and keeping track of voters, and getting them to the polls.[14]

But much of the day-to-day style of the traditional urban politician is clearly distasteful to the new reformers: they have generally eschewed the use of patronage and, with the exceptions of campaigns for housing code enforcement, they have avoided the extensive service operations to voters and interest groups which were central to old-style party organizations. For example, when election district captains and other officials of the Greenwich Village Independent Democrats, the reform group which deposed New York Democrat County Leader Carmine DeSapio in his own election district, were asked the same set of questions about their activities used in the New Jersey study, strikingly different responses were made.

SERVICES PERFORMED BY NEW YORK REFORM DEMOCRATS[15]

The Service	Percentage Performing It "Often
Helping deserving people get public jobs	0
Showing people how to get their social security benefits, welfare, unemployment compensation, etc.	5
Helping citizens who are in difficulty with the law. Do you help get them straightened out?	6

The successes of this class of new-style urban party politician have vindicated a portion of the classical strategy of urban party politics, the extensive reliance upon canvassing and other personal relations, and also have shown that under some circumstances it is possible to organize such activities with virtually no reliance on patronage and other material rewards. The reformers have tapped a pool of political activists used by parties elsewhere in the world—for example, in Great Britain—but not a normal part of the American scene. One might say that the reformers have "discovered" the British Labor constituency parties.

It is where material resources available to the parties are limited, for example, California, and where voter interest in these resources is low, that the new reformers are successful. In practice, however, the latter condition has confined the effectiveness of the reform Democrats largely to the more prosperous sections of cities; neither their style nor their programs seem to be successful in lower-class districts.[16] The areas of reform Democratic strength are generally *not* the areas which contribute greatly to Democratic pluralities in the cities. And, in many cities, the reformers' clientele is progressively diminishing as higher-income citizens move outward to the suburbs. Therefore, though fascinating and illuminating, the new reform movement must at least for the moment be considered as little more than a single manifestation in a panorama of urban political practices.[17]

CONCLUSION

The degree to which *old-style* urban party organizations will continue to be a part of this panorama is uncertain. Changes in the social composition of the cities promise to be a major factor in the future of urban politics. If, as seems possible, many cities become lower-class, nonwhite enclaves, we can be confident that there will be a continuing market for the services of the service-oriented old-style politician. Whether or not this is the case, many lessons can be culled from the history of party politics during the years of growth of the American cities—lessons which are relevant, for example, to studying the politics of urbanization elsewhere in the world.[18] In the nineteenth century, after all, the United States was an "emerging," "modernizing" nation, facing the problems of stability and democracy which are now being faced by countless newer nations.

NOTES

1. Frank J. Sorauf, "State Patronage in a Rural County," *American Political Science Review*, vol. 50 (December 1956), pp. 1046-56.
2. Angus Campbell, Philip E. Converse, Warren E. Miller, and Donald E. Stokes, *The American Voter* (New York, 1960), pp. 426-27. The statistic for nonsouthern cities was supplied to me by the authors.
3. Daniel Katz and Samuel J. Eldersveld, "The Impact of Local Party Activity on the Electorate," *Public Opinion Quarterly*, vol. 25 (Spring 1961), pp. 16-17.
4. Hugh A. Bone, *Grass Roots Party Leadership* (Seattle, 1952); Robert L. Morlan, "City Politics: Free Style," *National Municipal Review*, vol. 38 (November 1949), pp. 485-91.
5. Robert A. Dahl, *Who Governs?* (New Haven, 1961), p. 278.
6. *Ibid.*; Nelson W. Polsby, *Community Power and Political Theory* (New Haven, 1963); Raymond E. Wolfinger, *The Politics of Progress* (1974).
7. Raymond E. Wolfinger, "The Influence of Precinct Work on Voting Behavior," *Public Opinion Quarterly*, vol. 27 (Fall 1963), pp. 387-98.
8. Frost deliberately worded his questionnaire descriptions of these services favorably in order to avoid implying that respondents were to be censured for indulging in "machine tactics." Richard T. Frost, "Stability and Change in Local Politics," *Public Opinion Quarterly*, vol. 25 (Summer 1961), pp. 231-32.
9. James Q. Wilson, "Politics and Reform in American Cities," *American Government Annual 1962-63* (New York, 1962), pp. 37-52.
10. Phillips Cutright, "Nonpartisan Electoral Systems in American Cities," *Comparative Studies in Society and History*, vol. 5 (January 1963), pp. 219-21.
11. For a brief review of the relevant literature, see Fred I. Greenstein, *The American Party System and the American People* (Englewood Cliffs, N.J., 1963), pp. 57-60.
12. Joseph T. Klapper, *The Effects of Mass Communication* (New York, 1960).
13. James Q. Wilson, *The Amateur Democrat* (Chicago, 1962).
14. There is another interesting point of resemblance between old- and new-style urban party politics. In both, an important aspect of the motivation for participation seems to be the rewards of sociability. Tammany picnics and New York Committee for Democratic Voters (CDV) coffee hours probably differ more in decor than in the functions they serve. An amusing indication of this is provided by the committee structure of the Greenwich Village club of the CDV; in addition to the committees dealing with the club newsletter, with housing, and with community action, there is a social committee and a Flight Committee, the latter being concerned with arranging charter flights to Europe for club members. See Vernon M. Goetcheus, *The Village Independent Democrats: A Study in the Politics of the New Reformers* (unpublished senior distinction thesis, Honors College, Wesleyan University, 1963), pp. 65-66. On similar activities by the California Democratic Clubs, see Robert E. Lane, James D. Barber, and Fred I. Greenstein, *Introduction to Political Analysis* (Englewood Cliffs, N.J., 1962), pp. 55-57.
15. Goetcheus, *op. cit.*, p. 138.
16. DeSapio, for example, was generally able to hold on to his lower-class Italian voting support in Greenwich Village; his opponents succeeded largely by activating the many middle- and upper-class voters who had moved into new high-rent housing in the district.
17. Probably because of their emphasis on ideology, the new reform groups also seem to be quite prone to internal conflicts which impede their effectiveness. One is reminded of Robert Michels' remarks about the intransigence of intellectuals in European socialist parties. *Political Parties* (New York, 1962, originally published in 1915), Part 4, Chap. 6.
18. On the significance of the American experience with old-style urban politics for the emerging nations, see Wallace S. Sayre and Nelson W. Polsby, "American Political Science and the Study of Urbanization," Committee on Urbanization, Social Science Research Council, mimeo, 1963, pp. 45-48.

THE SILENT REVOLUTION
IN PATRONAGE

Frank J. Sorauf

With little fanfare and only quiet celebration the movement to install merit systems in place of the older patronage is well on its way to full victory. The federal government has almost completely been conquered by one form or another of merit appointment, while the traditional political machines, long the major consumers of patronage, are everywhere else in hurried retreat. And the scholars and administrators who for so long fought in the vanguard of the movement now savor a triumph in practical affairs of the sort rarely vouchsafed to intellectuals.

The case against patronage, based largely on the need for administrative expertise and professionalism, is overwhelming. But only rarely have the opponents of patronage stopped to worry about the effects on the parties and political system of abolishing it.[1] Some scholars of political parties have argued that patronage is important to the political process, but there has never been an attempt to compare the merit system's contribution to good administration with its supposed weakening of the party system in the total balance of effective government.

Such a comparison may not be necessary, however. Patronage is slowly dying out—more from its own political causes than from the campaigns of civil service reformers. However substantial the need of the parties for patronage fifty or even twenty years ago, the need is vastly less today. On the one hand, the organization, functions, and style of American politics, and the consequent need for patronage, have changed dramatically in the last generation; on the other hand, the nature and usefulness of patronage itself also have changed.[2]

Reprinted with permission from the Winter 1960 issue of *Public Administration Review*, a journal of the American Society for Public Administration, and with permission from the author.

USES OF PATRONAGE

Patronage is best thought of as an incentive system—a political currency with which to "purchase" political activity and political responses. The chief functions of patronage are:

Maintaining an active party organization. Experienced politicos maintain that the coin of patronage is necessary to reward the countless activities of an active party organization. The promise or actual holding of a political appointment, they report, is necessary to induce the canvassing of neighborhoods, mailing and telephoning, campaigning and electioneering, and other activities of the local party organization. Illustratively, many a city hall or county court house rests vacant on election day as its denizens go out to man the party organization.

Promoting intra-party cohesion. In the hands of a skillful party leader, patronage may be an instrument of party cohesion, edging defecting partisans back into the discipline of the party hierarchy and welding the differing blocks within the party into a unified whole. In one sense President Eisenhower's historic agreement with Senator Taft in Morningside Heights represents an attempt to enlist the support of the Taft Republicans in 1952 by promising them consideration in the party's appointments.

Attracting voters and supporters. The patronage appointment often may be used to convert the recipient (and a large portion of his family and friends) into life-long and devoted supporters of the appointing party. Gratitude for the job will win this support for the party, it is said, and a desire to retain the job by keeping the party in power will enforce

it. In some urban areas of Pennsylvania, experienced party men calculate that a well-placed appointment should net the party between six and eight voters. The same reasoning, of course, lies behind the appointment of representatives of special blocs of voters, such as ethnic, national, or religious groups.

Financing the party and its candidates. The cruder and more overt forms of this function of patronage have long been known to the fraternity as "macing" the payroll. In the heyday of patronage in American politics, something close to 5 per cent of the appointee's salary was thought a fair return to the party for its benefice. Patronage, always reward for past activity as well as inducement for the future, may also be used to reward a recent contribution to the party coffers.

Procuring favorable government action. Less commonly acknowledged, perhaps for its dubious ethics and legality, is the use of patronage to secure favorable policy or administrative action for the party or its followers. At the local government level it may involve the fixing of a traffic ticket, preference for certain applicants for public assistance, the calculated oversight in a public health inspection, or the use of public equipment to remove snow from private rights-of-way. By exploiting the appointee's dependence on the party, the organization reaps the political advantages of a preferred access to public policy-making.

Creating party discipline in policy-making. This last function of patronage redounds less to the advantage of political

Frank J. Sorauf

parties than to presidents and governors who use appointments to build support for their programs in legislatures. Franklin Roosevelt's wily use of the dwindling federal patronage, especially his delaying of appointments until after satisfactory congressional performance, scarcely needs more than mention. A number of governors still have at their disposal a vast array of political jobs to use in coordinating executive and legislative policy and in joining the separated powers of government.

But patronage may certainly be misused in ways that adversely affect the parties and political system. It may build up personal machines or followings that parallel and compete with the regular, formal party organization. Poorly administered, it may cause new resentments and hostilities, create more friction within the party than it eases. Also, patronage seldom can perform all of the six purposes at once since to use it for one purpose is to destroy its effectiveness for another. For example, appointments that solidify and activate local party organization may disturb centralized party unity at a higher level and impair party discipline within both party and legislature.[3]

Just how well patronage has performed the six functions for the parties over the years is a matter for considerable conjecture. Partisans usually claim patronage is the "life-blood" of American politics, and yet even among its most devoted and skillful users, many dissent and some are ambivalent. James Farley, for example, has boasted that he could build a major party without patronage,

and yet he dissented from the recommendation of the second Hoover Commission that rural postal carriers be taken from the patronage lists.[4] The scholarly studies of patronage and general political folklore indicate that it is fairly effective in maintaining an active organization and, to a lesser extent, in attracting voters and supporters, but that its value in performing the other functions is highly questionable. Political appointees do contribute money to the party treasuries but hardly enough to run a party today. As for the promotion of party cohesion, the intraparty bickering and bitterness occasioned by the division of the spoils is, to this observer, truly staggering.

DECLINE IN USEFULNESS

Regardless of the effectiveness of patronage in the past, it is today undergoing rapid changes, most obviously in its steady shrinkage. One observer has estimated that the federal patronage available to the Eisenhower Administration has ". . . not exceeded a fraction of one percent of the total federal establishment."[5] A precise estimate of the number of jobs still under patronage in city, county, and state administrations throughout the country would be impossible to come by, but all hands agree it is declining.

There do remain states where merit systems have made few inroads into patronage and where large numbers of positions (about 50,000 in Pennsylvania, for example) remain at least technically available for distribution by the victorious. But even in these instances the parties are using a steadily decreasing percentage of the jobs for political purposes because patronage as a political currency has been devalued. Merit systems make their greatest inroads into patronage in the well-paid, specialized positions where the call for expertness and training is greatest. The parties are left the less-desirable, poorly-paid positions generally. With continued economic prosperity and high levels of employment the economic rewards of these jobs, hardly princely in most cases, are less appealing than formerly. While low pay and chronic job insecurity plague the patronage job-holder, private employment has become progressively more attractive with rising wage levels, union protections and securities, unemployment compensation, pension plans, and fringe benefits. Viewed by most Americans as a short-term, desperation job alternative, the patronage position has lost considerable value as a political incentive.

Patronage also is losing its respectability. Its ethic—the naked political *quid pro quo*—no longer seems to many a natural and reasonable ingredient of politics. Parties often find that the attempt to clean political house after an election produces public outrage and indignation. The mores of the middle-class and the image of civic virtue instilled by public education extol the unfettered, independent voter rather than the patronage-seeking party-liner. The public-spirited citizen rather than the self-interested party worker is celebrated. And the public no longer tolerates the presence of political mediocrities in public service in the name of party loyalty.

Even the job-seekers themselves no longer accept the political obligations of their appointments as readily as once they did. Briefly, patronage has fallen into public disfavor for appearing to approach an outright political payoff, with the result that its usefulness to the parties has diminished.

CHANGES IN PARTIES AND POLITICS

The partial passing of the boss and the political machine has been perhaps the most obvious new development in party behavior. Depending heavily on the motive power of patronage, these machines long dominated big city politics and some county and state strongholds as well. They flourished especially in those urban centers inhabited by large groups of immigrants and minorities—groups not yet integrated into American life, often poor and insecure and bewildered by the traditions of American politics. The machine spoke to them in the simple terms of a job, of sympathy in city hall, and of food and fuel to soften the hardest times.

This is not to suggest that political machines have vanished or even that they will vanish within the next generation. But the machine, and the politics of the underprivileged on which it rests, is surely on the decline. Government and other private agencies have taken over the social welfare functions these organizations once provided. Furthermore, first and second generation groups, traditional recipients of the attentions of the machine, are disappearing, and their children and grandchildren now luxuriate in the

283

Frank J. Sorauf

prosperity and conformity of the suburbs, though in many cities their place will be taken for a time by immigrants from rural areas of the United States. In sum, rising levels of prosperity, higher educational levels, declining numbers of unassimilated groups, and greater concern by government for the unfortunate all point to a decline of the boss and machine and of the patronage they relied on.

Furthermore, party conflict since the 1930's has reflected social and economic appeals to a greater extent than in the preceding decades. Even though they do not yet approach the ideological fervor of European campaigns, American politics has become more involved with issues and less with the issueless politics of patronage, favor, and preferment. Campaigning, too, has shifted from the door-to-door canvass, local rallies, and controlled blocs of votes to the mass media and advertising agencies. Great, attractive candidates serve as the focus of these national campaigns. As a result the importance of the national party organization is increased—the center of party power shifting away from the local units just as clearly as the center of governmental power is shifting from the states and localities to the national government.

The new party worker. What is emerging, then, is a system of political organization more compatible with the middle-class values of suburbia than those of the ethnic or racial neighborhood of the urban center. Rather than relying on the organized party hierarchy, it depends more and more on the volunteer and *ad hoc* political groups and personal follow-

ings. In some states, such as California and Wisconsin, party leaders are converting this fleeting volunteer activity into more permanent clubs and party organization,[6] but the manpower of these changing parties contrasts sharply with the ward or precinct committeeman of the older machines. The new political men are far more likely than their predecessors to be motivated by belief, by loyalty to an attractive candidate (e.g., the Citizens for Eisenhower movement), by a sense of civic duty, or by a more generalized social and sporting enthusiasm. They view their political activity more as avocation than vocation.

The parties also have found fresh resources in the organized power of the interest group. It recruits voters for the favored party or candidate and provides campaign and financial assistance as well. Many a candidate today prizes the contacts and communication channels of the local labor union or chamber of commerce more highly than he does the face-to-face campaign. Voters in many corners of the country can testify that candidates rarely knock on their doors any more. Business and labor are major sources of party funds; the contributions of payrollers no longer suffice. Even the "new style" political leader, in contrast with the classic model of the boss, usually has closer ties to interest groups in the community. He may even have been recruited from one.

For these educated, secure, and even prestiged workers and leaders of the new parties, a political appointment holds little fascination. One sophisticated and experienced politician has written that

284

"Men and women are drawn into politics by a combination of motives; these include power, glory, zeal for contention or success, duty, hate, oblivion, hero worship, curiosity, and enjoyment of the work."[7] Today's political worker may more and more find his reward in the satisfaction of a deeply-rooted psychological need, the identification with a purposeful organization or a magnetic leader, the ability to serve an economic or professional interest, the release from the tedium of daily routine, or the triumph of an ideal. His "pay-off," instead of a political job, may be endorsement for elective office, membership on a civic commission, access to new and influential elites, or a reception in the White House gardens.

The new personnel needs of the party. These shifts in organization, functions, and personnel of the parties have meant that the patronage that does remain is not the patronage that the parties might easily use. The parties cry for trained, educated, experienced men of ability and affairs, albeit fewer men than formerly. The vast majority of patronage positions are poorly paid and generally unappealing to the men and women of skills and achievement the parties would like to enlist. Very likely the man placed on a trash collection crew will lack the social and political experience to be useful in today's politics, and his meager pay offers the party scant opportunity for fundraising. The middle-level job, potentially the most useful to the party in rewarding its more capable partisans, is rarely available for political appointment. These are the specialized, expert positions that are generally the first to be put under a merit system. When they do remain under patronage, their specialized qualifications are the hardest to fill from the rank and file of political job-seekers.

At the top, the party often has highly-placed positions available, at least in small number, to reward its leadership corps. Here, however, the party often fails to persuade its most capable men to give up, even temporarily, their positions in business and the professions for a political appointment. In turn, the party workers who would find the patronage position an attractive alternative to their private employment, lack the executive and administrative experience for the positions. Paul David and Ross Pollock write of these problems in the national government:

For positions at the higher levels, the party organization has only rarely been successful in convincing the administration that its nominees were sufficiently qualified. The administration, on its part, has had to go out and hunt, cajole, and persuade in order to recruit the kind of talent it wanted.... The supply of persons with the requisite competence and availability is simply not large enough in either political party, and there is little evidence to suggest that the supply is on the increase.[8]

As its usefulness to them declines, patronage imposes hard and worrisome choices on the party hierarchies. Often the parties' appointments to the plentitude of unattractive patronage jobs go to men and women with no particular record of service to the party and little promise for future serivce, or whose appointment will do little to integrate the party organization or build party cohesion. Their chief recommendation is their need for a job, and the party, functioning as employment bureau, hopes only for a little gratitude and possible support at the polls. The better paid, more enticing jobs are losing their incentive power for those partisans qualified to hold them, and the party finds itself haunted by the aggressive availability of unqualified jobhunters.

One is forced to conclude that the classic dependence of party on patronage is being undermined on both sides. Forced by the changing nature of American society and by new political problems and values, the parties are shifting to a new mode of operation that relies less than formerly on the incentives of patronage. Patronage, on the other hand, is declining in both quantity and quality, both in the number of jobs available and in their value to the party.

SHORT-TERM ADJUSTMENTS

Since party changes were not simply adjustments to the gradual demise of patronage, a further reduction in the supply of patronage in those states where the supply remains large will hardly alter the long-run development of the party system. It may, however, accelerate change in party operations or produce short-term side effects.

In the first place, patronage has persisted chiefly at the local levels and remains the bulwark of local party organization, a faintly anachronistic bulwark, one might add, in an era of centralized party and government. It is in these state and local party organs, despite their declining vigor and importance, that one finds the most vocal proponents of patronage—even of the remaining federal patronage, much of which is channeled through them. This concentration of patronage in the localities fortifies the local party and permits it to resist discipline or centralization by organs higher in the party structure.[9] Thus fortified, these decentralized pockets of political power also fight party cohesion and responsibility in legislatures and, paradoxically, often nullify the value of executive patronage in achieving legislative discipline.

Inevitably, these local units, as they lose their vitality and their part in major policy-making, become primarily dealers in patronage, converting it from a political tool to a political goal. When patronage declines there, a major resistance to party centralization and to issue-centered campaigns and candidates will die with it.

Secondly, restrictions on patronage weaken the Democratic party more than the Republicans. Patronage appeals more predictably to lower economic strata, to unskilled and semi-skilled workers, to urban dwellers, and to minority groups—all of the demographic groups which, studies show, support the Democratic party. Patronage as an incentive system comports with the economic needs, the understanding of the relationship between citizen and government, and the somewhat exploitative view of politics more common among lower social and economic groups than among the American middle class. Furthermore, the Democratic party also has greater problems in finding substitutes for it. The personal and financial support of the business community are not often at its disposal. The formation of a genteel party, dedicated to a philosophy of government and absed on sociability and civic virtue, falls more easily to the Republicans.

Thirdly, since the appeals of patronage are largely economic, its political value and usefulness are apt to be greatest in the remaining pockets of unemployment and economic hardship, for it is there that private employment fails to provide opportunities superior to patronage positions. In these areas, and in the country as a whole if widespread unemployment returns, patronage might enjoy a brief renaissance as a political incentive.

Finally, patronage has been involved in legislative-executive rivalry. Presidents of the United States, harassed by congressional attempts to control patronage through clearance systems and "senatorial courtesy," have been more willing to surrender it than has the Congress. State governors, however, are not so willing to abandon one of the few weapons they have over unruly legislatures.[10] Since the loss of patronage will certainly affect legislative-executive relations in the states more sharply than in the national government, one is justified in supposing that its further loss will make the task of gubernatorial leadership just that much more difficult.

IN CONCLUSION

To expect anything but a further contraction of patronage would be naïve. 1. Patronage does not meet the needs of present-day party operations. Activities requiring a large number of party workers—canvassing, mass mailings, rallies—are being replaced by radio and television. Political costs are so high that assessments on public salaries are minuscule beside the party's cost. 2. Patronage no longer is the potent inducement to party activity it once was. Public attitudes are increasingly hostile to patronage and the political style it represents. Employment in the private economy also provides an increasingly attractive alternative to patronage positions. 3. As a result, the incentives once provided by patronage are being replaced in the political system. The persons who can contribute most to campaigns, in skill and funds, seek different payoffs—prestige, power, or personal satisfaction rather than jobs.

Even though the further decline of patronage will certainly not destroy or seriously hamper the parties, it will produce political shocks and pockets of discomfort. It will probably hurt Democrats more than Republicans, will be slower and more crucial in economically distressed areas, and will weaken the influence of governors on legislative action more than the President's influence on Congress.

American political parties have, after all, been getting along without patronage to various extents for some time now, and they have survived. Even many large metropolitan cities, whose patronage needs the scholars emphasize, have managed without it. The political party has its causes and justification deep in the American political process and not in the dispensation of political privileges. Patronage is necessary to a certain type of party operation, but others can be maintained

287

without it. The old machines and local party organizations relied on patronage, but they were rooted in social and economic conditions that are disappearing. As they disappear, so will the parties and patronage they fostered.

Ultimately, the decline of patronage will, among a number of causes, speed the parties to further centralization, to the heightening of their ideological content, to a greater reliance on group participation in politics, to greater nationalization of the candidate image and party campaigning, and to the establishment of some modicum of party discipline.

There is something almost quaint in these days of big parties, big government, and advertising agency politics about a political institution that conjures up images of Boss Tweed, torchlight parades, and ward heelers. As the great day of patronage recedes into history, one is tempted to say that the advancing merit systems will not kill patronage before it withers and dies of its own infirmity and old age.

NOTES

1. One would, however, have to mention three specialists in public administration who have recognized and addressed themselves to the conflicting needs of party and administration. See especially Harvey C. Mansfield's paper on "Political Parties, Patronage, and the Federal Government Service," in the American Assembly volume, *The Federal Government Service: Its Character, Prestige, and Problems* (Columbia University, 1951), pp. 81-112. Also relevant are Richard E. Neustadt's review, "On Patronage, Power, and Politics," 15 *Public Administration Review* 108-114 (Spring, 1955), and James R. Watson, "Is Patronage Obsolete?"

18 *Personnel Administration* 3-9 (July, 1955).
2. Very few studies exist of the actual operation of patronage systems across the country. Among the few are: David H. Kurtzman, *Methods of Controlling Votes in Philadelphia* (published by author, 1935); Frank J. Sorauf, "State Patronage in a Rural County," 50 *American Political Science Review* 1046-1056 (December, 1956); and H. O. Waldby, *The Patronage System in Oklahoma* (The Transcript Co., 1950). In the absence of specific reports and data, one can only proceed uneasily on a mixture of political folklore, scattered scholarship, professional consensus, and personal judgment.
3. I have questioned the political usefulness of patronage at greater length in "Patronage and Party," 3 *Midwest Journal of Political Science* 114-126 (May, 1959).
4. The claim is in James A. Farley, *Behind the Ballots* (Harcourt, Brace, and Co., 1938), p. 237, and the dissent in the Commission on Organization of the Executive Branch of the Government, *Report on Personnel and Civil Service* (U.S. Government Printing Office, 1955), p. 91.
5. Mansfield, *op. cit.*, note 1 above, p. 94.
6. The literature on the California political clubs is rather extensive, especially in the non-academic journals, but the only general work on the volunteer movement in politics of which I am aware is Stephen A. Mitchell's *Elm Street Politics* (Oceana Publications, 1959).
7. Stimson Bullitt, *To Be a Politician* (Doubleday and Co., 1959), p. 42. The reader will, in fact, find all of chapter two a stimulating review of the incentives and motives of politics.
8. Paul T. David and Ross Pollock, *Executives for Government* (The Brookings Institution, 1957), pp. 25, 27.
9. The classic expression of this view is E. E. Schattschneider, *Party Government* (Rinehart and Co., 1942).
10. See Duane Lockard, *New England State Politics* (Princeton University Press, 1959) for reports of the value of patronage to governors in New England. For instance, he describes patronage as "perhaps the most important of these gubernatorial weapons" in Massachusetts (p. 160).

THE NEW-STYLE BOSS

Blanche Blank

A decade and a half have passed since Fiorello LaGuardia confidently asserted: "Within the next 10 years the political boss will be but a sad memory." As recently as [January 1961], Leo Egan of *The New York Times* wrote an article entitled: "The Political Boss, Going, Going —." It concerned "the changes that are making the boss, old-style or new, a thing of the past." But New York City is voting in a mayoralty primary this week and "bossism" is still the cry—at least of the Republicans and the "reform" groups behind Mayor Wagner. The fight has been billed as a final push against an already anachronistic enemy—Boss De Sapio.

I wonder. Destroying a candidate or a man-behind-the-candidate is not the same as the demise of an institution. But I would go further than this: Bossism may actually be nourished by urbanization,

governmental complexity, legal vacuums, political alienation, and the ubiquitous human drive for power.

Consider the *illusory* changes that so many feel have led to the end of the boss-machine era:

The development of the social welfare state. There is a popular idea that old-age assistance, unemployment insurance, welfare payments, hospital clinics, veterans' benefits, and other social services have taken the candy away from the tempter. Gone the day of the Christmas turkey! This is true, but enter the day of the fine print, the triplicate form, the long queue, the red tape and the surly official. The distribution of food and money is replaced by the distribution of advice and service. With more and more prizes in the hands of more and more self-contained bureaucracies, the need for an informed broker (the boss) increases. Take as an example a veteran who buys a home in New York State. He is entitled to reduce his assessed valuation for tax purposes by the amount of "eligible" funds used for his purchase. But to reap this yearly windfall he must know of it and have the literacy and determination to follow through. This entails filing forms and proofs of his bonus, mustering-out pay, insurance dividends and liability compensation. The directions are difficult even for a PhD. But an experienced boss who can take the citizen by the hand and guide him to something of value has something more than turkeys to offer.

In providing welfare services, the government (though destroying a few profitable practices for old-timers of *The Last Hurrah* vintage) introduces a whole new frontier for new-style bosses. In New York City there are more than 100 business licenses and countless performance standards required for landlords and tenants set up by housing, health and sanitary codes. A boss who has mastered the garbage removal, painting and fire requirements can attempt to influence the degree of enforcement in favor of his constituents. He can also harass his enemies. He can put his encyclopedia of who gets what, when and how at the disposal of the right people at the right time.

Reforms in election procedures. Every reform of the nomination and election process brings with it the promise of "death to the machine!" Yet each new elaboration simply demonstrates the machine's capacity for survival. The direct primary is the latest apotheosis of reform. It is supplanting the caucus and convention systems in an effort to wipe out bossism. But closer observation reveals that the boss still operates—by desig-

nating the very names that appear on the primary ballot. Jasper McLevy, the late Mayor of Bridgeport who claimed to have spent a lifetime fighting political machines, warned Connecticut in 1955 that its then newly-proposed primary law might actually increase the power of the bosses. It is too soon to evaluate his prediction; but in Hartford where nonpartisan primaries had been previously introduced in an effort to thwart machine politics, the Democrats simply adopted the frustrating practice of endorsing the top six vote-getters of the party as their candidates.

Massachusetts recently reverted to a "pre-primary convention." In 1959, California repealed its "cross-filing" primary after quite general public concession that its chief result was to obscure issues. (It had been introduced in 1913 by Governor Hiram Johnson's Progressive Republicans in a crusade to defeat entrenched political machines.)

The most recent and ironic example of reform backfiring occurred when Boss De Sapio won the 1959 *direct primary* contest for the district leadership. Post-election analysis indicates that he most probably would have lost had the old system of *indirect* elections been used. But just a few years before, political reformers had wrung from the boss himself a supposed new weapon in the arsenal of insurgency—direct primary elections of District Leaders in Manhattan.

The 50 or so election reforms instituted in Chicago over the last decade have certainly failed to oust its machine. And New York's excessive legalism concerning designating petitions (originally designed to prevent wholesale forgeries by the machine) has now become the bulwark of the machine. A dozen or more recent insurgent battles have been made difficult or impossible by requirements such as: petitions must appear on sheets of the prescribed shade of green; only black ink (no ballpoints); no abbreviations in date or address; no use of titles such as Mr. or Dr.; married women must use given first names; signatures must be identical with those on enrollment lists.

It has also been thought that the rapid extension of the merit system would wreck the bosses' ability to pay off in jobs. But while there may be a dent in the old patronage pot, it still carries more than enough meat and gravy to go around. To begin with, less than half of our states or smaller municipalities have anything that could reasonably be described as substantial merit coverage. In cities over 100,000 where the most dramatic merit reforms have occurred there are still significant gaps. In New York City alone the bench provides more than 300 seats in which political appetite, directly or indirectly, is satisfied. These judges in turn control close to 500 posts with salaries from $4,000 to $15,000 per year. Over one-third of Mayor Wagner's cabinet appointees have been active supporters.

Furthermore, exam publicity, eligibility requirements, grades, classification schedules, rating systems, salary and retirement rules, and the "rule of three" selection process are all useful to the boss. The personnel procedures that merit systems administer can all be manipulated. My point is that in each process—classifying a set of positions into a certain grade level, or even classifying them as competitive—there are individuals who will benefit or lose by the decision made. And the decision is made by a commission that is, after all, politically appointed (even if bipartisan). Furthermore, even when the decision is made by an administrative official who is himself a merit appointee, it is naïve to assume that he cannot be reached by the possibility of political influence. A salary raise, as well as retirement benefits, and classification acts are all *legislated* by groups who have political commitments.

The reduction of immigration. Immigration has been greatly curtailed, but the language and institutional ignorance that fed the immigrant into the machine has not been vastly reduced. In Manhattan alone, where Tammany is supposedly destined for oblivion, the population is about 17 percent Puerto Rican. Here is a *citizen* group with an alien language and culture—as much a prey to bossism as any old-time immigrant cluster. Any minority group that is socially or educationally underprivileged is likely to make up a hard core of machine support in certain politically important quarters. In ward 2 of Chicago's Negro-populated south side, boss William L. Dawson has lost little of his hold.

With the end of Prohibition it was thought that the era of free-wheeling gangsterism—with political machine connections—had died. Did it? In 1951, Sen. Estes Kefauver wrote: "A nationwide crime syndicate does exist in the US despite the protestations of a strangely

291

assorted company of criminals, self-serving politicians ... and others ... that there is no such combine." In 1960, we had further evidence of this at the Appalachian gangster conclave. Testimony taken over the years by the Senate Crime Investigating Committee is replete with reference to existing connections between political bosses and the underworld. In 1954, Albert Patterson, a candidate for State Attorney-General was shot to death in Phoenix City, Alabama, for promising to clean up politico-gangster corruption. While few political bosses today are out and out gangsters in the style of Kansas City's late Binaggio, many of them keep their lines of communication open.

Narcotics, gambling, non-taxed liquor and protection rackets have supplanted the old-time bootlegging.

Law and tradition dictate that much of the highly-skilled political work performed by the machine be *unpaid*. Even the most ardent reformer soon learns the need for patronage of one kind or another. Thus the spoils system. Witness the recent judicious distribution of federal plumss for deserving "insurgents" in New York. Yesterday's reformer becomes today's regular. The "reform" title hangs precariously indeed over some of Manhattan's current insurgent groups.

Finally, most people merely wish to be left alone. They can be counted on to rise only sporadically. This will undoubtedly be heightened by the trend toward urbanization, suburbanization, mechanization and bureaucratization. More and more of the public masks its frustration by withdrawing to manageable private concerns. The many thus continue to be ruled by the few. This is proving true in high literacy, high income suburbs like Westchester, where Republican boss Michalean reigns undisturbed; as well as in low income, low literacy areas such as Adam Clayton Powell's Harlem. On the one end the political ineffectiveness of the mass electorate may stem from social and geographic mobility; and on the other end from poverty and ignorance. In either situation, the boss does not generally have to persuade large numbers of fickle people. He needs only to manipulate his reliable regulars.

In short, the boss will continue to thrive as a power broker among the multitude of interest groups. The complexity of social benefit formulas, increasing urbanization, growing political alienation and an abiding human need for power and reward—these will prove the perennial allies of the "new bosses."

DALEY
OF CHICAGO

David Halberstam

In the political year 1968, Richard J. Daley surveyed the city of Chicago and was master of it. He exercised power as probably no man outside of Washington exercised it, and he was by most norms of the American ethic, particularly his own, a towering success. The poor of his city were afraid of him and the powerful of the nation deferred to him.

It was his city to an extraordinary degree, and now his party was coming to his city to choose a President. The more contested the nomination would be, the more the poor blacks and the long-haired white kids worked in the primaries to offset the Democratic party establishment, why, yes, the more powerful Richard J. Daley would be in August; and he was aware of this, aware that in his own way he could dominate the convention, and though there might be other men more popular, more handsome, more

beloved, the final decisions would be made by Mayor Daley. (Early in the year, when Robert Kennedy made his entrance into the race and a reporter asked a Daley man which hotel in Chicago Kennedy would be taking over, the Daley man answered, with the sense of certainty that only the very powerful have, "Bobby Kennedy isn't taking over anything in *this* city.") He would walk into the convention erect and powerful (particularly if his city were not in flames), and his words would be sought by the nation's foremost reporters, though surely they would be platitudinous, for he specialized in platitudes. He had learned long ago that if possible you spoke platitudes or you spoke not at all.

Everywhere there would be reminders to the guests that they were in Dick Daley's Chicago. In a profession where municipal officials keeled over like flies after one or two terms, especially if they were effective, thrown out by angry undertaxed constituents who felt themselves overtaxed, who hated the parking

From *Harper's Magazine* (August 1968), pp. 25-35. Reprinted with permission of the author.

293

and the air and their neighbors, Richard J. Daley reigned supreme, King Richard as he was called in Chicago.

Four times[1] he was elected, the fourth by his largest majority, 74 per cent. His years of success had virtually left Chicago without an electoral process, *that* was his achievement; in a city where few new buildings had been started before him, the sky was pierced again and again by new skyscrapers, each bigger and more gleaming than the last, and ever-grateful rich and aristocratic businessmen taught from the cradle to shun the Democratic party—that party of the machine and the Irish—competed to enlist in Republicans for Daley, vowed to give bigger contributions, while the most famous political scientists of Chicago, hawks and doves, liberals and conservatives, joined Professors for Daley. Municipal experts, technocrats with their measuring sticks, were in general agreement that Daley was the most successful Mayor in America—good cost accounting, good police department, good fire department, good social-economic programs. He was a politician with a smooth-functioning political machine in an age when machines were not supposed to function. (When one reporter for a local paper saw him at a meeting, a man who knew a machine when he saw one, Daley would say simply, "Organization, not machine. Get that. Organization, not machine.")

His city vibrated with those traditional American ingredients, vitality, energy, ambition, business drive, and racial failure, and it was because of these that

1. Six times, as of 1975. (*Ed.*)

Daley's role in history seemed curiously in doubt, for all his great achievements. In America now, when everything else failed, when the family failed and the churches failed and the system failed, the good Mayor would get the blame, not the Mayors of Natchez, Mississippi, or Clarksdale, Mississippi, or of thousands of other towns which had exported so many illiterate young Negroes North in the last fifteen years: the blame would be on the Mayor of the city which received them and which, as they had been failed once before, failed them again.

For Richard Daley presided over a city which had burned once and had a special tinderbox quality. It contained angry backlashing whites, some of the greatest backlashers in America who had finally managed to buy little homes in Chicago and paid their taxes there; and angry, frustrated, forelashing blacks. It was a city which contained one great Negro ghetto and another area which was not even a ghetto; it was a jungle, the kids alley-tough, totally outside the system, larger kids shaking down the smaller ones, youth gangs with organizational charts like the Army. Other cities were this bad, and some were worse, and in many of the older ways Richard J. Daley had done more for the Negro, to use that term, than many other Mayors. But there was also a suspicion that part of the problem was Daley, that his machine had been too smart for itself, and that finally Daley was perhaps not equipped to understand the complexity and the intense pressures of new times. Even his staff image seemed wrong, a point about which his staff was particularly sensitive. One of Daley's press people could point to a photograph of John Lindsay on the cover of *Life* and gloat over the headline, "Small acts and big plans," saying, "We could kill Lindsay with that. We could run against him and destroy him. Lindsay? What's he ever done? What programs has he got? Lindsay's people come out here for lessons in government."

It was not just Daley, it was America, with all the chickens, one hundred years or more in flight, coming home to roost. "Daley may well personify the Achilles' heel of America," one Negro critic said. "He's taken many positions not because he's outside the mainstream of America, but precisely because he's in it, which doesn't say a hell of a lot for either Daley or America."

For in a sense Chicago seemed to be the real capital of America, a strong, tough, vital city where the American business ethic worked, a city largely without reform influence ("We think of reform as being an effete Easterner idea," said one transplanted New Yorker). Nelson Algren, Chicago's uncrowned poet laureate, could write in his "Ode to Lower Finksville":

City of the big gray-flanneled shoulders
Fierce as a dog with tongue lapping for action
How come you spend all that great ferocity
On the windpipes of The Down, The Out and The Defenseless
And keep all that great lapping for over-fed real-estate hogs?

So Daley and Chicago seemed to symbolize America; he was ours, for better and for worse, in sickness and in health.

OTHER CHOICES, OTHER TIMES

Richard J. Daley is the product of the politics of another time. "I think one of the real problems he has with Negroes is understanding that the Irish are no longer the out-ethnic group," one Negro says. He would be doomed in the cosmetology of today's politics: those jowls, that heavyset look. He doesn't look like a modern municipal leader, a cost-accounting specialist; he looks, yes, exactly like a big city boss, right out of the smoke-filled room. "Daley will never really get a fair judging on his abilities as a mayor because of the way he looks," an admiring Chicago political scientist says. "He's much better than people think."

When he was first elected he spoke badly—"dese" and "dems"—but he has worked hard and now has very considerable control over most of his political appearances; there has also been a sharp decline in his malapropisms, though some Chicago reporters still collect them. Two of the best are *we will reach greater and greater platitudes of achievement,* and *they have vilified me, they have crucified me, yes they have even criticized me.* He is not good on the tube, but it is a mistake to underestimate his power and charm in person. "He exudes" one fellow Irishman says, "the confidence and power of a man who has achieved everything he set out to do and then a little more, but he also has the black moods of an Irishman and if you catch him in one of those it can be pretty frightening."

He dominates Chicago and he knows it, and this adds to his confidence. "People are always coming to me and telling me that they're going down to see the Mayor and tell him off," one Negro remarks, "and off they go, and of course he charms them completely and they come back and I ask, 'Well, brother, how did it go?' and they tell me, 'Why the Mayor's a fine man and we *know*'—get that, we know—'he's going to do the right thing.' " But clever, resounding speech is not his forte, and he has learned that the less you say now, the less you have to regret later, and indeed the problem may go away by then. He has made a political virtue out of being inarticulate. He has been satisfied with being Mayor, has consolidated his base there, has never let his ambition run away with him; this is part of the explanation for his power. He has sat there with a power base, slowly adding to it, incorporating new men as they rose, always looking for winners. Above all else Richard Daley loves power and winners. An aide of John Kennedy's remembers arriving in Chicago in 1960 for the first television debate, and Kennedy asking again and again, "Where's Daley, where's Daley," with no Daley to be found. "But after the debate," the aide recalls, "the first person to break through into the studio, with his flunkies around him like a flying wedge, was Daley. He knew he had a winner."

He was a poor Irish boy, born in a time when the Irish felt themselves despised in Protestant America. One reason, according to friends, that he was so close to Joseph Kennedy was that they both shared the same boyhood scars. Daley's father was a sheet-metal worker and an early union activist, blacklisted at several plants. There were few avenues open to an ambitious young Irish boy in those days and one of them was politics; though he is widely admired by all of Chicago's business giants today for his financial acumen, it is a fact of life, of which both are sharply aware, that he could not have made it in their world at that time.

More than most great men of power in America he is what he was. He lives in the same neighborhood where he was born, in the same house in which he has lived all his married life. He attends early Mass every day and observes the same basic tenets of the Catholic faith that he has based his life upon. His friends are the same small cluster of men, very much like himself, whom he has always known. His success has thrown him into the orbit of newer and more important men, but he has never crossed the line between association and friendship. His personal views remain rigid and he expects others to have the same; one reporter remembers a Daley son coming back from college recently with an unduly long haircut; Daley simply nodded at Matt Danaher, one of his deputies, and the boy was taken out for a trimming.

He is now the acknowledged master of the Democratic party machinery which gave him his start. The machine ethic was based upon hard work and loyalty; you worked your way up level by level. But loyalty rather than brilliance or social conscience or originality was the determining characteristic. It was and is a profession which abounded in limited men and hacks, of small men trying to throw around the power of bigger men, which often they only sniff at. Daley, apprenticing in a world of hacks, was and is no hack. He is an intelligent, strong-willed man, enormously hard-working. He set out within the party organization and mastered it, working his way up from precinct captain to committeeman to state legislator, a good one, easily distinguished from most of the men in Springfield, in his room every night studying the legislation. He was a young man who played by the rules of the game. He never frightened anyone, never looked too ambitious, accumulating political due bills all the time. He also mastered the art of finance as few active politicians in America have, eventually becoming director of revenue for Governor Adlai Stevenson.

In the view of several professional politicians, Daley helped protect Stevenson from less scrupulous politicians. He after all knew how and where the crooks might steal; it was the beginning of a relationship which would prove mutually beneficial to both until 1960 when Daley, given Stevenson's silence and Joe Kennedy's pressure, went for John Kennedy. As part of his loyalty ethic, however, Daley aided Stevenson's son, Adlai III, [now Illinois State Treasurer] in his start in politics, trying to give him good advice, suggesting that he play down his criticism of Vietnam. The other regular pols were bitterly opposed to young Stevenson. They considered him arrogant, uppity, and a man who had not done his apprenticeship. They were prepared to let him go on the slate this year for U.S. Senator, thus getting him out of Illinois; the machine has always preferred sending its reformers to Washington rather than

Springfield. Stevenson, an attractive and intelligent politician and a somewhat rumpled version of his father, instead went before the slate-makers and told everyone in a rather long speech—normally, one goes in, hat in hand for thirty seconds—that he was the best and strongest candidate for Governor. The regulars were appalled and threw him out.

Daley told him that he could still get on the slate for the Senate if he would plead loyalty on Vietnam. Back in he went, up came the question of Vietnam, out came Stevenson's doubts and his talk about conscience, and off the ticket he came. "Jesus, that guy is even worse than his father," one professional pol said. The result is that the Democrats are fielding a very weak ticket this year, with neither Stevenson nor Sargent Shriver on it. It was a case of divided loyalty for Daley, but apparently it would have required more of a fight than he was prepared to make. Not getting into futile fights may explain how he manages to conserve power.

CHICAGO'S BRAND OF TOUGHNESS

Chicago is rougher than other cities. Even today its more sophisticated citizens take a quiet pleasure in talking about not only its past sins but its present vices and the current power of the crime Syndicate. The city's rough edge is often a little hard for Easterners to understand. A few years ago a Negro alderman named Ben Lewis was shot down in cold blood. A correspondent for an Eastern magazine was immediately cabled by his New York office for a piece which would include, among other things, the outraged reaction of the good people of Chicago. There was no outrage at all, he cabled back. "The feeling is that if he's an alderman, he's a crook, and if he's a crook then that's their business."

The kind of money which focuses on reform politics in New York simply does not exist in Chicago and the machine has traditionally understood the reformers better than the reformers have understood the machine. Reformers have one district locally from which their candidates harass the machine (this year one of the ablest reformers, Abner Mikva, is running for Congress with the support of the machine, a truce not uncommon in Chicago politics), and indeed are occasionally placed on the ticket statewide to broaden its base and serve as a safety valve to keep reformers from going after the machine, though, as far as the machine is concerned, a U.S. Senate seat, and the Governorship are minor offices. The races for state's attorney and state assessor (who can investigate and harass the machine) are much more important.

Thus in 1948, the year that Stevenson was running for Governor and Paul Douglas for the Senate, a golden year, a liberal happened to run into Colonel Jacob Arvey, then boss of the machine. "How's the election going?" the reformer asked. "Fine fine, couldn't be better," Arvey answered. "The polls show Boyle [state's attorney] went way ahead."

The Chicago machine had prospered under the New Deal, prospered to the point of venality, until it made Chicago probably the most corrupt city in the country. Everything could be bought or sold. The police force was largely concerned with street-corner traffic courts and the downtown center of the city was dying fast. So a reform movement was started behind Martin Kennelly, a clean and handsome businessman. He ran in 1951 as a reform candidate and won. The reformers were delighted; so were the Syndicate and the machine. It became easier to steal than before; underneath the surface honesty almost everything went wrong. Kennelly was totally naïve about a very tough city. To this day, a lot of Daley critics, knowing his faults and failings, think of John Lindsay and see Martin Kennelly.

The local Chicago establishment was so disturbed about the Kennelly years that an informal meeting was held to decide what to do about the Mayor. The first thing, they decided, was to destroy the myth that they themselves had created of the Good Reform Mayor. So they decided to approach a nationally known magazine writer and have him come in to expose Kennelly. Tom Stokes was selected and a leading lawyer was duly sent to visit him. Stokes proceeded to give him a lecture on why a nice businessman with high morals and fine ideals could never govern a city as tough as Chicago; he could never understand the balance between what the city required and what the politicians and crooks would permit. Chicago needed, Stokes said, a tough professional politician who understood the underside of Chicago life and how to control it.

HIS SECRET CLOUT

Enter Richard J. Daley. When he decided to run for Mayor he already wore an important political hat, clerk of Cook County, which was like being Secretary of State for the machine; it allowed him to dispense much of the machine's patronage. Before making the race he reportedly promised Colonel Arvey that he would give up the organizational job (which he didn't and it became the secret of his success). The primary was particularly bitter and it was repeatedly charged that electing Daley would be like throwing the rascals back in.

"I would not unleash the forces of evil," he countered. "It's a lie. I will follow the training my good Irish mother gave me—and Dad. If I am elected, I will embrace mercy, love, charity, and walk humbly with my God."

The machine was split (in the same ward one precinct went for Kennelly 485 to 7, while another precinct went for Daley 400 to 10). A number of reformers such as Stevenson came out for Daley, and with the help of Bill Dawson, Lord of the Negro wards, Daley won. In the general election he was opposed by Robert Merriam, an attractive Republican candidate who gave him a hard race. It was a hard fought campaign, the question being, who's going to control Chicago, State Street or the Neighborhoods (the rich or the poor)? Daley won again, decided to be both Mayor and organization chairman, thus to a degree breaking with Arvey. Most of his success has stemmed from that decision; it is an extraordinary

achievement to hold both jobs with so little opposition for so long. (He was aided in the beginning by other pols, who underestimated him and felt he would be relatively easy to control.)

Daley's municipal ambition is backed up, to use the Chicago expression, with political clout. When he wants something done, it gets down. He knows every minuscule aspect of the city, both municipally and politically, knows the balance and has the political power to handle the people who don't measure up. As one Daley aide says, "I don't know how many times the Mayor told Bob Wagner there in New York to do the same thing, to go one way or another, either to be a reformer or to be like him, but to make a choice. But your city is different in New York—you people all have more illusions about yourselves."

From the time he took over almost thirteen years ago, Daley has steadily increased his power; where new power outside his sphere has risen up he has moved quickly and ably to incorporate it, to make it his. Where problems have arisen he has quickly appointed committees, often filled with former business foes, and then subtly moved the committees over to his own position. When there has been opposition, he has moved to embrace it (carrying always the threat of his real power if it didn't come along), to make it part of his consensus. Typically, several years ago the Republicans were prepared to run an excellent group of lawyers as judges. Daley went to them and said that if they ran as Republicans he would move Heaven and earth to beat them; if they

299

ran as Democrats he would guarantee there would be no opposition. Most ran as Democrats.

As his power increased, so did his ability to accommodate people, and his ability to tell them to get on the team or be frozen out. Though Daley was strongly opposed by State Street in his first race, he has since practically destroyed the Republican party as a force within the city. He has given the business leaders what they want, a new downtown area, an expressway, a decent police force, confidence in the city's economic future (and if the school system is deteriorating, their children can always go to private or suburban schools). In return he has had his projects carried out with their support, and has gotten their political backing and campaign funds. The result of this is that it has been very difficult for a serious Republican candidate to make a challenge. It takes an estimated $1.5 million to run for Mayor of Chicago and any candidate would have a hard time raising $200,000 to run against Daley.

The Democratic primary is the decisive election within the city, much more so than in New York, and within the primary, all other things being equal, the machine is the dominant force. For it still functions well. Each ward committeeman has about 500 jobs (the eleventh ward, Daley's own in the Bridgeport neighborhood, has at least twice as many), and that means that each committeeman has a base in his own area of 500 families or more from which to operate. In general, the appartus controls about 35,000 jobs and is considered to be worth about 100,000 votes in an election. Daley is

very good about seeing that every committeeman gets his fair share of patronage, but it all comes down from the Mayor; he watches the organization to see who can still cut and who can't. Through this system there is intense local control; if one block doesn't come through, everyone from top to bottom will know whose fault it is. The people just below Daley, the key committeemen, make their money selling insurance and real estate in their fiefs. But Daley has never been touched by scandal and probably never will be. The idea that he might be interested in money instead of sheer power would shock most Chicagoans. "It is Daley's greatest success that he has managed to convince the public that he is totally honest while at the same time conveying to the pols that he will permit clean graft so long as it is not abused and does not embarrass him," one newspaperman says. But even when there are abuses, he tries to take care of the offender; it is part of the ethic of loyalty. When he was first elected Daley had to clean out the Loop, which had become the center of crime. He carefully took all the hoods and semi-hoods who made their living there and put them in the Sanitation Department. About six years later the Sanitation Department began to go rotten and they had to be transferred again.

He has managed to keep the machine viable, to bring cost accounting to the city government, to keep up with many reforms in the New Deal tradition, and in the words of one political scientist, "to make the machine a limited instrument for social progress." He has bound together this unnatural consensus at a particularly difficult time, and part of the reason comes from the consensus itself; each member of it is aware of the others and of the counterpressure on the Mayor. This acts as a restraint; they will not push too far for fear of rocking the boat. Part of the reason, too, is that Daley simply works harder than his opponents. He is at early Mass when his enemies are still sleeping, and he is still working on city problems at night when they've all gone to bed or are out drinking. He pays enormous attention to detail; he goes over every job application, to a ridiculously low level. Finally he knows more about the petty details of Chicago than almost any of his critics. They, as Dr. Martin Luther King did, criticize the broad outlines of life in Chicago; he comes in armed with details of its daily life, what he is doing and what he would like to do but can't. "The Mayor could go on television tomorrow night and wave a wand to end discrimination but the next day life would be the same," says an aide.

He tries to control dissent in Chicago as much as he can, and outspoken critics from some papers and radio stations have occasionally left Chicago allegedly because of City Hall pressure; even in City Hall, when meetings are about to be called, there is what is known as the Ruly Crowd, made up of faithful followers ready to sit in at any meeting to keep out a potential Unruly Crowd. He avoids the press except on his own terms; reporters are avoided, though publishers are not; by Daley's maxim publishers have power and reporters do not. Besieged by magazine writers in the spring of this year he

consented to see most of them. He was very gracious to me, sounding a little like Martin Luther King talking about race; yet I had the sense of being a mosquito bite, which once scratched would never itch again.

There was a sense that Daley was an American genius of sorts, a pragmatic man with a sense of man's corruptibility. He was successful where social reformers might have failed. He embodied many of the qualities which distinguish Chicago; he was as tough, as shrewd, ambitious, and sentimental as that city. When the Negroes, in their anger, burned Chicago, his city, his sentimental love for the place was almost childlike. He despaired; how could they do that to his city, how could they do that to him after all he had done for them? Why didn't the Negroes come forth now and show to the world how much they loved Chicago?

But Richard Daley knew more than most men where power existed, and it did not exist among the black citizens of the city. Part of this was his fault, but it was very late in the game. Now sixty-six, in what is almost surely his last term as Mayor, concerned more than anything else with his place in history, he presided over a city seething with racial problems, of steadily intensifying polarization, of a school system which was often useless; and many of the black people of the city saw him more than anyone else in the city, or the country, as the symbol of what was wrong with America. (A young Negro playwright named Ronald Fair could write a bitter play, *The Emperor's Parade*, about an Irish mayor who brings over an imported Irish leprechaun for his greatest day, the St. Patrick's Day parade, and goes berserk when it is ruined by black civil-rights marchers.) It was one of the ironies of Daley's rule of Chicago that because he had succeeded so much in other areas his failures on race relations seemed so marked. Unlike other mayors, one sensed that he had the power to do something.

BLACK POWER, LIMITED

For Chicago, despite all Daley's successes, is like other American cities: a place which is rotting. The pattern is not unusual—whites leaving the inner city as soon as they can afford to, jobs leaving the city too; Negroes taking over more of their old areas, Negroes bitter about their lack of jobs, their lack of power, their shabby schools, becoming more violent, their violence driving out more and more whites. The Poles and the other ethnic groups are angry and tense about the blacks *because they get all the attention*, because the country *is being run for them, all the politicians have sold out to them*. The ethnic groups hold onto their houses, bought after long and hard saving, by sheer dint of organized neighborhood feeling against the Negroes. White Congressmen from Polish neighborhoods, old-style New Deal liberals, are backtracking fast on civil rights, attacking school bussing, telling their friends, *What can I do, I try and explain, but they won't listen, they just won't listen*. The liberals are worried about the city but are moving to the suburbs faster and faster, while the traditionally liberal University of Chicago

district becomes blacker and blacker. ("By the time the city is liberal enough to have a Jewish Mayor, it will have a black Mayor," one Jew says.) Those in our cities who are left to integrate with the blacks are those least prepared to understand and accept the problems of the blacks.

Perhaps 30 per cent of Chicago is black. Yet the black ghettos of Chicago are curiously powerless: they have little political bargaining power, and they have fewer jobs. A recent Urban League study on black power in Chicago showed that though Negroes composed 30 per cent of the population, they had only 2.6 per cent of policy-making positions in government and finance, and even that figure was probably optimistic.

Negro political leaders in Chicago have traditionally opted to play the machine's game, so that blacks in general have repeatedly been sold out by their own people; their representatives are ward politicians first, and Negroes second. "They can say no to us without checking higher up," one Negro said, "but they can never say yes without checking higher up." "I sometimes wonder," one white official remarked, "why so many of the Negroes on the City Council are so docile in this day and age, and then I realize that if they weren't docile they wouldn't be there."

The black community is thus divided against itself; its representatives are largely machine politicians interested in the traditional patronage and financial benefits, sensitive about intruding or being pushy in a white man's world, down-playing civil rights—just some of the boys mimicking the style of their white colleagues. "They're not even Toms," one Negro said. "There's no pretense at all to them. They play the game. That's what it's all about."

When on occasion a new Negro leader rises up and reflects power, Daley will try to accommodate and offer new and special privileges, with the alternative being a freeze-out. "So you have a tradition of people selling out, getting eroded. It's all too much for them," one white liberal who formerly served in the legislature said. "I know that white liberals will sit next to Negroes in the House and then the Negroes will occasionally encourage them on some liberal legislation. But when the vote comes the Negroes aren't there. So you ask them what the hell's going on, and they say, 'Look man, it's all right for you, you've got your own base, and you have something to fall back on. But this is all I've got, and if I don't do what they want, then I'm out of here.'"

All of this has probably tended to lull Daley's own view of reality. As one politician said, "The thing about him is that his machine is too successful for his own good. He allows these people so many jobs and so many positions and he thinks that he has real Negroes there and that the black community is satisfied. He doesn't realize that the community thinks that these people work for him, not for them. Then he sees the votes for him in the black wards and they're terrific votes because by the time the electoral process gets around, there's not much opposition and a lot of those people are scared to death anyway. So he decides that all this

talk by civil-rights people is just that, talk."

This, of course, is true only of the South Side, which is Chicago's older, more traditional ghetto. The South Side has some organizational form, some black representation. The West Side, in contrast, is a jungle. It is the port of entry for all the young illiterate blacks coming up from the South, and it is a wild, disorganized, and pitiful section. Those Negroes who make it go on to the South Side. Those who can't remain on the West Side, hopeless, without jobs, changing homes several times a year; the business establishments on the West Side are mostly all owned by whites who live elsewhere, the landlords are largely white and absentee, even the political machinery is controlled by whites, largely by Jews who once lived there and moved away, but have kept the political control. Inside it the kids are alienated and angry, totally outside the system.

After the murder of Dr. King the West Side burned. "Now," says A. A. Rayner, an independent alderman from the South Side, "they're building it back up just the way it was before, no decisions on the part of the people who live there, just the same people from the outside making all the decisions. If they put it up the same way, then it'll surely come down the same way again."

THE OUTLOOK FROM BRIDGEPORT

Daley would deal with these people if they had power, but they are so hopeless they are disinterested in the electoral proccess, their needs too great for the ballot. For twelve years they have gotten crumbs and the Mayor has manipulated them, confident that Chicago's Negroes have nowhere else to go in a showdown. If it is a choice between siding with them and with the white ethnic neighborhoods, which would have somewhere else to go (and with whom he has a basic sympathy and identity), he will edge more toward the whites. Thus black power in Chicago has stayed so small that finally in their anger and bitterness the blacks have a power, but it is a negative one, a power to destroy.

It is really a clash of two different cultures and ethics. Daley is from and of Bridgeport, a small Irish-American community which holds steadfastly to what it was. Going through it, the small bungalows, incredibly well kept up, sparkling with paint, the Blue Star flags in the windows, one has a sense of another time and place in America. Daley has lived in the same house for more than thirty years; he goes home for lunch every day. It is a neighborhood which has produced the last three Mayors of Chicago, and it has an unusually high percentage of people with city jobs. "Just about every house on the street has someone with political connections," one critic says. It is suspicious of outsiders and new ideas; Negroes do not walk its streets at night. Nor do they buy its property.

By dint of much effort, church centered, the property is kept up and the neighborhood is maintained. Negroes are not permitted to buy. A few years ago an unduly liberal resident sold to a Negro and riots resulted, windows were smashed, and the Negro's belongings were bodily moved out and the local Democratic organization moved two whites in the house.

Daley, of course, is better than Bridgeport, but he is still a part of it, and it influences the way he looks at social problems. He is deeply religious, but his religion is pre-Ecumenical, pre-John XXIII, where there is individual sin, but little social sin. He can tolerate small and petty graft, excuse an occasional roaring drunk, a failing of business virtue, but he cannot excuse adultery, and cannot understand or tolerate a man who fathers a family and then deserts it. He seems unable to understand the forces which create these failings.

He is a product of a time when the American ethic was to succeed, and those who didn't succeed at least respected those who did. He does not like poverty programs, in part because they represent a threat to his power—federal money going directly to black neighborhoods, without his control, diluting his base and creating a new base for an organization outside his machine, *financing his opposition.* Moreover, he doesn't think these people, what one lawyer calls "the underclass," are capable of leading and governing. "In his heart of hearts," one longtime associate says, "I think he would like to grab those people by the lapels, shake them and say *Get to work.*" Two years ago a nun who was a militant civil-rights activist on the West Side went to see Daley and pleaded with him to come out there, to see the conditions, to look at the schools, to see the children.

"Look, Sister," the Mayor answered,

"you and I come from the same background. We know how tough it was. But we picked ourselves up by our bootstraps."

WHEN KING CAME TO TOWN

The great challenge to Richard Daley's control of Chicago came in 1966 when Martin Luther King came to town. This became an almost classic conflict of two great forces: Daley with a tightly organized American political base—layer supporting layer of organizational structure, votes tangible, deliverable—pitted against a man whose power base was vague by traditional American terms, and was more moral than practical. In the immediate sense Daley certainly won, though the King people have a strong sense of social insight; it may be that years from now people will trace subsequent black victories and black awakenings to forces loosed by King's visit.

There is now some doubt among Chicagoans that Daley's victory was so wise. Some people feel that it was classic shortsightedness, that this time Daley really mixed the two jobs of politician and Mayor and viewed the challenge only as a politician, that King may have represented a chance to help save the city in spite of itself, that he might have helped give the kind of order to the black wards of Chicago that no white man can now do. "I'm not sure if Daley had to do it over again he wouldn't think twice," one reporter said, and then corrected himself. "No, that's me thinking. He'd do the same thing again."

King was unprepared for the immensity and complexity of Chicago. He and his people had never been noted for their organizational skill, but in the past they had operated in middle-sized Southern cities where they had a certain routine—find out who the best local people are, organize through them, pick out your targets, create your enemy, dramatize your fight against him, force them to make the mistakes.

In Chicago it was far more complicated. King just didn't have enough people. The city had different layers and different islands of Negro communities, and most of the existing black establishment saw King as a threat. ("Listen, don't tell us how well King's doing," a City Hall man told a reporter at the beginning of King's drive. "He had only forty people at his meeting last night and twenty of them were ours.")

As for Daley, he would be no Bull Connor; he would not be anyone's easy villain. Where King pushed, he would give way. Above all he would try and protect King and his people. Finally, King and his staff had no precise organizational plan of their own; it was their first venture into the North and they were deliberately biting off more than they could chew. If they could break Chicago, they could make it anywhere.

NO PROGRAM BUT A VISION

Early in their drive they invited Leon Despres, a white alderman who is Daley's foremost adversary in Chicago and a man who understands the Daley operation at least as well as the Mayor, to meet with them. Despres went before a large meeting and gave a precise description of how the machine worked—precinct by precinct, ward by ward, where it was vulnerable and what it would require in the way of hard work to beat it for aldermanic and legislative races. When he finished the crowd was enthusiastic. Then the Reverend James Bevel, a King deputy who was in charge of the Chicago program, a brilliant man but something of a mystic, said, "I believe in politics too. But if we do what this man wants then we're descending to the level of the opposition. We can't do that, we can't win and then end up like they are. That's not what we want."

Since Bevel was in charge of the program, the movement became largely speeches and street demonstrations; these demostrations had their effect, and indeed terrified the white community by unleashing so much hatred. But if King had gone deeper, trying to match the organizational root in 1966, anti-Daley black politicians would probably be having an easier time in 1968.

Daley studied King, watched him move, sensed that he would not respond in a traditionally political way. ("Daley was always a little relieved and grateful that King had not come up here to become Mayor of Chicago," one lawyer said.) Finally, after feeling King out, Daley had a meeting with him. The meeting surprised Daley. He expected King to arrive with a long list of specific proposals (after all, Daley always went places with specific proposals). Daley's own staff was carefully rehearsed, and each member re-cited just exactly what his department was doing, where each swimming pool was being built.

None of these statistics and briefings had very much effect on King, who was concerned with the broad social ills of Chicago, who felt that Daley treated symptoms rather than causes, and who suspected that Daley was more interested in his machine that his people. The meeting broke up with Daley sure he could take King. "That King," one of Daley's press people said, "he didn't have any program. We had all these programs and we said, 'Why don't you help us? Why don't you do something for your people? Why don't you support Mayor Daley's programs? If you went on television and endorsed them do you realize how much good it would do?' But, oh no, not him. And then that King left, and held a press conference and criticized the Mayor."

Even so, even without political power, King nearly brought Chicago to its knees. His street demonstrations touched off something very ugly in America. White racism exploded in the various ethnic neighborhoods. Day after day the scene repeated itself, the Negroes marching, the whites reacting with rocks and bricks, the replays on television, Daley's police forced again and again to arrest whites. Each day the establishment was more and more worried about the growing white racism.

Finally, King and Daley conferred again; it was the eve of King's proposed march into the tough Cicero neighborhood. As one white liberal described it, "The establishment would have given King almost anything not to make that march—it was worried sick what was going to happen. But King was too Christian, you know, and he was worried in his own mind about the Cicero march and what would happen to his own people and his responsibility for their lives—that's one difference between King and these younger people coming along now, they aren't going to worry very much about it—so he went into that room and the first thing he did was he gave away that Cicero march. They would have given him almost anything not to make it, and he gave it away at the beginning of the meeting." The result was a mild compromise of sorts—one of the usual citizens committees which sparkle throughout Chicago and America.

In the end, King's presence stirred many things in Chicago, including Operation Breadbasket (in which Negroes demanded jobs in proportion to their purchasing power, a very effective economic pressure). But though they encouraged others to challenge the system, and created forces which might someday help destroy the machine, it was a fact that King and his people had not developed a broad base in the poor black areas. In 1968 after King was slain, when the riots ensued and Richard Daley gave his shoot-to-kill order, the bulk of Daley's power was based upon the votes of poor blacks.

THE MAN WHO SWINGS
COOK COUNTY

William L. Dawson made Dick Daley Mayor. And probably Harry Truman and John Kennedy President. And endless other smaller officeholders. For generations Bill Dawson has controlled and brokered the black vote in Chicago's South Side, a vote which could swing Cook County, Illinois, and ultimately the nation. Congressman Dawson is a Negro politician of the old school. ("He thinks like a machine man, not like a black man," one critic says.) His part of the machine in the poor black wards of the South Side is particularly well run; machines run better among the poor than among the rich. It is tightly organized. It runs on the basic patronage and the tiny—infinitesimal to white America—economic favors, gifts which went out as a political force in white America some sixteen years ago.

His is an almost classic political story. He is a Georgia Negro gone North; he served in World War I, and was wounded there. (One of his few memorable speeches in recent years came during the Korean war when there was an amendment before the House which would allow reservists to pick their units by race. Dawson delivered an eloquent speech describing his own service, his own wounds and bad medical service, and asked America how long it would inflict second class status on those who were dying for it.) Back to Chicago to work as a tailor, he made a hesitant entry into Republican politics, for the Republicans in those days were the party of the Negroes. He became the most successful precinct captain the Republicans had, and soon an alderman. With the coming of the New Deal and Franklin Roosevelt, he switched to the Democratic party, like many other Negro politicians of that era. He became a part of the Kelly-Nash machine, and hence more and more of a professional politician. ("The Kelly-Nash machine, you know they got their money's worth out of people, you never dealt with them for free," says Sammy Rayner, Dawson's opponent. "They said to him come along, we'll take care of you, and they did and he has never wanted since.")

He soon dominated the entire South Side, and in his time he was considered a great spellbinding speaker. Yet though he has always been for civil rights in his career, he has been under increasing attack from other blacks in the past decade; they feel he has been silent on too many things, and too much of an organization man.

"He's from a different generation," one of his critics says. "He does some good things, but he does them under cover—it's as if he feels there's something to be ashamed about, a black man demanding things. He believes if you make speeches you make enemies." His opponents feel mainly that his organization has helped neutralize any new forces in

1. The Urban League report adds: "Exclusion of Negroes is not limited to legal and legitimate spheres of activity. Thirty years ago gambling was one of the few areas in which Negroes held tangible power. Although the Syndicate with its billion dollar a year Chicago operation was not included in this formal survey, it is worthwhile noting recent data on the structure of this organization which wields power and political influence. No Negroes held positions among the alleged thirteen leaders in the crime Syndicate. There are five Negroes in the Chicago Crime Commission's 1967 list of 216 major Syndicate members; only one of these is reputed to have even minor authority. . . ."

the black community. Even his seniority in Congress—twenty-five years and chairman of the important Government Operations Committee—has done the Negro little good, they believe. A recent Urban League report cited Dawson, though not by name, as symbolic of the frustration of black people in Chicago: ". . . theoretically he is in a more strategic position to influence government operations than any other Chicago Congressman. Yet only 2 per cent of the top federal jobs located in Chicago were held by Negroes in 1965. Such limits on the ability of an individual to act for major race ends is grounded in his dependency on the institution either to maintain his post or to gain minor racial concessions. . . ."

In recent years Dawson's power has been limited even within the machine. At one time he was a broker for all the Negro aldermen, but several years ago Daley, not wanting any subbrokers in Chicago, made alliances with other Negroes which broke part of Dawson's power. In addition there has been some criticism of Dawson by nonreform blacks who feel he has permitted Italians to take over the rackets in the South Side and hence sold out his own people.[1]

Dawson is old now; his age is listed at eighty-two, and some people believe he may even be ninety. He suffered a stroke several years ago and he does not see the public very often now. His office is often closed, he has little contact with civil-rights leaders. When a group of Chicago businessmen visited him in late May, they were stunned to hear him talk about Martin Luther King as if King were still alive. "That King is stealing money from these people and sending it to a bank in Geneva," he told them.

Thus by any normal standards, given the rising feeling in the ghettos, defeating Dawson in the primary should be relatively easy. It isn't. Though he does not campaign at all in the traditional sense, the machine virtually runs itself; there are some strong deputies to Dawson who find the present situation very profitable and are not about to see it disappear.

There are some chinks—the changing temper of Negroes, the increasing number of the Negro middle class, with the middle class votes strongly anti-Dawson (the District is gerrymandered to keep whites out). But much of the District is still poor. The Negroes live on welfare and in public housing ("high-rise vertical dungeons," one young Negro calls them) and they are frightened. They have been told over and over again they will lose their welfare and their housing by representatives of the organization, who also happen to sell them their insurance, visiting them monthly since Negro insurance is not sold long-term.

Thus the pols keep a close and friendly touch on the poor; they know every name and make sure every name votes. "Man, you whites think that King and those other preachers know these people," one black organization worker told a reporter recently. "They don't know these people. These people here, they don't want no talk. They can't eat that. You think any of these new preachers ever visited these people? They're too busy talking to white people like you. We talk to these people and we know them. We the ones get it done. Remember that. We the ones get it done." These poor housing developments turn out votes of twenty to one for the machine. . . .

MACHINE POLITICS
—OLD AND NEW

Theodore J. Lowi

The political machine is an institution peculiar to American cities. Like the militant party elsewhere, the American machine as a classic type is centralized, integrated, and relatively ruthless. But there the similarity ends.

Machines have been integrated from within, as fraternities; they do not arise out of opposition to the state or to a hostile class. The power of the machine rested upon being integrated in a dispersed, permissive, and unmobilized society. Integrated, however, in a special American way.

The most militant parties of Europe have depended upon homogeneity— enforced if necessary. Machines have developed ingenious techniques for capitalizing upon ethnic and racial heterogeneity. Militant parties have typically been based on common ends at the cen-

ter, holding the periphery together by fear. The machines were based upon a congeries of people with uncommon ends, held together at the center by logrolling and at the periphery by *fraternité, égalité*, and ignorance.

As to the significance of the machine for the development of the American city, the returns are still not in. Typically, it was the European observers who were the first to appreciate this unusual, American phenomenon. Ostrogorski, Bryce, Weber, Michels, Schumpeter, and Duverger each in his own way made an outstanding effort to appreciate the peculiarities of urban democracy in America. Harold F. Gosnell, in *Machine Politics: Chicago Model* (1937), was one of the very first Americans to join that distinguished company with anything approaching a systematic treatment of the subject. (By this standard, the muckrakers do not count.)

However, Gosnell was limited by the fact that there was, in his time, insuffi-

Reprinted with permission from *The Public Interest*, Number 9 (Fall 1967), 83-92. Copyright © by National Affairs, Inc., 1967.

cient experience with alternative forms of big city politics. Too few big cities in the United States had been "reformed" in sufficient degree to provide any basis for comparison.

In the 1960's, sufficient time has passed. The machine is nearly dead, and we have experienced lengthy periods of Reform government. We can now see the machine in perspective.

How does it shape up?

CHICAGO AND NEW YORK

We can begin to introduce perspective by immediately setting aside Gosnell's claim that the Chicago experience on which his book was based is representative. It is the very uniqueness of Chicago's experience with the machine that gives his study such value. It is New York that is the representative big city, not Chicago. Its representativeness derives from the fact that it has experienced Reform in a way that Chicago has not. In 1967, political power in Chicago still has an extremely strong machine base; political power in New York has an entirely new and different base. As New York was being revolutionized by the New Deal and its successors, the structure of Chicago politics was being reaffirmed. When New York was losing its last machine and entering into a new era of permanent Reform, Chicago's political machine was just beginning to consolidate. New York became a loose, multi-party system with wide-open processes of nomination, election, and participation; Chicago became a

tight, one-party system. New York sought to strengthen a weak mayor who already operated under a strong-mayor government; Chicago has had the opposite problem of an already strong mayor in a weak-mayor government.

To evaluate the machine we must ask whether, by surviving, machine politics in Chicago in any way distorted that city's growth and development. How much change would there have been in Chicago's history if the nationalization of politics had made possible in Chicago, as it did in virtually every other big American city, ways of "licking the ward boss" and altering precinct organization, means of loosening the hold of county organization on city hall, power for liberating the personnel and policies of the professional agencies of government? We cannot answer these questions for Chicago because the basis of machine strength still exists there, and the conditions for its continuity might well continue through the remainder of the century. However, we may be able to answer them, at least better than before, by looking at Chicago from the vantage point of New York's experience.

POPULISM AND EFFICIENCY

New York city government, like government in almost all large American cities except Chicago, is a product of Reform. It is difficult to understand these cities without understanding the two strains of ideology that guided local Reform movements throughout the past three-quarters of a century. *Populism* and *efficiency*, once the foundation of most local insurgency, are now almost universally triumphant. These two tenets are now the orthodoxy in local practice.

Populism was originally a statement of the evils of every form of bigness in the city, including big business, big churches, big labor, as well as big political organizations. Decentralization was an ultimate goal. In modern form, it has tended to come down to the aim of eliminating political parties, partisanship, and if possible "politics" itself.

Efficiency provided the positive program to replace that which is excised by populist surgery. The doctrine calls essentially for the centralization and rationalization of government activities and services to accompany the decentralization of power. Some Reformers assumed that services do not constitute power. Others assumed the problem away altogether by positing a neutral civil servant who would not abuse centralized government but who could use it professionally to reap the economies effected by rationalization and by specialization. That was the secret of the business system; and, after all, the city is rather like a business. ("There is no Republican or Democratic way to clean a street.")

While there are many inconsistent assumptions and goals between the doctrines of populism and efficiency, they lived well together. Their coexistence was supported by the fact that different wings of the large, progressive movement they generated were responsible for each. Populism was largely the province of the working class, "progressive" wing. Doc-trines of efficiency were very much the responsibility of the upper class wing. Populism resided with the politician-activists. Efficiency was developed by the intellectuals, including several distinguished university presidents, such as Seth Low, Andrew Dickson White, Harold Dodd, and, pre-eminently, Woodrow Wilson, who, while still a professor of political science, wrote a classic essay proclaiming the virtues of applying Prussian principles of administration in the United States.

These two great ideas were, by a strange and wonderful chemistry, combined into a movement whose influence forms a major chapter of American history. Charters and laws have been enacted that consistently insulate city government from politics, meaning party politics. It has become increasingly necessary, with each passing decade, to grant each bureaucratic agency autonomy to do the job as each commissioner saw fit, as increasingly appointments were made of professionals in each agency's fields.

On into the 1960's, the merit system extends itself "upward, outward, and downward," to use the Reformers' own rhetoric. Recruitment to the top posts is more and more frequent from the ranks of those who have made careers in their agencies, party backgrounds increasingly being a mark of automatic disqualification. Reform has succeeded in raising public demand for political morality and in making "politics" a dirty word. A "good press" for mayors results from their determination to avoid intervening in the affairs of one department after another. The typical modern mayor is all the more eager to co-operate because this provides an opportunity to delegate responsibility. Absolution-before-the-fact for government agencies has become part of the mayoral swearing-in ceremony.

Reform has triumphed and the cities are better run than ever before. But that is, unfortunately, not the end of the story, nor would it have been the end of the story even had there been no Negro revolution. The triumph of Reform really ends in paradox: *Cities like New York became well-run but ungoverned.*

THE NEW MACHINES

Politics under Reform are not abolished. Only their form is altered. *The legacy of Reform is the bureaucratic city-state.* Destruction of the party foundation of the mayoralty cleaned up many cities but also destroyed the basis for sustained, central, popularly-based action. This capacity, with all its faults, was replaced by the power of professionalized agencies. But this has meant creation of new bases of power. Bureaucratic agencies are not neutral; they are only independent.

Modernization and Reform in New York and other cities has meant replacement of Old Machines with New Machines. The bureaucracies—that is, the professionally organized, autonomous career agencies—are the New Machines.

Sociologically, the Old Machine was a combination of rational goals and fraternal loyalty. The cement of the organization was trust and discipline created out of long years of service, probation, and testing, slow promotion through the ranks, and centralized control over the means of reward. Its power in the community was based upon services rendered to the community.

Sociologically, the New Machine is almost exactly the same sort of an organization. But there are also significant differences. The New Machines are more numerous, in any given city. They are functional rather than geographic in their scope. They rely on formal authority rather than upon majority acquiescence. And they probably work with a minimum of graft and corruption. But these differences do not alter their definition; they only help to explain why the New Machine is such a successful form of organization.

The New Machines are machines because they are relatively irresponsible structures of power. That is, each agency shapes important public policies, yet the leadership of each is relatively self-perpetuating and not readily subject to the controls of any higher authority.

The New Machines are machines in that the power of each, while resting ultimately upon services rendered to the community, depends upon its cohesiveness as a small minority in the midst of the vast dispersion of the multitude.

The modern city has become well-run but ungoverned because it has, according to Wallace Sayre and Herbert Kaufman, become comprised of "islands of functional power" before which the modern mayor stands denuded of authority. No mayor of a modern city has predictable means of determining whether the bosses of the New Machines—the bureau chiefs and the career commissioners—will be

313

loyal to anything but their agency, its work, and related professional norms. Our modern mayor has been turned into the likes of a French Fourth Republic Premier facing an array of intransigent parties in the National Assembly. These modern machines, more monolithic by far than their ancient brethren, are entrenched by law, and are supported by tradition, the slavish loyalty of the newspapers, the educated masses, the dedicated civic groups, and, most of all, by the organized clientele groups enjoying access under existing arrangements.

ORGANIZED DECENTRALIZATION

The Reform response to the possibility of an inconsistency between running a city and governing it has been to assume the existence of the Neutral Specialist, the bureaucratic equivalent to law's Rational Man. The assumption is that, if men know their own specialties well enough, they are capable of reasoning out solutions to problems they share with men of equal but different technical competencies. That is a very shaky assumption indeed. Charles Frankel's analysis of such an assumption in Europe provides an appropriate setting for a closer look at it in modern New York; ". . . different [technical] elites disagree with each other; the questions with which specialists deal spill over into areas where they are *not* specialists, and they must either hazard amateur opinions or ignore such larger issues, which is no better. . . ."

During the 1950's, government experts began to recognize that, despite vast increases in efficiency flowing from the defeat of the Old Machine, New York city government was somehow lacking. These concerns culminated in the 1961 Charter, in which the Office of Mayor was strengthened in many impressive ways. But it was quickly discovered that no amount of formal centralization could definitively overcome the real decentralization around the Mayor. It was an organized disorganization, which made a mockery of the new Charter. The following examples, although drawn from New York, are of virtually universal application:

(1) Welfare problems always involve several of any city's largest agencies, including Health, Welfare, Hospitals, etc. Yet during more than 40 years, successive mayors of New York failed to reorient the Department of Health away from a "regulative" toward a "service" concept of organization. And many new aspects of welfare must be set up in new agencies if they are to be set up at all. The new poverty programs were set up very slowly in all the big cities—except Chicago.

(2) Water pollution control has been "shared" by such city agencies as the Departments of Health, Parks, Public Works, Sanitation, Water Supply, and so on. No large city, least of all New York, has an effective program to combat even the local contributions to pollution. The same is true of air pollution control, although for some years New York has had a separate Department for this purpose.

(3) Land-use patterns are influenced one way or another by a large variety of

highly professional agencies. It has proven virtually impossible in any city for one of these agencies to impose its criteria on the others. In New York, the opening of Staten Island by the Narrows Bridge, in what may be the last large urban frontier, found the city with no plan for the revolution that is taking place in property values and land uses in that borough.

(4) Transportation is also the province of agencies too numerous to list. Strong mayors throughout the country have been unable to prevent each from going its separate way. To take just one example: New York pursued a vast off-street parking program, at a cost of nearly $4,000 per parking space, at the very moment when local rail lines were going bankrupt.

(5) Enforcement of civil rights is imposed upon almost all city agencies by virtue of Federal, state, and local legislation. But efforts to set up public, then City Council, review of police processes in New York have been successfully opposed by professional police officials. Efforts to try pairing and busing on a very marginal, experimental basis have failed. The police commissioner resigned at the very suggestion that values other than professional police values be imposed upon the Department, even when the imposition came via the respected tradition of "legislative oversight." The Superintendent of Education, an "outsider," was forced out; he was replaced by a career administrator. One education journalist at that time said: "Often . . . a policy proclaimed by the Board [of Education], without the advice and consent of

the professionals, is quickly turned into mere paper policy. . . . The veto power through passive resistance by professional administrators is virtually unbeatable. . . ."

The decentralization of city government toward its career bureaucracies has resulted in great efficiency for the activities around which each bureaucracy was organized. The city is indeed well-run. But what of those activities around which bureaucracies are not organized, or those which fall between or among agencies' jurisdictions? For these, as suggested by the cases above, the cities are suffering either stalemate or elephantiasis—an affliction whereby a particular activity, say, urban renewal or parkways, gets pushed to its ultimate "success" totally without regard to its importance compared to the missions of other agencies. In these as well as in other senses, the cities are ungoverned.

THE 1961 ELECTION

Mayors have tried a variety of strategies to cope with these situations. But the 1961 mayoralty election in New York was the ultimate dramatization of the mayor's plight. This election was a confirmation of the New York system, and will some day be seen as one of the most significant in American urban history. For New York, it was the culmination of many long-run developments. For the country, it may be the first of many to usher in the bureaucratic state.

The primary significance of the election can be found in the spectacle of a mayor attempting to establish a base of power for himself in the bureaucracies. The Mayor's running mate for President of the City Council had been Commissioner of Sanitation, a position which culminated virtually a lifetime career of the holder in the Department of Sanitation. He had an impressive following among the sanitation men—who, it should be added, are organized along precinct lines. The Mayor's running mate for Comptroller had been for many years the city Budget Director. As Budget Director, he had survived several Administrations and two vicious primaries that pitted factions of the Democratic Party against one another. Before becoming Director he had served for a number of years as a professional employee in the Bureau. The leaders of the campaign organization included a former, very popular Fire Commissioner who retired from his commissionership to accept campaign leadership and later to serve as Deputy Mayor; and a former Police Commissioner who had enjoyed a strong following among professional cops as well as in the local Reform movement. Added to this was a new and vigorous party, the Brotherhood Party, which was composed in large part of unions with broad bases of membership among city employees. Before the end of the election, most of the larger city bureaucracies had political representation in the inner core of the new Administration.

For the 1961 election, Mayor Wagner had put his ticket and his organization together just as the bosses of old had done. In the old days, the problem was to mobilize all the clubhouses, districts, and counties in the city by putting together a balanced ticket about which all adherents could be enthusiastic. The same seems true for 1961, except that by then the clubhouses and districts had been replaced almost altogether by new types of units.

The main point is that destruction of the machine did not, in New York or elsewhere, eliminate the need for political power. It simply altered what one had to do to get it. In the aftermath of twenty or more years of "modern" government, it is beginning to appear that the lack of power can corrupt city hall almost as much as the possession of power. Bureaucracy is, in the United State, a relatively new basis for collective action. As yet, none of us knows quite how to cope with it.

WHAT IF . . . ?

These observations and cases are not brought forward to indict Reform cities and acquit Chicago. They are intended only to put Chicago in a proper light and to provide some means of assessing the functions of the machine form of collective action.

Review of Reform government shows simply and unfortunately that the problems of cities, and the irrational and ineffectual ways city fathers go about their business, seem to obtain universally, without regard to form of government or type of power base. All cities have traffic congestion, crime, juvenile delinquency, galloping pollution, ghettos, ugliness, deterioration, and degeneracy. All cities seem to be suffering about equally from the quite recent problem of the weakening legitimacy of public institutions, resulting in collective violence and pressures for direct solution to problems. All cities seem equally hemmed in by their suburbs and equally prevented from getting at the roots of many of their most fundamental problems. Nonpartisan approaches, even the approaches of New York's Republican mayor to Republican suburbs and a Republican governor, have failed to prevent rail bankruptcy in the vast Eastern megalopolis, to abate air or water pollution, to reduce automobile pressure, or to ease the pain of the middle-class Negro in search of escape from his ghetto.

The problems of the city seem to go beyond any of the known arrangements for self-government. However, low public morality and lack of what Banfield and Wilson call "public-regardingness" may be a function simply of poor education and ethnic maladjustment. The Old Machine and its abuses may just have been another reflection of the same phenomena. If that is so, then passage of more time, and the mounting of one socio-cultural improvement after another, might have reformed the machines into public-regarding organs, if they had been permitted to survive.

Are there any strong reasons to believe that real reform could have come without paying the price of eliminating the popular base of political action? Intimations can be found in the last of the machine-recruited leaders of Tammany, Carmine DeSapio and Edward Costikyan. Each was progressively more public-regarding than any of his predecessors. Indeed, Costikyan was a model of political

responsibility for whom the new New York had no particular use. However, for this question the best answers may lie in looking afresh at Gosnell's Chicago. With a scientific rigor superior to most political analysis of the 1960's, his book goes further than any other single work to capture what political behavior was like under Old Machine conditions. The sum total of his findings, despite Gosnell's own sentiments, does not constitute a very damning indictment of the Chicago machine—if contemporary experience is kept clearly in mind.

CHICAGO IN PERSPECTIVE

Even amidst the most urgent of depression conditions, the machine in Chicago does not seem to have interfered with the modest degree of rationality distributed throughout the United States. Take for instance the case of voting behavior on referendum proposals, the most issue-laden situation an electorate ever faces. Gosnell criticized the referendum as generally subject to fraud and other types of abuse, and most particularly so in Chicago during the 1920's and '30's. But even so, his figures show that the electorate, despite the machine, did not behave indiscriminately. The theory that universal suffrage provides no check against the irresponsible acceptance of financing schemes which pass the real burden on to future generations is simply not borne out in Chicago. Conservative appeals by the propertied were effective. Over a twelve-year period, including six fat years and six lean years, 66 local bond issues were approved and 48 were rejected. Those rejected included some major bond issues offered for agencies whose leaders had become discredited. Other types of issues show responsiveness to appeals other than local precinct or county organizations. As the antiprohibition campaign began to grow, so did the vote on the prohibition repealer. Clear irrationalities tended to be associated primarily with highly technical proposals involving judicial procedure or taxation; but this is true everywhere, and to much the same degree.

In a bold stroke, Gosnell also tried to assess the influence of the newspapers, the best source for rational—at least non-machine—voting decisions. For this particular purpose Gosnell's data were weak, but fortunately he was not deterred from asking important questions merely for lack of specially designed data. Factor analysis helped Gosnell tease out of census tract data and newspaper subscription patterns a fairly realistic and balanced sense of the role of the local newspapers. Gosnell was led to conclude that the influence of news media is limited, but that this was a limitation imposed far less by the machine than by the extent to which newspapers were regularly read. Newspaper influence on issues was measurably apparent wherever daily readership was widely established—the machine notwithstanding. Here again is suggested the possibility that real machine domination rested upon a level of education and civic training that was, at the very time of Gosnell's research, undergoing a great deal of change.

Taking all the various findings together, and even allowing for abuses that were always more frequent in cities than towns, and probably more frequent in Gosnell's Chicago than other cities, we can come away from Gosnell's analysis with a picture not at all at odds with V. O. Key's notion of the "responsible electorate."

Gosnell felt his book to be an indictment of machine politics. But today, looking at the Chicago experience from the vantage point of New York's, one feels less able to be sure.

GOOD GOVERNMENT
THROUGH
PARTY GOVERNMENT?

Edward N. Costikyan

For the first 165 years of this country's existence, the manner in which our cities were governed remained a local problem. The majority of our people lived outside city limits. Legislative apportionments conceived in an earlier, largely agrarian society insured rural domination.

Both of these conditions have changed: the majority of our citizens are urban and nor rural, and recent United States Supreme Court decisions require that their votes be counted on the same scale as those of rural residents. In the years ahead there will be an increasing predominance of urban and suburban voters, and an increasing national interest in adequate city government.

I have no blueprint for better city government, merely some tentative propositions.[My own] book has not attempted to formulate such a blueprint. Rather, I have been concerned with attempting to ana-

From *Behind Closed Doors*, copyright © 1966 by Edward N. Costikyan. Reprinted by permission of Harcourt Brace Jovanovich, Inc.

lyze and banish some myths about city government which my experience has taught me amount to little more today than mortmain—to little more, in truth, than a collection of dead myths that, when they are permitted to masquerade as reality, defraud those who in a reformist spirit accept them as a reasonable guide to urban political life. Reasonable they were for our grandfathers. Not for us. They must not be accepted as keys to reality any longer if genuine political reform is to be sustained in New York (or, I suspect, in any city at all comparable to New York).

Of course, the first step in the evolution of a new and better form of city government must be an honest appraisal of where we are, and a critical analysis of the assumptions that are supposed to lead us to the promised land.

If I am correct that the anti-political-party orientation of traditional reform doctrines is the product of the mistaken assumption that an early symptom of bad government was its cause, my conclusion, however correct, does not in itself provide a blueprint for tomorrow.

But it does suggest a hypothesis.

If anti-political-party good government has not achieved good government, would it be possible for a party-oriented theory of good government to achieve more progress?

I think it would. I would like to see it tried.

It must not be forgotten that the existence of the hierarchy of party officers has always acted as a check upon and balance to the power of the public official. The problem with party officers is never their existence but always their quality. The existence of such power in reliable hands can achieve the same kind of balance and consensual government the federal government has achieved through the Constitutional system of checks and balances.

Certainly, with a growing civil-service bureaucracy, which is increasingly dominating city government, some counterbalance is necessary. Indeed, the growing political power of the civil service has reached the point where the civil-service unions have almost filled the power position formerly occupied by the political parties. As Professor Theodore Lowi, of the University of Chicago, pointed out in an unusual speech to the New York League of Women Voters on May 27, 1965:

... the *Legacy of Reform is essentially the ushering in of the bureaucratic state.* The bureaucracies in New York City government—that is, the professionally organized, autonomous agencies—are the New

Machines. We may all like these better than the Old Machines, but they are Machines just the same. As with the Old Machines, the New Machines are based on fraternal loyalty, on trust built up over long years of probation and testing, on slow promotion up through the ranks, and on services rendered to members and to the public. As with the Old Machines, you have to join up before you can hope to have any influence. (Therefore the same words define each type of machine.)

The New Machines are different in that there are more of them, in that they are functional rather than geographic, in that they do not depend upon votes for their power, and in that they probably minimize graft and corruption. But these differences only help to explain their success as machines!

To a political scientist, the New Machines are machines because they are relatively responsible structures of power: that is, they shape the important public policies, yet the leadership is relatively self-perpetuating, and they are not readily subject to the controls of any higher, popularly based authority.

Bureaucratic power unchecked by any countervailing force has been able to dictate public policy over the objections of all other interested parties. For example, in New York the issue of civilian determination of charges of police brutality has grown and grown in importance. One political and civic group after another—including the New York County Democratic Party, the Liberal Party, the CDV, the Association of the Bar of the City of New York, the New York County Lawyers Association—pressed for a change in the system, which vested jurisdiction over such complaints exclusively in the police.

In 1965 every mayoralty candidate but one (Mr. William F. Buckley, Jr., of the Conservative Party) came out for some form of civilian review. Why did the city administrators resist these proposals? Professor Lowi again supplies the answer:

For some time now the Police Department has been suffering from acute illegitimacy in some impressive quarters of the community. As a consequence, the killing of the Negro boy by an officer last July touched off the worst Harlem riots in twenty years. A large part of the credit for stopping the violence goes to the formation of the Unity Council of Harlem Organizations and the demand of that organization for a review board totally independent of the Police Department. Considering the widely accepted rights and practices of legislative oversight of administrative agencies in Washington and the state governments, and considering such independent investigations as Hoover-type commissions and the like, the demand of the Negro leaders seems relatively modest. But not to Commissioner Murphy, who threatened to resign if such a board were set up. He cast the issue strictly in terms of the integrity of his organization, arguing that such intrusion would destroy police morale. Here is a 25,000-man organization, praised by Mr. Murphy as "one of the finest municipal departments in the world." Nonetheless it is too weak to withstand questions as to whether it is sufficiently close to the most pressing problems of the city.

Mr. Murphy's strategy was one I call "totalism." It is a vital strategy in bureaucratic warfare, and it is also used by rational conservatives the world over. . . .

Mr. Murphy resigned even at the faint effort of the City Council to set up a less independent *legislative* review. At all costs the professional agency must be left to itself to decide what is the public interest. All the mayor can do is to "regret" the passing of one bureaucratic boss and see to the appointment of the next, with the usual promise of "no interference."

So, here is the spectacle of New York politics today. On the one hand you have an array of bureaucrats who believe in their respective organizations, and leaders and who follow an established policy line especially when the organization itself is at stake. *The strength of each bureaucratic agency lies in its cohesiveness as a minority in the midst of vast dispersion of the multitude.* (Once these words fit the Old Machine to a T.)

There are countless other examples of the civil-service bureaucracy deciding important questions of *public* policy. In addition, in the vacuum created by the absence of any viable party structure, the civil-service establishment has increasingly assumed both the policy function and the political function of the old machine. I would today rather have John DeLury's sanitation men with me in an election than half the party headquarters in town.

This again is a natural phenomenon. For the party organizations existed in response to a functional need for what they could provide—the machinery to elect a candidate—in return for which the party expected to be heard by the people it elected.

It seems clear to me that there should be checks and balances upon the power of any chief executive, but that this restraint should be exercised by an organization over which the voters have control—through the power to select the officers of the organization in primary elections—rather than a civil-service union responsive only to the demands and special interests of its government-employee members.

The result of combining the party-leader role and that of the chief executive has been to prevent the party from performing its legitimate governmental function. Mayor Wagner's administration, in fact, demonstrated both extremes of an undesirable power relationship.

Until 1961, too much power in public areas was in the hands of party officers. Fluoridation, for example, could not pass until the party leaders lost their power to control the Board of Estimate. Until 1961, when Wagner toppled them, they controlled enough votes on the Board of Estimate to prevent a decision on the question. This condition existed in large part because of the historical relationship between the party and its mayor, and partly because the current mayor believed as a matter of policy that he should keep strictly out of questions of internal party leadership—until 1961.

After 1961, the balance went the other way. Party leaders were hobbled in making *their* decisions because the mayor exercised all party power. The designation of candidates for all major public offices, for judgeships, and even the selection of people to fill party offices such as county leader, was made by the chief public officeholder. The result was that the party officeholder became no more than a first sergeant executing orders. The

party organization more and more came to be at the disposal of one man—the mayor.

The mayor in turn suffered from a tremendous diversion of energy as he became more and more involved in internal party maneuvering. His *party leadership* role, it should be rememberd, was immune from any control. For mayors are nominated and elected, after all, to run the city, not the party, and in a primary the mayor's party activities are hardly an obviously relevant, let alone an effective, issue.[1]

I believe that the mayor, however, honestly felt on the basis of his experience and education that his course was the proper one. I do not think he was seeking the political leader's power for the sake of having more power (although he enjoyed exercising it), but rather because he believed it was essential *for the cause of good government* that he, and not the party officials, control the party structure.

In taking this position he was standing

1. The role of the President of the United States as leader of his national party is an entirely different phenomenon. For there is no national party in the sense that there are state and county political parties. The so-called national party is in effect a loose federation of state parties with no independent existence at all. It is either the political agency of the incumbent President or a caretaker for the next Presidential nominee of the party that is out of power.

It has none of the other attributes of a political party on the state level. It is not an independent fund-raiser, it controls and makes no nominations, and it simply fails to exhibit the characteristics of a continuing political institution.

firmly in the anti-party, good-government-fusion tradition of reform. But, the reform movement he embraced, and which helped elect him had moved beyond that old doctrine of reform to the party-oriented theory developed in the 1950's by the Lexingtonian clubs in Manhattan.

No small wonder that the mayor and the CDV were constantly at odds.

There was extensive speculation in the press and political circles when I resigned as county leader in December 1964 as to whether my resignation constituted a political split with the mayor. It didn't. I resigned because the practice of law and the practice of politics, both at the same time, had become too demanding. I had to choose which main road to follow. I chose the law.

But the mayor and I did have a basic disagreement as to the function of the party organization. The disagreement was never fully discussed between us, or even understood by me—at least not until after I had resigned and had an opportunity to reflect upon and analyze my experiences. But I had perceived some aspects of the disagreement while I was in office. At my club's annual dinner in June 1964 I spoke about it. Only a few people understood what I was talking about (the mayor was one of them). What I said was:

Twelve years ago we were on the threshold of a great new development in the Democratic Party. Almost alone and almost always lonely, this club forged its way as a pioneer in the drive to make the Democratic Party a better party. We believed in organization, but in better organization. We believed that the work of the Democratic Party and of party workers was *good* work for *good* men and women who believed in *good* government. Our principles were simple:

Political organization is a force for good government when good people staff it; and

Good people do not become bad ones because they are active in politics or have political power.

And so tonight we stand, almost as we did twelve years ago, at the threshold of a new struggle. This struggle is between those who believe the party organization is bad or at its best a necessary evil and those who still believe that better organization of good Democrats devoted to good government is a good thing.

It is a struggle between those who wish to weaken and divide our political party because they honestly believe the Party is a menace to good government and those, like ourselves, who believe that a strong organization is healthy, desirable, and an affirmative force for good government when it is staffed with good people.

Where do we stand in the coming struggle between those who would destroy party organization and those who would restore it in improved form?

I think the answer is clear. The same principles which have motivated this Club through twelve years of activity in the battle we have fought and won must lead us to join forces with those who believe that party organization is a good thing. For we have not done all of the work that we have done over these many years just to keep an evil—whether necessary or unnecessary—alive.

This conflict will increasingly affect city government in the years ahead. In

323

Edward N. Costikyan

more and more cities, the elected public officeholder is also the party leader. The civil-service establishment and other non-political power structures (like the "public authorities") are becoming increasingly powerful both on the policy and operational level. At the same time, more and more citizens, on a part-time basis, are involving themselves in internal party politics. And yet this development brings with it its own contradiction. As Professor Lowi pointed out:

On the other hand, you get the remains of a party, progressively absorbing individuals who have been taught that it is good *not* to believe in their organization. They have not been prepared to follow any established policy line, even when their organization is at stake. In fact the leadership enjoys only their distrust; there is heroism in this distrust, even when a truly distinguished, modern type is in power-for example, Edward Costikyan. So, the need for central leadership is greatest at the time it is becoming progressively weaker. And the situation is not likely to change as long as each new generation is trained in the old myths.

On the basis of my experience I cannot say with certainty that I am right and that Robert F. Wagner was wrong. A return to party government may conceivably bring with it a return to the old abuses as the former mayor feared (although I doubt it). From his point of view, he apparently believed he could not take the risk.

But I believe the risk is worth taking, given the nature of the changes in the composition of political parties since Boss

Tweed's day, the kind of people now involved in party politics, the control the voters have over the party through direct election of party officers, and the failures of present-day city government.

While no one can prophesy with certainty the results of a new form of party government, and while it is clear that *no* form of government will achieve utopia, I am sure that some new departure is necessary if city governments are to serve their proper function in the coming decades. I am also sure that the potential to be achieved if party organizations played their proper role in the governmental process has not been properly perceived or appreciated.

And so I offer as a hypothesis for achieving good government, a new form of party government. I believe the public officeholder must play a major role but not a dictatorial role in the party, especially on policy questions. I believe the party officeholder must play a major role, but not a dictatorial role, in the area of candidate selection—an area incidentally in which the public officeholder's views are to be taken with some skepticism since today's assemblymen, state senators and congressmen may be his competitor for higher office tomorrow.

When a state the size of New York must look to Massachusetts for a candidate for the United States Senate, as New York's Democrats did in 1964, it is conclusive proof either of the failure of the party to nominate the right kind of people to lower office ten or fifteen years ago or of its failure to develop them properly. In my judgment this failure is both that of the party leaders *and* of the public

324

officeholders, who were not anxious to encourage future competition for themselves.

I also believe there is a role to be played by the party officeholder in government. For example, in personnel recruitment, there has been an unfortunate separation between the two arms of government. Political sponsorship of an aspiring public servant is often as much of a liability as it is an asset.

"Quality" public officials are not supposed to come with political connections or recommendations. Three times I enjoyed the experience of learning of the appointment of an active member of my club to high office by reading about it in the *New York Times*. I could have found all three of them a lot faster than the city government did, if I had only had the opportunity to look.

Why shouldn't the party be asked first? Why not choose a man whose devotion to the party's positions on public issues has been evidenced by some prior political activity? Why ignore, in other words, the fact that good men have attached themselves to the party because of what it believes, because of its program? Why not encourage the participation of the right kind of public servant—or potential public servant—in political activity by using the political organization to the extent it can be used to recruit personnel?

This is not a plea for a return to the spoils system. It is a plea to encourage rather than discourage political participation by good citizens.

A second neglected area is that of information gathering. The political parties are well qualified to report on what the

standing and the new major and minor governmental problems are. There is no good reason why they should not contribute to the agenda of government. They know, usually with an intimacy the public officeholder cannot command, the problems the people face each day. And more often than not they have responded to these problems long before the problems have reached the press, the government bureaus, the City Council, or the mayor's office—long before, that is, they have acquired names like "juvenile delinquency," "*de facto* segregation," "urban blight," and the rest. Such party services as these are rarely used by government. They should be.

Finally, the party organization can play a major role in explaining governmental problems and policies to those affected by them. Sometimes an early explanation of why something can't be done immediately, with some indication of when it can be done, goes a long way to forestall the build-up and explosive expression of public resentment—a combination of factors that only makes government's job harder.

The results of the 1965 municipal election in which Republican-Liberal John Lindsay was elected mayor have relatively little impact upon the validity of the hypothesis I have been suggesting. To some extent, at least, the campaigns of both major candidates recognized that some of the functions the parties formerly performed were both valid and necessary in order to achieve good government, although neither suggested that the political parties should once again perform them.

Edward N. Costikyan

Thus, both Lindsay and Abraham D. Beame, the Democratic candidate, urged the creation of "local City Halls"—neighborhood offices to be staffed in part by volunteers and in part by city employees. It is clear that these offices were to perform some of the governmental functions which I have suggested the party should once again perform—information-gathering for the use of the mayor, and explanation to the voters of what their city administration can and cannot do, and why.

While neither candidate suggested that these local offices also act in the area of personnel recruitment, I believe that this function will inevitably be assumed if these local offices effectively perform the other functions assigned to them

Neither candidate, of course, suggested that the city-financed "local City Halls" were substitutes for the "machine," but they must have recognized it. And no one gave any attention to the impact of creating a political machine (inevitably these local offices will become local political headquarters in Mayor Lindsay's campaign for re-election, as he himself recognized in one incautious interview after the election) financed by city funds, immune from democratic control, controlled by the mayor, and staffed in part, at least, by city personnel.

If this is the only viable alternative to a system of party government—and no other alternative has as yet been suggested—then the argument for a new form of party government becomes that much more compelling.

Otherwise, the election left the valid-ity of the hypothesis I have suggested untouched.

Certainly the voters expressed no clear commitment to the old anti-political tradition of good government. For they elected Lindsay by a narrow margin, and a Democratic president of the City Council (the number-two man in city government), a Democratic comptroller (number-three), and a Democratic City Council by a large margin. Lindsay's was a personal victory, not a victory for a theory of government.

Clearly, the end result—a Republican-Liberal mayor surrounded by a Democratic administration with 16 out of 22 votes on the Board of Estimate and a veto-proof City Council does not appear to offer any likelihood of effective nonpartisan government. Nor does such a solution appear to offer any formula for good government.

It is perilous to leap to conclusions about the meanings of elections. Nevertheless, I believe it correct to say that the 1965 municipal contest in New York did not resolve the most important question facing New Yorkers:

Will responsible party government or "fusion" government serve the city best?"

The result of the election might be summarized in a sentence: The voters chose Lindsay but not "fusion," and they took out a Democratic insurance policy against what Lindsay might try to do.

In these circumstances, Professor Lowi's hypothesis, enunciated before the

326

1965 municipal struggle began, in the same speech quoted above, remains as cogent as ever:

A new type of *party machine* composed of responsible partisans is highly desirable, if attainable. There is nothing to *fear* in this, because the conditions for the *abusive* Old Machines is no longer exist. Moreover, it is also necessary. The party machine is necessary not only because it is a prerequisite to democracy but because the organized popular base offers the only chance of forging a *balance* among the specialized bureaucracies. The bureaucracies ought to be left to run the city. The party ought to be restored to help *govern them*.

Professor Lowi conditions his hypothesis on the question: Is such a new type of party machine composed of "responsible partisans" attainable? If the myths of

the past are banished, and regular participation of good citizens in the new type of party machine encouraged rather than discouraged, who can say such a machine cannot be built? The conditions for its creation exist today.

And if such a new machine can be built, as I believe it can, why should it not play a major role in the government of our cities? The tradition that cities are ungovernable is as false as the myth that political parties are necessarily corrupt. What *is* true is that cities and the political parties within them decay from the same kinds of citizen contempt and external and internal neglect. Neither the government nor the party rots because of any immutable law of life.

I believe we can save our cities and our parties if we want to, but I do not believe we can save one without saving the other.

❧ Bibliography ❧

In the area of machine politics in general and the city boss in particular the secondary literature alone is of such majestic bulk that no attempt will be made here to be inclusive. This is, then, a selective bibliography, *hors d'oeuvres* to whet the appetite and interest the reader in a larger feast upon a fascinating subject.

General works, old and new, include James Bryce, *The American Commonwealth* (1893); M. Ostrogorski, *Democracy and the Organization of Political Parties* (1902), vol. 2; Lincoln Steffens, *The Autobiography of Lincoln Steffens* (1931) and *The Shame of the Cities* (1906); Justin Kaplan's superb biography, *Lincoln Steffens* (1974); Samuel P. Orth, *The Boss and the Machine: A Chronicle of Politicians and Party Organization* (1919); Harold Zink, *City Bosses in the United States* (1930); J. Frank Kent, *The Great Game of Politics* (1923); J. T. Salter, *Boss Rule: Portraits in City Politics* (1935); Sonya Forthal, *Cogwheels of Democracy* (1946); Robert K. Merton, *Social Theory and Social Structure* (1957); Dennis Brogan, *Politics in America* (1954), chap. 4; Edward C. Banfield and James Q. Wilson, *City Politics* (1965), chap. 9; Alfred Steinberg, *The Bosses* (1972); Edwin J. Flynn, *You're the Boss: The Practice of American Politics* (1962); Joel A. Tarr, "The Urban Politician as Entrepreneur," *Mid-America* (January 1967); William V. Shannon, "The Age of the Bosses," *American Heritage* (June 1969); Richard C. Wade, "Urbanization," in *The Comparative Approach to American History*, ed. C. Vann Woodward; Monte A. Calvert, "The Manifest Functions of the Machine," in *Urban Bosses, Machines, and Progressive Reformers*, ed. Bruce M. Stave; James Q. Wilson, "The Political Economy of Patronage," *Journal of Political Economy* (August 1961); *The Annals* of the American Academy of

Political and Social Science, "City Bosses and Political Machines" (May 1964); Eric McKitrick, "The Study of Corruption," *Political Science Quarterly* (December 1957); James C. Scott, "Corruption, Machine Politics, and Political Change," *American Political Science Review* (December 1969). Two anthologies deal with specific eras: Bruce Stave, ed., *Urban Bosses, Machines, and Progressive Reformers* (1972), and Blaine A. Brownell and Warren E. Stickel, eds., *Bosses and Reformers: Urban Politics in America, 1880-1920* (1973).

The paradigm of city machines is, of course, New York's Tammany Hall, the most thoroughly studied organization in the literature of American urban politics. Tammany has had its share of detractors, among them William H. White, *Al Smith's Tammany Hall* (1928); Norman Thomas and Paul Blanshard, *What's the Matter with New York* (1932); Denis Lynch, *Boss Tweed, The Story of a Grim Generation* (1927); and Gustavus Myers's cool but devastating *History of Tammany Hall* (1917; reprinted in an attractive volume in 1971). Interestingly, Tammany has also had its apologists, adept with the whitewash, in William Gover's *The Tammany Hall Democracy of the City of New York* (1875); Euphemia Vale Blake, *History of the Tammany Society from Its Organization to the Present Time* (1901); Edwin Kilroe, *Tammany, a Patriotic History* (1924) (Kilroe was a great collector of Tammaniana, and his collection is available to scholars at the Columbia University Library); and Theodore Lothrop Stoddard, *Master of Manhattan, the Life of Richard Croker* (1931). Two delightful earlier works are Rufus E. Shapley, *Solid for Mulhooly: A Sketch of Municipal Politics under the Leaders, the Ring, and the Boss* (1881), and Matthew P. Breen, *Thirty Years of New York Politics* (1899). In 1928 M. R. Werner's *Tammany Hall* was published, a readable but not always accurate book. Roy V. Peel's *The Political Clubs of New York City* (1935) is indispensable.

More recent scholarship includes Seymour Mandelbaum's *Boss Tweed's New York* (1965); Alexander B. Callow, Jr.'s *The Tweed Ring* (1966)—a splendid gift for friend or relative; Rita Kramer's "Well, What Are You Going to Do about It?" [Richard Croker], *American Heritage* (February 1973); Warren Moscow's *What Have You Done for Me Lately? The Ins and Outs of New York City Politics* (1967) and *The Last of the Big-Time Bosses: The Life and Times of Carmine De Sapio* (1971). Important also are Edward N. Costikyan, *Behind Closed Doors* (1966); Alfred Connable and Edward Silberfarb, *Tigers of Tammany Hall: Nine Men Who Ran New York* (1967); Louis Eisenstein and Elliot Rosenberg, *A Stripe of Tammany's Tiger* (1966); Nancy Joan Weiss, *Charles Francis Murphy, 1958-1924: Respectability and Responsibility in Tammany Politics*

(1968); Richard O'Connor, *Courtroom Warrior: The Combative Career of William Travers Jerome* (1963); Arthur Mann, *La Guardia Comes to Power, 1933* (1965); Andy Logan, *Against the Evidence: The Becker-Rosenthal Affair* (1970); Robert Ernst, *Immigrant Life in New York City* (1946); Justin N. Feldman, "How Tammany Holds Power," *National Municipal Review* (July 1950); Theodore W. Lowi, *At the Pleasure of the Mayor: Patronage and Power in New York City, 1898-1858* (1964). Jerome Mushkat has an excellent study of Tammany in its early years, *Tammany: The Evolution of a Political Machine, 1789-1865* (1971); and the *New Yorker* magazine has published several interesting articles on New York politics, including Richard Rovere's "The Big Hello" (January 12 and 19, 1946), John McCarten's "Evolution of a Problem Child" (February 12 and 19, 1938), and Alva Johnston's "Scholar in Politics" (July 1 and 8, 1933).

Books and articles on the boss in Chicago include: Charles E. Merriam, *Chicago: A More Intimate View of Urban Politics* (1929); Harold F. Gosnell, *Machine Politics: Chicago Model* (1937); the books of Lloyd Wendt and Herman Kogan, *Lords of the Levee: The Story of Bathhouse John and Hinky Dink* (1943; reprinted in 1967 as *Bosses in Lusty Chicago*), and *Big Bill of Chicago* (1953); Bruce Grant, *Fight for a City; The Story of the Union League Club of Chicago and Its Times, 1880-1955* (1956); Alex Gottfried, *Boss Cermak of Chicago* (1962); Edward M. Levine, *The Irish and Irish Politicians* (1966); William F. Gleason, *Daley of Chicago: The Man, the Mayor, and the Limits of Conventional Politics* (1970); Peter Yessne, *Quotations from Mayor Daley* (1969); Mike Royko, *Boss: Richard J. Daley of Chicago* (1971); Humbert S. Nelli, "John Powers and the Italians: Politics in a Chicago Ward, 1896-1921," *Journal of American History* (June 1970); and Joel A. Tarr, *A Study of Boss Politics: William Lorimer of Chicago* (1971).

On other cities see Zane L. Miller, *Boss Cox's Cincinnati: Urban Politics in the Progressive Era* (1968); Lyle Dorsett, *The Pendergast Machine* (1968); Melvin Holli, *Reform in Detroit: Hazen S. Pingree and Urban Politics* (1969); James B. Crooks, *Politics and Progress: The Rise of Urban Progressivism in Baltimore, 1895-1911* (1968); Harvey Wheeler, "Yesterday's Robin Hood: The Rise and Fall of Baltimore's Trenton Democratic Club," *American Quarterly* (Winter 1955); George M. Reynolds, *Machine Politics in New Orleans, 1897-1926* (1936); J. Paul Mitchell, "Boss Speer and the City Functional: Boosters and Businessmen versus Commission Government in Denver," *Pacific Northwest Quarterly* (October 1972); Thomas J. Fleming, "I Am the Law," *American Heritage* (June 1969); Mark Foster, "Frank Hague of New Jersey: The Boss as Reformer," *New*

Jersey History (Summer 1968); William D. Miller, *Memphis During the Progressive Era, 1900-1917* (1957); Bruce M. Stave, *The New Deal and the Last Hurrah: Pittsburgh Machine Politics* (1970); Walton E. Bean, *Boss Ruef's San Francisco* (1952); James P. Walsh, "Abe Ruef Was No Boss: Machine Politics, Reform, and San Francisco," *California Historical Quarterly* (Spring 1972); Alexander B. Callow, Jr., "San Francisco's Blind Boss," *Pacific Historical Review* (August 1956); and Callow, "Legislature of a Thousand Scandals," *Southern California Historical Society Quarterly* (December 1957).

On the relation of urban politics to reform in general, see John G. Sprout, *"The Best Men": Liberal Reformers in the Gilded Age* (1968); C. W. Patton, *The Battle for Municipal Reform* (1940); Louis Filler, *Crusaders for American Liberalism* (1950); Richard Hofstadter, *The Age of Reform* (1955); Robert H. Wiebe, *The Search for Order* (1967); Samuel P. Hays, "The Politics of Reform in Municipal Government in the Progressive Era," *Pacific Northwest Quarterly* (October 1964); John D. Buenker, *Urban Liberalism and Progressive Reform* (1973); Buenker, "The Urban Political Machine and the Seventeenth Amendment," *Journal of American History* (September 1969); Buenker, "The Urban Machine Political Machine and Women Suffrage: A Study in Political Adaptability," *The Historian* (February 1971); Otis A. Pease, "Urban Reformers in the Progressive Era," *Pacific Northwest Quarterly* (April 1971); James Q. Wilson, "Politics and Reform in American Cities," in Ivan Hinderaker, ed., *American Government Annual, 1961-1962*; Lyle W. Dorsett, "The City Boss and the Reformer: A Reappraisal," *Pacific Northwest Quarterly* (October 1972); Allen F. Davis, *Spearheads for Reform: The Social Settlements and the Progressive Movement, 1890-1914* (1967); Arthur Mann, *Yankee Reformers in the Urban Age* (1954); J. Joseph Hutchmacher, "Urban Liberalism and the Age of Reform," *Mississippi Valley Historical Review* (September 1962); Daniel Patrick Moynihan, "Bosses and Reformers," *Commentary* (June 1961).

For more specific studies, see Jack Tager, *The Intellectual as Urban Reformer: Brand Whitlock and the Progressive Movement* (1968); J. Joseph Hutchmacher, "Charles Evans Hughes and Charles Frances Murphy: The Metamorphosis of Progressivism " *New York History* (January 1965); Allen F. Davis, *American Heroine: The Life and Legend of Jane Addams* (1973); Ari Hoogenboom, *Outlawing the Spoils: A History of the Civil Service Reform Movement, 1865-1883*; Hoogenboom "An Analysis of Civil Service Reformers," *The Historian* (November 1960); Hoogenboom, "Civil Service Reform and Public Morality," in H. Wayne Morgan, ed., *The Gilded Age* (rev. ed., 1970); Jeremy P. Felt, "Vice Reform as a

Political Technique: The Committee of Fifteen in New York, 1900-1901," *New York History* (January 1973); Burton W. Blassingame, "Frank J. Goodnow: Progressive Urban Reformer," *North Dakota Quarterly* (Summer 1970); Frank Mann Stewart, *A Half-Century of Municipal Reform: A History of the National Municipal League* (1950); James Weinstein, "Organized Business and the City Manager Movements," *The Journal of Southern History* (May 1962); Harold A. Stone and others, *City Manager Government in the United States* (1940); Frederick C. Mosher and others, *City Manager Government in Seven Cities* (1940); Leonard D. White, *The City Manager* (1927); and Don K. Price, "The Promotion of the City Manager Plan," *Public Opinion Quarterly* (Winter 1941).